Experiences of Intervention Against Violence

Cultural Encounters in Intervention Against Violence, Vol. 2

Carol Hagemann-White/
Bianca Grafe (eds.)

Experiences of Intervention Against Violence

An Anthology of Stories

*Stories in four languages from England & Wales,
Germany, Portugal and Slovenia*

*Geschichten in vier Sprachen aus England und Wales,
Deutschland, Portugal und Slowenien*

*Histórias de Inglaterra e País de Gales, Alemanha,
Portugal e Eslovénia, nas quatro línguas*

*Zgodbe v štirih jezikih iz Anglije in Walesa, Nemčije,
Portugalske in Slovenije*

Barbara Budrich Publishers
Opladen • Berlin • Toronto 2016

This project has received funding from the European Union's Seventh Framework Programme for research, technological development and demonstration under grant agreement no 291827. The project CEINAV is financially supported by the HERA Joint Research Programme (www.heranet.info) which is co-funded by AHRC, AKA, BMBF via PT-DLR, DASTI, ETAG, FCT, FNR, FNRS, FWF, FWO, HAZU, IRC, LMT, MHEST, NWO, NCN, RANNÍS, RCN, VR and The European Community FP7 2007-2013, under the Socio-economic Sciences and Humanities programme.

A CIP catalogue record for this book is available from
Die Deutsche Bibliothek (The German Library)

© 2016 by Barbara Budrich Publishers, Opladen, Berlin & Toronto
www.barbara-budrich.net

ISBN 978-3-8474-2043-9
eISBN 978-3-8474-1025-6 (pdf)

Die Deutsche Bibliothek – CIP-Einheitsaufnahme
Ein Titeldatensatz für die Publikation ist bei Der Deutschen Bibliothek erhältlich.

Verlag Barbara Budrich 🅱 Barbara Budrich Publishers
Stauffenbergstr. 7. D-51379 Leverkusen Opladen, Germany

86 Delma Drive. Toronto, ON M8W 4P6 Canada
www.barbara-budrich.net

Jacket illustration by Bettina Lehfeldt, Germany – www.lehfeldtgraphic.de
Artistic design: Ana Paula Mateus, Coimbra, Portugal
Typographical editing: Ulrike Weingärtner, Gründau, Germany – info@textakzente.de
Printed in Europe on acid-free paper by paper & tinta, Warsaw

Contents

Preface

The stories in this anthology emerged from interviews with women and young people about their experience of intervention when they were escaping a situation of abuse, neglect and/or coercion. For three years, the research project "Cultural Encounters in Intervention Against Violence (CEINAV)" studied how professionals in four countries – England & Wales, Germany, Portugal and Slovenia – intervene when confronting intimate partner violence, trafficking for sexual exploitation or physical abuse and neglect of children. Through cooperation with our associate partners, networks of specialized practitioners who work with victimized women or abused children and their families, we were able to contact women and young people who came from a minority or migration background and had travelled through a history of violence and intervention. We asked them to tell us who intervened, what had been helpful and what had not, or had even done them further harm. We also invited them to express how they experienced intervention in participatory art workshops and to take part in meetings to reflect on the interim results of CEINAV. We were looking for ways that the voices and perspectives of those who ought to be helped by intervention, but are often marginalized or silenced, could be heard.

In all their diversity this collection of stories does not claim to represent any general idea – in each story, the woman or young person speaks for herself or himself only – but offers an opportunity to see intervention from the other side. The stories have been extracted and condensed out of what was often a long interview, and focused around main points about which the interviewee felt strongly. Details that would have made the person identifiable had to be left out or changed, as research ethics require that publication should do no harm, and there was no way to assess the risk that might follow if she or he were known. Thus, the stories were crafted in a creative process and in their present form are always a merging of two voices: that of the interviewee, and that of the research team member. The key statements, the motto at the beginning, and the expressions of how things were perceived and felt, are the original words of the person whose interview it was, and all were asked for their permission to tell the story in this way.

We of the CEINAV research team are profoundly grateful to the practitioners who made it possible for us to meet these women and young people, often in the safe and familiar surroundings of the support services; even deeper is our gratitude to all those who shared their experiences with us. Together with our cooperation partners we are convinced that this anthology can be useful in education and further training as well as in educating the wider public, from the women and young people who may feel alone with their experiences to the stakeholder and policymakers who might gain a deeper understanding of what ethical professionalism is. We have translated all stories into English next to the original language as an invitation to think about how experiences may differ or be similar in different countries of Europe.

We dedicate this anthology to the 78 women and young people in four countries who found the time and courage to tell us about their experiences.

Vorwort

Die Geschichten in dieser Sammlung entstanden aus Interviews mit Frauen und Jugendlichen über ihre Erfahrung mit Intervention nach Misshandlung, Vernachlässigung und/oder Zwang. Drei Jahre lang erforschte das Projekt "Cultural Encounters in Intervention Against Violence (CEINAV)" wie Fachkräfte in vier Ländern – England & Wales, Deutschland, Portugal und Slowenien – bei Partnerschaftsgewalt, Frauenhandel oder körperlicher Misshandlung und Vernachlässigung von Kindern intervenieren. Durch Vermittlung unserer Praxispartner, Netzwerken von spezialisierten Fachkräften, die mit betroffenen Frauen oder Kindern und deren Familien arbeiten, konnten wir mit Betroffenen sprechen, die einen Minderheiten- oder Migrationshintergrund haben. Diese baten wir, uns zu erzählen, wer interveniert hatte, was hilfreich gewesen war und was nicht, oder was sogar weiteren Schaden angerichtet hatte. Wir luden unsere Interviewpartner auch ein, in einem Kunstworkshop visuell darzustellen, wie sie die Intervention erlebten, und an Treffen teil zu nehmen, in denen wir mit Fachkräften die Zwischenergebnisse des Projektes reflektierten. Wir suchten nach Wegen, wie die Stimmen und Sichtweisen derer, denen durch Intervention geholfen werden soll, die aber oft marginalisiert oder ausgeblendet werden, gehört werden könnten.

Trotz ihrer großen Vielfalt erhebt diese Sammlung von Geschichten nicht den Anspruch auf Vollständigkeit – in jeder Geschichte spricht die Frau oder der/die Jugendliche für sich persönlich – aber sie bietet eine Möglichkeit, Intervention von der anderen Seite zu betrachten. Die Geschichten wurden aus meist langen Interviews herausgearbeitet und mit einem Fokus auf Hauptpunkte verdichtet, die den Interviewten besonders wichtig waren. Details, an denen man die Person erkennen könnte, wurden ausgelassen und sämtliche Namen geändert, da die Forschungsethik verlangt, dass die Veröffentlichung keinen Schaden anrichten darf und das mögliche Risiko bei Wiedererkennung nicht abschätzbar war. Die Erzählung war daher ein kreativer Prozess und vereint immer zwei Stimmen: Die Stimme der/des Interviewten und die der Forscherin. Die Schlüsselaussagen, die Mottos zu Beginn, und Ausdrücke wie die Dinge empfunden wurden, sind immer die Originalstimme der interviewten Person, und jede/r wurde um ihre Erlaubnis gebeten, die Geschichte in dieser Art zu erzählen.

Wir vom Forscherteam sind den Fachkräften, die uns ermöglichten, diese Frauen und Jugendlichen zu treffen – oft in den vertrauten Räumen der Einrichtung – zutiefst dankbar. Besonders dankbar sind wir all jenen, die ihre Erfahrungen mit uns geteilt haben. Wir und unsere Kooperationspartner sind überzeugt, dass dieser Sammelband in der Aus- und Fortbildung wertvoll sein kann. Er kann ebenso der Information einer breiteren Öffentlichkeit dienen, angefangen bei den Betroffenen, die sich mit ihren Erlebnissen allein fühlen mögen, bis zu den Entscheidungsträgern, die vielleicht ein tieferes Verständnis erlangen, was ethische Berufsausübung heißt. Alle Geschichten wurden ins Englische übertragen und neben dem Original abgedruckt, und laden so zum Nachdenken darüber ein, wie Erfahrungen in den verschiedenen Ländern sich unterscheiden oder auch ähneln.

Wir widmen diesen Sammelband den 78 Frauen und jungen Menschen in den vier Ländern, die die Zeit und den Mut aufgebracht haben, uns ihre Geschichten zu erzählen.

Prefácio

Esta antologia constitui a súmula das narrativas a partir de entrevistas com mulheres e com jovens sobre as suas experiências e subjetividades nos seus encontros com os sistemas de intervenção durante o processo em que se libertavam de uma situação de abuso, negligência e/ou coerção. Durante três anos, o projeto de investigação "Cultural Encounters in Intervention Against Violence (CEINAV)" estudou a forma como profissionais em quatro países – Inglaterra e País de Gales, Alemanha, Portugal e Eslovénia – intervêm contra a violência nas relações de intimidade, no tráfico de seres humanos para fins de exploração sexual ou no abuso físico e negligência de crianças. Através da cooperação com associações parceiras, redes de profissionais especializadas/os que trabalham com mulheres vitimizadas ou crianças abusadas e as suas famílias, foi possível contactar mulheres e jovens de grupos sociais minoritários ou migrantes e que haviam viajado através de um historial de violência e de intervenção. Foi-lhes pedido para contar quem interveio, o que foi útil e o que não foi, ou até o que prejudicou. Foram ainda convidadas/os a participar em oficinas criativas e em reuniões para expressarem como experienciaram a intervenção e refletir sobre os resultados do CEINAV. Procuraram-se estratégias para que as vozes e perspetivas daqueles/as que deveriam ser ajudados/as, mas que são frequentemente marginalizadas ou silenciadas, pudessem ser ouvidas.

Na sua diversidade, esta coleção de histórias não afirma qualquer pretensão de generalização – em cada história, a mulher ou o jovem fala apenas por si – mas oferece uma oportunidade de conhecer a intervenção a partir dos seus pontos de vista. Cada história foi extraída e condensada do que foi uma longa entrevista, e foca-se nos pontos principais sobre os quais o/a entrevistado/a nutria fortes sentimentos. Foram retirados ou alterados detalhes que poderiam identificar a pessoa, visto que a ética requer que a publicação não provoque quaisquer malefícios, e não havia forma de avaliar o risco que poderia correr se ele ou ela fossem (re)conhecidos/as. As histórias foram construídas num processo criativo constituindo uma fusão de duas vozes: a do/a entrevistado/a e a do membro da equipa de investigação. Tentámos ser fiéis às palavras originais da pessoa entrevistada, tanto nas frases chave como no lema no início, para dar visibilidade às expressões de como as coisas foram percepcionadas e sentidas, e a todos/as foi pedida a permissão para contar a história desta forma.

Nós, da equipa de investigação do CEINAV, estamos profundamente gratas/os aos/às profissionais que tornaram possível o nosso contacto com estas mulheres e com estes jovens, que decorreu, na maioria dos casos, nos contextos seguros e familiares dos serviços de apoio; mais profunda é a nossa gratidão a todos/as as/os que partilharam as suas experiências connosco. Em conjunto com as associações parceiras, estamos convictas/os que esta antologia pode ser útil na educação e formação, assim como para o público em geral, desde mulheres e jovens que podem sentir-se sós nas suas experiências, a intervenientes e legisladores/as que podem ganhar uma compreensão mais profunda do que é o profissionalismo ético. Traduzimos todas as histórias para inglês, junto da língua original, como um convite para pensar sobre como as experiências podem ser diferentes ou similares em diferentes países da Europa.

Dedicamos esta antologia às/aos 78 mulheres e jovens que, em quatro países, encontraram o tempo e a coragem para nos falarem das suas experiências.

Predgovor

Zgodbe v tej publikaciji izvirajo iz intervjujev z ženskami in mladostniki o njihovih izkušnjah z intervencijo, ko so bežali iz situacije nasilja, zlorabe in/ali prisile. Tri leta je raziskovalni projekt »Kulturna srečanja v ukrepih proti nasilju (CEINAV)« preučeval, kako strokovnjaki v štirih državah – v Angliji in Walesu, v Nemčiji, na Portugalskem in v Sloveniji – intervenirajo, ko so soočeni z nasiljem v družini, trgovino z ljudmi za namene spolnega izkoriščanja ali fizično zlorabo in zanemarjanjem otrok. Prek sodelovanja z našimi pridruženimi partnerji, mrežami specializiranih delavcev, ki delajo z viktimiziranimi ženskami ali zlorabljenimi otroki in njihovimi družinami, smo lahko vzpostavili stik z ženskami in mladostniki iz vrst manjšin in migrantov, ki so izkusili nasilje in intervencijo. Prosili smo jih, naj nam povedo, kdo je interveniral, kaj jim je bilo v pomoč in kaj ne in kaj jim je mogoče celo še dodatno škodovalo. Pozvali smo jih, naj to, kako so izkusili intervencijo, izrazijo v participatornih umetniških delavnicah in sodelujejo na sestankih ocene vmesnih rezultatov projekta CEINAV. Iskali smo načine, da bi lahko bili slišani glasovi in perspektive tistih, ki naj bi jim intervencija pomagala, a so pogosto marginalizirani ali utišani.

Kljub vsej njeni raznolikosti ta zbirka zgodb ne predstavlja nikakršne splošne ideje – v vsaki zgodbi ženska ali mladostnik govorita le zase – pač pa nudi priložnost, da vidimo intervencijo z druge strani. Zgodbe so bile povzete in zgoščene iz pogosto dolgih intervjujev in se osredotočajo na glavne poante, o katerih so imeli intervjuvanci_ke odločna mnenja. Podrobnosti, po katerih bi osebo lahko prepoznali, so morale biti izpuščene in njihova imena so bila spremenjena, saj raziskovalna etika zahteva, da objava ne sme škoditi, ni pa bilo načina, da bi ocenili tveganje, ki bi sledilo, če bi bila oseba prepoznana. Tako so bile zgodbe izdelane v ustvarjalnem procesu in so v pričujoči obliki vedno zlitje dveh glasov: glasu intervjuvanca_ke in glasu članice raziskovalne skupine. Ključne izjave, moto na začetku in izrazi o njihovih dojemanjih in občutkih so izvirne besede intervjuvane osebe, pri čemer smo vse prosili za njihovo dovoljenje, da zgodbe povemo na ta način.

Člani_ce raziskovalne skupine projekta CEINAV smo globoko hvaležni strokovnim delavcem_kam, ki so nam omogočili, da smo se srečali s temi ženskami in mladostniki, pogosto v varnih in poznanih okoljih podpornih služb; še bolj pa smo hvaležni tistim, ki so z nami delili svoje izkušnje. Skupaj s partnerji smo prepričani, da je ta izbor lahko uporaben pri izobraževanju in nadaljnjem usposabljanju, pa tudi pri izobraževanju širše javnosti: od žensk in mladostnikov, ki se mogoče počutijo sami s svojimi izkušnjami, do deležnikov in oblikovalcev politike, ki bi jim to pomagalo do globljega razumevanja etične strokovnosti. Vse zgodbe smo prevedli v angleščino in jih objavili vzporedno z izvirnikom kot vabilo k razmisleku o tem, kako se izkušnje v različnih evropskih državah lahko razlikujejo ali pa so si podobne.

Ta izbor posvečamo 78 ženskam in mladostnikom v štirih državah, ki so si vzeli čas in so zbrali pogum, da so nam povedali o svojih izkušnjah.

Domestic violence

Stories and experiences of women

Domestic Violence

Stories and experiences of women

England & Wales

"I always compromised but when it got too bad my children helped me, then my friend"

Aafia's story

I came to the UK with my husband and children a few years ago. It was OK as I had a British passport so we were allowed to be here.

My husband was very abusive, mentally and sexually but I didn't tell anyone, not even my parents back home. I tried always to compromise. One day my son saw that I was very upset and I told him a little of what had been happening to me. He was very angry and a little later my daughter found out. They were both at university at this time and not living at home. So they tried to help, both of them, advising me what I should do. Then I also spoke to a friend and I asked her to tell me about a good lawyer. She spoke to another friend and gave me the number of this NGO, and she told me about a good lawyer.

So, I was thinking now, and preparing to leave my husband and my home. I was getting ready and when my husband threatened me again badly I waited until he had gone to work, and I left. I had somewhere to go on a temporary basis, and I went there. And then I stayed other places as well and I went to the lawyer and told her everything. So the lawyer advised me about my rights and what I could do to secure my position and made an application. I authorised someone else to act for me because I had to go back to my home country because I needed the support of my family. So now my husband became alert and he also came back to our home country and he quickly divorced me there so that he could avoid all the financial orders and division of assets that would happen in Britain.

So I came back to the UK. My family were very worried as I had nowhere to go to but I knew of somewhere I could stay for a couple of weeks and I had in mind the number of the NGO that my friend had given me. I thought I could always try and speak with them and ask them for help also and I did this. I was given an appointment to come and see someone. I told her about my situation. At that time there was no accommodation available and she said if I can wait they will contact me. So I continued to stay in temporary accommodation but I was still very afraid of what my husband had done and might do again and wondered if I should go to the police.

I spoke to my daughter about this and she said that I must go and speak to someone and get advice. So I contacted the NGO again and spoke with someone and she advised me to go to the police and offered to go with me. That was very helpful because I was becoming double-minded – whether to go - because it was going to affect my children as well. So the next day I went there with a support worker and I made a statement to the police. And I told the police that whatever little savings I had I was spending on my lawyers and the divorce. So I can't go to court again because I don't have any money left. So they were very supportive and said that because I am a victim, the Crown Prosecution Services are willing to help me and I don't have to pay anything for this criminal case against my husband.

And the police asked me to give, some of my information to other organisations like Victim Support and I told them yes and I had a call from Victim Support and she was very supportive.

Then the NGO called to say a room was available and I could move in the next day. I was so relieved that I finally have somewhere to go; I have a place of my own.

And looking back I did not seek help for a very long time. I always compromised but when it got too bad my children helped me, then my friend. She got me the lawyer and gave me the contact for this NGO. As for the lawyers, yes, they are really positive because they have been very encouraging and because I had very little knowledge of the law and British laws and everything. So they have been guiding me all along.

And this NGO has helped me, helped me to get back on my feet, and advised me to go to the police. So, because I have a place to stay with the refuge I am so happy and so glad that I can get all this help because if I was in my home country there is very little help available there except for your family if they are supporting you – if your family can help you. But in my home country there are no such organisations like these, like this NGO or the like – the police are not very helpful there as well... So I am very glad that I am in this country – this is the reason I am getting all this help. Yes.

I came to the UK a few years ago from my home country. It was an arranged marriage. My husband treated me very badly. He had a shop and I worked in that shop all day every day. When I wasn't working in the shop he locked me in the house and I had no permission to go or meet anyone on my own. He kept my passport hidden away. For a long time I tried to sort out the problems with him, I told him I needed some money for myself and that I needed to ring my mum sometimes but he refused me everything. I cried a lot because my mum was diagnosed with cancer and I desperately needed to know if she was all right but he kept me like an animal.

Then I found out I wasn't his only wife in the UK and he was leaving me alone at home for many nights and I was afraid. And I was alone there and many times I just thought let me out, I want to do something. I started maybe thinking about suicide as well to finish with myself, because it was such a hard life for me, here, with no family of my own to turn to and with my mum sick back in my home country and I couldn't even talk to her. Sometimes I felt so upset I just wanted to run away from there, take off my scarf, everything and just run out. But where would I go? And my husband said I will divorce if you keep saying these things - that I want to talk to my mum, or that I need money, or that I want to go out for a walk. He said, I will divorce you or I will kick you out from this country, because you are here because of me.

Sometimes I talked a little to people from the community who came into the shop so they knew I had some troubles but they said we can't help you like this. They said I had to tell the police, I had to take help from the police. But my husband was aware of these things and he kept saying don't call the police because the police are not good here. Nothing will happen to me but they will treat you very badly and so I was scared. But then last year I had a problem with my leg and I had to see a doctor and my husband took me there and the doctor referred me to a physiotherapist. When I got the appointment my husband went with me to the hospital and he treated me very badly in front of the physiotherapist because I think that physiotherapist noticed that maybe something is going wrong. And I think maybe the GP noticed something as well because he rang me to come in again to see him. And when I went he told my husband to wait outside and then he said I can help you.

And he phoned somebody and passed the phone to me and there was a lady speaking
my language and so I could tell her what was happening to me. She said I did not have to
stay with my husband, we will help you and you can come straight to us and I said, yes, I
wanted this help. So the GP had someone take me to a bus station because the help was
in another city and when I got to this other city someone was there to collect me and
they brought me here to this organisation and I have been here for a few months now.

The help I am getting here is very good. I have a place to live. I share a house but that's
OK, we're all together. And they tell everything to me, whatever I need, how to get the
money, they help me a lot in every way. I told my support worker I need a visa, I need a
passport because I don't know where these papers are. And I need to go back home to
see my mum because they let me use their phone and I called my mum and she is very,
very sick. So my support worker took me to a lawyer and that lawyer has made these
applications for me. And I told my support worker that I am very scared because where
I was living with my husband, in that shop and that house, everything where he has
registered, I think it is all in my name, all the bills, maybe credit cards and everything and
I am scared he can make trouble for me because he has got all the authority in his hands.
So, because I am an uneducated woman I don't know what to do, and I was like a servant
in front of him and he can do anything to me. I told this to my support worker and I asked
her to please help me. I said I want a divorce because he is a troubled person and it will
never be OK with him. So now I also have another lawyer who is helping me with these
things. But I don't know what will happen in the future. I don't think I have a very good, a
bright future. Because after here, where will I go? I have no home and no-one is here, my
family is not here and I have things buried in my mind and maybe people will think I am
not a good person because I broke up my home and I am not with my husband any more.
But the help here is good help and day by day I get stronger and I can see maybe I can
do something and move on, do things on my own and my advice now for other women
like me? I would say that if your husband is not good with you, don't stay with him for a
long time like I did. Leave him and go and live your own life. And when men do whatever
they want, if he has got more wives or a girlfriend, they just blame the lady, they push
the lady down. And when you get married you can't go back to your parents, you have
to compromise, sacrifice in your husband's house, you are just property and whatever
he wants he can do with me. You don't speak English, maybe we can't read or write,
we don't know about our rights here. But in this organisation, they give us good help,
English classes and computer classes, and we learn about benefits and financial support
so maybe there can be an independent life. For me, I think, I can be strong and do these
things but first I have to see my mum. The rest is OK, it is just that I can't cope with. And I
don't know long this visa will take, my papers are not complete and that's why I can't go
back to see her. This is the last wish of my life. I want see my mum.

"You need to understand our culture"

Fahima's story

I was born in the UK but my parents took me back to their home country when I was a child. Then when I was sixteen they got me engaged and forced marriage upon me when I was nearly eighteen. My husband was fifteen years older than me and I wasn't happy. If you don't love anyone, how can you marry? It really was completely forced. Then when I got pregnant with the first baby I wanted to come back to the UK to have the baby but my in-laws and my husband wouldn't give me permission. So I have two children and they were both born in my parent's home country.

I was not happy there because they control the ladies, they control you all the time, not just the husband but his mother and family as well. And I had to do all the work, all the cooking for all the family and look after my two kids as well. It was a very hard life. And my passport was gone. I said I want to apply for a passport, to go on holidays and take my children but my husband said, no, you can't do that, they're not your children, they're mine. You are just the mum and look after them but they are my children. And they did not even give me proper food or let me have permission to go to my mum's house to meet my parents. So things were very bad and I was very upset. So then I ran away, and I ran to my mum's house and I said I have no food, there is nothing in my house, and my kids are in bad condition too. Then my father, before he wasn't with me, but then he saw me. I had lost loads of weight and I was ill so he changed his mind. He came back to my house with me and he saw how I was forced to live, how my kids were forced to live and so he helped me get the passports and the tickets so that I could come and bring my kids here, to family here.

I flew with my kids to Heathrow airport and a relative met us there and brought us to where she lived and we lived with her for a few months. But because I was in a very bad condition, mentally and physically, I had to go to the doctor and it was the same doctor I had been registered with as a child. And this doctor she helped me a lot. She said I know you but what has happened to you? And she spoke my language because then my English was very poor. And so she said, I will help you. I will give you some medicines but you also must go this organisation and they can give you more help. So my relative took me to that organisation and they said, OK, we can help but it will be better for you to go to another place and that is how I came here.

That was four years ago. Now I am OK and live and work. I have my own house and I am doing all the things for myself and my children. But at first, I couldn't do anything. I thought I was useless, and I didn't know anything, about benefits, getting some place to live, how to travel and things. So my support worker, because you don't know about these things, and how to do these things, you need someone to tell you, and this organisation told me everything and I did language and IT courses as well. And she showed me how to make a budget on the money for your lifestyle, how we can do with the kids, and how your rent is coming in, going out, she told me every single thing and explained it very nicely. And that's very important if you're on your own. This learning process I think will never be finished, but I keep learning more things and I have friends and I have family, but at the beginning it was so hard and our cultural thing is too much because you know you can't go like this or do that.

I am OK now because my family here, we are more – we are Asian and Western as well – and we have our community doctors, like my doctor, who speaks my language as well even though I can now speak English. But at the beginning I was scared of everything because my brain was not working with me and I was afraid, even to go out, even to go shopping in the city centre. Sometimes my support worker was very good but sometimes she would push me and say if you can't do this, you don't need to live here, you have to go back then. And I was upset and told her I didn't like her saying that but she said sometimes she needed to be a little bit negative so I can learn and she made me do things on my own. Now she is my friend, but then I struggled. But you need to understand our culture. You have to sacrifice and compromise and men – they will never sacrifice or compromise. This is only for ladies, never for the man. Now I can't live my life like this, only for other people and I have learned this through this organisation and the help they have given me. There we were husband and wife, and he could do what he wanted. If he were to kill me they wouldn't worry. But my father, now he knows, and he knows about the forced marriage and he tells me he is sorry, it was a mistake and this is very important to me as well so now I will never go back.

"Slowly, slowly, I have been learning"

Hakima's story

So I am here because of the domestic violence. For many years I was upset and crying. Then I got pregnant again and one day my friend went with me to the hospital and I told her a little of what was happening. She gave me the number of this organisation and she said, you go there, they will help you. So I went home and I called the number and I told her what my troubles were and the help I needed. So she said, you can see a solicitor and she made the appointment and she went with me to see the solicitor because then I could not speak English. And so my husband had to leave the house and it got put into my name. But this organisation has helped me with everything. Because then I was scared all the time, I was scared to go out, to get on a bus, but here, first we got my visa sorted. I had three years, then another three years and next time, I can apply for indefinite leave to remain in this country.

I am better now because of all the help and everything. At the beginning they did so much because I could not. So they would ring and make appointments for me, with the GP or the hospital, or the solicitor and she would go with me to the appointments. And I saw the solicitor for the divorce so now I am separated and just living with my children. And I did English classes with this organisation and I went to the domestic violence group and this helped because before I had no confidence but they teach you how to become more confident and to learn how to do things on your own and slowly, slowly, I have been learning. And even they organise trips for us and the kids so we can be away together, somewhere different and this is good. I am comfortable with this organisation because they understand my language and my problems. When I talk I know I can tell her and she will not go outside and talk to other people. I think it's a very good organisation and it is just for the women. In my country women and men are separate. It is the same here and this is why I am comfortable with this organisation.

So it is good, but my husband still makes trouble for me. He has to see the children once a week at a leisure centre and when I go to collect them he makes trouble, or he makes trouble at the school or the house. And I call the police and sometimes they take a long time to come and say this is not an emergency but for me it is an emergency. And they never arrest him, just tell him to stop and he always says he will stop but he doesn't. And I go to court, again and again, I am in the court and last time the court says not to go there any more and it's not nice then because this is not good for the kids. It makes them scared. So now I am making another appointment with a solicitor and this organisation, they still help me even though it's been a long time.

"All these people who initially were so supportive believed him"

Lanika's story

Well if I start at my very beginning. The first help I attempted to get was through a local Helpline. They were absolutely useless! They just told me to go back and face my husband. They didn't question me, or allow for the possibility that it could be abuse. I tried that probably six or seven times over a period of four years. And I really feel cross that they let me down because back then I didn't know that what I was experiencing was abuse. I knew I needed help but I didn't know what my husband was doing to me was abuse, that's how confused I was.

I also tried my GP and said I was feeling down. I was referred for counselling. The counsellor listened to me but still did not name what I was experiencing as abuse or refer me anywhere. But she did get me to acknowledge that I was acting out the stereotypical role of a controlled Muslim woman. Then the school picked up that there was something wrong with my son, but instead of helping me they threatened me. They said if I didn't admit to my husband hitting my son then I was going to be in serious trouble with the police. They didn't even try to help me. All they did was call social services. If someone had said what your husband's doing is abuse I would have said YES!

Eventually I found a friend who I could confide in and trust. It was basically her that helped me to identify the abuse. It wasn't long before I went to the police. The first officer was really great. And then the next day I had a middle-aged policeman, and I was terrified because, you know, I'm scared of men anyway. And he turned out to be amazing too. I couldn't have asked for better. The same with the other officers – they were really, really, good and I had a woman. But the problem was I didn't realise that my husband had raped me. I thought rape was being dragged down the back of an alley, you know. I needed someone from the NGO there to explain to me what rape was. In the end the charges were dropped because I could not commit to rape.

It was the police who put me in touch with the NGO. They were very good at first because my case worker was able to reassure me, like my friend, and say this is not Islam; this is nothing to do with Islam. My caseworker gave me advice to go to court, go to a solicitor, and she did come to the solicitor with me and we got a restraining order so my husband couldn't contact me; he couldn't come to the street where I was living. I felt safe.

But after the solicitor was completely useless. I'm not blaming the NGO in any way but I thought the solicitors they recommended would be specialists in abuse and help me to find somewhere to live because I was still living with relatives and that wasn't good for me or my children.

In addition, the interaction with the NGO stopped almost straightaway – I had to chase and chase my case worker. I don't know how many hundreds or thousands of clients she's got, but it's obviously too many because none of us can ever get hold of her. And it shouldn't be that way. It should be them chasing you. Then I became aware of a local housing association and found they had a floating support service. I contacted them and they have been absolutely amazing - you know every time they made an appointment they've been there on the dot, if I've been in desperation they've come straightaway. And they've just organised a house for me and that's really helpful. So the housing association have been amazing, but I would like to see the NGO and the housing association talk to each other. They could have talked to each other straightaway and not left me in that hole. If the NGO had talked to the housing association I could have gone into emergency accommodation, which I'm only getting now, a year and a half after. And there have been other problems, like when I became aware that my case worker was going to a meeting where all the professionals were going to discuss my situation. I would have been alright with that, if it had protected me and the kids to some extent. But my ex-husband managed to convince some of the people there that he'd done nothing wrong and really it was all to do with me. The only way I could figure that they'd all spoken to each other was through that meeting. And that's what really got me; all these people who initially were so supportive ended up believing him.

So I think things could have been done better. Really it was my friend who had to do all the joining of the people together. She came everywhere with me. She talked to the professionals, talked to the housing association, talked to the NGO to get them to connect, to talk to each other. But in the end I was helped, despite the way I look, despite my religion, despite – all the things I worried about – that they would say, well you were married to a Muslim – what did you expect? But no, even the police were amazing, completely non-judgmental – they didn't blame you in any way, they did everything they could to help and – it was good that they called the NGO. At least now I can see the conditioning - how women are positioned in society, being a Muslim – all the mists have cleared at once.

Najprej sem pomoč iskala prek lokalnega telefona za pomoč v stiski. To je bilo povsem nekoristno. Rekli so mi, naj se vrnem in se soočim z možem. Niso me izprašali ali dopustili možnosti, da bi to lahko bila zloraba. To sem poskusila šestkrat ali sedemkrat v štirih letih. Zelo sem jezna, da so me pustili na cedilu, ker takrat nisem vedela, da je to, kar sem prestajala, zloraba.

Poskusila sem tudi pri svojem osebnem zdravniku, ki sem mu povedala, da sem potrta. Napotil me je v svetovalnico. Svetovalka me je poslušala, a tega, kar sem doživljala, ni imenovala zloraba, pa tudi napotila me ni nikamor. Me je pa pripravila do tega, da sem priznala, da igram stereotipno vlogo nadzorovane muslimanke. Potem so v šoli zaznali, da je nekaj narobe z mojim sinom, a namesto da bi mi pomagali, so mi grozili. Rekli so, da če ne priznam, da mož tepe sina, bom imela resne težave s policijo. Niso mi niti skušali pomagati. Vse, kar so naredili, je bilo, da so poklicali socialno službo. Če bi nekdo rekel, da je moževo početje zloraba, bi rekla 'ja'.

Sčasoma sem našla prijateljico, ki sem se ji lahko zaupala in se nanjo zanesla. V bistvu je bila ona tista, ki mi je pomagala prepoznati zlorabo. To ni bilo veliko pred tem, ko sem šla na policijo. Prvi policist je bil res super. Potem pa sem naslednji dan imela policista srednjih let in me je bilo groza, ker se že tako bojim moških. Pa se je izkazalo, da je tudi on čudovit. Ne bi si mogla želeti boljšega. In enako velja za ostale policiste – bili so zelo zelo dobri in imela sem tudi žensko. Toda problem je bil, da se nisem zavedala, da me je mož posilil. Mislila sem, da je posilstvo to, da te zvlečejo po stranski ulici. Nekdo tam bi mi moral razložiti, kaj je posilstvo. Na koncu so obtožbo opustili, ker se nisem mogla strinjati s posilstvom.

Policija me je povezala z nevladno organizacijo. Sprva so bili zelo dobri, ker me je moja socialna delavka lahko pomirila, kot prijateljica, rekla mi je, da to ni islam; da to nima nič opraviti z islamom. Svetovala mi je, naj grem na sodišče, in je šla z mano k odvetniku in smo dosegli prepoved približevanja. Počutila sem se varno.

*A kasneje odvetnik ni bil za nobeno rabo. Nikakor ne krivim nevladne organizacije, a sem
mislila, da bodo odvetniki, ki so jih priporočili, specialisti za zlorabo in da mi bodo pomagali
najti prebivališče, ker sem še vedno živela pri sorodnikih.*

*Poleg tega je interakcija z nevladno organizacijo skoraj takoj prenehala – kar naprej
sem morala loviti svojo socialno delavko. Potem sem izvedela za lokalno stanovanjsko
združenje in ugotovila, da imajo kratkoročno podporno službo. Stopila sem v stik z njimi
in so absolutno čudoviti – vsakič, ko smo se dogovorili za sestanek, so prišli točno; če sem
bila obupana, so prišli takoj. Rada bi videla, da bi se nevladna organizacija in stanovanjsko
združenje pogovarjala. Če bi se pogovarjali, bi lahko dobila krizno namestitev, ki jo bom
dobila šele zdaj, leto in pol kasneje. Bili pa so tudi drugi problemi, na primer, ko sem izvedela,
da moja socialna delavka hodi razpravljat o moji situaciji na večinstitucionalni posvet za
oceno tveganja (MARAC), kamor hodijo vsi strokovni delavci. S tem bi se strinjala, če bi se
mene in moje otroke do neke mere zaščitilo. A je mojemu bivšemu možu uspelo nekatere
ljudi tam prepričati, da ni storil nič narobe in da je vse moj problem. Edini način, kot lahko
sklepam, da so se vsi pogovarjali, je bilo prek tistega MARAC-a. In to me je res prizadelo; vsi
tisti ljudje, ki so mi bili sprva v veliko podporo, so na koncu verjeli njemu.*

*Tako da mislim, da bi stvari lahko bile narejene bolje. V resnici je bila moja prijateljica tista,
ki je morala povezati ljudi. Povsod je šla z mano. Govorila je s strokovnjaki, govorila je s
stanovanjskim združenjem, govorila je z nevladno organizacijo, da jih je pripravila do tega,
da so se povezali, da so govorili drug z drugim. A na koncu so mi pomagali ne glede na
to, kako izgledam, kljub moji veri, kljub – vsem stvarem, ki so me skrbele – da bodo rekli:
»Poročila si se z muslimanom, kaj si pa pričakovala?« A ne, celo policija je bila čudovita,
povsem neobsojajoča – na noben način me niso krivili, naredili so vse, da bi pomagali – in
bilo je dobro, da so poklicali nevladno organizacijo. Zdaj vsaj lahko vidim pogojevanje – kako
so ženske pozicionirane v družbi, muslimanke – vsa zameglenost se je takoj razblinila.*

"She always asked me what I "wanted

Marah's story

I came to the UK from my home country and it was very bad. My husband was very bad but he never let me see a doctor. Then I became pregnant and I said to my husband, I told my husband, now I must see a doctor, go to the hospital. And I had a friend, she lived in the same street and she must have seen me, how bad it was. So she told me about this organisation, she said, it is better if you go there, and they will help you. And she brought me here.

When I first came here, they asked me lots of questions but it was OK because they spoke my language and so I was able to tell them what was happening to me. They called the police but the police took a long time to come and then they did not help. So this organisation, they said they had no room in the refuge but they found a hotel and I stayed there, maybe three, maybe four days. Then I came to a refuge. My experience of the refuge was not really bad. Some of the workers are not good with the girls because they don't work properly to be nice. Their behaviour is not good and they are just proudly talking to us so, actually, I made a complaint, I was on a complaint; but because all Asian women stay there and they knew about Halal and things, I made lots of friends. And my support worker, she came to see me there and later in the hospital when I had my baby.

So then they asked me if I wanted to move to a house and, obviously I couldn't stay in this refuge forever! So I said I would choose an area and then my support worker looked for some place for me to stay there. That was four years ago so I am in this house for four years and I am settled now. But at the beginning, my support worker, she sorted out all the housing benefit and the child benefit. And they helped me with the English classes. It is the best place. And when I tell my inside feelings to my support worker, she has not shared this with another person and that is a good thing. It is good because they don't share and so my family, they don't know where I live. And they made an appointment for me to see a solicitor because I was not definite in this country yet and the solicitor needed to have lots of evidence which I showed him and it was OK because the solicitor also spoke my language. So now I have indefinite stay. And she always asked me what I wanted, she did not tell me do this or do that and so, when I moved, I said I wanted a big house, with trees. But this is a problem now because the rules have changed and I can't pay for the extra bedroom. So this organisation is helping me again.

And I said, I cannot work because my child is three and is not going to a full-time nursery yet. So I said to the Council, I will definitely pay you when I'm working. But at the moment I can't do any work and I am going to college so that I can improve my English.

So the help from this organisation is good and they also understand what is happening in Asian families. They know the husband can marry three times and live with three girls and this and that. My husband lived with another girl as well and has two babies. He never told me that but now I know. I am not saying that all Asian men are the same. Some are fantastic! But some are not good. And I really miss the refuge because of my old friends. They really helped me, made all the food like my mum did for me, it was like belonging. But this organisation is good too. Even now, if I have a problem and I need help, I can come to them and they help me.

"We've got rights. That's why our confidence is built"

Sabina's story

I learned about this organisation through leaflets and my friends. There were leaflets in the Asian supermarket and maybe at the doctor's too. And my friends knew because I think they had been in my situation. So when I first came to this organisation, they helped me with my problems. And I am very comfortable discussing my matters with the support workers because they know my language. This is important because at that time, I didn't know how to trust other people. But they really went deep down and understood. This is why I discussed my own life because I realised they needed to understand my case and then try to sort the problem out. And I came here with my children and said I have no place to stay. So first they found a hotel for us for a few days. And my support worker, she brought me food because then we were fasting and I needed my own food to break the fast. And she cooked this at home and brought it to us. Then they said there was a place in a refuge but I told them, I don't want to go there because my children are very upset and I don't think this will be good for them. So then they found me a flat. I think it is a Council flat because I am not paying any rent and we have been there now for one year. And they sorted out the child benefit because this was going to my husband but now it comes to me. And other benefits – at the Job Centre. And they help me with the solicitor so that I can be indefinite. I had another problem too. My children's school was very far away and they would take them there and pick them up. And now they are in another school, closer, and they are all together.

The support workers, I can talk to them and it is all confidential and private and this is really important because it's about my life, it's my own personal things. If I have shared, that person – the person I am sharing with has to be trustworthy. And they always discuss things first. Like this meeting, for example, today's meeting. My support worker, she phoned me and said, I know you've got children and I know you've got a busy life. But if you like, about this meeting, if you like to come I will put your name down. If you don't like, then just say no. So this is it. We have the rights. We've got rights to say, when I need help, you can help us. We've got rights. That's why our confidence is built. When I lived in the family, I can't build my confidence there. But the kinds of things now I've found that women can do and I think this is a good place. My confidence was very low when I first came here and now I am standing on my own two feet. When I came to this organisation, I found out that nothing is hard in life, just if the bad times come then we have to be strong. These ladies are running the big project and they are women like us and they understand our language, our culture.

Domestic Violence

Stories and experiences of women

Germany

"Sie haben mir gezeigt wie, und ich habe es selber geschafft"

Danielas Geschichte

Ich kam vor drei Jahren aus Osteuropa nach Deutschland und lebte ein Jahr mit meinem Mann hier. Unser Kind war bei meinen Eltern in einem anderen Land der EU. Die Familie meines Ex-Mannes lebt auch hier in dieser Stadt, und ich hatte sowohl mit ihm, als auch mit seiner Familie Probleme. Eines Nachts haben er und seine Familie mich geschlagen, danach habe ich Hilfe gesucht. Ich bin zur Polizei gegangen, denn das ist die erste Stelle, zu der man geht, wenn so was passiert, und sie waren sehr hilfreich. Der Polizist hat angeboten mit mir zu meiner Wohnung zu gehen, damit ich meine Sachen packen kann, und da verbot er meinem Ex-Mann mit mir zu sprechen sonst gibt es ein Verfahren gegen ihn. Für ein paar Tage konnte ich bei einer Freundin aus dem Deutschkurs für Migranten bleiben, und dann hat mir die Polizei von dem Frauenhaus erzählt und mich dorthin gebracht. Ich hatte vorher nie von so einer Unterkunft gehört, aber dort zu leben fühlte sich an wie eine Familie zu haben, die Atmosphäre dort ist so warm und voller Energie.

Am Anfang fühlte ich mich total verloren in Deutschland ohne mein Kind, und wusste nicht welchen Weg ich gehen könnte, ich hatte keine Papiere, kein Geld, nichts, und ich wusste ich kann nicht in mein Land zurückgehen, da bin ich noch mehr unsicher als hier. Aber die Polizei und die Betreuerinnen im Frauenhaus haben mir den Weg nach vorne gezeigt, Schritt für Schritt. Die Betreuerinnen haben gemerkt was ich brauchte noch bevor ich irgendwas gesagt habe, weil ich mir nie hätte vorstellen können, dass eine Lösung möglich ist. Sie fühlen das, in welcher Richtung sie helfen können, und fragen dann. Sie haben einen Weg gefunden ein Ticket zu bezahlen, so dass mein Kind zu mir kommen und bei mir leben kann, und das hat mir einen Grund zum Leben gegeben. Und wir haben eine Schule gefunden, sie haben mir geholfen, Sozialhilfe zu bekommen. Nachher haben sie mir beim Kindergeld geholfen, das ist ein bisschen schwer zu bekommen hier, und ich habe nicht so viel deutsch gesprochen. Der Frauennotruf hat mir einen guten Anwalt vermittelt, und nachher mit ihm zusammen Briefe geschrieben, damit ich aus dem Mietvertrag mit meinem Ex-Mann herauskomme und eine eigene Wohnung mieten kann.

Ich hatte Angst vor meinem Ex-Mann und seiner Familie und im Frauenhaus haben die mir gesagt: „Wir können so das machen, dass du einen Gewaltschutzantrag bekommst und dann kannst du mit dem Kind sicher hierbleiben".

"They showed me the way, and I did it myself"

Daniela's Story

I came to Germany three years ago from Eastern Europe and lived here with my husband for a year; our child was staying with my parents in a Western EU country. My husband's family also lives here in the same city, and I had problems both with him and with his family. One night both he and his whole family beat me, and that was when I looked for help. I went to the police as that is the first place to turn to when something like that happens, and they were very helpful. The policeman offered to go with me to our flat so that I could pack my things, and there he forbade my husband to speak to me, or he would be prosecuted. For a few days I could stay with a friend from the German course for immigrants, and then the police told me about the shelter and brought me there. I had never heard of shelters before, but living in the shelter felt like having a family, the atmosphere there is so warm, full of warm energy.

At first I felt totally lost in Germany without my child, and could not imagine what way to go, I had no papers, no money, nothing, and I knew I couldn't go back to my country, there I would be even less safe than here. But the police and the support workers in the shelter showed me the way forward, step by step. The support workers noticed what I needed before I even said anything, because I had never imagined that a solution would be possible. They just sense where they could help me and then ask. They found a way to pay for a ticket so my child could come to live with me, and that gave me a reason to live. And we found a school, and they helped me get income support. Later they helped me apply for the child subsidy, that's a bit difficult to get here, and I didn't speak much German yet then. The women's counselling centre put me in touch with a good lawyer, and then they had him write letters to get me out of the joint rental contract with my ex-husband so that I could rent a flat of my own.

I was afraid of my ex-husband and his family, and in the shelter they told me "What we can do, is for you to get a protection order, and then you and your child can stay here and be safe." The court process itself was very stressful for me. The most important thing was getting a protection not only from my ex-husband, but also from his whole family. But I couldn't face the idea of sitting in the same room, me alone with all of them. So first we wrote that I did not want to be in the same room with him and his family, but that didn't work. I didn't sleep then for a whole week, not at all, and then the shelter worker said she would come with me.

Das Verfahren war sehr anstrengend für mich. Das Wichtigste war, dass ich den Gewaltschutz nicht nur vor meinem Mann, sondern vor seiner ganzen Familie bekomme. Aber ich konnte mir nicht vorstellen, dass ich alleine noch mal denen allen gegenüber sitze. Erst mal haben wir in meinen Antrag geschrieben, dass ich nicht mit denen in einem Zimmer zusammen sein will, aber das hat nicht geklappt. Und eine Woche habe ich nicht geschlafen, gar nicht, und dann sagte die Betreuerin vom Frauenhaus, „ich komme mit". Der Anwalt war auch mit und hat mir so ein paar Tipps gegeben, wie ich das machen kann; er hat mir gesagt ich soll die überhaupt nicht anschauen, sondern nur das Gericht. Ich habe den Gewaltschutz dann unbefristet bekommen. Diese Chance, Gewaltschutz zu bekommen, war sehr, sehr wichtig für mich. Sonst könnte ich nicht ruhig auf die Straße oder zur Arbeit gehen. Heute habe ich immer noch irgendwie Angst, aber fühle mich meistens sicher.

In meinem Heimatland ist das ganz, ganz anders. Dort wäre ich auch zur Polizei gegangen, und die hätten mir vielleicht dabei geholfen meine Sachen zu holen und irgendwo anders hinzugehen, aber es gibt überhaupt keine Stellen zur Unterstützung von Frauen, also kann die Polizei auch nicht viel machen. Ich denke da geht es nicht um Kultur, es gibt überall solche Männer und Familien; aber das Sozialsystem fehlt.

Das hilfreichste, was mir gesagt wurde, war, dass ich es alleine schaffen kann. Sie haben mir gezeigt wie, und ich habe es selber geschafft. Das war sehr wichtig für mich, dass ich es alleine schaffen kann.

The lawyer was with me too and gave me good advice, how I could deal with this, telling me not to look at them at all, but only at the court. Now the protection order is unlimited. The chance to get such a protection order was very, very important for me; without that I could not be easy going to work or on the street. Today I am still somewhat fearful, but mostly feel safe.

In my home country, it is very, very different. There, too, I would have turned to the police, and they might have helped me get my things and go somewhere else, but there are no support services for women at all, so there isn't much the police can do. I think this is not a matter of culture, there are men and families like that everywhere; it is just the social welfare system that is lacking.

The most helpful thing anyone said to me was that I can make it on my own. They showed me the way, and I did it myself. That was very important for me, that I can make it on my own.

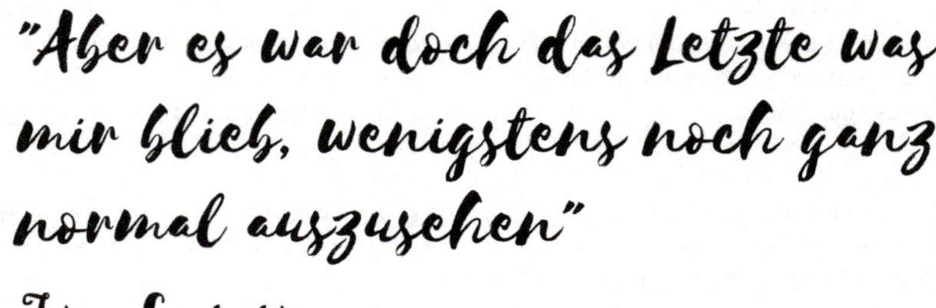

Obwohl ich schon lange in Deutschland lebe, war es schwierig für mich, aus der Gewaltsituation herauszukommen. Es hat viele Jahre gebraucht, Hilfe zu finden. Wenn es mit meinem Ex-Mann eskaliert ist, bin ich einfach immer raus gegangen um mich zu schützen. Schon vor einigen Jahren habe ich nach Stellen geschaut – natürlich wusste mein Ex-Mann nichts davon – und nur im Vorbeigehen die Schilder an den Häusern gelesen. Da ich nicht genau wusste, wo ich Unterstützung bekommen kann, habe ich erstmal nichts gefunden. Ich wollte auch nicht, dass meine erwachsene Tochter von der Situation weiß, und habe mit niemandem darüber geredet.

Die erste Stelle, zu der ich gegangen bin, war eigentlich für obdachlose Menschen zuständig. Am Anfang dachte ich, das Einzige was ich machen kann, ist eine andere Wohnung zu bekommen. Das war vor zwei Jahren. Sie konnten mir nicht weiterhelfen, weil ich ja mit meinem Ex-Mann zusammen eine Wohnung hatte. Ich glaube, ich sah denen nicht fertig genug aus. Aber es war doch das Letzte was mir blieb, wenigstens noch ganz normal auszusehen.

Ein paar Monate später dachte ich, dass es doch im Rathaus jemanden geben müsste, der mir helfen kann. Der Berater dort hat mir dann erklärt, dass es verschiedene Stellen gibt, und mich an eine verwiesen. Er war sehr nett und geduldig, manchmal melde ich mich heute noch bei ihm, wenn ich Hilfe brauche. Bei der Notübernachtung habe ich keinen Schlafplatz bekommen, obwohl ich von meiner Situation erzählt habe. Ich glaube es lag wieder daran, dass ich nicht so aussah, als bräuchte ich Hilfe.

Ich hatte dann aber auch eine Beraterin im Bezirksamt, die für mich über das "Geschützte Marktsegment" nach Wohnungen geschaut hat. Nach über einem Jahr habe ich erstmal einen Platz im Frauenhaus bekommen. Da war ich aber nur für ein paar Wochen, weil mir meine Beraterin in der Zwischenzeit eine Wohnung vermittelt hat. Ich habe das Gefühl, dass sie nur sichergehen wollte, dass ich es wirklich ernst meine mit dem Auszug und der Trennung von meinem Ex-Mann.

"But that was the last thing I had left — that at least I could maintain appearances"

Fatma's Story

Although I have lived in Germany for a long time already, it was difficult for me to escape the situation of violence; it took many years for me to find help. When things escalated with my former husband, I simply used to leave home to protect myself. I began looking for services that might help a few years ago already – of course, my husband did not know about that – and I read the signs on buildings. As I did not know exactly where to get the support I needed, I could not find the right place at first. I also did not want my adult children to become aware of the situation; I did not talk to anyone about this.

The first place I went to was actually responsible for homeless people. At first, I thought that the only thing I could do was to find another apartment. That was two years ago. They couldn't help me any further, because I was living in an apartment with my former husband. I think I did not look exhausted or battered enough to them. But that was the last thing I had left, that at least I could maintain appearances.

I few months later I thought that there should be someone in the town hall who could help me. The advisor there explained to me that there were various competent places, and he sent me to an emergency accommodation, where I could stay overnight. He was very nice and patient, sometimes I still phone him today when I need help. In the emergency accommodation I could not get a place to sleep, although I told them about my situation. I think the reason was again that I didn't look enough like I needed help.

But then I also had an advisor in the regional administration who looked for apartments for me through what was called the "Protected Market Segment". More than one year later, I was offered a place in the women´s refuge. But I stayed there only for a few weeks because my advisor had meanwhile found an apartment for me. My impression was that she simply wanted to be sure if it was my serious intention to move and to separate from my ex-husband.

Als ich das erste Mal beim Frauenhaus angerufen habe, war es für mich, als würde ich mit einem Engel sprechen. Natürlich ist es eigentlich selbstverständlich, aber mir ging es damals so schlecht, dass es sich eben so angefühlt hat. Im Frauenhaus hatte ich wenig Kontakt zu den Mitarbeiterinnen und keine Probleme, aber das lag auch daran, dass ich keine kleinen Kinder hatte und schnell eine andere Wohnung bekommen habe. Ich war ein leichter Fall für die, ich kam eigentlich nur zum Schlafen dorthin. Für die anderen Frauen war es viel schlimmer. Ich habe oft mitbekommen, wie sie geweint haben und nicht wussten, was sie machen sollten. Die Kinder müssen angemeldet werden, die müssen zur Schule gehen, und die Schule ändert sich, alles ändert sich... Aber die Mütter haben keinen Kopf dafür, sind frustriert und seelisch kaputt. Bei solchen Frauen sollten die helfen, und zum Beispiel Behördengänge zusammen machen. Es fehlen dort meiner Meinung nach Sozialarbeiter, Psychotherapeuten, Dolmetscher und eine Betreuung für die Kinder. Man muss immer alles alleine machen. Na wenn ich das alles alleine mache, was such ich da, wenn ich so stark bin und alles hab?

Es war ein großes Glück, dass ich meine Wohnung hier in meinem alten Bezirk bekommen habe. Sonst hätte ich eine andere annehmen müssen, in einem anderen Bezirk, weil das ja hier kein Wunschkonzert ist. Da hätte ich nicht immer „Nein" sagen können, obwohl ich es überhaupt nicht wollte. Das war schon ein ziemlich großer Druck.

Im Nachhinein denke ich, dass mir sehr geholfen hat, was mein Berater und meine Arbeitsvermittlerin zu mir gesagt haben. Sie hat mir immer gesagt: „Sie machen das. Sie haben so viel geschafft." Ich sage, wirklich? Weil so einen Moment ist man wirklich unsicher, weil man denkt, ich habe nichts mehr. Aber sie sagte es immer wieder und fragte mich auch, wie es mit meiner neuen Wohnung ist, ob alles ok ist. Und sie hilft mir auch mit Papierkram. Es hilft sehr, wenn jemand sagt: „Machen Sie den ersten Schritt und denken Sie an sich". Besonders wenn man in einer Zwickmühle ist und denkt, ist das richtig jetzt was ich mache, oder falsch? Vor allem wenn man das alles mit der Familie nicht besprechen kann und nur alleine alles im Kopf durchgehen lässt. Mein Hund hat mir auch sehr dabei geholfen durchzuhalten. Und dass ich wollte, dass meine Kinder mich wieder besuchen können. Das war so eine Antriebskraft, wo man sagt, du kannst jetzt nicht aufgeben, du musst, du musst. Weil wenn du zurück wieder nach Hause gehst, fängt wieder alles von vorne an. Und dann sagen die Stellen, oder die Leute die dir helfen wollen auch: „Dann wollen Sie ja gar nicht raus, dann brauchen Sie ja gar keine Wohnung. Sie sind doch gar nicht in Not". Und dann hat man später gar keine Hilfe mehr, wenn man das zweite Mal sowas braucht. Und man denkt dann: Zurück darf ich nicht, ich muss jetzt nach vorne, nicht zurück.

The first time I called the women's refuge, I felt like I was talking to an angel. Of course, it is perfectly normal, but at the time I was in such bad shape that this was really how it felt. In the women's refuge I didn't have much contact with the women working there and no problems, but that was also because I had no young children, and then I got an apartment quickly. I was a mild case for them and I actually only came there to sleep. For the other women, things were much worse. I often saw them weeping and not knowing what to do. The children have to be enrolled, they have to go to school; and school changes, everything changes. But the mothers do not have their heads free for all this, they are frustrated and mentally worn out. These women should be offered support, for example they should be accompanied to appointments with official authorities. As I see it, there is a lack of social workers, psycho-therapists, interpreters and people to take care of the children; you always have to manage everything alone. Well, if I can manage everything alone, what am I doing there, if I am so strong and have everything I need?

It was a great stroke of luck for me to get an apartment here in my old neighbourhood. Otherwise, I would have been compelled to take another apartment, in a different quarter, because it's not something like a musical request programme here. Then I would not have been in a position to say „No", even if I had not liked that apartment. That put me under quite a lot of pressure.

With hindsight, I think that it was very helpful to me what my advisor in the job placement agency told me. She always said: "You are going to manage that. You've mastered so many things", and I said to her: "Oh, really?" Because in such a moment you feel really unsure, because what you think is: "I've lost everything". But she said that again and again and she also asked me how things were going with my new apartment, if everything was o.k. And she also helps me with the paper work. It's very helpful if someone says to you: "Take the first step and think of yourself" – especially when you are between a rock and a hard place and you wonder: "Is that right what I'm doing now or is that wrong?" especially if you have no possibility to talk about all these issues with your family and have to let them go through your mind alone. My dog also helped me a lot to stand all this; and my strong will to get my children come and visit me again. That was such a driving power and then you say to yourself: "You cannot give up now, you have to get through it; you have to!" Because, if you go back home again, the whole game will start from zero again. And then those authorities or the people who want to help you will tell you. "But you don't want to leave actually, and so you are not in need of an apartment for yourself. You are not really in trouble." And later on, you will be completely left without any help, even if you need it a second time. And then you think: "I cannot go back, I have to go ahead, no way to return."

"Ich habe von keinem so viel Hilfe bekommen, wie hier"

Gabrielas Geschichte

Ich bin hierher gezogen, nachdem meine Ehe zu Ende ging, und hatte schreckliche Probleme, mit der Trennung klarzukommen. Es ging mir immer schlechter und schlechter, und ich wusste, dass ich Psychotherapie brauche, aber die Wartezeiten sind enorm lange, bei mir waren es 11 Monate, und damals hat mir keiner gesagt, dass es Möglichkeiten gibt, schneller an die Therapie zu kommen. Ich war hier neu eingezogen und kannte niemanden, keine Ärzte, keine Stellen, wo man gut informiert wird. Es war auch deshalb schwierig, weil ich keinen Mann als Therapeuten haben wollte, auf keinen Fall. Nach den Gewalterfahrungen in der Ehe hatte ich damals panische Angst vor jedem Mann.

Ich habe mehrere Einrichtungen angerufen, und was sehr wehgetan hat, die erste Frage war, ob ich Kinder hätte, und als ich sagte, dass ich keine habe, wollte die Frau gar nicht weiter mit mir sprechen. Ich musste mir anhören „Die Kollegin ist gerade nicht da, wir notieren uns Ihre Nummer und dann melden wir uns". Ich habe ein paar Tage gewartet, es hat keiner angerufen, dann habe ich woanders gesucht. Das habe ich auch mehrmals erlebt, dass mir gesagt wurde „in erster Linie muss den Frauen mit Kindern geholfen werden". Ich glaube, das Schlimmste war, vor allem, das war eine christliche Einrichtung, und da habe ich gehofft, dass sie mir helfen, aber das war wirklich das Schlimmste. So: „Haben Sie Kinder?" Und wie das gesagt wurde. Das Gespräch war sofort beendet für diese Dame.

Ich wusste zwar, dass es eine Frauenberatungsstelle gibt, aber am Anfang, weil ich vorher so schlechte Erfahrungen gemacht habe, habe ich mich einfach nicht getraut; ich hatte Angst, noch mal verletzt zu werden. Aber dann war mein Arzt in Urlaub und meine Psychotherapeutin im Urlaub, und da ging es mir wieder so schlecht, dass ich keinen Ausweg gesehen habe, und dann habe ich da angerufen. Ich war erst mal enttäuscht, weil das Gespräch nur 5 Minuten gedauert hat, aber sie hat mich gefragt, wie dringend das ist, und hat mir dann noch am selben Tag einen Termin angeboten. Dann hat sie über eine Stunde Zeit für mich genommen. Sie hat mir geholfen, mich zu beruhigen und ich hatte das Gefühl, ich habe alle Zeit der Welt, mit ihr über meine Probleme zu sprechen, und dass wir dann die Schwerpunkte finden. Und wie gesagt, von vornherein habe ich mich da überraschend wohl gefühlt; ich finde, die Frauen sind hier in der Beratungsstelle so kompetent.

"No one has ever given me so much help as I have received here"

Gabriela's Story

I moved to this town after my marriage had come to an end, and I had serious problems to cope with the separation. I was doing worse and worse, and I knew that I needed psychotherapy, but the waiting periods are so long, they were 11 months for me, and at that time, nobody told me there were other possibilities to get an appointment faster. I had just moved into this house and I didn´t know anybody, no doctors, no competent authorities to provide me with valuable information. It was also difficult because I didn´t want to have a man as a psychotherapist, by no means. After my experience of violence in my marriage, I had a panicky fear of every man.

I called several institutions and organisations and what was very painful to me, was when she first of all asked me if I had children, and when I said that I had none, that woman did not want to talk any further with me. I was just told: „The colleague is not in here at this moment, we are noting down your phone number and we will call you then. " I waited a few days, nobody called and then I sought elsewhere. I experienced several times being told: "First of all, women with children must be helped." I think the worst situation was the one I had in a Christian establishment, where I had hoped that they would help me, but that was the worst thing I had to undergo indeed. She asked me: "Do you have children?" – And the way she said it! The conversation was immediately terminated for that lady.

I did know that there was a women´s advice centre existing for women, but I simply didn´t have the courage to go there, because my previous experience had been so bad; I was afraid of being hurt again. But then, my doctor was on holiday and my psychotherapist was on holiday as well, and I was not doing well again so that I saw no other way, and so I called the people there. At first, I was disappointed that the conversation took only 5 minutes, but then she asked me whether it was urgent and she gave me an appointment on that same day. She gave me more than one hour of her time. She helped me to calm down and gave me the feeling that I had all the time in the world to talk about my problems with her and to find the focal points. And, as I just said, I felt surprisingly comfortable with her right from the start; I think those women there in the women´s advice centre are so competent. As I didn´t want to go to to a psychiatric clinic; she recommended me to take an appointment on a weekly basis; that was pure luxury to me. Then I told her that I was really out of money and have been; that was exactly at a time when I was in the worst financial situation

Da ich nicht in die Psychiatrie wollte, hat sie mir einen Termin jede Woche empfohlen, das war für mich der Luxus pur. Dann habe ich gesagt, dass ich wirklich sehr mittellos bin und war, das war gerade zu einer Zeit, wo es mir auch finanziell noch nie so schlecht ging. Und dann hat sie gesagt „Habe ich irgendetwas über Geld gesagt? Sie brauchen Hilfe, sie kommen nächste Woche wieder." Das war sehr schön. Weil sie mir so viel Hoffnung gegeben hat. Und wie die Frau mit mir umgegangen ist, das fand ich so wunderschön. Als ich nach 2, 3 Monaten erfahren habe, dass sie nur zur Vertretung da war, fand ich das sehr schade. Sie wollte gleich mit einer Kollegin sprechen, damit ich weitere Termine bekomme. Ich habe aber lieber versucht, alleine weiter zu kommen, und habe mich erst wieder bei der Beratungsstelle gemeldet, als ich wieder in das schwarze Loch gefallen bin. Ich habe wieder sofort einen Termin bekommen, und einmal in der Woche einen Termin; das zeigte mir, dass sie mir wirklich helfen möchten. Das merke ich daran, wie aufmerksam sie nachfragen, wenn sie einen Termin absagen oder verlegen müssen, dass sie immer fragen, ob ich warten kann, bis die Kollegin wieder da ist, oder ob ich dringend einen Ersatztermin brauche.

Ich habe von keinem so viel Hilfe bekommen, wie hier von der Frauenberatungsstelle. Neulich kam ich zum Termin und ich hatte mal wieder panische Ängste, und das hat keine 20 Minuten gedauert; meine Beraterin hat mir die ganze Angst so abgenommen, ich habe da solche Ruhe empfunden, das war der reine Wahnsinn. So was hatte ich noch nie im Leben gespürt. Und das ist mittlerweile so, dass ich schon überlegt habe, dass ich meine Psychotherapie, die ich von der Krankenkasse bezahlt bekomme, absage. Die Therapeutin ist nicht schlecht, am Anfang hat sie mir geholfen, aber mittlerweile habe ich das Gefühl, dass es nicht das ist, was ich brauche. Ich hatte inzwischen zwei Personen hier bei der Frauenberatungsstelle; hätte ich vor drei Jahren solche Therapeutinnen gehabt, dann gehe ich davon aus, dass mein Leben schon ganz anders aussehe würde. An den Fragen, die meine Beraterin hier stellt, sieht man sofort, dass das Frauen mit Erfahrung sind. Über einige Probleme der Vergangenheit, wie mein Mann mit mir umgegangen ist, konnte ich vorher gar nicht sprechen; das sind hier die ersten Personen, bei denen ich mich öffnen und diese Sachen ansprechen konnte. Das waren so schwierige Sachen, über die ich nie vorher gesprochen habe, die ich 25 Jahre quasi irgendwo versteckt habe und keinem erzählen konnte. Und jetzt habe ich so viel Vertrauen zu den Frauen bekommen und sie gehen so mit mir um, dass ich mich öffnen kann.

Ich weiß, dass das alles nur auf Spendenbasis funktioniert, deshalb habe ich gesagt „Ich kann zurzeit mir keine Spende leisten, wenn Sie Hilfe benötigen, was könnte ich helfen?" Sie sollen mir Bescheid geben. Und sie meinte „Ja, wirklich?" Ja, ok. Und dann habe ich so Briefe bekommen, die ich dann hier in der Umgebung in die Briefkästen werfen soll. Tue ich natürlich gerne. Und ich finde das ist eine Kleinigkeit im Vergleich dazu, was ich dank dieser Frauen gewonnen habe.

ever. And then she said to me: „Did I say anything about money? You need help, you will come back here next week." That was so nice; because she gave me so much hope. And the way this woman was dealing with me; that was so wonderful. When I learnt two or three months later that she was only working there as a replacement, I found that a pity. She wanted to talk to another colleague to get new appointments for me. But then I wanted to try to make progress alone, and I only contacted the advisory centre again when I fell into the black hole again. I got an appointment again immediately and then an appointment once a week; that showed me that they really wanted to help me. I noticed this in their way of attentively asking me when they had to cancel or postpone an appointment, and their always asking me whether I could wait until the colleague would be back again or whether I was in urgent need of an alternative date.

No one has ever given me so much help as I have received here in the women's advisory centre. Lately, I came to the advisory centre and was totally in panic again, and it did not even take 20 minutes; my advisor took away all the fears I had and I had such an experience of calmness then; that was so amazing. I had never felt anything like that in my life before. And meanwhile things have changed up to the point that I have already thought about cancelling my psychotherapy that is paid for by my health insurance. The psychotherapist is not bad, she helped me in the beginning, but meanwhile, I have the feeling that this is not what I need. By now I have had two counsellors here at the women's advisory centre; if I had had such psychotherapists three years ago, then I'm sure my life would be completely different. The questions my advisor asks me here can make you see instantly that they are women with experience. Before that I was completely unable to speak about some of the problems from the past, how my husband treated me; these women here were the first persons to whom I could open up and talk about these problems. These were so difficult matters which I had never talked about before, which I had hidden somewhere for 25 years and would not tell to anybody. And now I've got such a lot of confidence in these women and they treat me in a way that allows me to open up to them.

I know that everything just works on a donation basis and so I said: "Right now I can't afford to make a donation; if you need help in something, what can I do?" And that they should just let me know. And they said "Oh, yes, really?" Yes. Ok, then. And they gave me these letters and asked me to throw into the letter boxes here in the neighbourhood. I am pleased to do this, of course. And, as I think, this is just a very little thing compared to what I gained thanks to those women.

Ich bin zuerst bei dem Frauennotruf gewesen, weil ich schon immer so von ihm bedroht wurde. Beim Frauennotruf konnten sie mir damals nicht wirklich helfen, nur Gespräche anbieten. Darüber reden zu können war schon mal ganz gut. Aber dann nahm das solche Ausmaße an, dass ich wirklich gedacht habe, dass der mir was antut. Wir hatten zwei Wohnungen, ich in der Stadt Y, wo ich auch früher gewohnt habe, und er in Stadt T, wo ich auch zur Arbeit ging. Ich hatte bei ihm immer einen Koffer mit Kleidung und persönlichen Dingen, Ausweisen und Autopapieren und alles Mögliche, was man mal braucht. Ich ging 9 Stunden am Tag arbeiten, aber er wusste gar nicht, was Arbeit ist, und hatte den ganzen Tag nichts anderes im Kopf gehabt als nachdenken, wie er mich kontrollieren könnte. Ich sollte z.B. auf die Minute genau zu Hause sein. Der hat mich betrachtet wie seine Leibeigene, ich durfte nicht einmal mehr alleine einkaufen gehen. Aber dann hat er den Koffer mit all meinen privaten Dingen entwendet, und mir dann auch gedroht, dass er meinem erwachsenen Sohn, der noch in meiner Wohnung lebte, ernsthaft etwas antun wird. Da hatte ich richtig Panik und Angst und habe mich an die Polizei in Y gewandt, weil ich das gar nicht mehr alleine bewältigen konnte.

Die Polizei war erst mal verständnisvoll, sie versuchten, mich in einem Frauenhaus unterzubringen, aber da war wohl in der Region nichts frei, da habe ich mich entschieden, zu einer Verwandten zu fahren. Dann haben die mich auch noch begleitet, sind also hinterhergefahren, ob da jemand mir folgt, und haben mir das Gefühl gegeben, sie nehmen mich ernst. Sie haben auch gleich veranlasst, dass die Polizei in T den Mann sucht und eine einstweilige Verfügung noch in derselben Nacht ihm zustellt, dass er sich mir nicht nähern darf.

Die hat er natürlich nicht ernst genommen, er wusste, wo er mich suchen konnte, und ist am nächsten morgen vorbei und hat einen Zettel ans Auto gemacht und gehupt. Er hat danach immer weiter Drohbriefe geschrieben und mich auch wirklich gefährdet. Z.B. hatte er noch einen Schlüssel zu meinem Auto und hat daran manipuliert, die Reifen gelockert oder an den Bremsen was gemacht. Damit bin ich immer zur Polizei gegangen, aber nach diesem ersten Abend merkte ich,

I contacted the women's counselling centre first because he was always threatening me, but they couldn't really help me, except for talking, which was good as far as it went. But then his threats reached such a level that I really thought he would do something to me. I was working in City T, but we had both kept our own flat, mine in Town Y and his in City T, so I always had a suitcase in his flat with clothes and things I needed, documents and all sorts of personal items. I worked a 9-hour day, while he didn't even know what it means to work. He had nothing to do all day but think of ways to control me. For example he expected me to arrive home on the minute. He thought of me as his slave. It got to the point where he wouldn't even let me go to the store on my own. Then he stole my suitcase and threatened serious harm to my son, who was grown up but still living in my flat. And that was when I went to the police, because I realized I couldn't cope with this alone; I was in panic.

The police were very understanding and helpful, they called the shelters in both towns to see if I could stay there but there was nothing free; and then when I decided to stay with an older relative, they went with me and drove behind me to make sure he wasn't following. They gave me the feeling that they were taking me seriously. Right away they called the police in T, who that very night served him an injunction forbidding him to come near me.

But of course he ignored that, he knew where to look for me, and the next morning he taped a threatening letter to my car where I was staying and honked. He continued to threaten me, and even put me in real danger. He had a key to my car and manipulated it, for example loosening the nuts on the wheels or doing something to the brakes. Every time he did anything or wrote a threatening letter I went to the police, but after that first intervention I could tell that they were annoyed with me for bothering them, and they grudgingly just said "We'll add this to our files". So there was this injunction, and he ignored it, and that had no consequences. And that was when I became really very afraid, when I thought "Nothing will happen to him". It was a really terrible time for me, because I knew he is bigger and stronger than I am and he gets this crazy look in his eyes when he is angry.

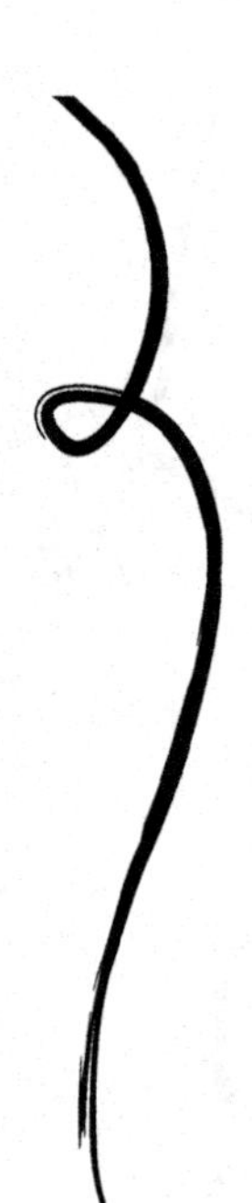

dass sie sich von mir genervt fühlten und etwas widerwillig sagten „Dann nehmen wir das zu den Akten". Da gab es diese Verfügung, und er hält sich nicht daran, und das hat doch gar keine Konsequenzen. Und das war auch das, wo ich richtig Angst hatte, wo ich gedacht habe „es passiert doch nichts". Es war eine richtig schlimme Zeit für mich, denn ich wusste, der ist größer und stärker als ich und bekommt so einen irren Blick, wenn er wütend ist. Bei der Arbeit war ich abgelenkt, aber abends und am Wochenende bin ich von einem Fenster zum anderen, monatelang, immer diese Bilder und Gedanken, wo ich einfach nur dachte, ich drehe durch.

Ich habe dann noch mal mit dem Frauennotruf Kontakt aufgenommen, sie haben mir auch eine Psychologin vermittelt. Einen Anwalt habe ich mir aus dem Telefonbuch herausgesucht, da habe ich bestimmt großes Glück gehabt, der hat mich richtig super vertreten und auch gut beraten. Der Richter war auch sehr auf meiner Seite und hat den Mann unter Druck gesetzt, die Wahrheit zu sagen und zuzugeben, was er getan hat. Das Verfahren dauerte mehr als fünf Stunden. Er hat dann eine Bewährungsstrafe bekommen mit Sozialstunden, und mir wurde Schmerzensgeld zugesprochen - Aber das hat nicht annähernd den materiellen Schaden ausgeglichen, den er angestellt hat.

Was bei mir so einen bitteren Beigeschmack hinterlässt ist, dass die Polizei nach der ersten Nacht mir nicht weiter geholfen hat; seine Drohungen und die Schäden, die ich berichtet habe, haben sie einfach nicht interessiert. Besonders bitter ist, dass ich all meine privaten Sachen nie wieder bekommen habe; ich weiß nicht, ob er sie versteckt oder vernichtet oder der neuen Freundin geschenkt hat. Die Möglichkeit muss doch bestehen, dass man sagt „wenn wir den jetzt da antreffen, dann gehen Sie da rein und holen gleich Ihre privaten Sachen da raus". Also in der Nacht hätte das doch geschehen können, ich wäre ja mit der Polizei auch in die Wohnung reingegangen. Es ist nicht nur der Wert der Verluste; ich möchte nicht, dass der noch was Privates von mir hat. Weil er mich auch immer kontrolliert hat, der hat mich kontrolliert bis auf die Unterwäsche. Und ich will das nicht, dass die Sachen in seinem Besitz sind.

Bei der Frauenberatungsstelle habe ich mich gut aufgehoben gefühlt, aber es wäre wünschenswert, wenn die noch mehr Möglichkeiten, Kapazitäten hätten, daran fehlt es ja wohl; die leben ja auch von Spenden. Es ist dort voll. Immer voll. Das sagt ja schon einiges, auch über unsere Gesellschaft. Ja, das würde ich denen wünschen. Es müsste mehr getan werden, dass die hier noch besser arbeiten können.

Ich hab mehrere Baustellen, aber da ist die Polizei das größte Problem eben in dieser Kette, was mich angeht. Also da müsste sich echt grundlegend was ändern. Die sind völlig unsensibel. Ich weiß nicht, ob die mit sowas auch überfordert sind oder ob die irgendwie eine Stelle dafür einrichten müssten, vielleicht eine Polizeibeamtin, die für sowas dann zuständig ist.

At work I was distracted, but in the evenings and on the weekend I paced from one window to the next, it went on for months that way, always with these images and idea in my head, and thinking I was about to crack up.

I went back to the women's counselling centre and they referred me to a psychologist who has helped me cope. I found a lawyer in the phone book who was really great, I really struck it lucky with him, he represented me really well and gave me good advice. The judge was also on my side and put pressure on him to speak the truth and admit to what he had done – the proceedings lasted over five hours. He got a suspended sentence under condition of community service, and he had to pay me compensation, but the compensation did not nearly cover the value of all the things he had kept or damaged.

It still leaves a bitter taste in my mouth that the police failed to help me after that first action. All the threats and acts of damage that I reported just didn't interest them. It's particularly bitter that I never got back all the things that were in his flat, very personal things, and I don't know if he has destroyed them, or hidden them or given them to his new girlfriend. It should have been possible to take me along, saying "If he's there you can go in and collect your personal belongings"; they could have done that in the first night, with police I would have gone to his flat. It's not a question of the value of what I lost, I just don't want him to have anything private of mine, because he was always monitoring me, right down to my underwear, and I don't want him to have those things.

The women's counselling center was very supportive and understanding, but they need more resources to give more help; they don't have enough staff to cover their hotline at night and depend on donations. It's full when I go there, always full, and that says something, about our society as well. They should be given more public funding so that they can do even better work.

I can see several problem areas, but for me the police are the biggest problem. There needs to be some fundamental change in that respect; they are not at all sensitive. Maybe they lack training or can't cope with these issues well; maybe there should be a woman in the police to respond to this kind of problems.

"Ich brauche keine Hilfe, wenn ich tot bin"

Jennys Geschichte

Ich hatte einen sehr schlimmen Konflikt mit meinem Ex und die Dinge sind einfach außer Kontrolle geraten. Die Kinder waren da und haben alles mitbekommen und dann hat er angefangen mich zu schlagen und solche Sachen. Und dann habe ich mir gedacht: „Das war's. Es ist mir egal ob er mich umbringt oder was auch immer passieren wird, genug ist einfach genug". Mein Sohn hat versucht zu stoppen was er sah und ist dann in Schock verfallen, er hat einfach nur gezittert und ich wollte schauen was mit ihm los ist. Und dann hat mein Ex die Tür geschlossen und meinte, dass er nicht mein Sohn sei. Dann sagte ich mir: „Das war's". Ich rannte in mein Zimmer, schloss die Tür – ich konnte zu dem Zeitpunkt kein einziges Wort Deutsch, ich war grade erst nach Deutschland gezogen – und dann rief ich die Polizei. Zu meiner Überraschung kamen sie innerhalb von 3 Minuten. Ich war so froh, denn wenn er mich gehört hätte wie ich die Polizei rufe und sie nicht rechtzeitig gekommen wären, bin ich mir sicher, dass an diesem Tag etwas sehr Schlimmes passiert wäre.

Er war geschockt als er sah, dass die Polizei da ist, also das war eine wirklich gute Hilfe, eine wirklich große Hilfe für mich. Sie haben mich gefragt ob ich bleiben will, oder an einen Ort umziehen den er nicht kennt, und ich entschied mich für eine Unterkunft die in der Nähe von einer Freundin ist. Was ich nicht gut fand war, dass die Polizei ihm einen Brief gegeben hat, in dem stand dass er nicht näher als 200 Meter an meine Wohnung ran darf, aber er war dann nur 5 Meter von ihr entfernt. Am nächsten Tag kam die Polizei um mich abzuholen und zum Bahnhof zu bringen. Es war wieder unheimlich aber es hat mich zum Glück niemand gesehen. Egal, es hat gut geklappt, ich bin zu der Unterkunft gegangen, aber meine Kinder wussten dass eine Freundin nicht weit weg wohnt und wollten bei ihr leben und bettelten: „Mama, können wir bitte dahin?". Und ich habe nachgegeben. Wenn man mich heute fragt, ich hätte das nie tun sollen.

Ich wohnte dann mit meiner Freundin. Ich hatte keine andere Wohnung, also fragte ich das Jobcenter und die sagten, dass sie keine Wohnung für mich frei hätten, und ich also für ein paar Tage bei meiner Freundin leben soll. Erst für einen Monat, dann für zwei Monate und ich war extrem belastet weil meine Kinder von der Erfahrung so gestresst waren. Außerdem haben meine Freundin und ihr Ehemann sich nicht gut verstanden und sich gestritten – und das war doch die Situation wegen der wir umgezogen sind! Ich wusste nie, dass er auch diese Art von Person ist.

"I don't need help when I'm dead."

Jenny's Story

i had a very bad conflict with my ex and the things just went out of control. The children were there and they witnessed everything and then he started beating me and stuff like that. And then I thought to myself "That's it. I don't care if he's going kill me or whatever going to happen, just enough is enough." My son tried to stop what he saw and then he got in shock, he was just shaking and I went to see what's wrong with him. And then my ex just closed the door to his room and said that he's not my son. Then I said "That's it". I ran in my room, closed the door, I couldn't speak any word of German at the time, I had just moved to Germany and then I called the police. To my surprise they came in 3 minutes. I was so glad because if he heard me calling the police and they didn't come in time, I'm sure that that day something very bad would have happened.

He was so shocked seeing the police were there, so that was a really good help, a really big help to me. They asked me if I wanted to stay, or move to a place unknown to him and I decided I would go to a shelter close to a friend of mine. What I didn't like was that the police gave him a letter that he's not supposed to be 200 meters around my flat but actually he was 5 meters away from the flat.
The next day the police came to pick me up and bring me to the train station. It was again scary but luckily no one saw me. Anyway, things went well, I went to the shelter, but my kids knew there was a friend not far away and they wanted to live at her place and begged "Mum, please, can we go?" and I gave in. If you asked me today I should have never done that.

I came and lived with my friend. I didn't have any other flat, so I asked the jobcenter and they said that they don't have any flats available for me so I should stay with my friend for a couple of days. It was a month and then a second month and I was in a really big stress because my children were in stress from their experience. Also, my friend and her husband didn't get on that well with each other and were having arguments – and that was the situation we moved to get away from! I never knew that he was that type of person as well.

I was suffering, my children too and then I went to my doctor, I explained the situation and then she said for me to find a psychologist for my children and for me. I found for my children but not for me.

Ich habe gelitten, und meine Kinder auch und dann bin ich zu meiner Ärztin gegangen, habe die Situation erklärt und dann sagte sie ich solle für mich und meine Kinder einen Psychologen finden. Für meine Kinder habe ich einen gefunden, für mich nicht. Ab dann wurde es besser und der Ehemann meiner Freundin wollte nicht, dass ich beim Jobcenter nach einer Wohnung frage, aber ich habe nicht mehr auf ihn gehört. Dann habe ich meine Beraterin getroffen und hatte so ein Glück sie zu treffen.

Ab dann hat ein neues Kapitel angefangen. Ich wollte, dass meine Adresse versteckt wird, weil mein Ehemann wusste wo meine Freundin wohnt und er Briefe vom Jugendamt bekommen hat. Ich habe das Jugendamt gebeten die Adresse zu verstecken. Aber sie sagten: „Das ist unmöglich, das können wir nicht machen." Dann hatten wir einen Termin vor Gericht. Ich fragte ob wir zu einem Gericht in einer anderen Stadt gehen können, weil ich nicht am selben Ort sein wollte. Also ja, das war gut, sie haben es geändert. Mit der Hilfe von der Beraterin und der Polizei bin ich für ein paar Tage in diese Stadt gezogen, bis das mit dem Gericht durch war.

Ich habe wegen ihm schon mal die Polizei gerufen, in dem anderen Land. Aber sie sind dem nie nachgegangen. Es war einfach nur ein weiterer Fall. Es ist ziemlich oft passiert, dass wir nicht gehört wurden wenn was passiert ist, und dann war es zu spät. Ich brauche keine Hilfe wenn ich tot bin, also macht was bevor es zu spät ist.

From there things were getting better and then the husband of my friend didn't want me to go to Jobcenter to ask for a flat but I didn't listen to him anymore. Then I met my counsellor and I was so lucky to meet her.

From then on a new chapter started. I wanted my address hidden because my husband knew that my friend lives here and then he got letters from the youth welfare office. I asked the youth welfare office to hide the address. And they said "it's impossible, we can't do that." Then we had a court meeting. I asked to go to a different court in a different city; I didn't want to be in the same place. So yes, that was good, they changed it. With the help of the counsellor and police I moved to that city for a couple of days until the court was finished.

I called the police on his account already in the other country. But they never investigated. It was like just another case. It happened really often that we were not heard at the time it happened, and then it was too late. I don't need help when I'm dead so take action before it's too late.

"Und die ganze Zeit läuft es falsch und ich berichtige das selber"

Katharinas Geschichte

Es bestand schon seit Jahren Gewalt in der Ehe. Das hat richtig angefangen ein Jahr nachdem ich mein Kind geboren habe und ich habe es gemerkt und dann habe ich gedacht „Mensch, jetzt hast du ein Kind". Meine Schwestern haben mir immer gesagt „Hör auf damit, lass das". Ich sollte, auch damals, so fing es an, ihn nicht heiraten. Und naja, ich habe es zum Wohle des Kindes doch gemacht und habe es versucht. Nachdem es so schlimm geworden war, habe ich es immer versucht mich scheiden zu lassen und ich habe gedacht „Ok, ich bereite meine Sachen vor und ich warte ab" und dann kam wieder Versöhnung. Er wollte generell nicht arbeiten, weil ich angeblich genug verdiene. So viel war das auch nicht muss ich sagen, ich habe alles getragen. Er hat Schwarzarbeit die ganze Zeit gemacht. Und dann, als es zuhause eskaliert ist, habe ich ihn gefragt „Wo hast du das ganze Geld hingebracht?" Er ist immer einmal im Jahr mit seinen Söhnen in sein Heimatland gefahren, meistens mit dem Kleinen und hat sich da was hochgezogen ohne dass ich es wusste. Und hat die ganzen Leute belogen, dass er angeblich nur 450 Euro verdient und im Endeffekt hat er gar nicht 450 Euro, der hatte fast 3000 bis 4000 Euro netto in der Hand jeden Monat. Ich habe das Geld nie gesehen. Und 2011 war es so schlimm, dass die Polizei angekommen ist und er einen Platzverweis gekriegt hat, weil er auch Schusswaffen hatte. An dem Tag bin ich auch geschlagen worden, bin ich im Krankenhaus gewesen und anschließend hat mir der Arzt gesagt, ich solle ihn anzeigen. Ich solle ihn endlich mal anzeigen. Das habe ich dann auch gemacht.

Und da hat einer von der Staatsanwaltschaft zu mir gesagt, ich sei nicht das Opfer, sondern mein Mann. Und „wir gehen nur nach den Vermerken der Polizei und nur das ist für uns maßgebend." Und in unserem Dorf ist auch bekannt, dass die Zuständigkeit ständig gewechselt hat, das hat meine Beraterin auch rausgekriegt und die werden auch nicht aktiv. Ein Stellvertreter war bis letztes Jahr im Frühling da und dann ist er in Pension gegangen, ich gehe davon aus, dass er die Vermerke auch bewusst gemacht hat. Und Hilfe habe ich von keinem gekriegt, sei es vom Jugendamt, sei es von der Polizei, von der Staatsanwaltschaft, die sind alle auf seiner Seite, weil er die Kinder hat. Meine Beraterin ist die einzige, die mir zuhört. Und die das auch so sieht.

"And things go wrong all the time and I correct them myself"

Katharina's Story

There was violence in this marriage for years. It really started one year after I had given birth to my child and I noticed it and I thought: „Well, now you have a child". My sisters always told me „Don't go on like that, let it be". Back then already, that is how it started, I shouldn't have married him. And well, I did it nevertheless for the sake of the child and tried it. After it became so bad, I was always trying to get a divorce and I thought, „Ok, I will get everything ready and wait and see" and then there was reconciliation again. He never wanted to work, because I supposedly earn enough money. It wasn't that much, I have to say, but I paid for everything. He did undeclared work all the time. And then, when it escalated at home, I asked him „Where did you put all the money?" He always used to go to his home country with the kids once a year, usually with the little one, and built something up for himself there without me knowing about it. And he lied to everyone that he would earn only 450 Euro, but effectively he didn't have 450 Euro but almost 3000 to 4000 Euro net earnings in his hands every month. I never saw this money. And in 2011 it was so bad that police came and gave him an order to leave our flat because he also had firearms. On this day he also beat me up, I was in the hospital and the doctor told me afterwards I should report him. I should finally report him. And that is what I did then.

And then one guy from the public prosecutor's office told me I wasn't the victim, but my husband. And „we just go by the police notes and only that is decisive for us." And in our village it's generally known that the responsibilities changed constantly, my counsellor figured that out, and they do not take action. One deputy was there until spring of last year and then he retired, I assume that he made these notes on purpose. And I didn't receive help from anybody, not the youth welfare office, not the police, not the public prosecutor's office; they are all on his side, because he has the children. My counsellor is the only one who listens to me. And who sees it the way I do.

He manipulated our older child. I was working, he was at home every day, and there was enough time for it. Last year when things were escalating I rented a post office box for my own mail and he went there three times and had them give him a duplicate key! I reported this to the police, but the public prosecutor brushed it off, allegedly because it is a marital dispute. Always „because of marital dispute", if it weren't a marital dispute, they would evaluate it very differently. But since it is a „marital dispute in a family" they always drop all charges.

Den Großen hat er manipuliert. Ich war berufstätig, er war jeden Tag zuhause, da war genug Zeit dazu. Letztes Jahr wo es so eskaliert ist habe ich ein Postschließfach beantragt und er ist dreimal zur Post gegangen und hat sich einen Zweitschlüssel geben lassen! Da habe ich auch eine Strafanzeige erstattet. Der Staatsanwalt hat das abgewimmelt, angeblich, weil es ein Ehestreit ist. Immer „wegen Ehestreit", wenn kein Ehestreit wäre, würden sie das ganz anders bewerten. Aber da es ein „Ehestreit mit Familie" ist stellen sie es alles ein. Seine Sachen stellen sie nicht ein, das geht alles auf Staatskosten, aber meine Sachen ja. Und das ist schon heftig muss ich sagen. Naja, ich wurde geschlagen, wurde misshandelt, mir wurden die Kinder weggenommen, ich habe gearbeitet, ich musste mein Haus verlassen, obwohl er Geld verdient hat, mir das nicht gesagt hat, und er kriegt alles.

Und die Richterin hat dann auch gesagt, ich wäre hysterisch gewesen. Ja ist ganz klar, wenn man angegriffen wird, dass man dann nicht sagt „Oh, da haben sie Recht, toll, klasse, danke schön". Da wehrt man sich automatisch als Frau, da wird man automatisch ja auch lauter, ich weiß nicht, wer sich das so gefallen lässt.

Alle erzählen von der Scheidung, aber so schnell kann man gar nicht, wenn man keinen hat, wenn man einen Job hat, mit den Kindern, die waren ja noch kleiner. Und mittlerweile hat der die Kinder auch so bearbeitet. Auch meine Rechtsanwältin hat gesagt, dass das manipulativ ist, so Sprüche kommen von keinem Kind, das wurde im Protokoll aber auch nicht erfasst. Und dann habe ich dieser Rechtsanwältin gesagt, sie soll eine Ergänzung hinzufügen, dann hat sie gesagt, sie mache keine Ergänzung, mein Fall sei viel zu schwer, sie möchte, dass sie Prozesshilfe kriegt, dass sie das bezahlt kriegt und sie möchte den Fall nicht noch weiter machen. Dann hat sie gesagt „Das ist alles bearbeitet, da müssen Sie vor das OLG gehen und da müssen Sie selber..." Es ist nicht erfasst worden im Protokoll. Und mein neuer Rechtsanwalt, der jetzt für mich zuständig ist, hatte mir damals gesagt, ich solle erst mal jemanden suchen für Familiensachen. In der Stadt dort wollte keiner Ärger mit der Richterin, darum wollte mich keiner vertreten.

Die ganze Zeit läuft es falsch und ich berichtige das selber. Ich wurde nicht angehört: Bei Gericht nicht, bei der Polizei nicht, beim Jugendamt nicht, nirgendwo! Die sagen einfach „Die ist emotional, die ist verrückt." Ich bin nicht verrückt! Das ist meine Art so. Mein Mann wurde sogar bei der ersten Gerichtsverhandlung aggressiv im Gericht und wurde gebeten, seine Stimme zu dämpfen. Steht sogar im Protokoll drinnen. Ich wurde nie richtig angehört. Ich weiß nicht, warum. Ich will einfach nur Hilfe. Ich habe einfach nur Hilfe gesucht. Die kriege ich bis heute nicht. Ich fühle mich so gefangen und ich weiß nicht, was ich machen soll. Das ist es ja. Im Endeffekt ist es alles für die Katz.

His cases they never drop, everything is paid by the state, but my cases. And that is really heavy, I have to say. Well, I was beaten, abused, my children were taken away from me, I worked, I had to leave my house, even though he earned money, which he didn't tell me, and he gets everything.

And the judge, she also told me that I was being hysterical. Well of course, if you are being attacked, you don't say, „Oh, you're right, awesome, great, thank you". You defend yourself automatically as a woman, you become louder automatically, I don't know who would put up with that.

Everybody is talking about divorce, but you can't do it that quickly, if you don't have anybody, if you have a job and the children, they were small back then. And in the meantime he influenced the children. My attorney said as well that it was manipulative, phrases like these don't come from a child, but they didn't put that in the documents. And then I told this attorney that she should make an additional note, but then she said she wouldn't do that, my case was too complicated, she wanted to get the court grant of legal aid so that she gets paid, and she doesn't want to take this case any further. Then she said, „It has all been processed, you have to go to the Higher Regional Court and do it yourself..." It wasn't put on record. And my new attorney, who is responsible for me now, he told me right away that first I should look for a lawyer for family matters. In the city nobody wanted trouble with the judge, so nobody wanted to represent me.

Things go wrong all the time and I correct them myself. Nobody heard me, not the court, not the police, not the youth welfare office, nowhere! They just say, „She is emotional, she is crazy." I'm not crazy! That's just how I am. My husband even became aggressive during the first hearing in the court and was just asked to lower his voice. It's even in the record. I've never been heard really. I don't know why. I just want help. I was just looking for help, and to this day I'm not getting any.. I feel so trapped and I don't know what to do. That's it basically. It's all for nothing in the end.

"Und da hatte ich wirklich so Fäuste unter dem Tisch"

Kornelias Geschichte

Ich komme aus einem EU-Land in Osteuropa, habe dort schon studiert und in Deutschland dann noch mal einen Abschluss gemacht. Ich habe mehrmals gehört, dass ich eine melodische Stimme habe, und dann fragen viele, „Ah, kommen Sie aus Frankreich oder so?". Und wenn ich antworte „Nein, ich komme aus dem Land F (in Osteuropa)" hat das Gespräch sofort eine andere Bahn genommen; das merkte man ihnen an, auch am Telefon. Das ist häufig so, ich habe das vor allem sehr deutlich zu spüren bekommen beim Arbeitsamt und beim Sozialamt.

Das Schlimmste war, als ich in einer Krisensituation mich an den psychiatrischen Notdienst gewendet habe; ich hatte wirklich ein ernsthaftes Problem und war suizidgefährdet und sie ließen mich da mit einer Praktikantin sprechen, die da gerade seit einer Woche Vorpraktikum gemacht hat. Das hat sie mir zum Schluss gesagt, also erstmal habe ich gedacht, ich bin wirklich im falschen Film. Die konnte mit meiner Erkrankung gar nichts anfangen, weil sie gar nicht wusste, was das ist. Und da hat sie mich nach meiner Ausbildung gefragt und dann habe ich gesagt, dass ich Magister in dem und dem bin. Und Sie meinte „Nee, Sie haben mich falsch verstanden, ich habe gefragt, wie viele Klassen Sie abgeschlossen haben". Das war der Hammer. In dem Moment hatte ich wirklich so Fäuste unter dem Tisch. Denn wir haben vorher darüber gesprochen, wir haben auf jeden Fall darüber gesprochen, dass ich an der Uni war. Ich war echt beleidigt, wie mit mir umgegangen wurde und ich sah keinen Sinn, mit dem Mädchen über meine Probleme zu sprechen, weil sie gar nicht kompetent dafür war ihr das zu erzählen. Da muss man Vertrauen haben, sich einer fremden Person gegenüber zu öffnen. Da spricht man über so persönliche Sachen und ich war damals, ich war wirklich schockiert und total enttäuscht.

Ich habe bei meiner Hilfesuche oder im Umgang mit Ämtern immer wieder erlebt, dass ich gefragt werde, ob ich Deutsch sprechen kann, ob ich Deutsch verstehen kann – nachdem ich angerufen habe. Und ich bin auch gefragt worden, ob ich mir vorstellen könnte, das Gespräch in der deutschen Sprache zu führen. Und ich glaube ein oder zwei Mal habe ich gehört, dass sie da keine Dolmetscher haben, um so ein Gespräch zu führen. Oder ich musste mir anhören, ich sollte froh sein, dass ich in Deutschland bin, weil mir in EU-Land F sowieso nicht so gut geholfen würde wie hier.

"And then I was really clenching my fists under the table"

Kornelia's Story

I come from an EU country in Eastern Europe, where I already studied, and in Germany, I got another diploma. I was told several times that I had a melodic voice, and quite a lot of people ask me then: "Oh, are you from France or so?" And when I answered "No, I come from Country F (in Eastern Europe)" the conversation took a different turn immediately; that was clearly noticeable, even on the telephone. This happens quite often, I had to experience this very clearly especially at the employment agency and at the social welfare office.

But the worst scene was when I was in a crisis situation and approached the psychiatric emergency service; I really had a serious problem and I was actually suicidal, and they let me talk with a student apprentice there, who was just in her first week of pre-study internship. That´s what she told me at the end of the conversation, well, at first I thought that I was completely in the wrong place there. She didn´t know at all what to do with my disorder, because she simply didn´t know what it was. And then she asked me about my education and training and I told her that I had a master´s degree in such and such discipline. And her answer was: "No, you have misunderstood me, I asked you about the number of school classes you completed." That was just about the limit. At that moment, I was really clenching my fists under the table. Because we had talked about that, we had definitely talked about my university studies. I was really offended by the way she was treating me and I saw no point in talking about my problems with this girl or telling her my story, because she had no competence in this field. It is important to have confidence in someone before opening up to an unknown person. Then you talk about such private matters, and in that situation I was really shocked and totally disappointed.

When searching for assistance or dealing with official authorities I have repeatedly experienced being asked if I could speak German and understand German – after I had called them by phone! And I was also asked if I could imagine holding the conversation in German language. And, I think, once or twice I was told that they had no interpreters for such a conversation. Or I was told that I should be glad to be in Germany anyway, because I could not benefit from such quality of assistance in the EU country F as I could in Germany.

"Helfen konnten sie mir erst, als es wirklich eskaliert war"

Laras Geschichte

Ich hatte das wahnsinnige Glück, ich kann's gar nicht anders sagen, Frau X zu treffen, damals war diese Frauenberatungsstelle noch ganz klein und unscheinbar auf der Y-Straße und ich hatte ihr das erzählt, hab dann aber gemerkt, so richtig geglaubt hat sie mir auch nicht. Ich hatte wirklich um Schutz gebeten, ich hatte wahnsinnige Angst vor meinem Ehemann, der hatte wirklich erzählt, er würde mich töten oder noch schlimmer, er würde lieber das Kind töten, als das Kind bei mir zu lassen. Der war auch sehr verzweifelt, weil von unserer Ehe aus Deutschland auch sein Aufenthalt abhängig war. Ich bin von meinem Pass her aus Deutschland, und er war es nicht. Da stand er noch mehr unter Strom. Und die Frau X hatte mir aber trotzdem noch den Rat gegeben, mich da beim Einwohnermeldeamt sperren zu lassen. Das habe ich auch getan, aber zu dem Zeitpunkt habe ich gemerkt, so richtig wusste Frau X auch nicht, wie sie mir denn helfen kann.

Helfen konnte auch die Polizei mir erst, als es wirklich eskaliert war. Vorher hat es mir keiner so richtig geglaubt. Haben ja alle gedacht „Ja, die Frau zieht hier ganz neu ein, was erzählt sie denn?". Nehme ich mal so an. Ich hatte schon Kontakt aufgenommen, nicht nur mit Frau X, auch mit dem Jugendamt, aber die konnten sich ja nur auf meine Erzählungen verlassen und es kommen ja wahrscheinlich oft Frauen, die einfach irgendwas erzählen, was dann am Ende übertrieben ist oder nicht stimmt oder was weiß ich.

Ja und dann Schlug das Schicksal zu: er hat mich irgendwie gefunden, meine neue Wohnung, ist am helllichten Tag hier mitten im Dorf in das Haus gestürmt, hat versucht unter viel Geschrei die Wohnungstüre einzutreten. Die Nachbarn bekamen das auch mit, es versuchte einer ihn zu bremsen, den hat er mit einem Messer bedroht und die ganze Straße bekam das dann mit als das alles eskalierte und ein Sondereinsatzkommando kommen musste. Und da ging das ja eigentlich erst los mit Frau X. Also mit Hilfe von Polizei und so.

Dann kamen ja hinterher sehr viele Gerichtsverhandlungen und Jugendamtstermine und Gerichtstermine und da kann ich wirklich nur sagen, ich habe das als wahnsinnig positiv erlebt. Also Frau X und auch andere Mitarbeiter, ich weiß nicht mehr, wie sie alle hießen, haben sehr eng mit der Polizei zusammengearbeitet, die haben mich wirklich mit Polizeischutz zu jedem einzelnen Gerichtstermin gebracht.

I had that unbelievable luck, I have no other words for it, to meet Ms. X, at a time when the women's advisory centre was still quite a small organisation and unimposing on that street Y, and I told her what was going on, but then I noticed that she couldn't really believe me. I had really begged for protection, I was terrified of my husband, he had actually told me that he would kill me or, even worse, that he would rather kill the child than have the child stay with me. He was also very desperate, because his right of residence also depended on our marriage contracted here in Germany. According to my passport, I am from Germany, but he wasn't. Therefore, he was even more under pressure. And Ms. X, she nevertheless gave me the piece of advice that I had better have the residents' registration office block access to my address. That's also what I did, but at that time I could tell that Ms. X didn't know either how she could help me at all.

So, and then fate struck. Somehow he found me in my new flat, and in broad daylight in the middle of the village he stormed into the house screaming and raging and tried to break down the door to the flat. The neighbors saw what was going on, one tried to stop him and he pulled a knife on him, and then the whole street caught on to what was happening, and the police had to send a special unit. And that was really the beginning with Ms. X, with the help of the police and so on.

Then there were a lot of court hearings and appointments at the youth welfare office and court trials, and everything I can say about this is that this was a really positive experience for me. Well, Ms. X and also other employees there, I have forgotten all their names, they worked with the police very closely, they really accompanied me to every single court hearing under police protection. When my child had to be interviewed, that was also done under police protection and then, this man was arrested and put in prison for 6 months, and when he was released again, they even went to the effort to go to that prison, and to interview fellow inmates. And there he had evidently threated that he was going to kill me and so on. And they really sensitized all people here, they monitored the kindergarten and they kept him under surveillance, too. Well, the experience I had here was very, very desirable and positive, it was the kind of experience that I think doesn't occur so often here in Germany, in fact I'm rather sure of that.

Als mein Kind befragt werden musste, auch mit extra Polizeischutz und der Mann ist dann inhaftiert worden: 6 Monate und als der wieder entlassen wurde, da haben die sich auch noch die Mühe gemacht, sind ins Gefängnis rein, haben Mitgefangene befragt. Und da hatte er wohl angedroht, er bringe mich um und so. Und dann haben die wirklich hier alle so sensibilisiert, den Kindergarten überwacht und ihn auch. Also hier habe ich wirklich sehr, sehr wünschenswerte, positive Erfahrungen gemacht, wo ich denke, das gibt es nicht oft in Deutschland, da bin ich mir sehr sicher.

Ursprünglich komme ich nämlich aus einer anderen Region und Polizei habe ich da nie so groß in Anspruch genommen, als ich in die Frauenhäuser gegangen bin. Und geholfen hat sie mir auch nicht. Hier, aus dieser Stadt, also wirklich, das ist schon sehr bemerkenswert, was ich hier erfahren durfte, und die haben mir wirklich auch Wege vermittelt mit dem Jugendamt, die zu jeder einzelnen Gerichtsverhandlung kamen, und hinterher konnte ich noch viele Male zu Frau X gehen und konnte mit ihr reden und hatte auch nie das Gefühl, verurteilt zu werden, solche Sachen halt.

Because, originally, I come from another region and I never really took recourse to the police before, when I went to those women´s refuges. And the police didn´t help me either. And here, in this town, well, really, this is very remarkable indeed, what I could experience here, and they really showed me ways to deal with the Youth Welfare Office, and they came to every single court hearing, and after that, I could go to Ms. X so many times again, and I could talk to her and I never had the feeling to be condemned or anything like that.

"Das einzige, wo ich mich nicht beherrschen kann, ist bei Nationalität"

Leylas Geschichte

Ich komme aus einem östlichen Mittelmeerland, bin aber schon viele Jahre in Deutschland. Ich lebte mit meinem Mann lange zusammen, aber ich musste mich von ihm trennen, weil er gewalttätig war. Er ist kein schlechter Mensch, aber psychisch sehr krank; ich muss mich von ihm fernhalten. Aber ich telefoniere mit ihm hin und wieder.

Im Frauenhaus habe ich nicht das Gefühl gehabt, dass ich wegen meiner Herkunft anders behandelt werde, weil, da sind so viele Frauen von überall her. Aber ich hätte nie gedacht, dass so viele deutsche Frauen – das muss ich jetzt so sagen, nicht weil ich einen Unterschied finde, Frau ist Frau überall, und Mann ist überall dasselbe - aber ich hätte wirklich nicht gedacht, dass so viele deutsche Männer das so oft machen. In den Frauenhäusern hab ich gesehen, es gibt viele. Das war eine Enttäuschung für mich, ne. Also hab ich wirklich gesagt, Mann ist Mann, überall dasselbe. Also, nicht anders. Aber ansonsten, aber ansonsten, wegen meiner Nationalität, ne. Das wäre ja, ich bin auch so ein Typ, wenn sowas ist, ich bin da nicht still. Das ist meine große Reizbarkeit. Da bin ich wirklich, dann sag ich ok, ich lasse es, schmeiße alles, können Sie alles haben, ich bin weg. Da überleg ich überhaupt nicht zweimal. Das ist nicht schön, aber da kann ich mich nicht beherrschen. Das einzige wo ich mich nicht beherrschen kann, das ist bei Nationalität, wenn es heißt die Scheißtürken oder so, das geht nicht. Und sowas habe ich eigentlich in Deutschland bislang nicht erlebt, bis auf ein paar Mal, und das ist schon über 30 Jahre her. Solche gibt es hier und dort, es gibt immer solche Leute.

Aber die Polizei, die machen sowas; die nehme ich deshalb gar nicht mehr ernst. Generell sind meine Erfahrungen mit der Polizei nicht so gut. Vor einigen Jahren hat mich mein Ex-Mann auf der Straße geschlagen und dann kam eben die Polizei. Und die haben ihn dann auf den Boden gedrückt, mein Gott, er hatte doch keine Pistole! Gegen Gewalt sollten die eigentlich sein. Und dann haben die mich ins Krankenhaus gefahren, weil mein Zahn kaputt gegangen ist, und mich einfach da gelassen. Und nach der Behandlung bin ich raus, und ich kenne die Ecke überhaupt nicht, das war in einem Außenbezirk irgendwo gewesen, kein öffentlichen Verkehrsmittel; ich hatte keine Tasche, ich hatte nichts.

I come from a country in the Eastern Mediterranean, but have lived in Germany for many years. I lived with my husband for a long time, but I had to leave him, because he was violent. He's not a bad person, but mentally very ill; I must keep away from him. But sometimes I speak with him on the phone.

In the women's refuge, I never felt that I was treated differently because of my origin, because there were so many women from everywhere. But I had never thought that so many German women – I must say it now, because I don't see any difference there, women are the same everywhere, and men are the same everywhere – but I had never thought that so many German men do this so often, too. In those women's refuges, I saw there were so many of them. That was a disappointment to me. Well, so I really said, men are men, the same everywhere. Well, no difference. But apart from that, apart from that – because of my nationality, no. That would be, well I'm the type of a person who ... if something like that happens, then I don't keep quiet. This is the point where I really get short-tempered. Then I'm really, then I say o.k., leave it now, I'll give up everything and just walk away. Then I don't think twice. This is not so nice, but I cannot keep my self-control then. The only thing I can't keep my temper about is blaming nationality, when they say 'bloody Turkish people' or so, that just won't do. And something like that, I actually haven't experienced it in Germany, except for a few times, but this was many years ago. People like that, you meet them here and there, you meet those people everywhere.

But the police, they do these things, which is why I no longer take them seriously. In general my experience with the police has not been so good. A few years ago, my former husband hit me out on the street and then the police came. And then they pushed him down to the ground, good Lord, he didn't have a gun, after all! They ought to be against violence, actually. And then they took me to the hospital, because my tooth was broken, and they simply left me there. And after the medical treatment, I came out of the hospital and I didn't know that quarter at all, that was somewhere out in the suburbs, with no public transport, and I didn't have my handbag with me, nothing. Honestly, I really found that was shit. It took me a few hours to come home, with such a lot of pain, on top of everything.

Das fand ich sehr, sehr, ehrlich gesagt, scheiße. Es hat ein paar Stunden gedauert, bis ich wieder nach Hause kam. Mit solchen Schmerzen, und das dann auch noch dazu.

Die haben ja nicht mal gefragt: „Ja, wo müssen Sie denn jetzt hin? Müssen Sie jetzt nach Hause? Vielleicht passiert Ihnen was?". Weder Polizei noch Krankenhaus! Ich würde sagen bei solchen Fällen sollte das Krankenhaus immer Kontakt mit dem Frauenhaus haben oder sowas. Und dann direkt anrufen und auch fragen, wo soll diese Frau jetzt hin? Wenigstens mal fragen: „Wollen Sie jetzt wirklich nach Hause gehen? Sonst haben wir für Sie eine Bleibe!". Vielleicht gehen viele wieder zurück nach Hause, weil in dem Moment, wo sollen die sonst hin? Aber ich finde die Frauen sollten vorher gefragt werden, vor allem wenn sie Kinder haben. Ich meine, welche Mutter würde dann gerne die Kinder alleine zuhause lassen? Wenigstens fragen: „Möchten Sie, oder haben Sie auch Kinder? Oder muss man die irgendwie mitnehmen?" Für solche Gespräche sollte es einen Sozialarbeiter im Krankenhaus geben.

*They didn´t even ask me: "Well, where do you have to go now? Do you need to go home?"
Neither the police nor the hospital asked these questions. I would say that in such cases,
a hospital should always be in touch with the women´s refuge or something like that. And
then they should call them and ask where the woman could go. They should at least ask
her: "Do you really want to go home now? Otherwise, we´ve got another place to stay for
you." Perhaps so many of these women go home then, because where should they go in that
situation? But, as I see it, those women should be asked before, especially when they have
children. What I mean is: what mother would want to have her children alone at home? They
could ask at least: "Would you like to, or do you also have children? Or do we have to take
them with you somehow, too?" There should be a social worker available in a hospital for
this kind of conversation.*

"Ihr Mann ist so lieb und der kann toll reden"

Marys Geschichte

Ich stand einfach da und ich wusste gar nichts. Nach der Trennung hatte ich nichts mehr und bin zur Versicherung gegangen. Da sagte die von der Versicherung „Sag mal, wir kennen uns doch von der Schule her, von den Kindern und so. Wieso bist du da und da? Wohnst du da jetzt oder wie?" Da habe ich ihr ein bisschen davon erzählt was passiert war. Sie sagte „Ja, ich habe gehört, dass dein Mann Dich fast umgebracht hätte und dies und jenes. Hast du schon eine Beratungsstelle besucht?" Ich fragte zurück was für eine Beratungsstelle, ich kannte das nicht und sie hat dann im Internet geguckt nach der Adresse, hat zwei gefunden und mir gesagt ich soll da anrufen. Ich habe die Adressen genommen, die Telefonnummern, sie hatte mir alles aufgeschrieben, aber ich habe das nicht gemacht.

Ich musste später nochmal zur Versicherung, sie fragte ob ich angerufen hätte und ich hab geantwortet dass ich mich nicht traue. Dann haben wir das gemeinsam gemacht, hat sie für mich angerufen aber diese Stelle war zu voll und da haben sie mich an diese andere verwiesen. Dort habe ich direkt einen Termin bekommen, ich glaube, das war das Beste, was ich machen konnte. Vorher hatte ich mir schon überlegt „am besten nicht mehr leben". Und dann ging ich zu dieser Beraterin und ich werde sie nie vergessen, sie hat mich komplett wieder aufgebaut.

In der Zwischenzeit ist mein Mann zum Jugendamt gegangen, und erzählte Geschichten. Ich würde klauen, wäre eine schlechte Mutter und dürfe die Kinder nicht bekommen. Ich wusste gar nicht, dass mein Mann da war. Als ich hinging und wollte mit jemand sprechen hieß es sie werden mit mir nicht sprechen. Ich habe gesagt das finde ich nicht in Ordnung, ich möchte, dass wir darüber sprechen. Da sagte sie „Wenn Sie was wollen, gehen Sie zum Amtsgericht."

Ich habe das meiner Beraterin erzählt und die sagte das geht gar nicht und hat selbst dort angerufen. Seitdem ging's schon ein bisschen, hat die Frau vom Jugendamt einmal ganz kurz mit mir gesprochen und dann kam wieder Stille. Die Briefe an meinen Mann sind immer zu mir gekommen und ich habe die – ich denke die sind ja vom Jugendamt, also gehen sie mich an – aufgemacht, und lese „Herr XY, Sie können sich jederzeit an mich wenden und einen Termin machen" und so. Er hatte mir damals immer schon gesagt „Du bist sowieso zu ehrlich und wenn was ist, du kommst sowieso nicht weiter. Ich bin Deutscher".

"Your husband is so sweet and he talks so nice"

Mary's Story

I just stood there and knew nothing at all. After the separation I had nothing and I went to the insurance company. The woman there said: „Tell me, don't we know each other from school, from our children and so on. Why are you in that place? Are you living there now or what?" Then I told her a little bit about what happened. She said: „Yes, I heard that your husband almost killed you and so on. Did you already go to a counselling service?" I asked her what kind of counselling service, I didn't know something like that. Then she looked for the address online, found two and told me I should call them. I took the addresses, the phone numbers, she wrote everything down for me, but I didn't do anything.

I had to go to the insurance company again later, she asked me if I had called and I said I don't dare. Then we did it together, she called for me but they had no free places left and then they referred me to this other facility. They directly gave me an appointment, I think that was the best thing I could do. Before I was thinking „I'd rather not live anymore". And then I went to this counsellor and will never forget her, she completely built me up again.

In the meantime, my husband went to the youth welfare office and told them some stories. I would steal, be a bad mother and shouldn't get the children. I didn't know at all that my husband was there. When I went there myself to speak with somebody, nobody would talk to me. I said this is not ok, I want to talk about this with you. Then she said: „If you want something, you have to go to the District Court."

I told my counsellor about it and she said that's not ok at all and called them herself. Since then it's a little bit better, the woman from the youth welfare office talked to me briefly and then there was silence again. The letters to my husband always came to me and – I was thinking they are from the youth welfare office, so they are for me – I opened them and read „Mr. XY, you can contact me any time and make an appointment" and so on. He was always telling me back then: „You're too honest anyway and when there's something, you won't get anywhere. I'm German." I'm not born German, of course, you can hear that in my accent. And he said: „The judges and everybody else will be on my side and kick you out. " He said that again and again and again. My husband applied for family counselling for example.

Ich bin nicht als Deutsche geboren, klar, das merkt man an meinem Akzent. Und er sagte „die Richter und alle werden auf meiner Seite sein und dich rausschmeißen." Das hat er mir immer und immer wieder gesagt. Mein Mann hatte zum Beispiel Familienberatung beantragt. Und diese Frau von der Familienberatung, die frisst meinem Mann aus der Hand. „Ihr Mann ist so lieb und der kann toll reden" sagte sie. Ja, das kann der auch. Der ist Profi im Reden.

Vor ein paar Monaten hatten wir einen Amtsgerichttermin und da wurde das Jugendamt natürlich eingeladen aus dem Dorf und mein Sohn hatte einen Beistand. Mit dem sollte ich mich nachher treffen, ich habe gesagt bitte ohne den Mann und nicht bei ihm zu Hause. Also kam der Beistand zu mir nach Hause. Ging ohne zu fragen durch die ganze Wohnung, der hat sich aufgeführt, als wenn er da Gott in meiner Wohnung war. Ich habe gesagt, das Schlafzimmer sei tabu, da ist er dann wenigstens nicht rein, aber überall sonst war er, hat sich alles angeschaut, in die Schränke geschaut und alles genau angeguckt. Das finde ich nicht in Ordnung, der hätte mich fragen sollen. Und dann mussten wir uns noch mit meinem Mann treffen. Ich habe gesagt an einer öffentlichen Stelle, also waren wir im Café. Die beiden duzten sich und rauchten zusammen und mein Mann schnitt mir Grimassen und der Beistand fand das lustig. Der sagte, Frauen dürfe man nicht trauen und Frauen darf man nicht decken. Also die haben mich fast kaputt gemacht.

Gut war nur, dass das Jugendamt gesagt hat, es waren noch wenige Monate, bis die Tochter 18 wurde, dass sie das nicht einsehen, mir das Sorgerecht zu entziehen. Bei dem Sohn sind es noch ein paar Jahre, aber da haben wir nun auch das gemeinsame Sorgerecht. Beide Kinder sind beim Vater, aber zumindest haben wir noch geteiltes Sorgerecht.

Ach ja und weil ich keine Arbeit hatte, bin ich zum Arbeitsamt gegangen. Ich wusste nicht, wie man das macht, weil ich noch nie arbeitslos war. Dort wurde alles aufgenommen und dann kam heraus ich hätte eine Sperre. Warum konnte mir aber keiner sagen. Meine Beraterin und die Opferhilfe haben sich dafür eingesetzt, dass ich wenigstens zur Tafel darf. Ich bekam einen „Bescheid" in dem aber wohl nur stand, dass ich gemeldet bin, nicht, dass ich bei der Tafel was bekomme. Die bei der Tafel haben mich ausgelacht und gefragt welcher Idiot mir das gegeben hat, das sei kein Bescheid.

Ich war mit dem Kind allein, hatte kein Geld, kriegte keine Hilfe vom Arbeitsamt, es gab nichts. Ziemlich genau fünf Monate bekam ich keine Hilfe und mein Nachbar, meine Schwiegermutter, mein Bruder haben mir ausgeholfen, mir Essen gebracht obwohl sie selbst kaum was haben. Ich hatte keinen Cent, musste betteln und Unterhalt habe ich natürlich auch nie gesehen. Wofür war ich denn dann arbeiten? Die Leute die auf der Strasse leben mit den Hunden, die bekommen jeden Tag die Tagesdosis oder wie nennt sich das? Die holen sich jeden Tag Geld ab vom Arbeitsamt. Und ich? Gehe arbeiten, arbeiten, arbeiten und ich habe nichts, keinen Cent und bekomme noch nicht mal einen Brief, dass ich von der Tafel was holen kann.

And this woman from the family counselling service, she's eating out of his hand. „Your husband is so sweet and he talks so nice", she said. Yes, he can do that indeed. He's an expert in talking.

A few months ago we had an appointment in the District Court, the youth welfare office from the village was invited as well of course and my child had a legal representative. I was supposed to meet with him afterwards, but I said please without my husband and not at his place. So this lawyer came to my house. Walked through the whole flat without asking, he acted like he was a god in my flat. I told him that the bedroom is taboo, at least he didn't go there, but everywhere else he looked at everything, looked in all the cupboards and examined everything very closely. I think that's not ok, he should have asked me before. And then we had to meet with my husband as well. I said in a public space, so we met in a café. They addressed each other by first names and smoked together and my husband pulled faces at me and the childrens' lawyer thought it was funny. He said one shouldn't trust women and one shouldn't cover up for women. They almost destroyed me.

The only good thing was that the youth welfare office said – it was only a few months until my older child turned 18 – that they don't see taking custody away from me. For the younger one it's still a few years, but we now have joint custody. Both children are with their father, but at least we have joint custody.

Ah right, and because I didn't have a job, I went to the job centre. I didn't know how to do that, because I've never been unemployed. They registered everything but then it came out that I'm blocked. But nobody could tell me why. My counsellor and the victim support tried to help me so that I can at least go to the soup kitchen. I received a „notification" which just said that I'm registered, but not that I could get anything from the soup kitchen. The staff there laughed at me and asked which idiot gave me this, it wasn't the certificate I would need.

I was alone with a child, had no money, didn't get any aid from the job centre, there was nothing. For about five months I didn't get any aid and my neighbour, my mother-in-law, my brother helped me out, brought me food even though they have very little themselves. I didn't have a cent, had to go begging and never saw any alimony. For what was I working then? The people who live on the streets with their dogs get their daily dose or how do you call it? They pick up money from the job centre every day. And me? I work, work, work and have nothing, not a single cent and I'm not even given a letter that would let me get some food from the soup kitchen.

"Das, was mein Mann sagte, wurde letztendlich befolgt"

Olgas Geschichte

Ich bin gebürtig aus Osteuropa und kam in den 1990er Jahren aus der ehemaligen SU nach Deutschland; heute sage ich, dass Deutschland meine Heimat ist. Mein Ex-Partner ist Südländer und kam als Flüchtling hierher. Ich habe immer voll gearbeitet und gut verdient, und wir haben uns ein gutes Leben aufgebaut. Das war immer von körperlicher und psychischer Gewalt begleitet, aber das kannte ich aus meiner Kindheit nicht anders.

Polizei war bei uns schon öfter, als die Kinder noch klein waren. Ich habe meistens gelogen und nur gesagt, dass ich angerufen habe weil die Kinder so geschrien haben, denn ich hatte nicht die Kraft und den Mut, über seine Gewalt zu sprechen. Ich hatte aber auch Angst; ich wusste nicht, wie soll ich mir helfen. Wie? Wie soll ich das; ich wusste nicht, wie ich das anfangen sollte? Wohin sollte ich gehen? Wie soll ich; wie? Gar nicht. Und da zog ich mich wieder zurück.

Ich konnte mich von ihm nicht trennen, und ich dachte, ich darf das überhaupt nicht, weil ich bei der Ausländerbehörde die Erklärung unterschrieben habe, dass ich ihn unterhalten werde. Denn die Gesetze waren damals so, dass er als Flüchtling erst zu mir ziehen konnte, als ich unterschrieben habe, dass ich für ihn aufkomme und er nicht vom Sozialamt leben wird. Deshalb dachte ich, ich kann ihn überhaupt nicht verlassen.

Ganz am Anfang, als ich noch schwanger war, mit großem Bauch, hat er mich einmal so geschlagen, dass ich dachte, das Kind wird überhaupt nicht geboren. Als ich so verzweifelt war, habe ich sogar bei der Ausländerbehörde angerufen und gesagt „Ich kann nicht mehr" und wollte diese Erklärung zurückziehen. Und der Mann bei diesem Amt sagte, „Naja, Frau X, so wollten Sie es haben". Und da habe ich den Hörer aufgelegt und gedacht: Da hat er auch Recht. Das war ich, ich wollte doch mit diesem Mann leben. Ich habe daran gedacht, dass meine Mutter das Gleiche erlebt hatte, und habe alles über mich ergehen lassen mit dem Gedanken „es kann nicht schlimmer werden. Schlimmer wird es in meinem Leben nicht mehr kommen". Da habe ich mich aber geirrt.

Erst als er die Kinder gegen mich eingesetzt hat, habe ich mich getrennt. Wir waren nicht verheiratet, und ich hatte immer das alleinige Sorgerecht gehabt, nur ich.

I was born in Eastern Europe and I came to Germany from the former SU in the nineties; today I would say that Germany is my home. My ex-partner is from a Balkan country and came here as a refugee. I always worked full time here and earned good money and we made a good life for ourselves. It always went along with physical and psychological violence, but that was what I grew up with as a child.

The police came to us several times when the children were still young. In most cases, I lied and I just said that I had called them because the children had been crying so much, for I didn't have the strength and the courage to talk about his violence. But I was also scared; I didn't know how to help myself. How? How should I ... I didn't know how to begin. Where should I go to? How should I, how? – Not at all. And then I retreated again.

I could not separate from him and I thought I wasn't allowed to at all, because I had signed that declaration at the immigration office that I would guarantee his living expenses. Back then as a refugee, the law was that he couldn't move to my town to live with me until I signed that I would support him and that he would not live on social welfare. Because of this I thought that I could not leave him at all.

Right at the beginning, when I was still pregnant, with a great belly, he beat me so badly that I thought that the child would not be born at all. When I was in such despair, I even called the foreigners' registration office and told them "I can't stand it any longer". I wanted to withdraw that declaration. And the clerk in that office told me: "Well, Mrs. X, that's how you wanted it to be". And then I replaced the handset and thought: "Yes, he is right. That was me, I wanted to live with this man". After that I turned inward completely. I remembered that my mother had been through the same, and I endured everything just thinking: "Things cannot get worse, impossible." But I was completely mistaken.

I separated from him only when he began to use the children against me. We were not married and I always had the sole custody of the children, me alone. He declared himself the father and the children bore his name, I had allowed this myself. But he was never worried about custody, that was never of any importance to him, all he said was: "It's your job to raise the children."

Er hat sich als Vater erklärt und die Kinder hießen nach ihm, ich habe das selber zugelassen. Aber er hat sich nie gekümmert um das Sorgerecht, das war ihm nie wichtig, er meinte nur: „Du bist dafür da, die Kinder zu erziehen". Wichtig waren ihm nur Geld und Haus und Auto. Bei der Trennung hat er aber das Sorgerecht beantragt. Und auf dem Jugendamt bekam ich zu hören: „Bereiten Sie sich darauf vor, dass er Ihnen die Kinder wegnimmt. Wir kennen auch andere Fälle und da ist es auch so passiert. Er kommt aus einem muslimischen Land und da ist es so, die Kinder gehören zum Vater". Dann klingelte für mich sofort die Alarmglocke: „Das ist schon öfter passiert".

Und ich denke schon, bei Eltern, die ausländische Wurzeln haben, hat das großen Einfluss. Egal, wo ich war, ob es das Gericht war, die Richter mehrmals, die Gutachter, alle wussten von dieser Situation. Alle. Die sprachen offen über Gewalt, sie wussten, was da abgelaufen ist, sie wussten auch wie schwer der Fall war. Es steht sogar in einem Bericht, wenn die Kinder beim Vater bleiben; die Mutter wird sie nicht mehr sehen. Beim Gericht sitzen alle professionellen Leute zusammen und reden „Das ist zu teuer, die Kinder unterzubringen; wenn die beim Vater bleiben, dann wird die Mutter die nicht sehen" und die reden und ich sitze da und denke, ich bin im falschen Film. Und da habe ich erst verstanden, dass Recht mit Recht nichts zu tun hat, weil das was mein Mann sagte, egal welche Gesetze waren, was er sagte wurde letztendlich befolgt. Er sagte nur „nein" und er ist dabei geblieben. Wenn er die professionellen Leute nicht sehen wollte, machte er die Tür zu und sagte „Die Kinder wollen die Leute nicht sehen." Und das Gericht sagt „naja, die Kinder haben gesagt, die haben Angst vor den professionellen Leuten, das ist so." „Die wollen nicht darüber sprechen, denen ist das zu viel". Ich glaube die Sachverständigen sprachen mit den Kindern nie richtig, der Vater hat schon von vornherein, wie sie das auch in den Unterlagen beschrieben haben, dafür gesorgt. Die bekamen nur ihn zu Gesicht und er sagte „Die Kinder haben Angst und die werden mit Ihnen nicht sprechen". Punkt. Alle gerichtlichen Verfahren, aber alle, sind so gelaufen.

Also mein Ex-Partner ist sehr charmant. Sehr charmant, ein gut aussehender Typ eben, Südländer, und das setzt er gezielt ein, auch bei den Frauen, z.B. bei der Anwältin. Auch bei der Gutachterin, die vom Gericht eingesetzt wurde. Bei ihr erlebte ich alles andere als Verständnis, alles andere als Mitgefühl. Sie hat mir nicht geglaubt, denn sie konnte sich nicht vorstellen, dass der schick angezogene, lachende, gut aussehende, charmante Mann überhaupt so sein könnte. Und sie meinte auch, ich könnte meine Kinder sowieso nicht so gut versorgen, weil ich arbeiten ging.

Und alle dachten: Sie ist viele Jahre mit ihm zusammen, jetzt kommt sie und erzählt ein bisschen über Gewalt und sagt, der Mann ist gewalttätig und der Mann sitzt da und grinst und die Kinder lieben ihn und keiner wollte das vertiefen, es sollte die Sache zügig gemacht werden und abgeschlossen sein. Auch die Richter waren überfordert, die wollten auch keine kompetente Entscheidung treffen. Ich erlebte eine Angst vor Entscheidung, vor Durchsetzung, Angst, etwas Falsches zu machen, weil alle jetzt von Integration sprechen, alles sollte freundlich ablaufen, alle sollen wir diesem Bild entsprechen.

What mattered to him were the money, the house and the car. But when we separated he applied for custody. And at the youth welfare office they told me: "Be prepared, he will take the children away from you. We know other such cases and that is what happened. He comes from a Muslim country and there the children belong to the father." Immediately, the alarm bell began to ring for me: "that has happened already several times".

And I really think that when the parents have foreign roots, this has a strong influence. No matter where I've been, whether in court, with the judges several times, the experts, they all knew about this kind of situation; all of them. They spoke about violence openly, they knew what had happened there, they also knew about the seriousness of the case. It was even written in one of the reports; it says: if the children stay with the father, the mother won't see them any more. At court, all the professionals sat together and talked, saying: "It is too expensive to take the children into care; if they remain with the father, the mother won't see them any more". And they talk while I'm sitting there and I listen to them. And then I think I must be in the wrong film. And that was when I understood that the law has nothing to do with justice, because finally, regardless of the laws, what my husband said decided what would happen. He just said "No" and he stuck to it. When he didn't want to see those professionals, he closed the door and said: "The children do not want to see those people, and that's how it is." And the court said "They don't want to speak about it, it's too much for them." Those experts, they have never really talked to the children, that's what the father had arranged for right from the start, as it was also described in the documents. They only saw him and he said: "The children are afraid, and they won't talk to you." Full stop. All judicial proceedings, really all of them, went like this.

Well, my ex-partner is a very charming person. Very charming, a handsome Mediterranean type to say it flatly, and he uses this purposefully, with women also, for example with the lawyer. And also with the expert who was appointed by the court. What I experienced with her was anything but understanding, anything but sympathy. She didn't believe me, because she couldn't imagine that this smartly dressed, laughing, handsome and charming man ever could be like that. And she also thought that I could not care for my children properly anyway, because I was working. And all of them thought: She lived with him for so many years and now she comes along and tells us a little bit about violence and says: this man is violent, and the man is sitting there and grinning, and the children love him, and nobody wanted to go any deeper, the matter was to be dealt with speedily, to be closed and completed. It was too much for the judges as well, they did not want to take a competent decision either. What I saw was that they were afraid to take a decision, to impose something, to attack, there was a big fear of doing something wrong, because everyone talks about integration now, everything has to go on in a friendly manner, we are all expected to fit into this pattern.

"Wir haben viel durchgemacht wegen ihm"

Sarahs Geschichte

Ich hatte die Familie verlassen und endlich einen Platz gefunden wo ich bleiben konnte, als das Verfahren anfing.

Die Richter verhörten die Kinder. Sie sagten die Kinder wären von mir und meiner Betreuerin beeinflusst, sie wären nicht sie selbst und könnten nicht frei sprechen. Diese Dinge haben mich wirklich verrückt gemacht, weil ich meine Kinder nie beeinflussen würde! Weil die alles gesehen haben was passiert ist, es erlebt haben, wie soll man da die Fakten ändern? Wenn man versucht denen was zu erzählen macht man das kaputt, also dachte ich, dass ich nie mit ihnen darüber rede, sie auf ihre Art reden lasse, so wie Kinder halt Dinge erzählen. Also die Leute vom Gericht haben sich geweigert die Zeugenaussage der Kinder aufzunehmen und gesagt, dass die Kinder noch ein weiteres Mal befragt werden. Also haben die das so gemacht und es ist genauso geendet wie davor, nichts hat sich geändert, aber diese Dinge dauern lange, alles nochmal und nochmal durchzugehen, also das war wirklich Stress für meine Kinder und für mich auch.

Die Leute vom Gericht wollten einen Gutachter bestellen, der dann mit den Kindern redet. Also sagte ich, dass das ok wäre. Manchmal denke ich, ich war dumm, ich hätte das nicht erlauben sollen. Aber weil der Ehemann meinte, ich würde meine Kinder beeinflussen und sie hätten Angst die Wahrheit zu sagen – was natürlich nicht stimmte – habe ich nachgegeben. Um zu beweisen, dass wir nichts zu verstecken hatten. Manchmal denke ich, es war eine schlechte Entscheidung, weil die Kinder gelitten haben. Es war so als würde niemand sie ernst nehmen.

Und dann wurde mir dieser Anwalt für Kinder vorgestellt. Oh mein Gott, wir haben viel durchgemacht wegen ihm. Ich ertrage es kaum daran zu denken was er da in einigen Gesprächen vom Stapel gelassen hat. Er war derjenige, der meine Kinder beeinflusst hat! Er kam in meine Wohnung, setzte sich hin, und an dem Tag wusste ich, dass hier irgendwas falsch läuft. Er sah so unprofessionell aus, die Art wie er mit meinen Kindern geredet hat, und mich dabei ignorierte. Wie auch immer, ich dachte „lass ihm die Befragung", die nur dafür da war uns kennenzulernen, also keine echte Befragung. Er hat alle möglichen unangemessenen Fragen gestellt, alles aus der Vergangenheit, „nur um uns einander vorzustellen". Ich habe mit meiner Betreuerin geprüft, ob das der echte Anwalt für Kinder war oder jemand der von meinem Ex geschickt wurde, aber es war der Echte.

"He put us through a lot"

Sarah's Story

I had left and finally found a place to stay and then the proceedings started.

The lawyers interrogated the children. They said that the children were influenced by me and by my counsellor, they weren't themselves, they couldn't speak freely. These things really made me crazy because I would never influence my children! Because they've seen everything that happened, experienced it, and how can you change the facts? If you try to tell them something you'll ruin it so I thought I'll never talk to them about it, I just let them speak in their own way, the way kids tell things. So the court people refused to take the testimony the children gave and instead said that the children had to give yet another interview. So they did and again it was the same outcome as before, nothing changed, but these are things that take a long time, to go through it again and again, so this was really stress for my children and for me as well.

The court people wanted to appoint an expert to talk to the children. So I said that was fine. Sometimes I think I was stupid, I should not have allowed that. But because the husband said I was influencing my children, they were afraid to tell the truth – which was not true of course – I gave in. I let these people talk to my children anytime and anywhere. To prove we had nothing to hide. Sometimes I think this was a bad decision, because the children suffered. It was like nobody was taking them seriously.

And then this children's lawyer was introduced to me. Oh my God, he put us through a lot. I can hardly bear thinking about what he came up with in some conversations. He was the one who was influencing my children! He came to my flat, sat down, and that day I knew that something is going wrong here. He looked so unprofessional, the way talked with my children, ignoring me all the time. Anyway, I thought "let him have this interview" which was just for getting to know us, so not a real interview. He asked all sorts of inappropriate questions, all about the past, "just to get to know each other". I checked with my counsellor, if this was the real children's lawyer or rather someone sent by my ex, but he was the real one. And he continued to see the children and interrogate them over and over, sometimes spontaneously calling on the phone "I want to speak to your children" and I let him in. He called my ex and gave the phone to my son to talk to him without my permission, without letting me know. So that went for a whole year, him asking them questions and influencing them.

Und er hat die Kinder weiterhin gesehen und immer wieder befragt, manchmal spontan am Telefon gesagt „Ich will mit deinen Kindern sprechen" und ich habe ihn reingelassen. Er rief meinen Ex an und gab meinem Sohn das Telefon um mit ihm zu reden, ohne meine Erlaubnis, ohne mir Bescheid zu sagen. Also das lief ein Jahr lang, dass er Fragen stellte und sie beeinflusste.

Einmal bin ich zu meiner Anwältin gegangen und habe erklärt, dass mir die Situation unangenehm ist. Und dann entschloss ich mich nochmal mit meiner Betreuerin hinzugehen. Ich fragte „Kannst du mit mir kommen?", weil ich denke wenn man alleine geht, aus meiner Erfahrung, wenn man alleine geht nehmen sie einen nicht ernst, und wenn man jemanden mitnimmt wie eine Therapeutin oder eine Betreuerin reagieren sie anders, was nicht fair ist, aber so ist das nun mal. Ich fühlte mich nicht gehört.

Dann hatte ich auch mit dem Jugendamt Probleme, die haben mir nicht geglaubt oder was passiert ist, ich fühlte mich als würden sie nur meinem Ex und seinem Anwalt glauben. Mein Ex kam zu allen Terminen, eigentlich wollte er diesen Fall einfach nur gewinnen, aber zum Glück hat er diesmal nicht gewonnen und ich war froh. Er hat überhaupt keine Bestrafung bekommen für all das, was er getan hat, aber was soll ich machen?

Once I went to my lawyer and explained that I wasn't comfortable with this situation. And then I decided to go again with my counsellor. I said "can you come with me?" because I think when you go alone, from my experience, when you go alone they don't take you seriously and when you take someone like a therapist or a counsellor, they react differently, which actually is not fair, but that is how it is. I felt like I'm not heard.

Then I had problems as well with the youth welfare office, they didn't believe me or what happened in my situation, I felt like they were believing my ex and his lawyer. My ex came to all the appointments, actually, he just wanted to win this case but fortunately this time he didn't win and I was glad. He didn't get any punishment at all for what he's done but what can I do?

"Später ist zu spät"

Sonjas Geschichte

Es hat sehr lange gedauert, ehe ich Hilfe suchte. Ich hatte schon einige Male Kontakt zur Polizei und auch einmal zur Beratungsstelle, aber ich konnte über die Verhältnisse zu Hause nicht erzählen, denn ich habe mich dermaßen geschämt, dass ich das nicht über meine Lippen gebracht habe, darüber zu sprechen. Das ist was Privates und ich weiß nicht, Sie ziehen sich aus vor fremden Leuten. Dann zog ich mich zurück. Außerdem, bei diesem Mann dachte ich, das ist die Liebe meines Lebens, und mit ihm wollte ich bis zum Ende zusammen sein. Deshalb hat das so lange gedauert, und ich habe mich an ihn so geklammert, weil ich mit Familie so viele unerfüllte Wünsche verbunden habe. Ich habe mit meinem Partner alles erreicht, was zu erreichen ist, wenn es um Geld geht. Also uns ging es wirklich super, aber zwischen uns war nichts. Außer Sex, was ich für eine Art von Liebe hielt. Ja und in der Arbeit war ich geschätzt und anerkannt und ich dachte „Wieso kann man diese Anerkennung zuhause nicht erreichen, gerade mit Leuten, die man liebt?"

Hilfe habe ich erst gesucht, als meine Kinder mich psychisch und auch körperlich angegriffen haben. Weil ich glaubte, dass ich als Mutter versagt habe. Zu Hause hatte ich nur noch Angst, das Falsche zu sagen oder zu tun. Dann habe ich bei der Erziehungsberatung professionelle Hilfe gesucht. Und das Erste was ich dort gesagt habe war „Ich habe versagt, ich bin eine schlechte Mutter". Der Berater dort hat mir nur zugehört und hat dann nur einen Satz zu mir gesagt „Was wollen Sie, Frau X, in Ihrem Leben?" Und er hat natürlich auch mehr gesagt, aber das ist geblieben, nur dieser einzige Satz. „Was wollen Sie?" Und „Sie sind bestimmt keine schlechte Mutter, denn Sie sprechen hier darüber". Und das war das erste Mal, dass überhaupt Verständnis da war, ein kleines bisschen. Ich kam wieder nach Hause und ich hatte nur im Kopf dieses „Was willst du, was willst du in deinem Leben, was willst du?" Das war das Hilfreichste, denn es hatte in meinem Leben noch nie jemand gefragt, was ich will. Dass ich mir von anderen etwas wünschen soll, war für mich total neu, obwohl das normal und menschlich ist, aber für mich war es das eben nicht. Und das ist sehr oft in meinem Kopf, jeden Tag, also ich habe ein Etui auch jetzt und in diesem Etui war das „Was willst du?" Jeden Tag.

In meiner Familie waren alle sehr besorgt um mich, und meine Schwester hat dann den Termin bei der Frauenberatung gemacht und hat mich dorthin begleitet. Jede zweite Woche war ich bei der Beraterin. Ja und sie war vorsichtig mit mir, ich glaube zwei Jahre hat das gedauert, und ich wuchs an diesem „was willst du?".

"Later is too late"

Sonja's Story

*It took a very long time before I went looking for help. I had been in contact with
the police several times and also once with the advisory centre, but I could not talk
about things as they were at home, because I was so much ashamed that I could not
bring myself to speak about this. Then I withdrew. And, what is more, with this man,
I thought he was the love of my life and I wanted to be with him until the end. That's
why it took so long and I clung to him, because having a family was associated with
so many unfulfilled wishes for me. I achieved everything with my partner that could
be achieved, as far as money was concerned. Well, we were really doing well, but
there was nothing between us. Except for sex, which I thought was some kind of love.
Yes, indeed, and at work I was respected and recognized and I thought: "Why is it
impossible to gain this recognition at home, especially with those you love?"*

*I only started looking for help when my children started to attack me psychologically
and physically, because I thought that I had failed as a mother. At home, it got to
the point where I was constantly afraid to say or do the something wrong. Then I
looked for help at the educational counselling centre. The first thing I said there was
"I have failed. I am a bad mother." The advisor there just listened to me and uttered
one single sentence: „What is it that you want in your life, Mrs. X?" He certainly said
more than this, but this one sentence stuck. "What do you want for you" And: "Most
certainly, you are not a bad mother, because you are talking about this here." And
that was the first time I found understanding somehow, just a little bit. I came back
home and all the time I had was this one sentence in mind: „What is it that you want
in your life, what do you want for yourself?" That was the most helpful thing I have
ever experienced, because in my whole life nobody had ever asked me what I wanted.
Wishing something for myself from others, this was totally new for me, even though it
is something normal and human, but it was simply not something normal for me. And
it came to my mind so often, every day, well, I had like a little box in my mind, and I
still do, and in this box there was this question: What is it that you want? Every day.*

*In my family, they were all very concerned about me and then my sister made an
appointment for me at the women's advisory centre and she accompanied me on the
way there. I went there almost every week, I had a consultation hour with my advisor
every second week. Yes, and she was careful with me, I think it took two years or so,
and I was growing along with this "What is it that you want?" The more often we met,
the more I was also disclosing from myself. And there was something that attracted
me to her so much, she listened to me, and at the same time, I found myself and saw
the way ahead.*

Je mehr wir uns trafen, desto mehr gab ich auch von mir preis. Und in ihr war etwas, was mich so hingezogen hat, sie hat mir zugehört, gleichzeitig fand ich mich selber und fand einen weiteren Weg. Das war sehr erstaunlich für mich. Und sie hakte irgendwo ein, fragte mich und ich wurde nachdenklich und ging. Und so ging das jedes Mal. Ich nahm viele Sachen mit, die in meiner Seele weiter arbeiteten wie „Wie ist das? Wie komme ich dazu, dass sich zuhause absolut nichts geändert hat?". Meinen Mann habe ich einmal angesprochen, ob er zur Beratungsstelle gehen würde und er sagte „für Bescheuerte wie Dich kann das gehen", aber für ihn kam das gar nicht in Frage. Also über private Probleme zu sprechen war für ihn Verrat.

Dann kam der Punkt, wo er mich so geschlagen hat, dass ich wusste, ich muss mich für das Leben entscheiden, denn wenn ich bleibe, werde ich nicht mehr lange leben. Nach dieser Nacht bin ich zur Polizei gefahren. Als ich die Tür geöffnet habe, liefen mir schon die Tränen und ich konnte fast nicht reden. Ich sagte nur, dass sie ihn weg von mir halten sollen, und dass ich nicht mehr will, dass er mich schlägt. Und die Polizei war sehr effektiv. Die haben den Bericht ernst genommen, die haben alles aufgeschrieben und sie haben gesagt „Sie warten, der Tag vergeht, wir kommen um 10 Uhr, wir nehmen ihn und wir gehen." Und so war es auch. Nur mit dem kleinen Unterschied, dass er in der Zeit zu den Kindern gegangen ist und was er da gesagt hat, das weiß nur er. Er war alleine mit ihnen und hat wohl erzählt, dass er mich liebt und dass alles nicht so passiert ist, dass ich übertreibe.

Eine Polizistin hat mit mir gesprochen und hatte viel Verständnis. Sie hat mich ständig gefragt, „Sie wollten das?" und die Fakten mussten stehen; der ganze Verlauf, wie ich da geschlagen worden bin. Aber immer wieder zurück an mich „Wollen Sie das?" weil die genauso wie ich wusste, dass das eine Entscheidung für mein Leben ist und dass schwere Konsequenzen auf mich zu kommen.

Die haben ihn weggenommen, aber alles andere blieb offen. Es gab keine Institution, keine Person, die mich weiter begleitet hat. Die Polizei hat ihm zwar verboten, sich mir zu nähern, aber er hielt sich nicht daran. Der stand jeden Tag vor der Glastür, die Kinder konnten ihn sehen, und er sagte jedes Mal „Du kannst doch den Kindern nicht den Vater nehmen." Für mich war dies eine völlig neue Situation, und ich dachte auch, ich könnte den Kindern den Vater wirklich nicht nehmen. Für mich hieß es „Solange ich lebe, da ist der Vater." Und an der Stelle habe ich mich auch geirrt. Weil im Rückblick gesehen dies die Stelle war, um die Gewalt zu unterbrechen. Aber er ging weiter seinen Weg, wie er ihm immer gegangen ist. Ich war nicht soweit, die Polizei zu rufen, weil ich immer noch dachte, an diesem Mann ist etwas Gutes, es kann nicht so viel Böses sein. Das ist der Vater von meinen Kindern.

Die Kinder sahen ihn zweimal die Woche durch das Jugendamt. Sie bekamen von ihm Handys und haben mir gesagt, was ich zu tun und zu machen habe. Ich bat das Jugendamt in dieser Zeit um Hilfe, ich habe unendlich viele Dokumente ausgefüllt.

That was an amazing experience for me. And she would only step at one particular point, asking me a question, and I began thinking and took the question with me when I left. And that´s how it was every time. I took so many things along with me which continued to work in my soul, like the questions: "How is it? What is it that makes me think that nothing has changed at home, absolutely nothing?" I talked to my husband once and asked him if he wanted to go to an advisory centre and he said: "That might work for crackbrained people like you." But that was out of question for him. Well, talking about private problems, that was treason in his eyes.

And then there was that point when he battered me so badly that I knew that I had to take a decision for my life, because if I stayed with him, I would not survive much longer. After that night, I drove to the police. And then, when I came through the door there, tears were already rolling down and I was almost unable to speak. I just told them that they should keep him away from me and that I could no longer bear him beating me. And the police were very effective. They took my report very seriously, they noted everything down and they told me: „You are going to wait for us, the day will pass by and we will come at 10.00 o´clock, we will take him and go away." And that´s how it happened indeed. With the only single difference that he went to the children during that time and what he told them there, he´s the only one who knows it. He was alone with the children and had probably told them that he loved me and that everything had not happened this way and that I was carrying it too far.

A police officer who talked to me showed a lot of understanding. She constantly asked me: „Did you want that?" and the facts had to be set forth; the entire situation as it took place, how I was battered. But she always returned the question to me: "Do you want that?" because she knew it, exactly as I knew it; that would be a decision for my life and would have serious consequences for me.

They ordered him to leave, but everything else remained unsolved. There was no institution, no person, who continued to assist me. It is true that the police forbade him to approach me, but he did not obey. Every day, he stood before the glass door, the children could see him and every time he said: "But you cannot deprive your children of their father." That was a completely new situation for me, and I also thought that he was right; I could not deprive my children of their father indeed. To me, this was "As long as I live, he is their father." And concerning this point, I was wrong, too. Because, looking back at everything, that was the point where violence had to be stopped. But he followed his own path as always. I had not arrived at the point to call the police, because I still thought that there was something good in this man, there could not be such a lot of evil in him. He is the father of my children, after all.

The children saw him twice each week through the youth welfare office. They were offered mobile phones by him and they told me what I was allowed to do and what not. During that time, I asked the youth welfare office to help me; I filled in an awful lot of documents. I said to them: "I need assistance, this asks too much of me, there is violence, please help me, please help me, otherwise this will turn for the worse."

Ich sagte „Ich brauche Unterstützung, ich bin überfordert, da ist Gewalt, helfen Sie mir bitte, helfen Sie mir bitte, sonst wird das schlimm ausgehen." Das war die große Enttäuschung. Es hätte alles schnell gehen müssen, aber es ging alles sehr langsam. Antrag stellen; es hieß erst „eine Woche", die nächste Woche verging, ich rief an „Nein, die Sitzung ist nicht passiert". Übernächste Woche. Dann vergeht der nächste Monat. Nach drei Monaten war ich in der Klinik, und die Kinder waren schon bei ihm.

Sofort als er das Haus verließ, das wäre der entscheidende Punkt gewesen, Hilfe zu leisten. Später ist zu spät. Und da nahm alles seinen Lauf, Gewaltlauf, wie das auch vorher war, ja. Und ich alleine konnte da gar nicht mehr richtig unterbrechen, ich konnte nur zusehen, dass ich mich da - wie ich sagte lebendig - retten kann.

Was sich verändern müsste? Auf jeden Fall das Jugendamt, das ist sehr wichtig. Wenn Frauen Hilfe brauchen, dann brauchen sie die sofort. Sofort und auf der Stelle. Wenn man von Gewalt spricht, psychischer und physischer Natur, da muss Hilfe sofort kommen. Da müssen professionelle Leute da sein. Nur dann kann es gelingen, die Kinder zu retten, vor allem es geht um sie, für die Zukunft, damit sie keinen seelischen Schaden tragen. Also dass die Schäden begrenzt werden – weil Schäden sind schon eingetreten, aber dass die Schäden begrenzt werden. Jetzt sind die Kinder ausgeschlossen aus meinem Leben und ich aus ihrem. Sie sind dem Vater ausgeliefert, der mit Gewalt erzieht und sie weitergibt… in die nächste Generation.

There was that big deception. Everything should have gone quickly, but things went pretty slowly in fact. Filing an application; first they said "one week", and then, the next week passed by; I phoned them and the answer was: "No, the meeting has not been held." The week after next. Then the next month passed by. Three months later I was in hospital and the children were already with him.

What should be changed? The youth welfare office in any case, this is very important. When women need help, they need help immediately. If you talk about violence, whether it is psychological or physical, then help must come immediately. Then professional people have to be there. This is the only way to save children; it is especially about them, for their future, to save them from suffering psychological harm. Well, it is a matter of limiting harm. For harm has already occurred, but it has to be limited. Now the children are excluded from my life and I am excluded from theirs. They are at the mercy of their dad, who raised them with violence and passes it on... to the next generation.

"Mein ganzes Gehalt ging drauf"

Theresias Geschichte

Hier in dieser Stadt bin ich angekommen, weil ich auf der Flucht vor meinem Ehemann war. Ich hatte da vorher aber schon drei Frauenhäuser durch und der hat mich jedes Mal gefunden mit drei Kindern im Schlepptau und dann bin ich zufällig im Nachbardorf gelandet, habe mich beworben und habe zufällig, also bei der Caritas hier, eine Stelle bekommen. Also bin ich dorthin gezogen. Vorher war ich in drei Frauenhäusern. Das ist alles jetzt sehr lange her, aber was ich da erlebt hab, das war also wirklich, ich kann es nicht anders bezeichnen, katastrophal und unverschämt und ausbeuterisch. In einem einzigen Zimmer habe ich mit meinen drei Kindern da gewohnt und es war eng, dreckig und schmutzig. Und dafür mussten wir so wahnsinnig viel Geld bezahlen. Viele Frauen hatten keine Arbeit, denen tat das nicht weh, die wurden dann sofort zum Sozialamt geschickt. Aber bei mir war es ja nun so, ich hatte ja Arbeit und mein Gehalt; und mein ganzes Gehalt ging drauf. Und dann bin ich trotzdem in diesem Frauenhaus runtergesunken auf Sozialhilfeniveau und musste mein ganzes Gehalt da abgeben. Alles und noch viel mehr und das Sozialamt musste mir dann Geld fürs Essen geben. Also das fand ich schon unverschämt für die Gegenleistung, die man bekam. Es war ja kein Luxushotel.

Das hat mir damals wirklich keiner geglaubt, aber für das gleiche Geld hätte ich in irgendeine billige Pension in einer anderen Stadt gehen können und hätte mich da verstecken können. Da hätte ich es ein bisschen würdevoller gehabt als in so einem Frauenhaus. Das habe ich schon als sehr schlimm empfunden. Da steht man dann am nächsten Morgen und dann sagen die einem hier mit so tausend komischen Briefen in der Hand „So, wir haben schon beim Sozialamt angerufen, zu dem und dem Bearbeiter müssen Sie". Und das sind überdimensionale Preise gewesen. Wenn die Leute Hilfe brauchten bestand die Hilfe darin, zu sagen „Ja, da ist das Sozialamt und da ist das Jugendamt". Es war ein Schutz, klar, aber mich hat auch erschüttert, dass mein Mann mich jedes Mal gefunden hat und danach habe ich nie wieder eins gesehen und möchte das auch nicht.

Wissen Sie, wenn man mit drei Kindern da steht in einer fremden Stadt und ich hatte nichts. Sie müssen sich wirklich vorstellen, ich bin hier angekommen, ich hatte mein altes Auto, meine drei Kinder mit ihren Schultaschen und das Nötigste zum Kleiden, und das war's. Und ich glaube zu der Zeit hatte ich noch 1500 Mark heimlich gespart. Und wenn Sie damit irgendwo ankommen, egal, wo Sie ankommen, man fühlt sich erbärmlich.

"My entire salary was spent for this"

Theresia's Story

I came to this town because I was fleeing from my husband. But at that time I had already gone through three women's refuges, and he found me every time with three children in tow. Then I landed in that neighbouring village by chance, applied for a job and got one, by chance, here at the Caritas organisation. That was why I moved there. I had stayed in three women's shelters before. All this is a long time ago, but what I had experienced there, that was really, well, I cannot describe it differently, that was catastrophic and shameless and exploitative. I lived there with my three children in one single room and it was narrow, dirty and dingy. And we had to pay so much money for this. Many women were without any job, that was not so painful for them, they were immediately sent to the social welfare office then. But in my case things were different because I had a job and my pay; and I had to spend all my pay for this. So despite earning money from my work, in that women's refuge I sank to the income level of social welfare and I had to leave all my pay there. All of it. and even a lot more than that, so the social welfare office even had to give me money for food. Well, to me, this was quite an exorbitant demand for what I received in turn there. For it was not a luxury hotel, after all.

Nobody wanted to believe me this at that time, but I could have gone to any cheap guesthouse in a different town and could have hidden away there. I could have lived there with some more dignity than in such a women's refuge. To me, this was a terrible experience. Then they stand there the next morning and tell you, with something like a hundred strange letters in their hands "Well, now, we have already called the social welfare office, you have to go to such and such person who is in charge for you". And the prices were excessive. When people needed help, the help they received consisted just in saying: "Yes, the social welfare office is over there and the youth welfare office is over there." Yes, it was a safe place, to be sure, but what appalled me was that my husband always found me. After that I never saw a women's refuge again and I don't ever want to see one again.

You know, if you have three children and you stand there in a town you don't know; and I had nothing. Just imagine: I arrived here, I had my old car, my three children with their school bags and the basic essentials of clothing, and that was everything. And I think I had saved an amount of 1,500 German Marks secretly at that time. And if you arrive somewhere with only this in your hands, no matter where, then you feel wretched. You feel like creeping into a mouse hole.

Man möchte sich in einem Mauseloch verkriechen. Die Frau X wusste, ich hatte gar nichts außer einer nackten Wohnung und dann hatte die auch in Dorf W eine Wohnung aufgetan, wo der Besitzer verstorben war und hatte seine ganze Einrichtung der Kirche gespendet. Und Frau X hatte mich dann zu dieser Kirche geschickt und dann konnte ich mir da auch wirklich sehr viele sehr gute Sachen rausholen, das werde ich nie vergessen. Waschmaschine, alles so Sachen, die man wirklich braucht. Und ich stand dann da und auf einmal kriegte ich wirklich einen richtigen hysterischen Anfall. Diese Frau von der Kirche die stand da und war ganz lieb und versuchte mir alles zu zeigen und mir auch zu sagen „Nehmen Sie ruhig, was Sie brauchen" und die haben mir das sogar noch gebracht. Und dann fing ich an zu begreifen, dass ich das doch alles hatte; dass das jetzt alles weg ist. Mein Mann hatte, schon während ich im Frauenhaus war, die Sachen verkauft. Das muss man sich mal vorstellen. Die mir gehörten! Und dann kriegte ich wirklich so einen hysterischen Lachanfall draußen auf dem Bürgersteig, ich konnte gar nicht... also das war mir so unangenehm, das ist mir auch nie wieder passiert und hinterher fing ich richtig an zu weinen. Also wenn Sie fragen „Wie haben Sie sich gefühlt?" also man fühlt sich wie das. Ganz furchtbar.

Ms. X knew that I had nothing but a bare flat completely unfurnished, and then she even found out about a flat there in Town W, where the proprietor had died and had left his entire home furnishing and fittings to the Church. And Ms. X, she sent me to the woman at the church, and I could really get a lot of things from there, I will never ever forget this: a washing machine and all those things which you really need. And then I was standing there and, suddenly, all at once I actually began laughing hysterically. The woman from the church was standing there and she was quite nice and gentle and she tried to show me everything and also to explain to me: "Please have no fear to take everything you need." And they even brought the things to my new flat. And then I slowly began to realize that I had had all of this before, and that everything I had was gone. My husband had sold all those things while I was staying in the women's refuge. Just imagine that! The household goods and objects that belonged to me! And then I really got that attack of hysterical laughter outside there on the sidewalk, I could simply not ... well, that was so awkward to me, and it never ever happened to me again and then I really started to weep. Well, if you ask me "How did you feel then?" Well, you feel like .... Completely awful.

"Ich habe keinen Fehler gemacht"

Zeras Geschichte

Ich komme aus einem arabischen Land aus einer sehr großen Familie. Mein Mann war sozusagen schon immer da. Mit 16 wurde ich zwangsverheiratet. Ich habe zwar versucht nein zu sagen, ich wollte das nicht, aber ich musste es tun, um meine Familie, meinen Bruder, Onkel, Cousins und Schwestern zu schützen. Später, um meine Kinder zu schützen. Ich habe Abitur gemacht und danach eine Ausbildung gelernt und spreche noch einige andere Sprachen und inzwischen ein bisschen Deutsch. Eine Weile habe ich einen guten Job gehabt und gearbeitet. Nach ein paar Monaten fing es aber an, dass mir mein Mann verboten hat zu arbeiten. Es geziemte sich nicht für unser Ansehen.

Ich konnte weder meinem Mann, noch der Familie vertrauen. Es passiert zwar in allen Ländern, dass gelogen und taktiert wird, aber dort wo wir herkommen ist es noch schlimmer. Diese Leute lügen immer und sind gefährlich.

Ich habe schon ein paar Mal versucht zu meiner Familie zu gehen und zu sagen „bitte, ich kann das nicht. Ich will das nicht, ich kann nicht mit ihm zusammen sein." Aber er setzte meine Familie unter Druck. „Wenn Du nicht zurückkommst, bringe ich Deinen Bruder um "Meine Mutter hatte deswegen Angst und hat mich immer beschworen „geh zurück, Zera, geh zu ihm zurück". Also ging ich zurück.

Bevor ich nach Deutschland kam ist schon einiges passiert. Es gibt in meinem Heimatland keine Hilfe. Wenn man welche findet, dann keine richtige. Niemandem kann man vertrauen und immer ist alles die Schuld der Frau.

Die ersten 10 Jahre die ich in Deutschland war, war ich nur zu Hause, wie eingesperrt. Nichts war anders als in meinem Heimatland. Ich wusste nicht, dass es Hilfe für Frauen gibt, ich wusste nicht mal, wo die Innenstadt oder die Sparkasse oder irgendwelche Ärzte waren. Ich habe eins meiner Kinder hier in Deutschland bekommen, aber immer wenn ich zu einem Termin musste kam er mit. Ich war selber wie ein kleines Kind: Alleine wäre ich draußen verloren gewesen. Wenn Besuch kam sagten wir „Hallo" und dann musste ich den Raum verlassen. Es war ein Gefängnis, glaub mir, ein Gefängnis. Mir fehlen die Worte dafür. Ich durfte nicht entscheiden was ich anziehe, oder esse, ich habe Schläge bekommen, für alles was ich benutzen wollte musste er die Erlaubnis geben. Wenn er sagte er möchte bei mir liegen und ich sagte ich will nicht, gab es Schläge. Ich musste auch ins Krankenhaus, aber ich konnte doch nicht sagen „ich kriege Schläge".

"I haven't made any mistake"

Zera's Story

*I come from an Arabian country and from a very big family. My husband has always
been there, so to speak. I was forced into marriage at the age of sixteen. I certainly
tried to say 'No', I did not want that, but I had to accept it to protect my family,
my brother, my uncle and cousins as well as my sisters. Later, it was to protect my
children. I finished high school and then I had went through vocational training, and I
speak some other languages and, meanwhile, a little bit of German, too. I had a good
job and worked for a while. But after a few months, my husband began to forbid me to
work. It did not befit our reputation, he said.*

*I could neither put any trust in my husband nor in my family. It is true that people tell
lies and do radical manoeuvring in all countries in the world, but in our home country,
this is even worse. Those people always lie and they are dangerous.*

*I had tried several times to go to my family and to explain to them: "Please, I cannot
do that. I don't want to do that, I cannot stay with him." But he put my family under
pressure: "If you don't come back, I will kill your brother." My mother was scared
about this and she never stopped imploring me: "Go back, Zera, go back to him." And
so I returned.*

*Before I came to Germany, quite a lot of things had already happened. You cannot get
any help in my home country. And if you find it, then it is not true help. There is nobody
you can trust, and it is always the woman's fault.*

*The first ten years living in Germany I was staying at home the whole time, as if I
were locked up. Nothing was different from the situation in my home country. I did
not know that there was help available for women; I did not even know where the city
centre or the savings bank or any kind of doctors were. One of my children was born
here in Germany, but always when I had to go to an appointment, he came along with
me. I felt like a little child myself: I would have been lost outside on my own. When
people came to pay us a visit at home, we said "Hello" and then I had to leave the
room. It was like being in prison, believe me, it was a prison. I have no words for this.*

*I was not allowed to make my own decisions on how to dress, or what to eat, and I
was beaten; and he had to give his permission for everything I wanted to use. When he
said he wanted to sleep with me and I said I didn't want to, I was beaten. I had to go
to the hospital, but I could not admit and say "I am beaten", could I?*

Mein Kind hat irgendwann im Jobcenter gesehen, dass es Integrationskurse gibt und gesagt „schicken Sie meiner Mama so einen Brief, die braucht das". Das hat mir viel geholfen. Ich war von den 6 Monaten vielleicht 2 nicht da, wenn ich blaue Augen durch die Prügel hatte, aber er musste mich oft genug gehen lassen, weil er wusste, dass ich dieses Zertifikat brauchte und die Sprache schwer zu lernen ist.

Eines Tages hat er mich wieder geschlagen und meine Tochter hat die Polizei gerufen. Die haben mir gezeigt dass es einen Frauennotruf gibt und ein Frauenhaus, dass ich da Schutz finden kann. Als mein Sohn im Grundschulalter war, hat auch er nachts die Polizei gerufen, weil er nicht wusste, was er damit auslöst. Natürlich leugnete mein Mann alles, aber mein Sohn sagte „doch, er hat sie geschlagen". Daraufhin habe ich auch die Wahrheit gesagt und die Polizei hat ihn rausgeworfen. Wo er geschlafen hat, weiß ich nicht, doch dann rief die Familie wieder an und ich ließ ihn zurück. Diese Geschichte hatten wir immer wieder. Immer wieder Polizei, immer wieder raus, wieder zurück. Einmal hat die Polizei auch mich weggeschickt, ins Frauenhaus in einer anderen Stadt. Aber ich habe gesagt das hilft mir nicht. Für eine andere Frau mag das richtig sein, aber nicht für mich.

Drei Mal war ich im Frauenhaus und habe festgestellt, dass das nichts für mich ist. Ich will nicht weglaufen. Wenn ich gehe, dann hat er was gegen mich in der Hand. Dann habe ich einen Fehler gemacht. Ich musste um mein Gesicht zu wahren bleiben. Außerdem hat er meine Familie unter Druck gesetzt bis die mich anflehten zurück zu gehen. Ich habe mit meinem Körper und meiner Seele für die Sicherheit meiner Familie bezahlt. Erst die meiner Eltern, dann die meiner Kinder.

Gewendet hat es sich, als er versuchte mich bloßzustellen. Er hat mich beschatten lassen, um mir eine Affäre nachzuweisen und mich vor der ganzen Familie bloßzustellen. Ich habe das Spiel mitgespielt und den Spieß umgekehrt. Er fand nur heraus, dass ich nie fremdgegangen bin. Er hatte nichts gegen mich in der Hand, aber ich hatte jetzt etwas gegen ihn in der Hand. Jahrelang habe ich alles erduldet, aber das ging zu weit. So etwas macht man nicht mit einer Frau, die einem Jahrzehnte zur Seite stand. Die Prügel habe ich ausgehalten, die Seitensprünge, alles, was noch passierte, das war in der Familie „normal". Aber nun hatte er endlich einen Fehler gemacht und ich nicht.

Ich bin selber zum Amtsgericht gegangen, habe diesen Zettel genommen und gesagt „Ich will mich scheiden lassen". Verboten oder nicht verboten in meinem Heimatland, ich kann sterben, aber ich kann nicht zurück zu diesem Mann. Er versuchte mich zu überreden zurück zu kommen, er hat versucht die Kinder zu kaufen, er hat seine Familie geschickt mich anzurufen und zurück zu bekommen, aber ich habe mich scheiden lassen. Was mir dabei geholfen hat waren die Termine hier in der Beratung. Der Kontakt mit meiner Beraterin hier hat mir sehr viel Stärke gegeben. Ich brauchte Vertrauen, einen Menschen dem ich vertrauen kann. Und dann eine Chance zu arbeiten, etwas zu tun, mit dem ich nach vorn sehen kann. Ich habe einige Praktika und Fortbildungen gemacht, aber Arbeit zu finden ist sehr schwer. Ich wünschte mir, dass es mehr Chancen für Frauen wie mich gäbe.

One day, one of my children saw in the job centre that they offered integration courses and she told them: "Please send a letter to my mum, she needs that." That helped me a lot. I didn't attend the courses throughout the whole 6 months, but missed about 2 months or so in all, whenever I had black eyes from the beatings, but he had to let me go quite often, because he knew that I needed this certificate and that the language was difficult to learn.

One day he had beaten me again and my daughter called the police. They showed me that there was a Women's Emergency Hotline existing as well as women's refuge, where I could find shelter. When my son was at primary school age, he also called the police at night, because he didn't know what he would provoke by doing this. He didn't know anything about pressure and threats. Of course, my husband denied everything, but my son confirmed it again: "Yes, he has battered her." Then I also told the truth and the police threw him out. I didn't know where he slept that night, but then the family phoned me again and I let him return. We had this same story again and again. The police came again and again, he was expelled and he came back again. Once, the police sent me away, too, into the women's refuge. They told me that I should go far away, into a women's shelter of another city. But I said to them that this wouldn't help me. I haven't made any mistake. This might be the right thing for other women, but not for me.

I stayed in the women's refuge home three times and I realised that this wasn't the right thing for me. I don't want to run away. If I go away, then he can use this against me. In that case, I would admit having made a mistake. I had to stay to save face. And what is more, he put my family under pressure, until they begged me on their knees to return to him. For the safety of my family, I paid for this with my body and my soul; at first for the safety of my parents and then for the safety of my children.

The turning point came when he tried to show me up. He had tailed me in order to furnish proof of me having an affair and to show me up before the entire family and then he wanted to blackmail me. I took part in the game and turned the tables. Everything he could find out was that I was never unfaithful. He had nothing to use against me, but now I had something to use against him. I had endured everything for years, but that was going too far. You don't do this with a woman who has stood by your side for decades. I endured the floggings, the infidelities, everything that happened, that was "normal" in the family, but finally, he made a mistake and not me.

I went to the local court on my own, I took this paper and I told them: "I want a divorce." Whether it is forbidden in my home country or not, I can die, but I cannot return to this man. He tried to persuade me to come back to him, he tried to 'buy' the children, he sent his family to call me and to get me back, but I got divorced. What helped me most was the appointments here in the advisory centre. The contact I had here with my advisor made me very strong. I needed trust; someone whom I could trust. And then I needed a chance to work, to do something that would allow me to look forward. I completed some practical training and further education programmes, but it is very hard to find work. I would very much like to see more chances for women like me.

Domestic Violence

Stories and experiences of women

Portugal

"Quatro anos à espera de julgamento foram uma tortura"

História de Adelina

Sofri violência doméstica nos meus dois casamentos. Durante a primeira relação, que durou 8 anos, tive a minha primeira filha. Separámo-nos porque ele tinha um problema com drogas e era violento e por isso decidi ir viver com a minha mãe. Enquanto estava com a minha mãe, conheci outro homem e depois fui viver com ele. Ficámos juntos 15 anos. Durante esse tempo, ele foi extremamente violento em muitas ocasiões. Senti-me muito isolada. Ele metia as pessoas de fora no coração e ninguém acreditava que ele me estava a maltratar. Até pensavam que eu é que era má com ele! Uma vez, eu queria mostrar a toda a gente que eles não estavam a ver as coisas como elas eram e decidi meter-me debaixo do comboio. Deitei-me na linha mas o comboio parou. Tinha tanto medo do meu marido que não conseguia pensar direito. Não sabia o que fazer. Deixei de ser eu.

Durante esses 15 anos chamei a polícia várias vezes mas depois ficava cheia de medo porque já sabia que ele me ia bater ainda mais. Perguntei-me muitas vezes de que servia estar a pedir ajuda. Os vizinhos também chamaram a polícia várias vezes. A polícia chegava e eu ouvia-os cá em baixo a falar e a rir. Nem sequer subiam para ver se eu estava viva ou morta. Uma vez ele bateu-me num sítio público e voltaram a chamar a polícia. Uma senhora que tinha visto tudo insistiu que queria ser minha testemunha mas o polícia disse: "não, não é preciso testemunhas, nós vamos fazer um relatório e não é preciso mais nada." Eu não sabia nada de tribunais. Não sabia que era preciso meter um advogado. Portanto, ele levou advogado, eu não levei. Os quatro anos à espera de julgamento foram uma tortura. No final, o tribunal disse que tinha sido apenas uma troca de palavras. Ele ficou de pagar uma multa ao tribunal e mais nada. No final disto tudo, eu continuava a viver com ele porque não tinha forma de o pôr fora de casa. Durante esses quatro anos, fui a uma instituição e puseram-me numa casa de abrigo. Ele descobriu onde eu estava, foi lá e bateu-me. Mais tarde, soube que o tribunal lhes tinha pedido para fazerem um relatório mas negaram que eu tinha lá estado.

Não entendo estas injustiças e sou revoltada, se for preciso, digo à frente de qualquer pessoa que me vou revoltar. Eu sinto que as organizações lutam mas elas também têm dificuldades. As coisas estão a ficar muito graves.

"Four years waiting for trial were torture"

Adelina's Story

I suffered from severe domestic violence in my two marriages. The first one lasted 8 years and during that time I had my first child. We separated because of his drug use and his violence and I went to live with my mother. While I was with her, I met another man, and then I went to live with him. We were together for 15 years. During this time he was extremely violent on many occasions. I felt very isolated. To other people he was very charming and nobody believed that he was maltreating me. If anything they thought I was the one who was mean to him. One time, I wanted to show everyone that they weren't seeing things right so I attempted suicide by lying on the train tracks. The train stopped and didn't hit me. I was so afraid of my husband and didn't have the ability to think clearly. I didn't know what to do. I wasn't myself anymore.

During those 15 years I called the police and went to the station several times but when I got home I was already afraid because I knew I was going to get beaten up even more. I would ask myself why I even bothered seeking their help. The neighbours also called the police a few times. The police would get to the house and I would hear them talking and laughing downstairs. They didn't even check if I was dead or alive. One time he hit me in a public place and the police was called again. A lady who witnessed this incident insisted that she wanted to be my witness however a police officer said: "no, we don't need a witness, we will make a report and that's it." I knew nothing about courts. I didn't know I had to hire a lawyer so he got a lawyer but I didn't. Those four years waiting for trial were torture. In the end, the court said that what had happened was a mere exchange of words. He was sentenced to pay a fine to court, nothing else. At the end of this process I continued to live with him because I had no way to kick him out of the house. During those four years I went to an institution and was placed in a shelter. He found out where it was, went there and hit me. I later also found out that the court had asked for a report from this institution but they denied that I was ever a client there.

I don't understand why this is so unfair and I am outraged, if need be I will tell anybody that I will protest. I feel that the organizations fight but they also have many challenges, I know the challenges that they have. Things are getting very difficult.

"Ele é quem devia sair de casa"

História de Beatriz

Tenho 60 anos. Nasci e cresci no Brasil. Perdi a minha família quando tinha 7 anos. A minha mãe morreu e o meu pai dividiu-nos como gatinhos. Só voltei a encontrar a minha família em 1997, quando me fui despedir do meu pai e da minha irmã que estavam doentes e morreram pouco depois.

Quando tinha 19 anos conheci um homem português. Ele enganou-me, prometendo arranjar-me trabalho. Disse-me para ir temporariamente para casa dele para ele depois me levar ao meu novo emprego. Isso nunca aconteceu e eu acabei por ficar presa naquela casa. Ele maltratou-me desde o primeiro dia. Quando eu lhe disse que estava grávida, as agressões físicas começaram. Viemos para Portugal quando eu estava grávida do meu segundo filho. Ele era muito agressivo comigo e com as crianças. Uma vez ele bateu no nosso filho de três anos com um cinto. Foi um crime! Eu fui fazer queixa e o polícia disse que não queria interferir entre pai e filho. Noutra situação eu fui ao hospital mas não contei que era vítima de violência doméstica porque tinha muita vergonha. Os meus patrões começaram a notar o abuso constante e diziam-me: "por amor de Deus, faça queixa dele!" Eu não fiz queixa porque tinha medo dele. Ainda hoje tenho.

Uma vez, bateu-me tanto que me partiu os dentes todos e a minha cara ficou toda deformada. Eu fui à polícia dessa vez. O polícia disse: "ele está no país dele e na casa dele, se não está bem, vá para o seu país." O polícia tratou-me como se eu fosse uma prostituta. O sistema de justiça aqui é muito racista. Numa altura, fui também procurar ajuda a uma instituição. Eles não fizeram nada. A única coisa que queriam era que eu fosse para uma casa de abrigo, mas isso é tão injusto! Ele é quem devia sair de casa.

Ao longo dos anos, fiz várias queixas na polícia e nada aconteceu. Acabei por ir a uma organização brasileira e arranjei ajuda psicológica e legal. Com a ajuda deles foi finalmente possível apresentar uma queixa-crime. Naquela altura, eu estava muito deprimida. O polícia disse: "você não está bem, se está a ser tratada por um psiquiatra." E eu disse: "estou a ter consultas porque tenho uma depressão profunda, não é por estar maluca!" Nessa altura eu qualificava-me para receber o estatuto de vítima mas não recebi absolutamente nenhum apoio do governo. O meu maior apoio foi a psicóloga da organização brasileira.

"He is the one who should leave the house."

Beatriz' Story

I'm 60 years old. I was born and raised in Brazil. I lost my family when I was 7 years old. My mother passed away and my father gave my siblings and me away as if we were kittens. I only reunited with my family in 1997, when I went back to Brazil to say goodbye to my father and my sister who were sick and died shortly thereafter.

I met a Portuguese man when I was 19 years old. He promised to get me a job and tricked me into moving temporarily to his home telling me that he would take me to my new employer. This never happened and I became imprisoned in his home. He never gave me a day of happiness. He always used me. He has maltreated me severely from day one. When I told him I was pregnant, the physical aggressions began.

We came to Portugal when I was pregnant with my second child. Not only was he aggressive towards me, he was also aggressive towards our children. One time he beat our child on his third birthday with a belt. That was a crime! When I reported it, the police officer said that he didn't want to interfere between father and child. One other time I also went to the hospital but didn't disclose the domestic violence because I was extremely ashamed of it. My employers started to notice the constant abuse and they used to say: "for heaven's sake, report him!" I didn't report him at that time because I was afraid of him. Even now, I am afraid of him.

One time he beat me so much that he broke my teeth and my face became deformed. I went to the police that time. The police officer said: "he is in his country and his home, if you are not well, go back to your country." The police officer also treated me as if I was a prostitute. The justice system here is very racist. At some point I went to an institution looking for help. They didn't do anything. The only thing they wanted me to do was to leave home and go to a shelter but that is so unfair! He is the one who should leave the house.

Throughout the years I made several complaints in the police but nothing happened. I finally went to a Brazilian organization and was able to get juridical and psychological help. With their help I was finally able to make a criminal complaint. At that time, I was profoundly depressed.

A única solução que me dão para acabar com a violência é ir para uma casa de abrigo mas eu não quero mesmo fazer isso. Eu não vou deixar a minha casa! Tenho 60 anos e tudo o que tenho foi comprado com o meu dinheiro. Eu trabalhei noite e dia para ter o que tenho. Ele nunca comprou nada. Ele é quem tem de sair, não eu! Isso é muito injusto.

Neste momento, tenho três queixas-crime e três processos no tribunal contra ele. As minhas testemunhas já foram ouvidas mas ainda nada foi feito. Ele continua em casa e continua a bater-me. Na sociedade portuguesa, há muito preconceito contra as mulheres brasileiras. Eles tratam todas as mulheres brasileiras como se fossem prostitutas.

The police officer said: "You're not well, you are being treated by a psychiatrist." I said: "I am seeing a psychiatrist but that is because I have a profound depression. It's not because I'm crazy." At this time, I was entitled to be given the status of the victim, but I got absolutely no governmental help or support. My main source of support is the psychologist I met in the Brazilian organization.

Again and again the only solution I am given to stop the violence is to go to a shelter but I really do not want to do that. I'm not going to leave my house. I am 60 years old, everything that is in my house was bought with my money. I worked day and night to have what I have. He never bought anything. He is the one who has to leave, not me! It is very unfair.

Currently I have three criminal complaints and three different lawsuits going on against him. My witnesses have already been heard but nothing has been done so far. He goes on beating me. He is still at home. In Portuguese society there is a lot of prejudice against Brazilian women. They treat all Brazilian women as if they are prostitutes.

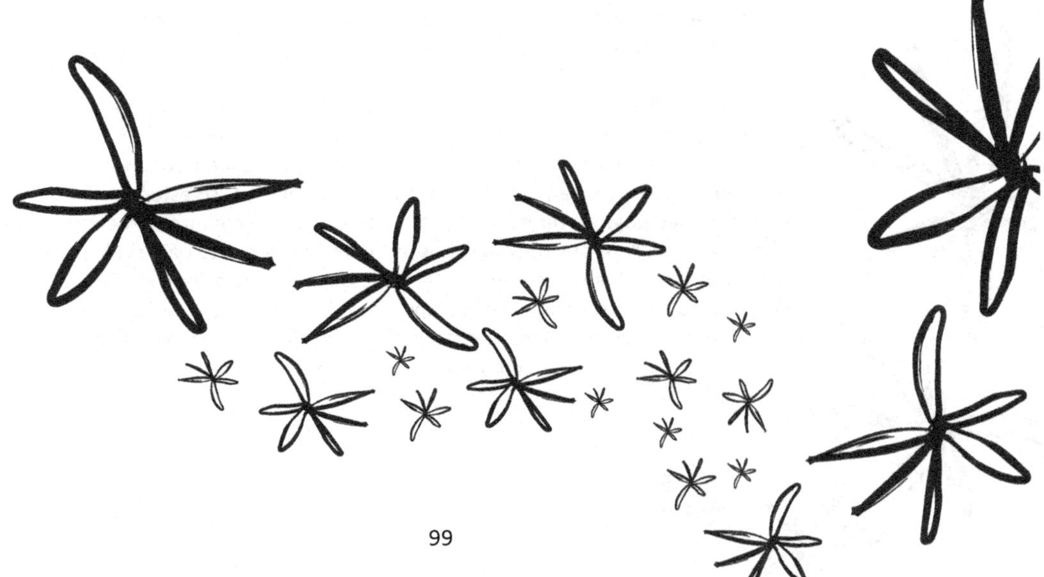

"Aconselharam-me a não levar os meus filhos"

História de Carmen

Tenho 42 anos e sou cigana. O meu pai prometeu-me quando eu tinha 11 anos. Depois casamos de acordo com a nossa tradição quando eu tinha 13 e ele 18 anos. Eu não gostava dele. Uma semana depois de casarmos ele começou a bater-me no meio da rua. Ele batia-me todos os dias. Eu perdi dois bebés e depois fiquei novamente grávida do meu primeiro filho quando tinha 17 anos.

Fui ao hospital algumas vezes. O meu marido vinha sempre comigo e dizia-me sempre para dizer que me tinha magoado ao cair de umas escadas abaixo. Uma vez, na triagem, mandaram-me para um psiquiatra. O psiquiatra disse: "você tinha nódoas negras nesta data, tinha nódoas negras nesta data, você está a vir aqui muitas vezes!" O meu marido ficou chateado e o doutor chamou a segurança para o levar lá para fora. Quando cheguei a casa ele bateu-me muito. A família toda estava contra mim. Eles perguntaram: "porque é que chamaste a polícia?" Eu não chamei! Eu neguei tudo ao doutor!

O meu pai tirou-me da escola quando eu era muito pequena. Quando os meus filhos cresceram eu tentei voltar à escola mas não consegui fazer muito porque a minha comunidade ia à escola fazer escândalo: "tu és cigana, não tens de estudar, tu tens o teu marido, tu tens isto, tu tens aquilo..." O meu marido costumava levar-me e buscar-me. Um dia puxou-me pelo cabelo quando me ia buscar e insultou-me. A minha professora insistiu para eu pedir ajuda à minha assistente social.

Tentei ir trabalhar mas a minha família interferiu outra vez e tive de me vir embora. Numa ocasião ele destruiu todo o meu material escolar incluindo um diploma que eu tinha acabado de ganhar. Pensei: "tenho de me ir embora, estou farta, não posso fazer nada aqui!" Estava tão cansada! "Não posso estudar, não posso trabalhar, não posso fazer nada da minha vida!" No dia seguinte os meus vizinhos disseram-me: "nós ouvimos os gritos, ele bate-te tanto, isto não é vida para ti." Os meus filhos estavam completamente dessensibilizados com a violência. Eles tinham visto aquilo durante tanto tempo. Era normal para eles. Quando eu tentava falar com eles e perguntar se eles queriam vir embora comigo, eles diziam que só iriam embora com a mãe e com o pai.

"They advised me not to bring my children"

Carmen's Story

I am a 42 years old Roma woman. My father arranged my marriage when I was 11. We then got married according to our tradition when I was 13 and he was 18. I did not like him. A week after we got married he hit me badly in the middle of the street. He hit me every single day. After two miscarriages I got pregnant with my first child at 17.

I went to the hospital a few times. My husband always came with me and would instruct me to say that my injuries were due to falling down a flight of stairs. One time the triage staff at the hospital sent me to a psychiatrist. The psychiatrist said: "you had bruises on this date, you had bruises on that date, you are coming to the hospital very often!" My husband got mad and the doctor called security to take him outside. When I arrived home he beat me very badly. The entire family was against me. They asked: "why did you call the police?" I didn't! I denied everything to the doctor!

My father took me out of school when I was young. When my children grew up I tried to return to school but I couldn't go very far because my community went to the school to make a fuss: "you are Roma, you don't have to study, you have your husband, you have this, you have that..." My husband used to drop me off and pick me up from school. One day he pulled me by the hair when he picked me up and insulted me. They started to notice I went to school bruised. My teacher urged me to ask my social worker for help.

I tried to work and my family interfered again so I had to leave. At some point he destroyed all my school materials including the diploma I had just obtained. I thought: "I have to go away, enough is enough, I can't do anything here!" I was so tired! "I can't study, I can't work, I can't do anything in my life, I am tired!" The next day my neighbours told me: "we hear the screams, he hits you so much, this isn't a good life for you." My children were desensitized to the beatings. They had seen it for so long. It was normal to them. When I tried to talk to them and ask if they would go away with me, they said that they would go away with me and their dad.

I had a social worker from social security and so I opened up to her. I told her I could not stand it anymore. I told her about what happened at school. She told me to meet with the staff of a shelter. When I went there they informed me of my rights and the assistance they could give me. However, my children had to stay behind.

Eu tinha uma assistente social e abri-me com ela. Disse-lhe que já não aguentava mais. Contei-lhe o que aconteceu na escola. Ela disse-me para me reunir com umas senhoras de uma casa de abrigo. Quando fui lá, elas informaram-me dos meus direitos e da assistência que me podiam dar. No entanto, os meus filhos tinham de ficar para trás. Elas aconselharam-me a não levar os meus filhos porque tinham tido lá uma senhora cigana com os filhos de 10 e 12 anos e eles ligaram à família. Depois dessa reunião fui para casa e, no dia seguinte, mudei-me para lá. Só levava a roupa do corpo. Nunca mais vou esquecer o dia em que fui embora. Levei os meus filhos à escola. Eu sabia que os ia deixar. Dei-lhes um abraço muito apertado, tão apertado! O meu filho mais novo disse: "mãe, eu não quero que tu sofras mais". Eu já tinha chegado ao meu limite!

Eu sofri tanto quando fui para a casa de abrigo. Chorei tanto. Eu tinha apoio psicológico e muita ajuda mas tive de fazer tantas mudanças! Tive de mudar de número de telefone. Cortei o cabelo. Usei calças pela primeira vez. Estive nessa casa de abrigo uma semana. Era na mesma cidade onde eu vivia e, uma vez, vi um primo na rua, por isso pedi para me mudarem para mais longe. Quando cheguei à nova cidade não tive ajuda económica nenhuma durante 2 meses. Nunca me senti descriminada. Sempre fui bem tratada. Eles trataram-me da mesma maneira que tratavam as outras senhoras. Eu fiz uma grande amizade com as doutoras da casa de abrigo e elas continuam a ajudar-me até hoje. Elas continuam a dar-me imenso apoio e vão ao tribunal comigo, por exemplo.

Eu fiz uma queixa contra o meu marido e o caso foi para tribunal. Participei nas sessões por videoconferência. Eu já lhes contei a minha vida toda e, de cada vez que há uma sessão, saio a chorar, um caco. A certa altura o representante do Ministério Público perguntou-me: "o que é que quer disto tudo?" Eu disse: "o que eu quero... eu não quero que nada de mal aconteça ao pai dos meus filhos." Não pedi pena de prisão nem nada disso. Eu disse: "só quero que ele aceite. Se ele um dia me vir na rua que não me faça mal. Quero que ele aceite que os meus filhos me vejam e que tenhamos uma relação saudável. É isso que eu quero."

O que eu diria a outras mulheres é que saiam desse sofrimento. Elas vão ter tudo de novo, ainda melhor. Saiam dessa situação! Eu sei que se ficasse com o meu marido ia ser fatal. Naquela raiva dele, ele ia-me matar. Por isso, se estiverem nessa situação, saiam!

They advised me not to bring my children because they had had a Roma lady with her 10 and 12-year-old children and they called their father and the entire family went there. After the meeting I went home and in the next day I moved there. The only clothes I had were the ones I was wearing. I will never forget the day that I left. I took the children to school. I knew I was going to leave them. I held them so tight, so tigh. My youngest child said: "mom, I don't want you to suffer anymore." I had reached my limit, I was going crazy.

I suffered so much when I went to the shelter. I cried a lot. I had psychological support and a lot of help but I had to deal with so many changes! I had to change my phone number. I cut my hair. I wore pants for the first time. I was in the first shelter for one week. It was in the same city where I lived and I saw a cousin in the street so I asked to be placed far away. When I got to the new city I didn't have financial assistance for 2 months. I never felt discriminated against. I have been very well treated. They treated me in the same way the others were treated. I maintained my relationship with the shelter staff and they help me to this day. They continue to help me a lot and go to court with me, for example.

I made a complaint against my husband and the case is now in court. I participate in the sessions through videoconference. I told them all my life there and every time there is a session I leave crying, a wreck. At some point the prosecutor asked me "what do you want from all this?" I said: "what I want... I don't want nothing wrong to happen to the father of my children." I didn't ask for a jail sentence or anything: "What I want is for him to accept. If one day he sees me in the street I don't want him to harm me. I want him to accept that my children can see me and that we can have a healthy relationship. That's what I want."

What I would tell other women is to get out of that suffering. They will have everything again, even better. Get out of that situation! I know that staying with my husband was going to be fatal. In his rage, he would have killed me. So if you are in that situation get out!

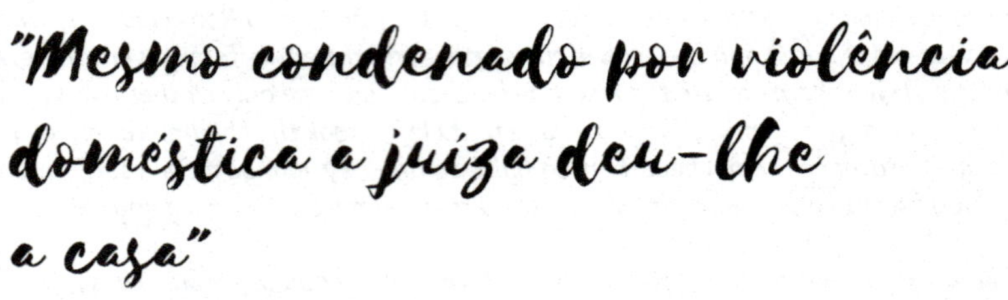

"Mesmo condenado por violência doméstica a juíza deu-lhe a casa"

História de Celeste

Tenho 72 anos. Casei muito nova, conheci o meu marido aos 15 anos, ele tinha 19. Teve sempre mau feitio. Eu estava sempre com a ideia "com o tempo, vai melhorar". E foi indo assim. Tenho dois filhos e ele também lhes batia. Tínhamos problemas de dinheiro, ele tinha muitas dívidas e foi chamado a tribunal por isso.

A partir de certa altura, as coisas começaram a piorar. Decidi pedir ajuda. Mas, sinceramente, não me senti bem recebida. Na altura, marcaram-me um atendimento com um psicólogo. Cheguei lá, disseram que o psicólogo não podia, porque tinha tido qualquer problema, de maneira que ficava para outra vez. Marcaram outro dia, cheguei lá, também não estava. A certa altura, desisti. Ao longo dos anos, fui à polícia várias vezes e fiz sempre queixa. Sentia-me sempre mal, cada vez que ia à polícia. Ele era muito cuidadoso para não deixar marcas à vista, e as queixas nunca deram em nada. A polícia chegava e ele negava tudo. A certa altura, decidi que tinha que encontrar alguém que me ajudasse. Fui à lista telefónica e procurei o número de apoio às vítimas. A senhora que me atendeu deu-me o número de uma ONG. Então, telefonei, e estou muito satisfeita com o atendimento que tenho tido. Estão ali sempre para me ajudar em tudo o que for preciso. Finalmente, há quatro anos, o meu marido ameaçou-me que me matava. Nessa noite, temi pela minha vida, resolvi chamar a polícia. Quando chegaram, foram comigo dentro de casa para eu ir buscar as minhas coisas. E levaram-me a casa da minha filha.

Na ONG, recebi todo o tipo de apoios. Também me pediram apoio jurídico à Segurança Social mas depois nomearam um advogado para o divórcio, outro para a partilha, outro para a pensão de alimentos. Três ou quatro advogados. Apresentei queixa e ele foi condenado a dois anos de pena suspensa por violência doméstica. O divórcio foi decretado recentemente. Mas ele continua lá em casa. Mesmo condenado por violência doméstica, a juíza deu-lhe a casa a ele. De maneira que tive de meter recurso de revisão da sentença. O processo está pendente porque ele está incomunicável e nunca aparece em tribunal. Entretanto, continua a usufruir dos nossos bens. Eu gostava de voltar para a minha casa. Apesar de tudo o que se passou, é a minha casa.

"Even condemned for domestic violence the judge gave him the house"

Celeste's Story

I am 72 years old. I got married very young, at 19 years of age. I met my ex-husband when I was 15 and he was 19. He always had a bad temper but I always held to the idea: "with time he will get better." I have two children and he beat them too. We struggled financially, he contracted a lot of debt and was sent to court for that.

At some point, things got worse. I decided to seek help for the first time. However, honestly, I didn't feel very welcomed. When I first got in touch with them, they scheduled a psychological appointment but when I got there, they told me the psychologist had had a problem and could not see me. They scheduled a new appointment but when I got there, the psychologist wasn't there again. I gave up. Throughout the years I went to the police a few times and made several complaints. I felt badly when I went there. He was very careful not to leave marks on me so my complaints never went anywhere. The police would call him in and he would deny everything. At some point I decided that I had to find someone to help me. So I looked in the phonebook and found a support number for victims. I called and the lady gave me the number of an NGO. I called and am very satisfied with the help that I have there. They are there for me for everything that I need. Finally, four years ago, my husband threaten to kill me. That night I was afraid for my life and decided to call the police. When they arrived, they escorted me back inside the house so I could get a few of my belongings. They took me to my daughter's house.

At the NGO, they gave me all kinds of support. They also assisted me in getting legal representation from social security. However I was given a lawyer for the divorce, another one for the division of belongings, another for spousal support… Three or four lawyers. I pressed charges and he was condemned to a suspended jail sentence of 2 years for domestic violence. Recently, we also got divorced. However, he continues to live in our house. Even condemned for domestic violence the judge gave him the house. So I had to ask for a new revision of this decision. This process is pending because he is unreachable and never shows up in court. In the meantime, he is benefitting from all our goods. I would like to go back to that house. Despite everything that happened, it is my house.

"Conhecer a CPCJ e ter uma ajuda durante um ano foi uma coisa boa"

História de Malika

Nasci e cresci na Argélia. Dois anos depois de acabar o meu curso, fui para a Grécia porque os meus pais estavam lá a viver. Uma rapariga que vive sozinha não é lá muito aceite. Ao início fazia limpezas, porque não falava grego. Uns meses depois, comecei a falar um bocadinho grego e trabalhei num centro de beleza. Conheci o pai do meu filho porque ele era um dos amigos dos meus pais. Estava sempre em nossa casa, como se fosse de família. Começamos uma relação e viemos para Portugal. Quando cheguei cá a Portugal, pfff… Tudo mudou! Casei cá. Só tive autorização de residência 5 anos depois. Estava a sofrer. O meu filho nasceu cá, mas não tinha autorização de residência, tinha que ter paciência.

Podia aceitar ser empregada do meu filho e do meu marido, mas queria receber uma coisa em troca. Só respeito, não queria mais nada mas ele não me respeitava. Muitas vezes ele falava com a minha mãe e dizia palavras feias para a minha mãe, porque sabia que a minha família era o meu ponto fraco. Eu não estava habituada àquele comportamento. Na minha família as pessoas respeitavam-se. O meu pai tratava a minha mãe como se fosse um ser humano, não uma serva. O meu pai veio visitar-me quando ainda estava casada e viu como ele nos tratava e disse: "tens família na Grécia, deixa-o sozinho e vem embora".

O meu marido controlava tudo. Se um dia estivesse a ver a televisão e aparecia uma notícia de violência doméstica, ele mudava logo de canal. Mesmo um programa árabe que falasse de violência, que falasse de uma mulher também vítima, ele dizia: "tu não tens o direito de ver isto". Eu fazia as compras rapidamente porque senão ele ficava nervoso. Ele era muito violento e cruel e batia-me todos os dias. Em todo o lado há estas associações de apoio a vitimas. Mas em Portugal, onde?

Um dia, estava em casa e bateram à porta. Eu abri a porta e era um polícia. Ele disse: "temos aqui uma queixa contra a senhora". Eu perguntei: "Posso saber porquê?" Ele disse: "A senhora sai e deixa o seu filho sozinho em casa". Eu disse: "não, não é verdade isso". Fomos falar na Comissão de Proteção de Crianças e Jovens (CPCJ) e eles ajudaram-me durante um ano.

"Knowing CPCJ and having help for a year was a good thing"

Malika's Story

I was born and raised in Algeria. Two years after I got my degree, I went to Greece because my parents had been living there. A girl who lives on her own is not something people accept very well. In the beginning I worked as a janitor because I did not speak greek. A few months later, I began to speak the language and started to work at a beauty center. I met my son's father because he was my parents' friend. He was always at our place and was part of the family. Eventually we started a relationship and moved to Portugal. When we came here, everything changed! We got married here. I only had a residence permit five years later. I was suffering. My son was born here but I didn't have a residence permit, I had to be patient.

I could accept being my son and husband's maid but I wanted something in return. All I ever wanted was to get some respect but he did not respect me. Many times he said bad words to my mother because he knew that my family was my weak spot. I was not used to this behavior. In my family people respected each other. My father treated my mother as a human being not as a servant. When we were still married my father came to visit us and when he saw the way he treated us he said: "you have family in Greece, leave him alone and come back".

My husband controlled everything. If I was watching TV and something about domestic violence came up he would immediately change the channel. Even if it was an Arab TV show that spoke of violence or a woman victim, he would say: "you don't have the right to watch this". I had to do the grocery shopping quickly otherwise he would get very angry. He was extremely violent and cruel and hit me every day. I knew that everywhere there are associations to help victims of domestic violence. But in Portugal, where?

One day I was at home and someone knocked on my door. I opened the door and it was a police officer. He said: "there has been a complaint against you." I asked: "May I know why?" He said: "You leave your child alone at home". I said: "that isn't true." We talked at the Commission for Protection of Children and Youngsters (CPCJ) and they helped me for a year.

Um dia, estava tão desesperada que saí de casa e fui ao hospital porque era o sítio que eu conhecia melhor por causa da doença do meu filho. No hospital, fizeram soro, depois decidi voltar para casa por causa do meu filho. No hospital, não me perguntaram nada sobre o que se estava a passar. Quatro dias depois, o meu marido foi buscar uma peça para o carro que estava na oficina. Sabia que ele ia demorar e fui com o meu filho para a CPCJ. Eu só tinha a mala, a autorização de residência e o passaporte. Na CPCJ estava toda a tremer, estava toda marcada. Estava a presidente da CPCJ e mostrei-lhe o corpo todo e ela chamou a polícia e a ambulância. O polícia disse "fique descansada que tem segurança aqui no hospital". Esta foi a primeira vez que os médicos me perguntaram alguma coisa sobre violência doméstica. Algumas enfermeiras até choraram porque já tinham reparado que eu estava sempre triste mas pensaram que era por causa do meu filho.

Enquanto eu estava no hospital, a presidente da CPCJ ligou para uma ONG que tem uma casa de abrigo. Foram lá buscar-me, fui lá dois meses. A associação tratou dos documentos, tratou do meu filho, medicamentos, tudo. Na primeira casa de abrigo foi difícil; eu não podia sair porque era perto de onde eu vivia. Eles também me tiraram o meu telemóvel. Durante um mês não soube nada de minha família, se estavam vivos ou mortos. Sentia-me muito mal, até cheguei a um momento e disse "olha, preferia ficar com ele e não criar problemas nenhuns". Eu queria muito saber notícias da minha família e a diretora da casa de abrigo disse-me que a minha mãe e o meu irmão andavam à minha procura no hospital. Então eu pedi para ligar para uma prima minha que vive na Grécia mas longe dos meus pais, e ela disse que o pai do meu filho tinha sido preso. Quando saí de casa, o pai do meu filho tinha ido para a Grécia atrás da minha família. Duas semanas depois, começou a ficar mais agressivo e queria matar o meu pai. Ele foi preso lá. Mais tarde fui visitar a família para apresentar a queixa também lá. Em Portugal também já foi condenado a termo de identidade e residência.

Depois mudei para outra casa de abrigo mais longe para poder recomeçar a minha vida. Três meses depois a doutora conseguiu arranjar uma vaga numa creche. Com 5 anos, foi a primeira vez que o meu filho foi à creche. Antes, ele era mais agitado, agressivo e batia a toda a gente. Mas agora está melhor porque mudou tudo.

Estou muito satisfeita com a ONG, a escola e o hospital. Todos mostram muito respeito por mim. Conhecer a CPCJ e ter uma ajuda durante um ano foi uma coisa boa. Eu fiz bem sair de casa antes de fazer uma coisa má. Esta é a coisa importante para mim. A palavra mais útil que eu ouvi da NGO foi "tu és muito forte".

One time I was so desperate that I left home and went to the hospital because it was the place that I knew best because my son had a medical condition. I was put on an IV line, but then decided to go back home because of my son. At the hospital, they did not ask me what was going on. Four days later, my husband went to fetch a part for the car at the repair shop. When I had that chance to leave, I took it. I ran away with my son to CPCJ. I only had my handbag, residence permit and passport with me. When I got there I was shaking and was bruised all over. The CPCJ director was there and I showed her all the marks in my body and she called the police and an ambulance. The police officer said: "don't worry, there is security at the hospital". This was the first time the doctors asked anything about domestic violence. Some of the nurses even cried because they had noticed I was sad before but they assumed it was because of my son's condition.

While I was at the hospital the CPCJ president called an NGO that runs a shelter. They picked me up and I stayed with them for two months. The NGO took care of my documents, my son's wellbeing, the medications, everything. In the first shelter it was very difficult; I could not go out because it was near where I lived. They also took my mobile phone. For a month I didn't know anything about my family, if they were dead or alive. I felt so bad that I even said: "I prefer to go back to him than to cause any trouble". I really wanted to know news of my family and the director told me that my brother and mother had been asking about me at the hospital. I asked to call a cousin of mine who lived in Greece but far away from my parents. My cousin told me that my husband had been arrested. When I left home, he went to Greece after my family. Two weeks later he became aggressive and threatened to kill my father. He was arrested there. I also went to Greece and pressed charges against him. In Portugal he was also subject to a statement of identity and residence.

I then moved to a shelter farther away so I could restart my life. Three months later the director found a vacancy at a childcare centre. At 5 years old, it was the first time my son went to childcare. Before, he was very agitated, aggressive and hit everybody. Now he is doing much better because everything changed.

I am very pleased with the NGO, my son's school and the hospital. Everyone has been very respectful with me. Knowing the CPCJ and having help for a year was a good thing. I am glad I left home before I did something bad. This is something very important to me. The most useful thing I was told at the NGO was: "you are a very strong person".

"A ONG foi 100% sigilosa e isso foi extremamente importante para mim"

História de Maria dos Anjos

Casei há 40 anos e tive dois filhos. Após um ano de casada, a situação começou realmente a ficar muito difícil. Ele é uma pessoa alcoólica e tornou-se muito agressivo fisicamente, ao longo do nosso casamento. Só recorri uma vez ao hospital mas não falei da violência.

Tentei várias vezes pôr termo ao relacionamento, mas não consegui, por três razões: a principal é o meu marido não aceitar; a outra é falta de apoio familiar, porque, na altura, o conceito familiar que tinha era: "as crianças vão sofrer muito" com a separação. Outra razão e talvez a mais complicada foi o facto de que fui criada com muito amor numa casa com muita paz, em que nunca se ouvia uma discussão. De maneira que quando vi aquela situação de embriaguez, eu ficava a tremer, não sabia lidar com aquilo. Cheguei a ir para casa dos meus avós. Recebiam-me, mas diziam sempre: "Olha, perdoa, dá uma outra oportunidade". Depois, chateada com o meu marido que me perseguia por todo o lado, os telefonemas constantes: "é marido e está arrependido". Ele também era muito ciumento e começou por me afastar das pessoas amigas. E, lentamente, fui perdendo tudo. Senti-me só. Uma das coisas que me deixa imensa pena foi ele ter destruído todas as minhas fotografias. Uma vez foi a destruição completa da casa toda. Quando cheguei a casa, deparei-me com um terramoto! Chamei a polícia, mas, depois, com medo, fui pedir para retirar a queixa.

Também tive outra situação terrível, que foi ele tentar abusar sexualmente da minha filha, é uma coisa que me dói muito. Fui ao Tribunal de Menores e, também, mais uma vez, tive que lá ir dizer que foi um mal-entendido. Ele fez perseguições tremendas! Quando os meus filhos ficaram mais crescidos, ele era muito mau para eles. Expulsou o mais velho de casa, com 16 anos. Os meus filhos diziam-me "Mamã, não pode continuar a viver assim!" E acompanharam-me a uma IPSS. Imediatamente queriam participar. Oficializar. Eu então desisti. Porque eu, de certeza que, se levasse avante um divórcio, ele matava-me, tenho a certeza absoluta! E nós vemos isso todos os dias na tv.

"At the NGO, it was 100% confidential and that was extremely important to me"

Maria dos Anjos' Story

I married 40 years ago and had two children. A year after I got married my situation became very difficult. He was an alcoholic and became very physically aggressive throughout our marriage. I went to the hospital once but did not disclose the violence. I tried several times to end the relationship but was unable to. There are three big reasons: the main one is that my husband never accepted the idea. Secondly, I lacked familial support; at the time the idea was that "children will suffer tremendously" with a separation. Finally, maybe the most complicated reason is that I was raised with a lot of love and in a peaceful home, in which there was never an argument. Hence, when I saw the drinking problem of my husband, I became very frightened and did not know how to deal with it. I became an easy target for him. Today we are still together but we always have many problems. When I was younger I fled to my grandparents' house. They sheltered me but kept telling me: "Look, forgive him, give him another chance". He chased me and called me constantly when I left. My grandparents said: "he is your husband, he is sorry for what he did." He was also very jealous and I ended up losing all my friends. Slowly I lost everything. I felt so lonely. On one occasion, he destroyed most of the furniture and the contents of the house including the destruction of all my photos. When I got home I thought there had been an earthquake. I called the police but quickly went back and took it back because I feared his reaction.

Another terrible situation was that he tried to sexually abuse my daughter. This is something that hurts me a lot. This went to the Court but once again I went back and said it was all a misunderstanding. He made tremendous threats! When my children grew older he was very mean to them. He kicked our son out of the house at the age of 16 and we maintained a relationship in secret. My children said: "Mom, you can't go on like this." They accompanied me to an IPSS. However, when we started to tell our situation, they immediately said that they had to inform the authorities. I immediately gave up. I am absolutely sure that if I pursued a divorce he would kill me, I am certain of that. We see situations like that on the TV all the time.

Com a morte de um dos meus filhos, o sol apagou-se para sempre. Isolei-me um ano inteiro. Um dia decidi visitar um centro de formação profissional e fiz lá uns cursos. Contei a uma das formadoras o que se passava e ela disse: "Não se preocupe, porque ninguém vai fazer nada que não queira, sem o seu consentimento." Mandaram-me para uma ONG e, passado pouco tempo, recebi um telefonema a marcar um atendimento. Garantiram-me que na ONG era 100% sigiloso e isso foi extremamente importante para mim. Deu-me impressão de estar num confessionário. Eu era uma concha, uma amêijoa tão fechada!

Na ONG, ganhei uma força tremenda em termos de defesa com o meu marido. Toda a gente me pode telefonar, porque eu não lhe admito que me proíba. Tenho tomado posições perante ele, de força, de poder. Pelo menos fazer-lhe sempre sentir que sou gente e não um objeto. E isso não tem preço, para mim. Foi na ONG que eu aprendi. Antes, achava que estava sozinha; eu pensava que situações como a minha só aconteciam nos filmes. A ONG deu-me tudo que eu não conhecia, há de haver alguma coisa para cada uma no seu próprio caso encontrar o seu próprio caminho. Procurem, perguntem que podem encontrar.

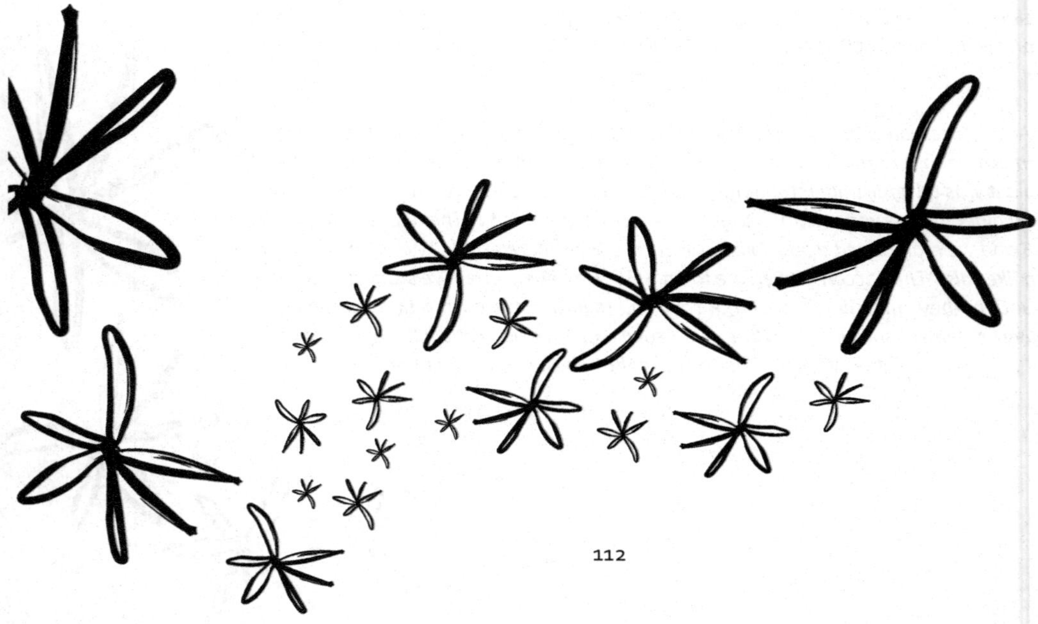

When my child died it was as if the sun never rose again. I isolated myself for an entire year. One day I decided to go out and stumbled upon a community centre. I started to enrol in some professional development courses there. One time I disclosed what was happening to an instructor and she said: "Don't worry because nobody will do anything that you don't want, or without your consent." They then referred me to an NGO and they called me back shortly to schedule an appointment. They guaranteed that the NGO was 100% confidential and that was extremely important to me. It was as if I was in a confession booth. I was like a clam before. I was so closed off!

With the help of the NGO I became much stronger and I am able to defend myself against my husband. I now am able to talk with friends on the phone again and I don't let him forbid me. I have been able to stand my ground with him. At the very least I make him realize that I am a person, not an object. That to me has been invaluable! I learned all this at the NGO. Before I thought I was alone; I thought that situations like mine only happened in the movies. At the NGO, they taught me a lot I did not know. There is always something to help each woman find her own way. Look and ask around, because you may find the help that you need.

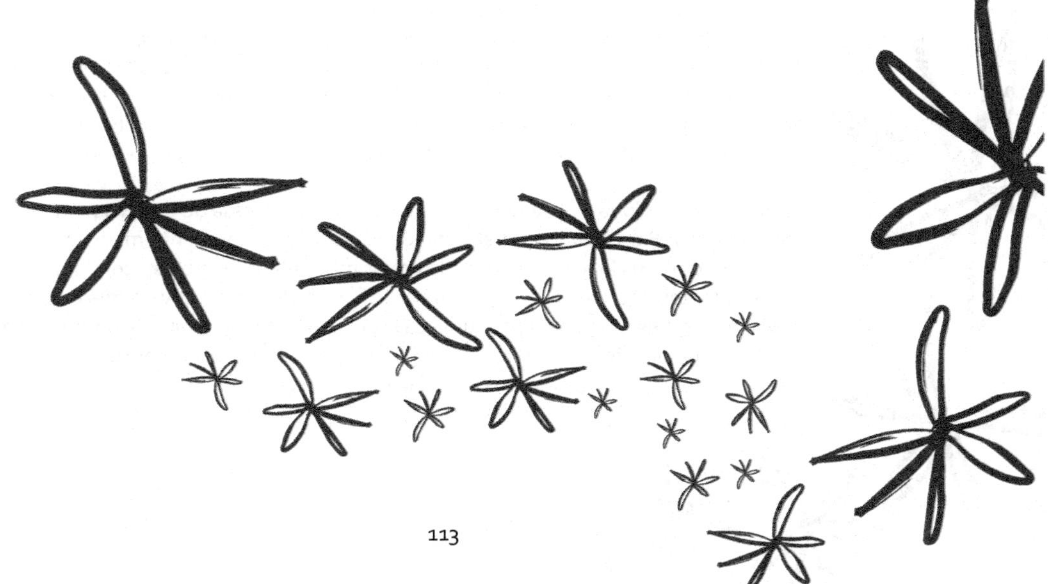

"Tive muito medo quando fui levar os meus filhos ao pai"

História de Maria

Nasci na América do Sul e casei lá com um português que tinha emigrado para o meu país. Já estou em Portugal há vários anos. Quando cheguei a Portugal, começámos o nosso negócio. Ele pôs o negócio no meu nome. Pronto, trabalhávamos, da manhã até noite, de madrugada, todo o dia. Sem eu saber, ele foi criando dívidas. Era meu marido, eu confiava nele e assinava tudo o que ele me dava. Eu era a dona, mas não sabia das contas. Ele só me dava 20 euros por dia. Confrontei-o e ele disse-me que eu é que tinha de resolver. Comecei a planear pagar as dívidas. Pedi um empréstimo e comecei a pagar as dívidas. Depois disse-lhe que não queria mais nada em meu nome. O nome dele ficou limpo. Eu fiquei muito revoltada! Disse-lhe que devíamos cada um seguir a sua vida. Depois disto, ele ficou muito agressivo e ciumento. Começámos a ter problemas.

Continuávamos a viver na mesma casa, mas vidas separadas. Arranjei um novo emprego. A minha patroa disse-me que eu estava a ser vítima de violência doméstica porque viu que ele era muito controlador. Então, deu-me o número de apoio às vítimas. Em vez de ligar, fui lá diretamente à IPSS. Contei à psicóloga.

Um dia, bateu-me com uma força que você não imagina! À frente do meu filho de três anos. Na minha família, nunca vi ninguém bater. E a dizer: "de agora para a frente, vai ser assim, vou começar a bater-te. Vais caminhar, vais trabalhar e não tens carro, vais estar comigo sempre, e nem telemóvel, nem nada, é assim". Eu fiquei com muito medo. Antes disto, eu tinha encontrado um revólver que ele tinha escondido em casa. Eu escondi noutro lugar e naquele dia ele estava sempre a perguntar-me pelo revólver. A minha sorte é que ele não o encontrou. Fechei-me no quarto com os meus filhos e fiquei doente vários dias, com vómitos.

Voltei à psicóloga e ela aconselhou-me a ir para uma casa de urgência: "você tem que sair. Para proteger os seus filhos." E eu, a viver com tanto medo, aceitei. Trouxe os meus filhos. O meu medo era os meus filhos, não os ter comigo. Na casa disseram: "onde você vai, vão os seus filhos". Primeiro estive numa casa de urgência, 15 dias. Depois fui para uma casa de abrigo. Gosto muito da nova cidade. No princípio foi difícil, mas agora é como uma grande família. Temos de aprender a viver umas com as outras.

"I was very afraid when I took my children to their father"

Maria's Story

I am from South America and married a Portuguese man who was an immigrant in my country. I have been in Portugal for several years. When we got to Portugal we started our own business. He put the business in my name. We worked from the morning until night, every day. Without my knowledge my husband contracted a lot of debt in my name over the years. I trusted him and signed everything he gave me. I was the owner but I did not manage the money at all. He only gave me 20 euros per day. I confronted him with this debt and he told me that I should solve it. So I initiated some instalment plans to pay my debt. After this I told him I did not want anything else in my name. His name was clean. I was very outraged by this. I told him that we should both go our separate ways. He started to get aggressive and jealous. Our problems started then.

We continued to live in the same house but were living separate lives. I found a new job. My boss started telling me that I was a victim of domestic violence because of his controlling behaviour. She suggested I called a help line. Instead of calling I went directly to an IPSS. I told the psychologist what was going on.

One day he got very jealous. He hit me with unimaginable strength. He hit me in front of my 3 year-old son. I had never seen anybody in my family hit anybody. He said: "from now on this is how it will be, I will start to hit you. You will walk, you won't have the car, you will be always by my side, no cell phone, nothing. This is the way it will be." I became very scared. Before this happened I had found a gun that he hid in the house. I hid it somewhere else and that day he was always asking me about the gun. My luck was that he didn't find it. I locked myself in the room with the children and was very sick and vomiting for several days.

I went back to the psychologist and she advised me to go to a shelter. I was so afraid that I accepted. The next day I left to the shelter with my children. I made a formal complaint that day. My biggest fear was not having my children with me. They told me at the IPSS: "Wherever you go, your children will go with you." I went first to an emergency shelter for 15 days and then I went to a more permanent shelter. I really like my new city. At first it was hard but now it is like a big family. We had to learn how to live with each other.

Fiz a denúncia de violência doméstica. Agora tenho três advogados diferentes: um para a violência, outro para os meninos, outro para as dívidas. Fui só uma vez a tribunal pela violência doméstica. Também fui ao Tribunal de Família porque ele disse que queria ver os filhos. Ficaram decididas as visitas do pai. Ao mais pequenito, porque o mais velho disse que não quer ir passar a noite com ele. Ele ainda tem medo do pai. O pai faz-lhe muitas perguntas sobre onde vivemos e se eu tenho namorado. Mal dormi na noite antes de os levar ao pai. Tive muito medo quando fui levar os meus filhos ao pai; isto foi o mais difícil. E a pensão que ele paga é muito pequenina. Só ao fim de muitos meses comecei a receber o subsídio da Segurança Social para os meus filhos. Eles estão bem, agora, não têm problemas, também estão bem na escola. Eu acho um bocado injusto. Trabalhei tanto e fiquei com as dívidas todas às minhas costas. Ele continua na casa. E eu trabalho tanto e não consigo poupar nem para os meus filhos nem para uma casa.

Ao fim disto tudo, o mais importante para mim foi ouvir "nós estamos aqui, você conta connosco". É muito importante ouvir isso de alguém, que eu estava sozinha neste país, não tinha ninguém, não tinha feito amizade com ninguém.

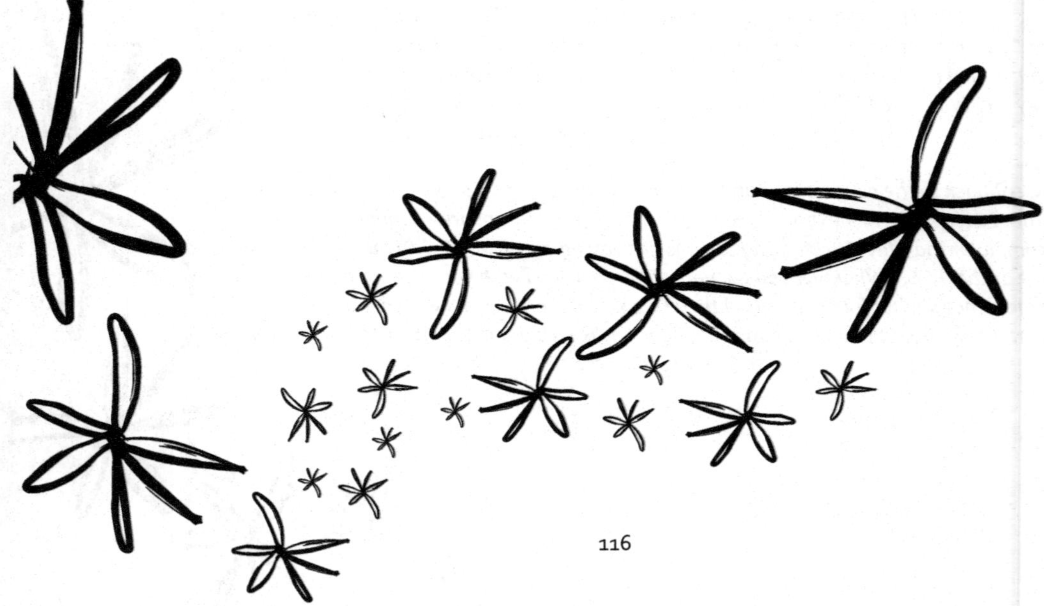

I made a complaint for the domestic violence. Right now, I have three different lawyers: one for the domestic violence complaint, one for the children and one for the debt. I only went to court for the domestic violence once. I also went to family court because he said he wanted to see his children. The family court determined the visitations with the father. The youngest goes with his father overnight. The oldest said he didn't want to go overnight. He is still afraid of his father. His father asked him a lot of questions about where we lived and if I had a boyfriend. I barely slept the night before I took them to their father. I was very afraid when I took my children to their father; this has been the hardest part. He pays very little for each child. I just started to receive some money from social security for the children. My children are doing very well they don't have any problems. They are doing well at school. I feel that it is unfair. I worked so hard and now have all the debt on my shoulders. He kept the house. I continue to work hard but am unable to save any money for my children or for a house.

At the end of all this, the most important thing I heard was "we are here for you, you can count on us". It is very important to hear this from someone because I was alone in this country; I had nobody, I had no friendships.

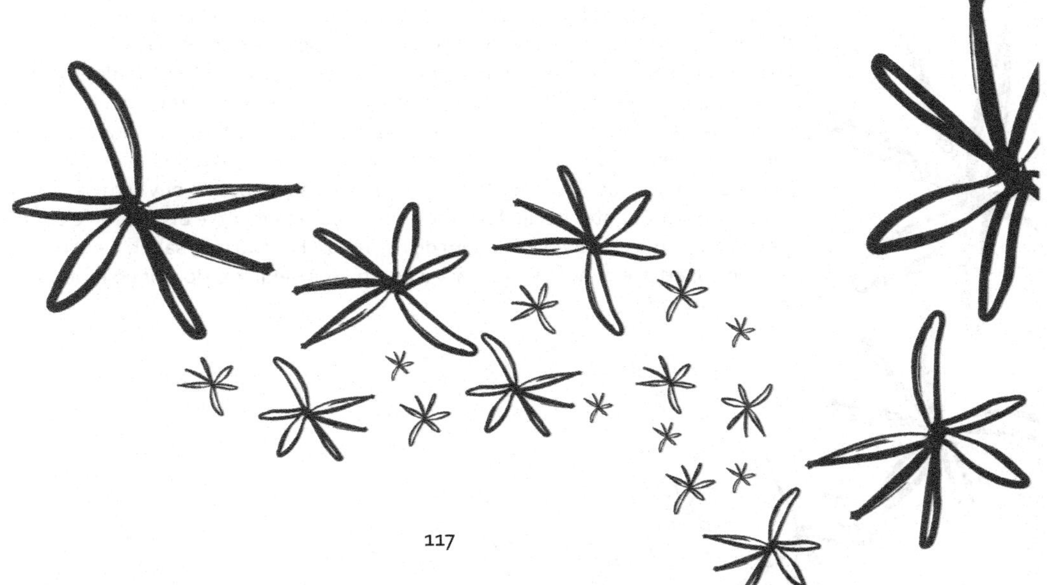

"Todas aquelas horas no hospital e as crianças sem comer"

História de Natasha

A história é simples. Fui a única filha dos meus pais, nascida na União Soviética. Naquela altura, eu tinha tudo. Fiz o 12º ano e universidade. Naquela altura, estava a trabalhar. Quando vim para Portugal, não consegui arranjar emprego na minha área porque o Ministério de Educação não permitiu, por causa da Língua. Acho que é justo. Nós não falamos muito bem português.

Encontrei o meu ex-companheiro aqui, em Portugal. Já o conhecia há algum tempo. Então, ele fez a proposta para vivermos juntos, por causa do futuro, para vivermos felizes. Tudo uma bela história. Decidimos comprar um apartamento e começámos a trabalhar duro e muito. Sem folgas, sem feriados. Tivemos 2 filhos. Apesar do dinheiro, vivemos sempre num barraco. O meu filho mais velho começou a ter problemas respiratórios. Eu disse: "Vamos arranjar alguma maneira, qualquer coisa para melhorar a nossa vida", mas ele recusou. Fiquei zangada, saí de casa, fui viver com uma amiga, e levei o meu filho. Ele apareceu logo, regressamos àquela 'casa'. Os meus pais também diziam: "Natasha, o teu filho precisa de pai." Não reparei logo no início da nossa relação, mas aquela pessoa, por exemplo, não dá flores, não dá beijinhos, não dá abraços. Não festejamos aniversários, nem as festas, nada. O dinheiro era tudo. Quando estava grávida do meu primeiro filho, ele empurrou-me uma vez e eu, de costas, bati no cantinho da parede. Saí para a rua, toda a noite, a chorar. Pensei: "Volto para o meu país. Mas como? Não tenho dinheiro e tenho esta barriga." Voltei para casa. Ele começou a chamar-me nomes, a tratar-me sem respeito nenhum, como se eu fosse criada dele. Quando eu já tinha a legalização, começou a ficar mais agressivo: "Tu, aqui, não és ninguém. É tudo meu. Tu não tens nada. Queres ir embora? Vai. Os filhos ficam comigo." O meu filho mais velho, muitos meses antes de eu sair de casa, disse: "Ó mãe, diz ao pai para ele não nos bater, quando tu não estás em casa." Quando ouvi isto decidi ir ao advogado. Mas antes decidi falar com o meu companheiro e disse-lhe: "eles são pequeninos, mas também precisam de respeito." Ele não quis saber. E eu, um dia, de cobertor e almofada, fui para o quarto dos meninos, dormir no tapete.

"All those hours at the hospital the children had nothing to eat"

Natasha's Story

My story is simple. I was an only child born in the Soviet Union. At that time I had everything. I completed high school and went to college. When I came to Portugal I wasn't able to find a job in my area because the department of education didn't allow me to work because of the language. I think it is fair. We don't speak Portuguese very well.

I met my ex husband here in Portugal. I had known him for a while and he suggested that we live together to have a better future and also to live happily. It seemed like a beautiful story. We decided to buy an apartment and so we started to work a lot and very hard. We did not take time off or holidays. We had two children together. Despite all the money we earned, we lived in a shed. My oldest son started to have respiratory problems. I told my husband: "let's find some way to have a better life" but he refused. I was so angry that I left to a friend's house with my son. He came after us and we moved back "home". My parents also said: "Natasha, the boy needs his father." I didn't notice this in the beginning but he was the kind of person who doesn't give flowers, doesn't give kisses, and doesn't give hugs. We didn't celebrate birthdays or have parties, nothing. Money was everything. When I was pregnant with my first son he pushed me one time and I hit the wall. I left the house all night and cried. I thought: "I am going back to my country. But how? I have no money and a big belly." I returned home. He then started calling me names, treating me with no respect, as if I was his servant. When I became a legal immigrant he became much more aggressive. He would say: "In this house you are nobody. Everything is mine. You don't have anything. You want to leave, go ahead. The kids stay with me." A few months before I left, my oldest son also told me: "mom, ask dad not to hit us when you are not home." When I heard this I decided to seek a lawyer. However I thought I should talk with my husband first and I told him: "the kids are little but they need respect." He didn't care. One day I picked up my blanket and pillow and went to sleep in the kids' bedroom floor.

One day he opened a window and pushed me out of it and held my head down. He then started to hit me and slam my head against the wall. I though: "I am going to fall. This is the end for me." My son came to hold my legs and my husband kicked

Um dia, ele abre a janela, puxa-me para o lado de fora, com a cabeça para baixo. Ele começou a bater-me e a bater a minha cabeça contra a parede. Eu pensei: "Eu vou cair. Este é o meu fim." O meu filho veio segurar-me nas pernas e ele deu-lhe um pontapé! Consegui passar as minhas pernas para dentro e comecei a gritar: "Deixa-me em paz. Tenho 2 filhos." Ele olhou para mim com uns olhos, parecia um lobo, e disse: "Tu percebeste?!"

Depois disto, telefonei ao meu patrão a dizer que não podia ir trabalhar. Logo, liguei para a nossa associação de imigrantes, e avisei também. Fui logo para a PSP, apresentar queixa. Quem me recebeu foi muito simpático, só disse: "Agora, vai para o hospital, depois volta." Fui para o hospital, sozinha, porque os meninos estavam na escola. Consegui, depois, ir buscar o mais velho e pedi a uma amiga que fosse buscar o mais novo e o trouxesse ao hospital. Entrei às 2 e meia, e saí só às 11 da noite. Todas aquelas horas no hospital e as crianças sem comer e eu com tanta dor de cabeça! Os meninos ficaram lá comigo até às 11 da noite. Sem comida, sem nada. Depois, voltámos à esquadra da PSP, à noite, preenchemos todas as papeladas, todos os documentos, tudo, tudo. Mais uma hora e meia com estas coisas. As crianças estavam, nas cadeiras, a dormir, enquanto preenchemos tudo. A minha dor de cabeça continuava. Estava sentada e só me apetecia chorar, chorar. Depois, o polícia disse: "Agora, vocês vão para uma casa de abrigo". Ele disse que ia mandar aquela queixa-crime para o tribunal, para sair ele de casa. Mas ele ainda lá está.

Os meus filhos ficaram na esquadra, enquanto eu fui a minha casa, com apoio da PSP, buscar as minhas coisas. Algumas, porque ele não deixou levar tudo. Mesmo com a polícia. Depois fomos para a casa de emergência e ficámos lá 3 dias. A Diretora da Casa era simpática. Ela ligou para as escolas, a avisar que os miúdos não iam estar presentes e assim. E da sua parte, ela fez tudo o que é possível. Enquanto estávamos na casa de abrigo, a mãe de um amigo do meu filho mais velho mandou-me uma mensagem a dizer: "Se precisar de ajuda, qualquer coisa, disponha." Nessa casa abrigo ficamos doentes porque estava muito frio. Eu paguei os medicamentos. Depois mudámo-nos para uma casa de abrigo noutra cidade onde ainda vivemos.

Em relação à queixa de violência doméstica, eu odeio falar, ir para a reunião a falar com a minha advogada, porque ela, como nós dizemos, não é peixe, nem é carne. Não se o que ela faz. O tribunal decidiu que ele devia sair de casa, mas ele não saiu. Não podemos voltar para lá, porque ele pode ficar com os meus filhos, porque não tenho nenhum papel de tribunal, para o afastar a ele dos meus filhos e de mim própria. Só a questão das responsabilidades parentais está resolvida. Ele não tem interesse nos filhos, porque ele já mandou uma primeira mensagem: "filhos e carro para ti, apartamento para mim." Ele fez a troca. Já arranjei outra advogada de uma outra associação. Espero resultados.

*him too! I managed to get my legs in and then started to scream. I told him: "leave me
alone! I have two kids, don't you understand?" He looked at me in such a way, he looked like
a wolf, and said: "Did you understand?!"*

*After this I told my boss I would not go to work that day and I also called the immigrant
association to let them know. I went to the police to make a complaint. The officer was very
nice and only said: "Now you will go to the hospital and then you come back." I went to the
hospital alone because the children were at school. I then picked up my older son and asked
a friend to pick up the little one and bring him to the hospital. I was at the hospital from
2:30pm to 11pm. During all those hours at the hospital the children had nothing to eat and
my head hurt so much! My kids were there with me until 11pm. We didn't have food, we
didn't have anything. We then went back to the police office and filled out all the paperwork
and documents for another hour and a half. The children fell asleep at the police station.
My head continued to hurt very badly. I wanted to cry and cry and cry. After the paperwork
was done the police officer said: "now you are going to a shelter." He said he would send the
complaint to court so that my husband had to leave our home but he is still there.*

*The police took me home to get some of my things while the children stayed at the
police office. Even with the police there he only let me take a few things. We went to the
emergency shelter and stayed there 3 days. The director of the shelter was nice. She called
the children's schools to let them know the children would be absent and all that. She did
everything to help us. The mother of one of my child's friends also sent me a text that said:
"If you need help, anything, let me know". While we were at the emergency shelter we got
sick because it was very cold. I paid for our medicine. We then moved to a long-term shelter
in another city where we still live.*

*In regards to the court complaint, I really hate talking with my lawyer because she, as we
say, she is neither meat nor fish, I mean, I don't know who she is or what she does. The court
decided that he should leave the house, but he didn't. We can't go back to the apartment
because I have no paper from the court and no way to protect the children and me. The
children's custody is the only thing that has been solved. He has no interest in the children
because he already sent me the text: "children and car to you, apartment to me." He has
made his choice. I already found another lawyer to represent me. I expect results.*

"Com a ONG, comecei a sentir-me muito mais segura de mim"

História de Olívia

Fui casada durante mais de 30 anos. Temos dois filhos, já adultos. O casamento foi uma tortura. Dantes eu julgava que aquilo era normal. Mas depois mudei e comecei a ver que não era normal, digamos que, há 10 anos atrás, comecei a abrir os olhos. Era a bebida, o mau feitio. Não, aquilo não era normal.

Sofria de violência doméstica, não física. Mas hoje, analisando, acho que até é bem pior, porque se tivesse havido uma violência física, eu há muito tempo que já poderia ter tomado outras atitudes. Era uma coisa mais visível. Era agressivo neste aspeto: manipulava-me de tal forma, que eu não podia fazer nada. Quando chegava a hora de ele vir para casa, ficava tão nervosa que dizia aos meus filhos: "atenção, o pai vem aí, não podemos mexer em não sei quê." Mas aquilo ia piorando. O beber também ia piorando. E eu dizia : "Um dia eu acabo com isto".

Primeiro, fui a uma IPSS. Mandaram-me ir para o acompanhamento das famílias de alcoólicos. E eu fui. E eu vi que me iam ensinar era a viver com um alcoólico. E não era isso que eu queria. Eu não queria aprender a viver com um alcoólico. Eu não queria era viver com um alcoólico. E então não insisti. Um ano depois, comecei a ir a uma ONG. Foi uma pessoa amiga que já tinha andado lá e que me indicou. Liguei para lá, e foi a psicóloga que me atendeu. Eu era assim: "Eu não tenho violência... violência..." A psicóloga disse: "Mas venha na mesma. Venha na mesma e vamos conversar." E depois foi-me dando assim umas dicas: "Sabe que violência doméstica não é só física." Portanto, foi-me abordando, foi-me abordando, até que me abriu. Nunca me disseram: "Afaste-se dele". Mas fui percebendo que eu tinha que me afastar, que é diferente. Foi uma decisão minha. A coisa mais importante que me disseram na ONG foi que eu teria que, primeiro, gostar de mim. E deram-me "o meu trabalho de casa" que era cuidar de mim. Foi a maneira de me fazer perceber que tinha que olhar por mim e que devia perder tempo a fazer isto, comigo, e que tinha direito a isso.

Numa altura em que ele, alcoolizado, destruiu uma série de coisas em casa, chamei a polícia. Chamei, mas não na presença dele, e quando a polícia e a doutora do INEM chegaram, ele ficou muito atrapalhado, a dizer que, realmente, não devia ter feito, mas aquilo foi um escape dele ou qualquer coisa. Mas viram bem que ele que estava alcoolizado.

"At the NGO, I started to have a lot more confidence in myself"

Olivia's story

I was married for more than 30 years. We have two children, already adults. The marriage was torture. Over the course of those years I had changed so much that I thought the relationship was normal but when I started to realize that it wasn't that normal, maybe 10 years ago, I started to open my eyes. I saw in his drinking, in his bad temper, that the relationship wasn't normal.

I suffered from non-physical domestic violence. Looking back, I think it was even worse than physical. If there was physical violence, I would have done something a long time ago, because it was visible, I could have taken a stance. But he manipulated me in such a way that when it was time for him to come home I would start to get nervous and say to my children: "watch out! Dad is here! We can't do this, we can't do that." With time, things kept getting worse and worse, his drinking also got worse. I used to say: "One day I will stop this".

I first went to an IPSS. They sent me to a support group for families of alcoholics and I went there. When I got there, my feeling was that they would teach me how to live with an alcoholic. I did not want that! I did not want to live with an alcoholic so I gave up. I never went there again. One year later, I started to go to a NGO. A friend who had gone there recommended it me. I called and talked with the psychologist. I remember telling her: "I don't have violence exactly..." She said: "Come anyway and let's talk" As time went by she gave me some tips: "you know, domestic violence isn't just physical." So she talked with me and I started to open up. They never told me: "you have to get away from him". With time I realized that I had to move away, which is different. It was my choice. The most important thing they told me at NGO was that I had to love myself. First of all, love myself. They told me my homework was to take care of myself. It was a way to make me understand that I had to look after myself and I could waste time on myself. I had the right to do it.

At some point I called the police after he ruined a lot of things in the house while intoxicated. I didn't call in front of him. When the police and paramedics arrived he was embarrassed and started saying that he really should not have done that, but "it was a form of escape" or something like that. They could clearly see he was intoxicated.

Nessa altura, pedi ao Ministério Público para ele fazer um tratamento compulsivo, e então a delegada de saúde conversou com ele, se ele concordava em fazer um tratamento. Aí sim, começou a fazer o primeiro tratamento. No hospital, foi muito bem tratado, andava muito bem. Andava mesmo muito bem.

Andei um ano na ONG, e comecei a sentir-me muito mais forte. Muito mais segura de mim. E cheguei a confrontá-lo muitas vezes, diretamente: "Vamos partir para o divórcio". Ele não aceitava o divórcio. Batia com as portas, não havia diálogo. Ele sentia-me a fugir-lhe das mãos. Ele começou a sentir-me areia nas mãos dele. Nesse ano, ele foi para um segundo tratamento. Depois de vir, chegou a fazer muitas asneiras. Chamei a polícia muitas vezes. E ele dizia aos polícias: "Olhe, ela toma isto, toma isto, toma aquilo", eram os medicamentos dele. Ele chegou a mostrar os medicamentos dele aos polícias, a dizer que eu estava com uma depressão enorme. E eu estava num descontrole, porque eles olhavam para mim e estava ele mais calmo do que eu. Os polícias diziam: "Por muito que acreditemos, minha senhora, não podemos fazer nada. Não estamos a apanhá-lo em flagrante, ele está muito mais convincente e está muito mais coerente a falar do que a senhora". Num período de 3 meses, foram tantos os episódios de violência que eu cheguei a ir mostrar as marcas à Medicina Legal. Fui lá todas as vezes que ele me tinha deixado marcas, está lá tudo registado. Nesse período, foram 67 vezes que eu chamei a polícia. Eu implorava aos polícias: "levem-no daqui", "não podemos porque não há flagrante, não há nada". Até que, depois de eu chamar tanta vez, cheguei a pôr-me à frente dele, a dizer: "Dá cabo de mim. Faz! Não sejas cobarde para depois ninguém ver, faz". Porque ninguém acreditava em mim!

Finalmente, ele foi chamado ao Ministério Público e o Ministério Público decretou-lhe o afastamento de residência. Eles disseram: "Se ele estiver a incomodá-la, chame a polícia. Porque ele ainda não está com a pulseira, não podemos controlar o afastamento dele." E ele não cumpria. Não vivia mais já em casa, mas não saía da minha porta. E eu fui outra vez ao Ministério Público saber: "então, foi decretada a medida de afastamento e e e continua ali? O que é que se passa?" E, então, puseram-lhe a pulseira electrónica.

Hoje, sinto-me uma mulher feliz. Apesar de tudo, sinto-me realizada, feliz. Só tenho pena dos anos perdidos. Não voltam. Nem vão estorvar. Quanto mais tenho a minha liberdade, mais quero viver para ela. O que recomendaria a outras mulheres é pensarem, acima de tudo, primeiro nelas. Que é o meu lema: agora, sou eu. Não sou egoísta. Há sempre alguém no fundo, mas primeiro eu. E que ninguém seja submisso a ninguém. Que ninguém merece ser maltratada fisicamente, nem psicologicamente.

At that time I asked the prosecutor to send him to compulsory alcohol inpatient treatment. The doctor talked with him before him being admitted, to see if he agreed to do the treatment. That's when he started his first treatment. He was very well treated there. He was doing very well. I was going to the NGO for about a year and I felt much stronger. I started to have a lot more confidence in myself. I confronted him many times directly: "Let's get divorced." He didn't accept a divorce. Every time I brought up divorce he would start slamming doors, there was no dialogue. He started to feel as though I was sand escaping his hands. In that year, he went for a second alcohol inpatient treatment. After he returned, he started to cause a lot of trouble. I called the police many times. He would tell the police: "Look: she takes this medication and that medication". He would show his medication to the police and tell them that I was extremely depressed, that I was out of control and they looked at us and he looked a lot calmer than I did. The police said: "As much as I want to believe you, we can't do anything. We are not catching him in flagrante. He is a lot more convincing and coherent than you." In a period of three months there were so many episodes of physical violence and I went to forensic medicine several times to document my bruises. During this period I called the police 67 times. I implored the police officers: "please take him away!" They said: "we can't do it because it isn't flagrante, there isn't anything." It got to a point when, after calling the police so many times, I got in front of him and said: "Finish me! Do it! Don't be a coward so that nobody sees what you do. Do it!" I said this because nobody believed me!

Finally he was called to go to court and the prosecutor decided that he should move away from the residence. They told me at the courthouse: "If he bothers you again, call the police." At the time he still didn't have the bracelet so they could not control his behaviour. And he didn't comply with the restraining order. He didn't live at the house anymore but he didn't leave my door. So I went to the prosecutor again: "the order was decided but he continues there! What is going on?" That day they finally put his bracelet on.

Today I feel happy. Regardless of everything, I feel accomplished, happy. I only regret the lost years. The more I have my freedom, the more I want to live for it. What I would recommend other women to do is to, first of all, think about themselves. That is my motto now: it's me. I am not selfish. There are always people on the background but first it's me. Nobody should be submissive; nobody deserves being physically and psychologically maltreated.

"Acho injusto que eu é que tive de sair de casa e começar do zero"

História de Rosa

Nasci num país da América do Sul. Vim para Portugal há 8 anos e, agora, tenho cidadania portuguesa. Conheci o meu ex-marido português, no meu país. Ele voltou a Portugal por razões familiares e namoramos 3 anos pelo telefone. Ele regressou ao meu país para casarmos e depois voltámos os dois para Portugal.

Atacou-me três vezes, durante a nossa relação de 7 anos. A primeira vez, bateu-me muito e deixou marcas no meu corpo. Ele dizia que me ia mandar de volta para o meu país se eu o deixasse. Ele tratava-me como se eu fosse mercadoria dele. Na cabeça dele, ele trouxe-me aqui e podia mandar-me de volta quando quisesse. Mas eu não queria voltar. Eu não tomei a decisão de deixar tudo e todos para que alguém determinasse quando eu deveria voltar. Eu queria voltar quando eu achasse que era tempo de ir, não por causa dele. Eu tinha os meus objetivos, queria estudar. Naquela altura, resolvi falar com um advogado para saber que opções é que eu tinha se nos divorciássemos, mas não lhe contei sobre a violência doméstica. O advogado disse-me para ficar com o meu marido até ter cidadania portuguesa.

A segunda vez foi pouco depois de a minha filha nascer. Através da TV e da senhora para quem eu trabalhava, fiquei a saber para onde devia ligar. Desta vez, liguei para o 144 e eles mandaram-me ir a uma IPSS onde tive uma psicóloga durante 6 meses. Quando cheguei, eles informaram-me das minhas opções e disseram que eu podia ir para uma casa de abrigo, se quisesse. No entanto, nessa altura, eu não estava preparada para sair de casa com uma bebé tão pequenina. Decidi ficar com ele e ver. A psicóloga ajudou-me a lidar com a situação em casa.

A terceira e última vez que ele me atacou foi numa manhã de Janeiro. Acordámos, estava tudo tranquilo e ele começou a discutir por uma fatura de telefone de 26 cêntimos. Começou a agredir-me e foi buscar uma faca. A menina assistiu a tudo. Eu corri para o quintal da vizinha e pedi-lhe para ela chamar a polícia. Ele pegou no carro, saiu e foi trabalhar. A menina foi para a escola na carrinha. A polícia marcou-me uma consulta de medicina legal no hospital.

"I think it is unfair that I had to get out of the house and start from scratch"

Rosa's story

I was born in South-America. I came to Portugal 8 years ago and now have Portuguese citizenship. I met my Portuguese ex-husband in my country. He returned to Portugal for family reasons and we kept a long distance relationship for three years. He then went to my country so we could get married and then we moved to Portugal.

He attacked me three times during our 7-year relationship. The first time, he hit me a lot and left marks in my body. He said that he would send me back to my country if I left him. He treated me as if I was his commodity. In his mind, he thought he brought me here and he could take me back whenever he wanted. However, I didn't want to go back. I didn't decide to leave everything and everyone so that someone else determined when I should go back. I wanted to go back when I felt it was time to go, not because of him. I had my goals, I wanted to study. At that time I decided to talk with a lawyer about my options in case we got a divorce. When I met with the lawyer, I didn't disclose the domestic violence. The lawyer told me to stay with my husband until I obtained Portuguese citizenship.

The second time he hit me was shortly after our child was born. Through the TV and from a lady I was working for, I learned where I should call. So this time, I called the line 144 and they sent me to an IPSS where I had appointments with a psychologist for 6 months. When I went to my first appointment they told me that I could go to a shelter if I wanted. At this time, however, I was not prepared to get out of my house with a baby so small. I decided to stay with him and hoped for the best. The psychologist helped me to deal with the situation at home.

The third and final time he attacked me was in one morning, in January. Everything was fine until he started an argument about a phone bill of 26 cents. He started to hit me and then went and got a knife. Our daughter saw everything. I ran out and asked a neighbour to call the police. He got in the car and left for work and our daughter went to school in the school bus. I went to the police office and they scheduled an appointment in forensic medicine. The next day I went to the appointment with a friend. The doctor mocked me about me being hit by my ex-husband.

Eu fui à consulta com uma amiga no dia seguinte. O médico gozou connosco à cara podre. Ele disse: "Levou porradinha do marido, foi?!" Estavam lá outras senhoras e ele tratou-nos a todas assim. Eu desta vez não tinha marcas nenhumas porque fugi de casa quando ele estava a correr atrás de mim com uma faca. Para ter provas tentei falar com a vizinha que ouviu o que se passou. Liguei-lhe várias vezes e tentei enviar uma carta mas a morada estava errada e nunca consegui entrar em contacto com ela para ela ser minha testemunha.

Naquela altura, mudei-me temporariamente para casa de uma amiga. Já não aguentava mais os insultos constantes, os ciúmes dele, sempre a controlar-me, e as ameaças de morte. Tinha tanto medo que ele me fizesse alguma coisa que cheguei a fazer um seguro de vida; pelo menos, se ele me matasse, a minha filha não ficaria sem nada. Nas duas semanas a seguir eu não sabia o que fazer. Eu já tinha encontrado um apartamento para me mudar mesmo antes de ele me ter batido. Mas, mesmo que eu mudasse para o apartamento novo, ele iria ficar a saber onde era. Foi aí que eu falei de novo com a psicóloga da IPSS que ofereceu ajuda imediatamente e sugeriu que eu fosse para uma casa de abrigo. No dia seguinte, a psicóloga e dois polícias à paisana foram a casa dele e ajudaram-me a levar as coisas. Na casa de abrigo, encontrei muita ajuda. Ajudaram-me com a creche para a menina, emprego, apoio psicológico, etc. A minha maior preocupação sempre foi que a minha filha estivesse bem.

Em relação à queixa, deram-me uma advogada da segurança social mas eu nunca vi essa advogada, nunca tive muita confiança que me fosse ajudar. O caso ficou arquivado por falta de provas. O tribunal agora disse que a minha filha tem de visitar o pai fim-de-semana sim, fim de semana não. Nós encontramo-nos na estação de comboio para ele levar a menina. Tem sido pacífico, ele tem muito medo, é um lugar público, e agora que a polícia e os tribunais estão envolvidos, ele tem medo. Ele não vem certinho. Diz que fica muito caro e então espera pelas férias para a vir buscar. Não seria por mim que a menina teria impedimento de ir com o pai. O que foi comigo, foi comigo. Com ela é diferente.

Sinto-me grata pela ajuda que tenho recebido. Não sinto que tenha sido tratada de maneira diferente de uma portuguesa. Quem mais me ajudou foi a psicóloga da IPSS, a casa de abrigo e a minha patroa. Apesar de todas as ajudas, acho injusto que eu é que tive de sair de casa e começar do zero e agora tenho bastantes dificuldades económicas.

There were other women there and the doctor treated them all the same. At this time I did not have any marks on my body because I ran away. In order to gather evidence I tried to get in touch with my neighbour and I tried calling her numerous times and I sent her a letter but I was never able to find her and have her as my witness in court.

In those days, I moved temporarily to a friend's house and I had already found an apartment to move to. I was decided to move there even before he hit me. I could not stand his constant insults, jealousy, his controlling behaviour, and his death threats. I was so afraid for my daughter and me that I got life insurance so that if he killed me at least my daughter would have something. In the two weeks following the incident I did not know what to do. Even if I moved to the new apartment he would soon find out where it was. I decided to talk with the psychologist of the IPSS again. She immediately offered help and suggested that I moved to a shelter. In the following day, the psychologist and two undercover policemen helped me move out. I found a lot of help at the shelter. They helped find a day care for my daughter, I found a job, psychological support, etc. My main worry has always been the wellbeing of my daughter.

In regards to the claim, I was given a lawyer by the social security department but I never even saw that lawyer. I never trusted that she could help me. Eventually my case was archived for lack of evidence. The family court has recently decided that my daughter has to visit her dad every other weekend. We meet at the train station so he can take the girl with him. It has been peaceful. I was never against my daughter having contact with her dad. What happened with me is one thing. With her it is different.

I feel grateful for the help that I have received. I don't feel as though I am treated in a different way from Portuguese women. The greater sources of help have been the IPSS psychologist, the shelter and the lady I worked for. Despite these supports, I think it is unfair that I had to get out of the house and start from scratch. I have a lot of economic difficulties.

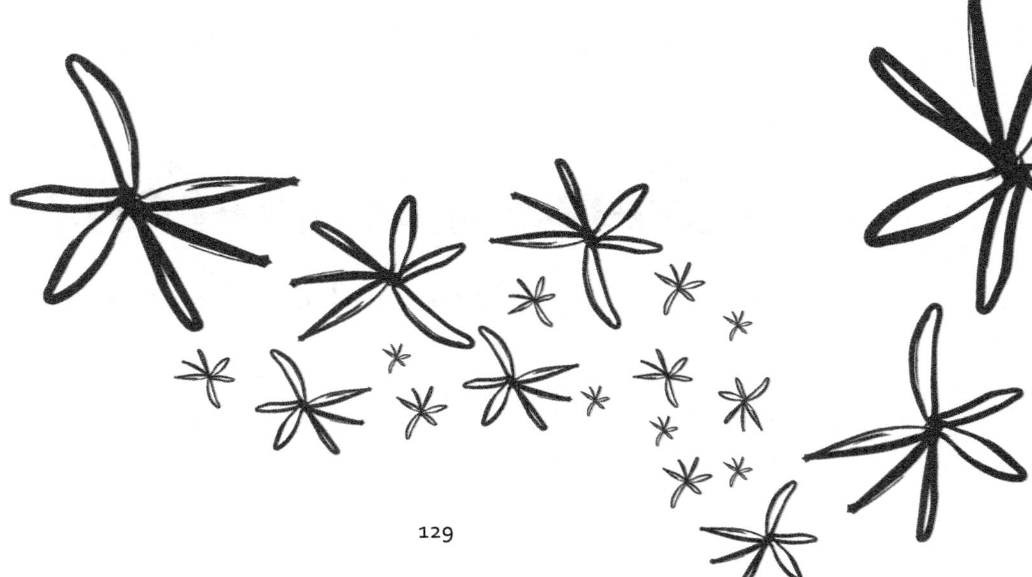

Domestic Violence

Stories and experiences of women

Slovenia

"Polž je hitrejši"
Amelijina zgodba

No, prva stvar je bila, da sem sploh ugotovila, da moram govoriti o tem. Potem pa sem potrebovala kar nekaj časa, da sem šla na policijo, le informativno, potem pa sem končno podala prvo prijavo. Nisem vedela, da potem oni avtomatično kontaktirajo center za socialno delo (CSD), zato sem skoraj padla na rit. Ker ko sem končno končala s policijo, nisem bila niti pripravljena niti zainteresirana, da nadaljujem s CSD-jem.

Mož se je za nekaj mesecev odselil, a ko se je vrnil, se je nasilje nadaljevalo in eskaliralo, zato sem ga tedensko prijavljala policiji. In ker me je CSD obvestil, da je to absolutno nasilje v družini, ker imava majne otroke, in da lahko sicer izgubim otroke, sem začela obiskovati CSD. Potem sem poiskala celo psihoterapevtko in tam sem ugotovila, da imam pravico reči ne, da sem tudi jaz človek, da imam iste pravice. In potem sem se mu enkrat fizično uprla, a me je prijavil policiji in CSD-ju – potem so mi rekli, da bom obravnavana kot oseba z nasilnimi dejanji in da sem zato na poti, da izgubim otroke in da moram poiskati strokovno pomoč. Zato sem se obrnila na Društvo za nenasilno komunikacijo (DNK) in to je bila najsvetlejša točka v mojem življenju. Pri CSD-ju in policiji me je vedno bilo strah, kaj pa če izve, kako bo reagiral. Toda pri DNK nisem imela zadržkov, da povem, karkoli hočem. In tako sem začela redno hoditi tja, hvala bogu za DNK, oni so me rešili, pa izvedela sem tudi, da obstajajo različne oblike nasilja.

Ko je prišla policija (včasih po eni uri), so bili nevljudni, žaljivi, sarkastični, leni, indiferentni, 'pametni'. Izjave, kot so: »Ne vem, gospa, čudno se mi zdi, da se vam ne vidijo modrice.« Ali: »Ja, veste, glejte, to ni priča, ker je vaša mama.« Potem: »Gospa, on se želi le pogovoriti z vami, rad bi razrešil stvari.« Policija je bila očitno na njegovi strani in ti komentarji so me potrli. Čutila sem, da bi raje bila ponovno pretepena, kot da bi šla na policijo. Le enkrat je dobil prepoved približevanja in še to le za 48 ur.

Potrebovala sem deset let, da sem se prepoznala kot žrtev nasilja v družini, a sem nato ugotovila, da sem tudi žrtev policijskega nasilja. Z grozo sem ugotovila, da ker so bili v situacijo vpleteni majhni otroci, bi bila dolžnost policije, da pokliče nujno službo CSD-ja, a v vseh tistih letih, tega niso naredili niti enkrat. Kasneje sem izvedela, da tudi CSD ni opravil svojega dela, kot bi moral. Imeli so toliko razlogov za intervencijo, saj so vedeli, kaj se dogaja, a niso ukrepali. Vedeli so, da nima rednih stikov z otroki, da je izklopil plin v naši hiši, da je ukradel moj pralni stroj, da ni redno plačeval preživnine. CSD niti enkrat ni sklical multidisciplinarnega tima (MDT).

"The snail is faster"
Amelia's Story

Well, the first thing was that I just found out that I needed to talk about it. And then it took me some time to go to the police for information purposes only, and after that I finally made the first complaint to the police station. I did not know that they automatically contact the Centre for social work (CSW), so I was almost thrown on my ass. Because when I was finally done with the police, I was not ready and neither interested to go further with the CSW.

My husband moved away for several months, but when he came back the violence resumed and escalated, so I had complaints to the police station on a weekly basis. And since CSW informed me that this is about family violence, because we have small children, and that I can lose my children otherwise, I started to visit CSW. Then I even found a psychotherapist and there I realized that I had the right to say no, that I am also a human, that I have the same rights. And then once I physically resisted, but he reported me to the police and to the CSW - they then told me that I will be treated as a person with violent acts and that I am therefore on track to lose my children and that I have to seek professional help. So I turned to the Association for non-violent communication (DNK) and this has been the brightest point in my life. At CSW and the police I always had this fear, what if he finds out, how will he react. But with DNK I felt free to say whatever I wanted. And so I started to go there regularly, thank God for DNK, they saved me, I also learned that there are different forms of violence.

When the police came (sometimes after one hour), they were rude, offensive, sarcastic, lazy, indifferent, smart. Statements like: "I do not know, ma'am it seems weird to me that your bruises are not visible!" Or, "yeah, you know, see, this is no witness, because she is your mother." Then: "Madam, he only wants to talk with you, he would like to solve things." The police were clearly on his side and these comments collapsed me. I was in the position to rather be beaten again than to go to the police. He only once got a restraining order and only for 48 hours.

It took me 10 years to recognize myself as a victim of partner violence, but I realized that I'm also a victim of police violence. In horror, I realized that, because small children were involved in the violent situation, it would be the duty of the police to call the urgent service of the CSW, but in all those years they did not do this even once. Later I found out that also the CSW has not carried out their work as they should. They had so many reasons to intervene, as they knew what was happening, but did nothing.

Sklicali so ga šele na pobudo DNK in v vseh teh letih smo imeli tri MDT-je. Do takrat nisem vedela, da je kaj takega sploh možno. A itak ni bilo nobenega velikega učinka.

Kar se tiče zdravnikov, sem bila v veliki zadregi. Že ko je policija prišla na vrata, te vsi sosedi gledajo in se počutiš kot kriminalec. Potem prideš k zdravniku in imaš nekaj na obrazu, modrico, ljudje te malo čudno gledajo, potem pa te zdravnik vpraša, od kod ta modrica, ti pa se hočeš samo skriti. Samo enkrat sem šla k zdravniku, ko sem bila hudo pretepena. A to je bila napaka, ker me potem niso jemali resno. Moje prijave so padale ena za drugo, vse po vrsti, čeprav sem pogosto imela priče, ker nisem imela zdravniških potrdil.

Po treh letih je bil mož obsojen na eno leto pogojne kazni na dve leti preizkusne dobe. Takrat sem že bila v varni hiši, ker so stvari šle tako daleč. Ko sem končno dobila lastno stanovanje in sem prišla pod pristojnost novega CSD-ja, so po nekem formalnem postopku moj naslov sporočili možu. Po treh letih pravnega boja sem se uspela ločiti Na CSD-ju me obravnavajo kot osebo, ki uporablja fizično nasilje nad otroci, ker je moj bivši mož CSD-ju in policiji rekel, da otroke tuširam z mrzlo vodo. Bili so zelo zelo pristranski. Zdaj na CSD vedno hodim s svetovalko DNK.

Celoten proces je razgaljanje in mesarjenje in zasliševanje in ponavljanje, da ti gre vseskozi na bruhanje. Mislim, polž je hitrejši. In potem če imaš srečo, dobiš obsodbo, s katero ne moreš nič. Institucije me dojemajo in obravnavajo kot noro, če se lahko tako izrazim. Vedno sem poslušala, kakšne pravice ima on, kaj moram upoštevati, kaj mu moram ponuditi, kaj moram dovoliti, nič pa ni bilo rečenega, kako lahko pomagajo meni. Razen civilne pritožbe, za katero seveda nimam denarja, včasih nimam denarja celo za plenice za otroke. Sicer moraš biti naravnan na neko vnaprejšnjo igro, v kateri moraš sprejeti njena pravila. Sodnik mi je rekel, da je danes zelo priljubljen trend, da ženske zlorabijo prijavo nasilja, da bi dobile otroke.

Moj oče je iz nekdanje jugoslovanske republike, mama je Slovenka, jaz sem se rodila in živim tu v Sloveniji. Še vedno pravim, da mi končnica mojega priimka, ki je tipična za nekdanjo jugoslovansko republiko in daje vedeti, da nisem Slovenka, ni pomagala.

Zavedam se, da bi vse lahko bilo precej drugače, če bi vsak dobro opravil svoje delo. Da bi res dobili jasno sliko, kaj je dovoljeno in kaj ne, kaj je prav in kaj ne. Stoprocentno sem prepričana, da v tem primeru ne bi imela teh nočnih mor, ki sem jih doživela. Usposobljenost osebja bi morali povečati.

They knew that he did not carry out regular contacts with children, that he turned off the gas in our house, that he stole my washing machine, that he did not pay alimony regularly. Multidisciplinary team (MDT) was not even once convened on their initiative. DNK was the initiator of MTD and we had three MDT over the years, until then I did not know that such a thing was possible at all. But there was no major effect anyway.

With regard to doctors, it was so embarrassing. Already when police come to the door, all the neighbours watch and you feel like a criminal. Then you have come to the doctor and you have something in your face, a bruise, and people look at you a little bit weird and then the doctor ask you where you got this bruise from, and you just want to hide. Only once I went to a doctor when I was badly beaten. But this was a mistake, because they didn't take me seriously. My complaints fell one after another, all in a row, although I often had witnesses.

After three years my husband was sentenced to 1 year on 2 years' probation. I was then already in a safe house because things had progressed so far. When I finally got my own apartment and I moved to the new CSW, they reported my address by some formal procedure to my husband. After three years of legal struggle, I managed to separate. At CSW they treat me as a person who uses physical violence against children, because my ex-husband told the CSD and the police that I shower the children with cold water. They were very, very, very biased. Now I always go to CSD accompanied by the DNK counsellor.

This whole process, it's deconstruction and butchering and interrogation and repetition that you already repulsed all along. I think, the snail is faster. And then if you're lucky, you get a conviction with which you can do nothing. I am perceived and treated by the institutions as an insane person, if I can say this. I've always heard about what rights he has, what I have to consider, what I have to offer him, what I have to allow, but there was nothing said about how I can be helped. Apart from civil appeal for which I don't have money of course, I don't have money sometimes to buy diapers for the children. Otherwise, you have to be in a certain mode of anticipated game, in which you have to accept how you have to play. The judge said to me that the trend today is anyway very popular that women abuse a violence appeal in order to get the children.

My father is from former Yugoslav republic, my mother Slovene, but I was born and live here, in Slovenia. I still say that the typical ending of my surname marking me as being from the former Yugoslav republic, and thus not a Slovenian was not helping me a lot.

I realize that all could be much different if each one was doing his/her job. In order to really get a clear picture of what is allowed and what is not allowed, what is right and what is not right. I am 100% sure that in that case I wouldn't have these nightmares that I experienced. The qualification of personnel should be increased.

"… in ne povzdigujejo glasu, da ti povejo, kaj bi morala storiti"

Ljiljanina zgodba

Sem iz nekdanje jugoslovanske republike na jugu. Mi imamo malo drugačne navade. Ženske se poročijo tako, da družine sklenejo dogovore. Tako sem se tudi jaz zaročila, se poročila in potem je šlo vse navzdol. Tam sem rodila prvega otroka, ki je umrl. Že takrat sem ga hotela zapustiti. A so starši rekli, da se bo sčasoma spremenil in da se moram navaditi nanj. On je bil tu (v Sloveniji), delal je, jaz pa sem ostala tam dol. Potem sva oba prišla v Slovenijo.

A je začelo z alkoholom in potem je bilo vsak dan slabše. 28 let življenja z njim je bilo kot v zaporu, še posebej 15 let, ko sva živela tu. Zlorabljal me je fizično, psihološko, tudi ekonomsko in prek otrok. Leta 2011 sva se s hčerko končno odločili, da odideva, a nisva imeli kam. Klicali sva varno hišo, a niso imeli mest, bila je polna. Problem je bil, da nisem hotela iti brez hčere, a tam ni bilo mest za obe. Potem pa mi je moja svetovalka na zavodu za zaposlovanje povedala, da obstaja študentska varna hiša. Vedela je, da se dogaja nekaj zelo hudega, ker mi nikoli ni dovolil, da bi šla na zavod sama. Vztrajala je, rekla mu je, da če znam slovensko, njemu ni treba biti tam. A je on vztrajal in mislim, da se ga je bala. In ko sva se odločili oditi, je rekla, da bi morali poiskati varno hišo SRCe. Hči je našla njihovo številko na internetu. Nisem mogla brez nje, da bi jo pustila tam ali na cesti.

Preselili sva se tja, hvala bogu, je bilo dovolj prostora. Hči je ostala tam, medtem ko sem jaz za devet mesecev šla v drugo državo in se nisva videli. Ko sem se vrnila, sva imeli stanovanje. Potem so se začeli problemi, ne problemi, bilo me je preveč strah za hčerko. Hotela je ven, jaz pa sem se bala, da bo začela piti, kot njen oče. A je preživela devet mesecev sama in ni imela nobenih problemov. Potem sem poklicala SOS telefon in so mi povedali, kam naj grem. Dali so mi številko te nevladne organizacije in odkar sem jih poklicala, se mi je življenje stoprocentno spremenilo.

Težko se mi je bilo odpreti nekomu, ki ga nisem poznala. A ti ljudje, posebej moja svetovalka, ki sem ji posebej hvaležna, me je vedno spodbujala, da nadaljujem. Zdaj sem drugačna oseba, ni me strah, prej sem se bala lastne sence. Zdaj se lahko borim zase. Še vedno me je strah bivšega moža, a ne kot na začetku. Zdaj nama ne povzroča težav. Z veseljem prihajam na Društvo za nenasilno komunikacijo (DNK), vem, da se bom nečesa naučila. Vesela sem, da imajo delavnice. Nimam prijateljev, a tu so skoraj kot prijatelji, ker so tako zanesljivi.

"... and not raising their voices to tell you what to do"

Ljiljana's Story

I come from a former Yugoslav republic in the south. We have a little bit different customs. Women get married so that families make a contract between them. In my time I got engaged, I got married and from that day on it all started to go downhill. I bore my first child there, and it died. Then I already wanted to leave him. But my parents said that he was going to change in time that I had to get used to him. He was here (in Slovenia), he worked, and I stayed down there. Then we both came to Slovenia.

But he started with alcohol and since then every day it was worse. 28 years of living with him were like a prison, especially the 15 years when we lived here. He abused me physically, psychologically, also economically, and through the children. In 2011 me and my daughter finally decided to leave, but there was nowhere we could go. We called a safe house, but they did not have places, it was full. The problem was that I did not want to go without my daughter, but both of us could not be there. Then there was one lady at the Office for Employment, my counsellor, and she told me about the student safe house. She knew that something very bad was going on, because he never let me go to the Employment office by myself. She insisted, she said to him, if she can speak Slovenian, you do not have to be here. But he insisted and I think she was afraid of him. And when we decided to go, she said we should find this »Heart« safe house. My daughter found the number on the internet. I could not go without her, to leave her there or on the street.

We moved there, thank God, there was enough space there. My daughter remained there while I went to another country for 9 months and we didn't see each other. After I came back, we had a flat. Then problems started, not problems, I was too much afraid. My daughter wanted to go out, and I was afraid that she would start drinking like her father. But she has spent 9 months alone and had no problems. And then I called the SOS phone and they told me where to go. They gave me the number of this NGO and since I called them my life has changed 100%.

It was difficult to open up myself to someone whom I did not know. But these people, especially my advisor, I'm particularly grateful to her, she always encouraged me to go on. I am a different person now, I'm not afraid, before I was afraid of my own shadow. Now I can fight for myself. Still, there is fear of the former husband but not as much as in the beginning.

Kar tako mi pomagajo, na primer pri iskanju stanovanja. Ne bi ga našla brez njihove pomoči. Ljudje res potrebujejo take institucije. Poslušajo te in ne povzdigujejo glasu, da ti povejo, kaj bi morala storiti. Ker nam je dovolj tega povzdignjenega glasu. Tu, ko prideš, so vsi prijazni, tako da se počutiš čisto kot doma.

Zdaj sem srečna, da sem, kar sem, in da sem odšla. Zdaj sva varni. Moj partner je na začetku povzročal težave, sin je rekel, da je pisal vse možne stvari in kaj nama bo naredil. A sčasoma se je pomiril. Zdaj pravijo, da je nekje v EU. Bomo videli v prihodnosti, kot človek je v redu, če ne pije. A trezen je bil le dva dni v letu. Žal mi je, da ni bil kaznovan, za to mi je žal. Vsaj en dan bi moral čutiti, kako je, če nekomu tolikokrat uničiš življenje.

Po pomoč sem šla le na DNK: na začetku sem se bala, zdaj pa vedno pokličem, če sem v težavah. Nikoli ničesar ne storijo brez mojega soglasja, dvakrat premislijo, preden kaj storijo. Nič niso naredili prehitro, vedno to, kar sem potrebovala, ob pravem času, vse je bilo, kot je moralo biti. Največja pomoč je, da se vsi smejijo, nobenih zagrenjenih obrazov, ko prideš, to me je pritegnilo. Pazite na te institucije, ker so zelo pomembne.

Ponosna sem na svojo domovino, a ne na njene zakoreninjene navade. Nikoli si ne bi želela, da bi se moja hči vrnila tja, da bi živela tako življenje. Oče in mati ti rečeta, kaj moraš narediti. Poročijo te. Dobiti dobrega moža je loterija. Zdaj počasi napredujejo, a moja generacija je veliko pretrpela. Te navade bi morali opustiti. Če se ženske nekega dne čutijo ogrožene, bi morale enostavno oditi. Nič drugega, se mi zdi. Zdaj lahko rečem tudi to. Medsebojno spoštovanje je pomembno, a tradicija je nekaj drugega. Kdo bi želel živeti z nasilno osebo? To je nekaj, kar je treba izkoreniniti, ne glede na to, kaj ljudje pravijo.

He does not make problems for us now. I'm coming to DNK with joy, I know that I will learn something. I'm happy that they have workshops. I don't have friends, but here, they are almost like friends, because they are so reliable. Just like that, they are helping me, for example with finding a place to live. I couldn't find this without their help. People really need such institutions. They listen to you, and not raising their voices to tell you what you are supposed to do. Because we have enough of this raised voice. Here, when you come, everybody is nice, so that you feel completely at home.

Now I'm happy that I am what I am and that I have left. We are now safe. My partner made problems at the beginning, my son said that he wrote all sorts of things and what he would do to us. But in time it calmed down. Now they say he is somewhere in the EU. We will see in the future, as a human he is ok if he does not drink. But he was only sober on two days in the whole year. I'm sorry that he was not punished, this I'm sorry for. He should have felt for only one day how it is if you wreck somebody's life so many times.

The only place I went for help was DNK: I was afraid at the beginning, but now I always call if I'm in trouble. They never do anything without my consent, they think twice before they do anything. They did nothing too fast, always what I needed in time, everything was just as it had to be. And the biggest help is that everybody is smiling so no bitter faces when you come, that attracted me. Watch over these institutions, because they are really important.

I'm proud of my birth country but I'm not proud of those deep rooted customs. I would never want my daughter to return there, to live such a life. Your father and mother tell you to do so and so. They marry you there. If you get a good husband, that's the lottery. Now there is slowly some progress, but our generation has suffered a lot. These customs should be abandoned. If women one day feel in danger, they should just leave. Nothing else, I think. Now I can also say this. To respect each other is important, but the tradition is something else. Who wants to live with a violent person? It is something that should be rooted out, whatever people say.

"... Ti ljudje se ne zavedajo, da je ločitev zelo težka"

Marijina zgodba

Problemi so se začeli, ko je najina hči začela zmenkovati s fantom druge veroizpovedi, česar mož ni odobraval in je za to krivil mene. Šla sem na center za socialno delo (CSD) po informacije, vprašat, kaj naj storim, in svetovalka je rekla: »Ne zmenite se zanj, ni vam ga treba poslušati.« Moj mož nikoli ni šel na CSD, pa tudi nikoli ni bil povabljen. Takrat sem tudi prvič hodila na Društvo za nenasilno komunikacijo (DNK), a le za kratek čas.

Nasilje je trajalo in se stopnjevalo deset, enajst let. Potem pa me je enkrat, ko sem bila sama doma, zelo hudo pretepel in me zadrževal v stanovanju cele tri dni. Uspela sem se izpogajati, da mi je dovolil poklicati v službo in sporočiti, da me ne bo. Vodja je nekaj posumila in obvestila hčer, ki je prišla do stanovanja in prosila soseda policista, naj neformalno posreduje in se pogovori z možem, kar je tudi storil. Potem me je končno izpustil, tako da sem šla k zdravniku, ki mi je rekel, da moram to prijaviti CSD-ju, kar sem tudi storila. Oni pa so spisali prijavo in jo poslali policiji, čeprav sem jih prosila, naj tega ne naredijo.

Nekaj časa po tem je hotel, da grem z njim na sodišče vložit zahtevek za ločitev. Ker sem zavrnila, je postal nasilen, a mi je vseeno uspelo iti v službo, ker je posredoval sin. Toda potem me je prišel iskati v službo in sem obvestila CSD, ki je obvestil policijo. Policist je rekel: »Gospa, če vam je kaj naredil, mi povejte. Morate povedati. Nič ne moremo, dokler nam ne poveste, kaj se je zgodilo. Vas je pretepel, vas je žalil?« Vse sem zanikala. Zrastla sem v družini, kjer se o tem ne govori, govorimo si, potrpi, jutri bo bolje, drugače ... Ne vem, na nek način sem ga ljubila, mlada sem bila, ko sem ga spoznala, dolga leta sva živela skupaj. Zdaj ga bom pa prijavila policiji? Tega nisem mogla storiti. Ko si žrtev, te je strah povedati. Prvič, sram te je kazensko ovaditi svojega moža. Potem te je sram pred otroci, kako te bodo gledali, kaj bodo rekli sosedi. Tega nisi zmožen povedati naglas, nisi se sposoben braniti.

Potem sem začela intenzivno hoditi na DNK in klicati SOS telefon, kjer so mi zelo pomagali. Stali so mi ob strani, šli z mano na sodišče in mi pomagali pripravljati pritožbe. Ženske bi težko šle skozi to same brez teh organizacij. Po enem letu smo končno prišli do sodišča. Na zaslišanju je bilo jasno, da mož laže o raznih informacijah, a ga je sodnik izpustil.

"These people are not aware that divorce is very difficult"

Marija's Story

Our problems began when our daughter started dating one guy who was of another faith and my husband did not approve of it, for this he blamed me. I went to the Centre for social work (CSW) for information to ask what to do, and the consultant said, "Ignore him, you do not need to listen to him." My husband never went to CSW and also they never invited him. That's when I first went to Association for non-violent communication (DNK) as well but only for a short time.

The violence lasted and intensified for ten, eleven years. Then once, when I was home alone he beat me severely and kept me in the apartment for a full three days. I managed to negotiate that he allowed me to call the place where I work, that I will not come in. My boss suspected something and informed my daughter, who came to the apartment and asked a neighbor who is a police officer to intervene informally and talk with my husband, which he did. Then he finally let me go, so I went to see a doctor, who told me that I need to report it to CSD, which I also did. They however wrote a report and sent it to the police, even though I asked them not to do that.

Some time after that, he wanted me to go with him to court to file for divorce. Because I refused, he became violent, but I still managed to go to work, because my son intervened. Then, however, he came to control me at my working place, and I informed the CSD, who informed the police. The police officer said, "Ma'am, if he did anything to you, tell me. You need to say. We cannot do anything until you tell us what happened. Did he beat you, did he insult you?" I denied everything. I grew up in such a family that does not speak about that, it is like, have patience, tomorrow will be better, it will be different ... I do not know, I loved him in a way, I was young when I met him, we lived together for long years. And now I will denounce him to the police? I couldn't do that. When you are a victim, you're afraid to tell. Firstly, you are ashamed to criminally charge your own husband. And then you are ashamed of your children, how will they look at you, what will the neighbors say. You are not able to say it out loud, you're not able to defend yourself.

Then I started to intensively go to DNK and SOS Help-line, where I was helped a lot. They stood by me, went with me to the court and helped me to prepare complaints. Women would have difficulty go through this alone, if it were not for these organizations. After one year, we finally arrived at the court.

Mož je dobil pet mesecev pogojne kazni na dve leti preizkusne dobe. Ni dobil prepovedi približevanja. Vendar je sodnik na koncu možu vseeno rekel: »Gospod, če mislite imeti ženo, partnerko, to ni dobro. Ne smete je pretepati. Nasilje je kaznivo.« A sploh ni poslušal do konca. Kar odšel je. Ne zdi se mi prav, da ga nihče ni ustavil.

Potem sem vložila ločitveni zahtevek. Glede odvetnika pa vem, da če pridem z zahtevo po ločitvi, pričakuje, da sem trdna. Jaz pa sem prišla in rekla: »Rada bi se ločila, a nisem prepričana.« Rekel je: »Gospa, kaj zdaj? Hočete ločitev ali ne?« Bila sem zelo prestrašena. Mislim, itak sem bila prestrašena, v solzah. Je to zato, ker ga ne plačam sama, ampak država? Vendar bi moral imeti malo boljši odnos. Nisem prišla kupit ali prodat hiše. Bila sem tam, prestrašena, strah me je bilo za svoje življenje, za svoje otroke, za nami so leta skupnega življenja. Bila sem izgubljena.

Tudi nad sodnico sem bila razočarana. Napisala sem besedilo o letih najinega skupnega življenja. Nekako sem hotela, da bi sodnica to prebrala pred njim, ker se mu nisem upala povedati, da je bilo to, kar mi je storil, narobe. Sodnica je rekla: »Kaj, kaj počnete, kakšna pisma, kaj ste napisali? Kaj mislite?« Rekla je: »Se želite ločiti ali ne? Zdaj se odločite. Če ne, bom odkorakala skozi vrata. Pet minut imam.« Mislim, ti ljudje se ne zavedajo, da je ločitev zelo težka. Ni tako, kot da sem prišla v trgovino po liter mleka. »Vzemi ali pusti!« Tako je bilo. Tam je bila uboga oseba, ki ne ve niti svojega imena, ki ji je bilo žal, da se je to zgodilo, njen svet je razpadal.

Sicer pa se mi v tistem času ni zdelo prav, da je CSD interveniral brez mojega soglasja in moj primer poslal policiji, a sem danes hvaležna za to, da so. Imeli so prav, jaz sem bila tista, ki bi morala ustaviti situacijo. Verjetno si nikoli ne bi upala nič storiti in bi še vedno trpela. Zato se ne moreš odločiti. Prav je, da institucije, ko zaznajo, da nekdo počne nekaj narobe, da obstaja nasilje, to prijavijo, in zdi se mi, da bi to lahko bilo narejeno še bolje. Vendar pa bi zame bilo lažje, če bi to storila moja osebna zdravnica. A moja zdravnica je govorila: »In vas je pretepel, a ni važno.«

Še vedno hodim na DNK. Zaupam jim in zaupam sebi. Če jih ne bi bilo, bi bila še vedno na tleh. Dejansko nisem povsem razumela, kaj se mi dogaja, dokler niso rekli, da ni bilo prav to, kar mi je delal, da bi nasilje morali ustaviti.

At the hearing, it was clear that my husband is lying about various information but the judge let him go. My husband got 5 months to 2 years of imprisonment on probation. He didn't get any restraining order. But still the judge eventually told my husband: "Mister, if you will ever have a wife, partner, this is not good. You do not fight. The violence, this is criminal." But he did not listen until the end. He just went. For me it does not seem right that no one stopped him.

Then I filed for divorce. As for the lawyer, I know that if I came to file for separation he expects that I'm stable. But I came and said, "I would like to divorce but I am not sure". He said, "Ma'am, what now? You want or don't want to divorce? "I was very scared. I mean, I'm scared anyway, all in tears. Is it because he is not paid by me, but by the state? But he should have a little better attitude. I'm not coming to buy or sell a house. I'm there all scared, scared for my life, for my children, for years a common life. I'm lost.

About the judge I was disappointed too. I drew up a text about years of our common life together. Somehow I wanted the judge to read this before him, because I did not dare to tell him that what he did to me was wrong. The judge said: "What, what are you doing, what letters, what did you write? What are you thinking?" She said: "Do you want to be separated or not? Now you decide. If not, I will go through the door. Five minutes I have." I mean, these people are not aware that divorce is very difficult. It is not that I came to the store to buy a liter of milk: "Take it or leave it!" It was like that. But there is a poor person who does not even know her name, she was sorry that this has happened, her world is falling apart.

Otherwise, at that time, for me it didn't seem right that the CSD intervened without my consent, and sent my case to the police, but today I'm grateful that they did it. They were right, I was the one who had to stop that situation. I'd probably never dare to do anything, and would still suffer. So you are not able to decide. It is right that the institutions when they detect that someone does something wrong, that there is violence, report this, and it seems to me that this could be done even better. Yet for me it would be easier if my personal physician did that. But my doctor would say: "And he beat you, but never mind."

I still go to DNK. I trust them, and I trust myself. If it was not for them, I would be still on the ground. I actually did not quite understand what was happening to me until they said that it was not right what he was doing to me, that violence should be stopped.

"Vse je trajalo predolgo"

Sarina zgodba

Sem ločenka, mati treh otrok. Niso bili rojeni v Sloveniji, le jaz sem bila rojena tu, a so se starši leta 1994 odločili, da se vrnejo v svojo domovino. Leta 2006 sem se preselila nazaj v Slovenijo, ker tam ni bilo nobene kakovosti življenja. Uredila sem vse papirje, a je trajalo nekaj časa, da so otroci sprejeli to idejo. Potem sem se ločila od njihovega očeta in kasneje spoznala svojega novega partnerja, ki je bil potem nasilen do vseh nas. Imela sva razmerje na daljavo, potem sva se poročila in je prišel za nami v Slovenijo. Pol leta je bilo vse v redu, potem pa se je postopoma začelo, a tega sprva nisem prepoznala.

Imela sem rojstni dan, bila sem v službi, ko sem prejela klic od policije. Rekli so, da so otroke zadržali v šoli in da je bilo prijavljeno nasilje v družini. To je bil zame popoln šok. Na policijski postaji so bili socialni delavci, ki so rekli, da otroci ne bodo šli domov, da jih bodo tisti dan zadržali in potem … Ne vem, ne spomnim se več, kaj so rekli, kam bodo šli … A ne domov. Bilo me je strah: Kaj, kako, otroci ne grejo domov? Seveda so mi to razlagali, govorili so, a se tega sploh ne spomnim. Kot bi se gledala iz druge dimenzije. Jokala sem, policisti in socialni delavci so govorili, a nisem slišala njihovih glasov. Tako so v tistem obdobju otroci živeli v drugem mestu, v mladinskem centru. Ne spomnim se, kako se imenuje, pozabila sem.

Ko sem vprašala, kako dolgo bodo otroci odsotni, niso rekli nič določenega … Nekaj tipa: kolikor bo potrebno. Nisem vedela, ali se bodo vrnili do naslednjega šolskega leta. Grozno sem se bala vsega. Ni bilo nobenega konkretnega odgovora, saj so rekli, da bodo lahko hodili v šolo tam, da bodo prišli domov, ko ocenijo, da bo varno za otroke.

Center za socialno delo sem vprašala, zakaj morajo vzeti otroke, zakaj njega ne pošljejo stran … ker je nasilje v družini, zakaj ne gre on stran? To ni okej in meni jasno … A nisem dobila nobenega posebnega odgovora. In policiji nisem mogla povedati, kar sem hotela, pač pa le dejstva. Nisem hotela živeti brez otrok. Tista dva meseca, ko so bili tam, sem samo skušala ugajati CSD-ju, narediti vse, kar so hoteli od mene, le da bi mi vrnili otroke. Grozno sem se počutila. Sploh ne vem, kako sem funkcionirala, tako je, kot bi imela nekakšen blackout glede tega časa. Imela sem dva živčna zloma.

"Everything took too long"

Sara's Story

I'm divorced, a mother of three children. They were not born in Slovenia, only I was born here, but my parents decided in 1994 to return to their home country. In 2006 I moved back to Slovenia, there was no quality of life down there. I organized all the papers, but it took time for the kids to accept the idea. Then I divorced their father and later I met a new partner, who was then violent towards all of us. We had long distance relationship and then we married and he followed us to Slovenia. For half a year everything was fine, and then step by step it started, but I did not recognize it first.

It was my birthday and I was at my workplace and there was a phone call from the police. They said that the children were being kept in school, and there was a report about violence in the family. That was a total shock for me. At the police station there were social workers and they said that the children won't go home, that they will keep them that day and then... I don't know, I don't remember any more what they said where they would go... But not home. I was afraid: What, how, children don't go home? Of course they were explaining it to me, they talked, but I can't recall that at all. As if I was looking at myself from another dimension. I cried and policemen and social workers talked but I didn't hear their voices. So for that period the children stayed in another town in the Youth Centre. I don't remember how is it called, I forgot.

When I asked how long would the children stay away, they did not say anything certain... something like, as much as will be necessary. I didn't know whether they would come back until school next year. I was terribly afraid of everything. There was no concrete answer, as they said that they would be able to go to school there, that they would come home when they estimate that it would be safe for the children.

I asked the Centre for Social Work why they have to take away the kids, why he is not sent away... because, there is violence in the family, why does he not go away? This is not ok and it is not clear to me... But I did not get any particular answer. And to the police I could not tell what I wished, but just the facts. I did not want to live without my children. That whole two months when they were there, I was just working on pleasing the CSW, to do everything they wanted from me, just to bring back the kids. I felt awful. I don't know at all, how I functioned, it is as if I have a sort of black-out about that time. I had two nervous breakdowns.

Od CSD-ja nisem dobila nobene posebne pomoči, razen da so me poslali na DNK (Društvo za nenasilno komunikacijo). Stalno sem se bala, ker so nekoč nepričakovano prišli preverit, ali so otroci v redu. Da bi govorili z njimi in malo z nama. Naredila sem vse, da so končno napisali sklep, da se otroci vrnejo domov.

A s pomočjo DNK sem se počasi postavljala na noge. Imela sem grozne dni, če vprašate mojo svetovalko. Prvi dan sem se skregala z njo. Potem pa sem ure jokala. Nisem mogla sprejeti tega, da so otroci šli stran, moj bivši pa je doma. Najprej je bil aretiran, potem pa je prišel domov. Če bi mene vprašali, bi njega morali izseliti, saj je on bil problem, otroci pa bi bili doma. Bilo je super, da nas je socialna delavka poslala na DNK, ker so pomagali meni in otrokom. Tja sem hodila enkrat ali dvakrat na teden, kot bi hodila v zdravilišče. Nekoč je bilo doma spet nevzdržno in po službi sem počakala, da je šef odšel domov in potem sem si rekla: »Sara, če boš sedaj poklicala DNK, boš rešena, sicer to ne bo šlo nikamor.« In tako sem poklicala in vprašala svojo svetovalko, če se spomni, da mi je govorila o ločitvi. Rekla je: »Ne spomnim se, a če sem to rekla, potem sem to tudi mislila.« Rekla sem, da hočem ločitev in naj mi pomaga napisati tožbeni zahtevek za ločitev. Zame je bilo to olajšanje, ko sem videla, da razmišlja enako kot jaz, da je bilo to nasilje, da me ne bi smel ogrožati.

Želela bi si boljše komunikacije s policijo. Na primer, ko sem prišla podat izjavo, nikoli nisem dobila uradnega zapisnika, nimam pojma, kaj so zapisali, samo po spominu. V vsem tistem času je ta moški imel predvsem pravice, pravico do tega ali onega, pravice na vse strani. Jaz pa sem imela samo dolžnosti. Vse je predolgo trajalo. Ne vem, kako sem vmes živela. A moraš živeti in delati, tega ne moreš kar prespati, kar bi naredila, če bi lahko. Le da bi prišel datum, ko moram tja in tja. To je vse predolgo trajalo, predolgo. Kar pa se tiče sodišča, se je to končalo šele po dveh letih.

Dobil je maksimalno kazen, tako da nas od takrat pusti pri miru: dve leti pogojnega zapora na pet let preizkusne dobe in tri leta prepovedi približevanja. Edino, kar sem prosila tožilca, je bilo, naj naglas pove – da bi lahko tudi on slišal – da obsodba velja za cel svet, ne le za Slovenijo. Tj., da kjerkoli bi se mi hotel približati, biti nasilen, bi njegova pogojna kazen veljala. Kjerkoli na svetu, če bi bil agresiven do mene ali kogarkoli drugega. Dejansko so mu morale institucije povedati to, naj se zaveda, da tega ne sme in naj odide. Ni imelo smisla, da jaz to govorim.

I did not get any particular help from CSW except that they sent me to DNK (Society for non-violent communication). I was constantly afraid, because once they came unexpectedly to check if the children were ok. In order to talk to them and to us a little. I did everything so that they finally wrote the conclusion to bring the children back home.

But with the help of DNK I was slowly getting to my feet again. I had terrible days, if you ask my advisor. I had quarrels with her on the first days. Then for hours, I cried. I could not accept that the children were away and my ex was at home. He was first arrested, but then he came home. If I was asked, he was the one who should be thrown out, as he was the problem, and the kids would have been home. It was great that the social worker sent us to DNK, they helped me and they helped the children. I went there once or twice a week, it was like a SPA centre. One day it was unbearable at home again and after the job I waited for the boss to go home and then I said to myself: »Sara, if you're going to call DNK now, you shall be rescued, and otherwise this will go nowhere«. And I called and asked my advisor if she remembers that she talked to me about divorce. And she said »I don't remember but if I said that then I have meant it.« And I said I wanted a divorce, and her to help me to write a lawsuit for divorce. For me, it was a relief when I saw that she was thinking the same way as me, that that was violence that he was not allowed to endanger.

I would wish for better communication with the police. For example, when I came to give the statement, I never got the official notes, I have no clue what they wrote down, just by memory. In all that time, this man had above all rights, the right to this or to that, rights all around. I only had duties. Everything took too long. I don't know how I lived in between. But you have to live, and work, you cannot just sleep it over, which I would do if I could. Only for the date to come, when I had to go there and there. Too long all this has taken, too long. As for the court, that only ended after two years.

He got the maximum sentence, so that since then he leaves us in peace: two years of prison changed into five years on probation and three years of restraining order. The only thing I asked the prosecutor for was to say out loud – so that also he could hear – that the sentence is valid for the whole world, not only in Slovenia. That is to say, wherever he would try to come close to me, to be violent, that his probation sentence is valid. Wherever in the world, if he was aggressive towards me or anyone else. In fact, institutions were needed to tell him that, now you listen, this you cannot do, now you go. There was no point for me to talk about that.

"Mislim, da je povsem prav, da
službe intervenirajo"

Zoranina zgodba

Rojena sem bila v Sloveniji, a izviram iz druge republike nekdanje Jugoslavije, moji starši so od tam, sicer pa živijo v Sloveniji. Tudi svojega partnerja sem spoznala tam, zaročila sva se, ko sem imela komaj petnajst let. Kasneje sva se poročila in sva bila poročena vrsto let. Zavedala sem se, da sem zelo mlada, a sem nekako bežala iz domačega okolja. Moj mož je bil pogosto pijan in je postajal vse bolj nasilen do mene; nasilen je bil tudi do najinih otrok, predvsem ko me ni bilo doma. Ko smo se vrnili v Slovenijo, smo najprej živeli v najetem stanovanju, a smo kasneje od občine dobili stanovanje s subvencionirano najemnino za mlado družino.

Na začetku sem iskala pomoč v kliniki za zdravljenje alkoholikov v upanju, da bi bil pripravljen iti na zdravljenje, a je bilo zaman. Enkrat, ko je bil še posebej nasilen, sem hotela poklicati policijo, a se je vrnil, me udaril in vrgel telefon na tla. Enostavno nisem mogla pritisniti zelenega gumba za klic. Nekajkrat sem poskusila, a enostavno nisem mogla pritisniti zelenega gumba, ker sem se takrat bala.

Obrnila sem se na center za socialno delo (CSD), kamor sem hodila na pogovore dva ali tri mesece. Tudi on je hodil, a le ko je bil spodbujen. Potem sem se obrnila na sosedo, ki je tudi bila v zelo težki situaciji, in sem jo prosila za nasvet. Predlagala mi je Društvo za nenasilno komunikacijo (DNK). Pomoč njihove svetovalke je bila neprecenljiva. Stala mi je ob strani kot druga mama ali če se izrazim drugače, lahko bi rekla, da je takrat bila moja prva mama, ker mi lastna mama ni mogla dati takih informacij. Zame je res bila na prvem mestu. Zdelo se mi je, da jo lahko pokličem za najmanjšo podrobnost in da je bila pripravljena, da me posluša in mi pomaga najti rešitev.

Potem sem vložila zahtevek za ločitev. Ko je dobil pošto, je znorel in me pretepel. Naslednji dan je hči šla v šolo in ker je bila bleda kot stena, je učiteljica opazila in poklicala psihologinjo, ki jo je vzela iz razreda in se pogovorila z njo. Hči ji je povedala, da je bila prestrašena, ko je vse to videla na lastne oči, in da se boji za moje življenje. Potem je šola obvestila DNK, ta pa policijo brez mojega soglasja. Svetovalka me je potem poklicala in mi rekla: »Zorana, ne prosim za tvoje dovoljenje, saj sem policijo že obvestila, a prijavo bova napisali skupaj.«

"I think it is quite right that the services intervene"

Zorana's Story

I was born in Slovenia but I have roots in another former Yugoslav republic, my parents are from there, who otherwise live in Slovenia. Also I met a partner there and we got engaged when I was only 15. We married later, and have been married for many years. I was aware that I was very young but I was kind of running away from the home environment. My husband was often drunk and became increasingly violent towards me; he was also violent towards our children, mostly when I was not home. When we returned to Slovenia, we lived first in rented accommodation but later we got an apartment with subsidized rent for a young family from the municipality.

At the beginning I was looking for help in the clinic where they treat alcoholics in the hope that he would be prepared to go to treatment, but to no avail. Once, when he was particularly violent, I wanted to call the police, but he came back, hit me and threw the phone on the floor. I just could not push the green button to call. I tried several times, but I just couldn't press the green button, because I was afraid then.

I turned to the Centre for social work (CSW), there I went to talk for two or three months. He was going as well but only when he was urged. Then I turned to the neighbor, who also was in a very difficult situation and I asked her for advice, she recommended me Association for non-violent communication (DNK). Their adviser's help was invaluable. She stood at my side as a second mother or to put it another way, we could say she was the first mum at that time, because my own mom could not give such information. She was really in the first place, for me. I find that I could call her for every detail and she was willing to listen and help me how to find a solution.

Then I filed papers for divorce. When the mail came for him he got crazy and beat me. The next day my daughter went to school and because she was pale as a wall, the teacher noticed and called a psychologist and she was pulled out of class and began to talk. The daughter told her that it was frightening to see it all with her own eyes and that she fears for my life. Then the school informed DNK and the DNK informed the police, without my consent. Adviser then called me and said to me:"Zorana, see, I do not ask you for permission, I have already informed the police, but the report we're going to do together."

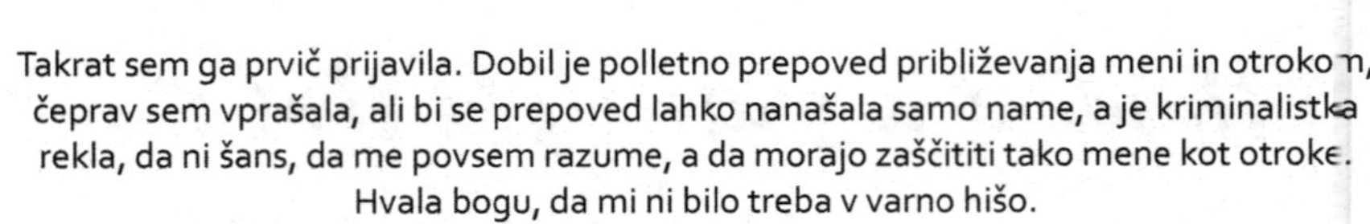

Takrat sem ga prvič prijavila. Dobil je polletno prepoved približevanja meni in otrokom, čeprav sem vprašala, ali bi se prepoved lahko nanašala samo name, a je kriminalistka rekla, da ni šans, da me povsem razume, a da morajo zaščititi tako mene kot otroke. Hvala bogu, da mi ni bilo treba v varno hišo.

Zelo pogosto sem bila v stiku s svetovalko DNK, hodila sem dobesedno vsak dan, celo dvakrat na dan, da sva se ukvarjali s projekti in načrti, kako in kaj narediti. Pomagala mi je tudi narediti načrt za poplačilo dolgov, ki sem si jih nakopala zaradi njega, skupno več kot 20.000 evrov. Sledil je ločitveni postopek na sodišču. To je bilo trpljenje, a mi je svetovalka DNK stala ob strani in me je spremljala na obravnave. Najhujše breme je bilo, ko sem ga po prepovedi prvič videla, v sodni dvorani je bil tudi najstarejši otrok, ne pa tudi mlajši, saj sem jih prosila, naj ga ne peljejo na sodišče. Moj odvetnik je zahteval 150 evrov preživnine na otroka, a je sodnic rekla, da bi bilo glede na to, da nikjer ni delal, primerneje 100 evrov na otroka na mesec. Za nasilje v družini je bil obsojen na dveletno pogojno kazen na štiri leta preizkusne dobe.

Ker nisem imela druge izbire, sem ga morala tožiti zaradi preživnine, ker je devet mesecev ni plačeval. Dejansko bi morala prositi za povišanje preživnine, ker 100 evrov na otroka ni dovolj. Zelo sem razočarana nad našim sodiščem, ker mu že tri leta pošiljajo pošto na moj naslov, čeprav ni več prijavljen na tem naslovu in kljub dejstvu, da sem sodišču pisala, naj neha. Zdaj je na drugem kontinentu a je slovenski državljan in če bi sodišče želelo, bi lahko izvedelo naslov njegovega novega prebivališča in pošte ne bi več pošiljalo na moj naslov. Najhujše je, da je to ena banalna stvar, ki je ne morejo storiti.

Sicer pa sem bila v vsem tem času pogosto bolna. Priznam, da ko sem bila na pogovorih na sodišču, mi je zdravnik dal pomirjevala. Ne da bi me poživil, pač pa malo pomiri, ker ponoči nisem spala. Včasih celo ves teden, spala sem lahko le dve uri na noč in sem potrebovala nekaj, da bi me malo sprostilo. Vendar pa me zdravnik nikoli ni vprašal o nasilju v družini.

Mislim, da je povsem prav, da službe intervenirajo. V tistem trenutku si lahko na koga jezen. A ko potem še enkrat trezno razmisliš, veš, da so delovali za tvoje dobro in ti verjetno rešili življenje. Še danes hodim na DNK, ker se pojavijo določene stvari, ki jih ne znaš razrešiti sam. Zgodijo se stvari, kot sem že omenila, recimo preživnina, skušajo mi pomagati, svetovati, kaj storiti. Po mojih izkušnjah bi rekla, če slišim, da ima kdo problem, bi ga napotila na DNK.

This was the first time that I reported him. He got a six-month ban on approaching me and the children, even though I asked if the prohibition can be only to me, but the criminal officer said not a chance, that she fully understands me but that they must protect both me and the kids. Thank God that I did not need to go to the safe house.

I was in contact with the DNK counselor quite a lot, it was literally every day, even twice a day that I came and we worked together on projects and plans, how and what to do. She helped me also to make a plan to repay debts which I have accumulated from him, a total of more than 20,000 euros. The divorce procedure in court followed. That was a live in suffering, but my DNK counselor again stood on my side and walked with me to the debate. The heaviest burden was when I first saw him after the ban, also the older child was in the court, but not the younger, as I asked them not to take him to court. My lawyer requested EUR 150 maintenance per child but then the judge said that in view of the fact that he has not worked anywhere, we landed at EUR 100 per child per month. For domestic violence, he got two years to four years' probation.

Since I had no other choice, I had to sue him in respect of maintenance because he has not paid for 9 months. I should actually ask that maintenance be raised, because 100 EUR per child is not enough. I am very disappointed in our court because they sent him mails to my address for three years now, even though he is no longer registered at this address and despite the fact that I wrote to the court to stop this. He is now on another continent and is also a Slovenian citizen and if the court wished they could just find out his new registered address, and not to send his mails to me. The worst thing is because it is one banal thing they can't do.

Otherwise, all this time I was often sick. I admit, when I was in court at the talks, my doctor gave me sedatives. Thus, not to pick me up, but to calm me a little, because I do not sleep at night. It was the whole week sometimes, I could only sleep two hours at night and I needed one that really, to chill me a little. But the doctor never asked about the violence in the family.

I think it is quite right that the services intervene. You can be mad at someone at that moment. But then, when you soberly think again you know that they only acted for your good and that they saved your life probably. I go to DNK until today, because certain things come up that you don't know how to solve by yourself. Things come up, as I mentioned earlier, for the maintenance, they are trying to help, what to do in this case. So I would say from my experience if I hear someone has a problem, I'd refer her/him to the DNK.

Child physical abuse & neglect

Stories and experiences of young people with intervention

Child physical abuse & neglect

Stories and experiences of young people with intervention

England & Wales

Jhanelle's story

I was being badly abused at home. Sometimes I'd go to school and there would be marks but my father always told me what to say and when I said this to teachers, they didn't ask any more. Things got so bad that when I was about thirteen years old, I decided that I didn't want to live any more so I attempted to kill myself. When that didn't work, I knew I was in big trouble. That's when I ran away. Some people, they were strangers, they helped me and called the police. When the police came they took me to an office and asked me lots of questions. Then after that they took me to social services and I met my social worker. She didn't talk about serious things, she just joked around and tried to make me feel comfortable. I liked that. Then she explained that they would need to find another family for me. She asked me what kind of family but I didn't know so she put me into a family where she thought I'd feel comfortable. I did, because they were like my skin colour, so I didn't stand out from the rest of them. But first, the social worker told me I had to see a doctor for a medical examination. So she and the police officer took me to the hospital and the doctor just gave me a basic check, you know, ears, throat and things like that. Then a photographer came as well because they needed to take photographs of all the marks on my body so I had to take off my clothes. I was OK with this but I didn't understand why the doctor had to stay in the room. All the others were women but he was a man and I didn't like him being there because I'm scared of men but nobody asked me about this.

After we left the hospital, the social worker took me to meet the foster family. I had questions. I wanted to know how it works, what carers are supposed to do because I didn't want to be in an abusive family again. So she told me, I didn't have to feel afraid. They wouldn't hit me or anything and she said, if something does go wrong I have to tell her. So this was good. And my foster mum is good. I am still with this family now. They have children of their own. One of them has been very mean to me and used to make me feel like an outcast, saying I had no home of my own and stuff like that; but it happened too often and now I just don't care, it doesn't bother me anymore. That's how it goes. At least I'm happy there compared to when I first came which is nearly three years ago now.

But now I have a bit of a problem with the police. When they first interviewed me, I didn't
want to tell them. I'd never told anyone before about what had happened with me and
what my dad had done to me. But I knew I had to say it because it was the right thing
to do and I knew I didn't want to go back to my dad. But then they told me I had to do
another interview the next day and I felt that was kind of like rushing me. And I really
hated that because I felt I needed at least a few months' break. I needed to have a break
to get away from all that, so that I can talk properly, not when all of my brain was stressing me. It made me want to exaggerate things because I was so scared and didn't want to
go back. So it was too rushed and I felt I had no choice. They said I had to tell them everything while it was all fresh in my memory; they said that otherwise I would forget everything but I can still remember to this day, so how does this work?! I wasn't given a chance
to just say no. Because I was new to it all and I'm a bit timid and shy. I wasn't given the
space I needed. It was all rushed.

Now I don't know what's happening with my dad. I know he was arrested but they let
him go with some bail conditions. I've been waiting now for almost three years to see if
there's something with the court. No-one tells me anything. I saw the police again last
year and she said they were still trying to go through the process, the prosecution, to
gain evidence to use but nobody asks me what I want. I don't want my dad prosecuted
and when I reach the age of eighteen I'm going to cancel all this. I think he's learned his
lesson. He's been through a lot himself. There are reasons why people do the things they
do. So it's like at the beginning it all happened too fast and now everything is all happening too slowly. When they rushed me, I'm like he's my dad, but now that I've had time,
I've thought about it, I am like, well, this is not what I want. I would feel so guilty. If they
asked me now, I just hope I can cancel it, that's all.

"My foster family is the best but I am still scared for the future"

Ljena's story

I came to the UK about a year ago from a European country, but it is not part of the European Union. I didn't know I was coming here. I was having a lot of trouble with my family and so a relative helped me and this is how I came to the UK. I was in a park and I heard a woman on her mobile phone, she was speaking my language and I asked her to help me.

She was scared at the beginning. You know if someone comes up to and says please, take me to your home tonight. But then talking with her, she changed her mind and she took me for the night but she said in the morning you are going to social services.

Next day she took me to social services and left me there. The people were nice but I didn't understand the language, so that was a big problem. They took me to some hostel. It was evening by then and I hadn't eaten. So I went out to get some food and when I came back the doors were locked. And they had to come back to let me in. Then my social worker took me to a place. We had to go on the train and this place was part of the Home Office but when we got there, my social worker left. She said she had another case. I didn't understand what was going on. I was alone there. Some time later, there was an interpreter and I had an interview and after that someone took me to another house. There were other people in this house. I stayed in a room by myself but the other people were very nice. I just had my clothes and my shoes which were in a poor condition. So they washed my clothes and they gave me food which was good. I hadn't eaten all day at that point and my social worker had used my money for the train fare but someone from the Home Office gave me a few pounds. The next day a new person came to take me somewhere else. I still didn't know what was going on but they brought me here, to Children's Services here where I am now and then everything changed.

My new social worker explained everything to me. They had to do an age assessment and after that, they had to find me a temporary foster place. So all day I sat with my social worker. She made calls to people on a list to see if anyone wanted me. It was a Friday and people said no, I was too old, they wanted a younger child, or they wanted a boy. Then one family said, yes, they wanted me and my social worker took me there.

The first night I was scared, I couldn't sleep because I had no experience of foster care so I didn't know what it would be like. Then I relaxed a bit. I could see they were good people.

After the weekend, my social worker and a key worker came to take me to a different house, to share this house with another girl, also from my country. It was a nice house and I liked it but there was a problem. The girl I was sharing with went to sleep at a friend's house every night and I am too scared to sleep on my own. After two nights I said to my social worker, I cannot stay here so then they brought me back to the foster family and I have been with them ever since. Then the Home Office called me for another interview and this time was so different. My social worker and my key worker were both there and they spoke to the solicitor. Everything was explained to me that I need to apply for permission to be in the country and everybody helped me. And my foster family helped me, they explained more even though I still couldn't speak much English but somehow we communicated.

I think foster families, at least my foster family, is the best one. My family will always be my family, with problems or not, you know...But this family is like choosing. Like going to the shop and choosing the best. I chose the best family. I am very glad to have them. Only when people see us and they see how our colour is, you know, they say, no, you can't be their daughter. And I say yes I am their heart daughter, so it doesn't matter that they didn't give birth to me.

Now I have taken English classes and I am in college. Everything here has been good, except for the health people. With all I have been through, all the stress, I am very sick and they cannot find what is wrong with me. And I think they do not want me here. One doctor, who was not English, he was Chinese, he asked me why am I here in this country? I felt very bad but my foster dad was with me and he asked, is this a medical question? And now I feel too that my solicitor has let me down. He did not call me to explain that my visa will soon expire. This will be on my birthday when I will be eighteen and no longer a child. This will be the worst birthday ever. I don't want to be eighteen, in this country, being a child is good. Good! Now I am scared for the future. That's the only thing, because I don't know what happens now that I am an adult and that makes me scared.

"It's good with this family because we're the same colour so I don't stand out"

Lorianna's story

I don't really remember much of my early childhood but at around age five I went into care. I can remember that, I remember moving in with my carer and going to primary school from there. And I've been with that same family ever since so I call my foster mother 'mum' and my foster sister 'sister'. I think of them as my family. There have been ups and downs but I guess that's what happens in any family.

When I was younger it seemed like there were always social workers around - probably because I was too young to make my own decisions. But it felt to me that they were there too often. It would have been better if they'd stayed away more and just let me be, like, more of a normal child. So I felt crowded by them. And often they didn't make decisions fast enough. So, like, if there was a sleepover, my mum would have to go to the social worker, then the social worker would have to go back to my mum and by the time they'd made a decision, it was too late and the sleepover had already happened. On the whole, though, I think they were ok. If I needed anything at school like books or money for a school trip, they just sorted it out. And they would always ask me if there was anything I wanted to talk about, anything about home or school or stuff. School is good. I like it because I've got lots of friends there. When I was younger I had to go to meetings every so often. I didn't like that because it was always during classes and then the other kids would ask me where I'd been. I never said anything to them but I did tell my social worker I didn't want to go any more. So then they had the meetings without me. That was better and now I write down anything I want to say and they can discuss that. And they always tell me what was said in the meetings and that I can see the minutes if I want to – but I never do. But sometimes they say I have to be involved in making decisions even though I don't want to. Then they say to me it's kind of like, it's because it's my choice.

So really I think it's all been ok for me. I've been with the same carer all the time and that's good – also because we're the same colour so that means I don't stand out. If we were different and I went to school or something it would be like, oh, what's happened here?

And it's better to grow up in your own culture, knowing what your background's like and stuff so it's good that social workers put me here with this family. The only thing I would say about the social workers is that they change too often. It's like, you know, you've got to build up the trust, so if they just keep going and coming it's kind of – the trust kind of goes because they're going to leave soon. Then you don't know who you're going to get, are they going to be better or worse than the next one, so…it's kind of hard to talk to new people and you don't really remember them. I remember the one I've got now and the previous one but I don't properly remember anyone else.

"Moja rejniška družina je super, a me je vseeno strah glede prihodnosti"

Ljenina zgodba

V Veliko Britanijo sem prišla pred kakšnim letom iz evropske države, ki ni članica EU. Nisem vedla, da bom prišla sem. Imela sem veliko težav s svojo družino, zato mi je sorodnik pomagal in tako sem prišla v Veliko Britanijo. Bila sem v parku in sem slišala žensko, ki je po mobitelu govorila v mojem jeziku, zato sem jo prosila, naj mi pomaga.

Na začetku jo je bilo strah. Saj veste, če nekdo pristopi k tebi in reče: »Prosim, vzemite me k sebi domov nocoj.« Potem pa si je v pogovoru premislila in me je vzela za tisto noč, a je rekla, da bom zjutraj šla na socialo.

Naslednji dan me je peljala tja in me tam pustila. Ljudje so bili prijazni, a nisem razumela jezika, kar je bil velik problem. Peljali so me v nek hostel. Takrat je bil že večer in nisem še jedla. Zato sem šla ven po hrano in ko sem se vrnila, so bila vrata zaklenjena. Morali so se vrniti, da so me spustili noter. Potem me je moja socialna delavka nekam peljala. Morali sva na vlak in ta ustanova je bila del Ministrstva za notranje zadeve, a ko sva prispeli tja, je moja socialna delavka odšla. Rekla je, da ima drug primer. Nisem razumela, kaj se dogaja. Sama sem bila tam. Čez nekaj časa je prišel tolmač in imela sem razgovor, potem pa me je nekdo peljal v drugo hišo. V tej hiši so bili še drugi ljudje. Bila sem sama v sobi, a ostali ljudje so bili zelo prijazni. Imela sem le svoje obleke in čevlje, ki so bili v slabem stanju. Zato so mi oprali obleke in mi dali hrano, ki je bila dobra. Cel dan nisem jedla, moja socialna delavka pa je moj denar uporabila za karto za vlak, a mi je nekdo z Ministrstva za notranje zadeve dal nekaj funtov. Naslednji dan je prišla nova oseba, ki me je odpeljala nekam drugam. Še vedno nisem vedela, kaj se dogaja, a so me pripeljali sem v službo za otroke, kjer sem zdaj, potem pa se je vse spremenilo.

Moja nova socialna delavka mi je vse razložila. Morali so oceniti mojo starost in mi potem najti začasno rejniško družino. Tako sem cel dan presedela s svojo socialno delavko. Klicala je ljudi na seznamu, da bi videla, če bi me kdo vzel. Bil je petek in ljudje so rekli 'ne', češ, da sem prestara, hoteli so mlajšega otroka ali pa fanta. Potem pa je ena družina rekla 'ja', hoteli so me in socialna delavka me je peljala tja.

Prvo noč me je bilo strah, nisem mogla spati, ker nisem imela izkušenj z rejništvom, zato nisem vedela, kako bo. Potem sem se malo sprostila. Videla sem, da so dobri ljudje.

V ponedeljek sta prišla socialna delavka in odgovorni delavec; odpeljala sta me v drugo hišo, ki naj bi si jo delila s še eno punco iz moje države. Hiša je bila lepa in mi je bila všeč, a sem imela težavo. Punca, s katero sem si jo delila, je vsak večer šla spat k prijatelju, jaz pa se preveč bojim, da bi spala sama. Po dveh nočeh sem svoji socialni delavki rekla, da tam ne morem živeti, zato so me potem pripeljali nazaj k rejniški družini, kjer sem ostala do danes. Potem me je Ministrstvo za notranje zadeve poklicalo na še en razgovor, a tokrat je bilo zelo drugače. Moja socialna delavka in odgovorni delavec sta bila oba prisotna in sta govorila z odvetnikom. Vse so mi razložili: da moram zaprositi za dovoljenje za bivanje v državi in vsi so mi pomagali. In tudi moja rejniška družina mi je pomagala, še več so mi razložili, čeprav še vedno nisem znala kaj dosti angleško, a smo nekako komunicirali.

Mislim, da so rejniške družine, vsaj moja rejniška družina, najboljše. Moja družina bo vedno moja družina, s problemi ali ne, saj veste ... A pri tej družini je nekakšna izbira. Kot bi šel v trgovino in izbral najboljšo. Izbrala sem najboljšo družino. Zelo sem vesela, da jih imam. Le ko nas ljudje vidijo in vidijo naše barve, saj veste, potem rečejo: »Ne, ne moreš biti njihova hči.« Jaz pa rečem, da sem njuna hči po srcu, tako da ni važno, da me nista rodila.

Hodila sem na tečaj angleščine in zdaj sem na kolidžu. Vse tu je bilo dobro, razen zdravstvenih delavcev. Glede na vse, kar sem prestala, ves stres, sem zelo bolna in ne morejo ugotoviti, kaj je narobe z mano. In mislim, da me nočejo tu. En zdravnik, ki ni bil Anglež, bil je Kitajec, me je vprašal, zakaj sem v tej državi. Zelo hudo mi je bilo, a je bil rejnik z mano in je vprašal, če je to medicinsko vprašanje. Zdaj se mi pa zdi tudi, da me je odvetnik pustil na cedilu. Ni me poklical, da bi mi razložil, da mi viza kmalu poteče. To bo na moj rojstni dan, ko bom dopolnila osemnajst let in ne bom več otrok. To bo moj najslabši rojstni dan. Nočem biti osemnajst, ker je biti otrok v tej državi dobro. Dobro! Zdaj se bojim za prihodnost. Edino to, ker ne vem, kaj se zgodi zdaj, ko sem odrasla, in to me plaši.

"I know that all of what the social workers have done has been good for me"

Robert's story

I was quite young when I came to the UK with my brothers. We came from Africa. Our mum had already died back home and we came here to stay with an auntie. And we all lived with her in this house – I don't remember how long - but then she took ill and an ambulance came to take her to the hospital. She died there but nobody told us. I went with my brother to the hospital. Then he found out that she'd died and he said they should have told us. They should have told us how ill she was so that we had a chance to see her and say goodbye before she died but we didn't and that really upset me. I wish I knew why they didn't tell us.

Then somebody came to the door of the house. They were social workers and they said we had to go into a placement because there was nobody else to look after us. They wanted to keep us all together so we had two temporary placements and then they moved us to my old place. Only my youngest brother is still there. The social workers drove us there and said this is where you are going to live. This is permanent, with a nice family. They said they had to go to court to get a piece of paper. I didn't go and I don't remember anything else about it but it wasn't an adoption. It was just something so we could stay with this family permanently. They had other kids and foster kids. For me, that was a bit difficult because I didn't like to socialise and because they came from a different part of Africa so I had to get used to the food and everything. This was challenging but it was a still a good placement. My oldest brother went to college and my youngest brother went to school. I went to a special school. A mini-bus picked me up every day. My teacher knew I was in care but to me, I think that should be up to the young person. If he wants, if he or she wants to tell they are in care, of course, I mean if they want the teacher to know but it should be the decision of the young person. I was bullied in school because I was black. We told the teachers but I don't think they did enough so me and my friends we had to stand up for ourselves.

Just over two years ago I was moved into a semi-independent place. I learned to cook and to budget. That was good and I liked the area. Then I had to move from there so my social worker applied for housing for me and I got a direct offer

That's where I am now. It's like a small place but it's mine. I only share the hallways with
other people. But I don't like the area. I don't know it and everything is too expensive
there. And it's too far from where I know and where my friends are. So it costs too much
on the bus. I only get – I have to sign on at the Job Centre even though they know I am in
college, I still have to go and sign on and if I don't they'll stop my benefits so I'm going to
have a word with my social worker - he's my personal adviser now and he's good. We sat
down together and agreed a Pathway Plan. It says what I want to do and all that. He's my
first point of contact. Well, I usually first come here to this Centre because they know me
really well and they always help. They call my personal adviser and then I go and meet
with him. He helps me sort out any problems I've got even though I'm an adult now.

So I think that social workers are really good. The only thing I would say is that it was too
quick when they first took us into care. They should have waited, you know, to give us
a chance to get over the emotion of losing someone. But I think when you're younger
some of the decisions, some things they do for your own good. Not only for your good,
for others too. You only see this when you grow up and understand more. And they
share information. I'm ok with that if it's with my permission or if they do it because of
protection, they share information for protection. So I know that all of what the social
workers have done has been good for me and my personal adviser, the personal adviser I
have now, he's also African so he knows about racism and he says if somebody's bullying
you because of race, we won't stand for it. Tell the police and give them my contact
number. So in this way, change is coming. My experience has been good but I know it's
not good for all young people. Social workers need to spend more time with them – and
with the foster carers to be sure the foster carers really want them. This is what I would
recommend.

"My behaviour started changing, because I felt that someone cared"

Saafir's story

I was taken into care when I was still quite young. I'd been living with my mum but it turned out she wasn't very well and was not coping with me. So social services got involved and said my only option was to go and live with my dad and my step mum but shortly after I moved in with them my dad became abusive – he was physically and verbally abusive to me. My step mum used to look after me quite a lot and she would have a go at my dad but it didn't stop him. So I think my step mum talked to my mum and she called social services. Then social services came and spoke to my dad and I think they wrote something down about marks on my body but I don't remember them speaking to me. The next time they came with the police and told me they were taking me away. They said I had nothing to worry about, that they would take me to some nice people who would look after me. I was happy about leaving my dad.

I remember going to court. The judge talked to me about where I wanted to live and I said I wanted to live with my mum but then they said that wasn't possible so the judge asked me, if I couldn't live with my mum, did I want to stay with my foster family. So I said, yes, I did because at that time I was getting on well there. My foster parents had a son of their own who was about my age and we played football together. I liked that and I stayed with that foster family for a long time. I still had social workers who visited and they also let me visit with my mum but then I started to worry about my dad and my behaviour changed. I became very angry. I was angry all the time with everyone, and I used to lash out. And it was because of this that I was kicked out of school and there were lots of tensions at home. I tried to talk to my social workers about this but they kept changing so none of them really got to know me and they didn't really support me. So then my foster mum was angry with me all the time too and I thought, it's all my fault that no-one wants to help me, even at the new school which was not mainstream, it was a school for kids with anxiety or anger issues. I asked for help but they said there was no more help to give.

Then my nan came and said she could have me but I didn't want to live with her so then I had lots of short placements. I would be a couple of months here and a couple of months there but the placements always broke down because my behaviour was so bad.

Eventually they got me a psychologist and he spent a lot of time with me. I think he cared a lot for me and he thought I needed a lot of support. Then my behaviour started changing back, because I felt that someone cared in social services. And I got a new social worker who was nice and understanding, someone who listened to my views but I think that's also because I was older by then, and more attention was paid to what I thought was best for me. And I got this placement, where I am now and I've been here for more than a year, that's the longest placement since my first carer. Everything is much better now and I have loads of friends. I've done my exams and got a temporary job before I go to college, and I'm looking ahead to semi-independent living, learning to budget and to stretch your money to buy appropriate food and stuff. And one of the social workers told me about another service, an advocacy service they said I should use if there's ever a problem social services can't help me with. So I wanted to see the court papers and the rest of my files but my social worker didn't think that was a good idea, at least for now. But I think it is, because everybody has told me a different story and I know everyone has a different view on the situation, I just want to know the true view, to see the hard copy on paper. Now my social worker is going to go through everything with me, and help me go through my whole life, what's happened, where I've been living, so that I'll have like a book for when I leave care, like a book full of memories.

I think social services have got better which means that I can deal with things better. Like right now, I'm thinking about my culture, my religion. I remember my mum wanted me to be a Christian and my dad wanted me to be a Muslim and no-one ever gave me the choice to pick for myself, so I'm thinking about that now. To me each culture has a different belief system. Christians can be quite passionate about their religion and Muslims are very strict, like you know, woman is the cleaner and man is the worker. I think that's wrong so right now I'm thinking about being Christian and now that I'm older, I'm seen as a young adult, I think social workers pay closer attention to my views and recently my social worker remembered what job I want in later life and that was good because it made me feel like he actually knew stuff about me. And another time I was helping another kid because sometimes social workers don't know what to do and I could see this kid was desperate. She wanted to believe her parents but at the same time she wanted to know what was right and when I was younger I was stuck in the same mind frame. So I told my social worker it's best if I talk to her and he said that was very mature of me, even though I know he didn't want to admit it! But I think it's good for older kids to talk to younger kids so they can hear stuff from someone who has been through it too. Yes, I think there should be more of that because social workers can't know all that stuff but for kids who are still trapped in a certain mind frame, their parents can still manipulate them into believing certain things. So if they talk to another kid who's been through that, it's more helpful to get them out of that trap.

"They always say they listen to you but they don't"

Saba's story

I was in and out of care since I was born. I would live with my mum for a bit then, when she couldn't look after me, I'd go into care for a while. Then one day, when I was still really young I remember being taken to a foster family and that's when I realised I wouldn't be going back to my mum. And I remember being so scared. I was just standing on the doorstep of this foster home but nobody explained or talked to me. Even though I was so young, I think I would have understood if someone had just talked to me.

Then I was moved to a new school. I was such a quiet child. I was like a retard, just didn't know what was going on with my life, you know. I don't remember much about the foster family but one day a social worker came and asked me where I wanted to live, with my mum, my dad or the foster family. I didn't really know my dad then. They said I'd had some contact with him but I couldn't really remember so I put my mum first and my dad last, with the foster family in the middle. A little while after that I was in school one day and I looked out of the window. I saw a man and a woman. I didn't know it at the time but it was my dad and step-mum. They said that my step-mum was going to adopt me and that I would live with her and my father and their other child who was a few years older than me. When I first went there it was all fun and games, you know. It was like a new family and they treated me like their daughter. Social workers came to the house a lot, at least until the adoption was finalised. Then everything changed and they started to abuse me, and I had no end of household chores to do. One day two social workers came to the house and they talked to me and said I had made allegations at school. I don't actually remember making any allegations but, anyway, I denied it. My parents were in the house, just next door and I got so scared. So the social workers went away again, telling me it was wrong to lie and I wasn't to do it again.

After that, my dad took me out of school and when someone called round about this, they said I was being home-schooled. Nobody asked any more questions. The abuse got worse and it went on for years. I never left the house but when I was a bit older I found a telephone directory and I called Children's Services myself. I told them what was happening to me. I had to speak very quietly as my dad and step-mum were in the house. Shortly after that two women came to the door. I don't think they were social workers.

I think they were police or something because my father didn't want to let them in but they said they had a right so he had to let them into the house. They came and found me and took me out of the house to their car. We sat in the car and I remember telling them everything. They said I would not be going back home. One of them then went and spoke to my dad, then the three of us drove off in the car. They took me to an office where I had an interview, I think it was with the police and, after that, a medical check. So then a social worker talked to me and said they would find a foster mum and get me back into school. I liked going back to school but I hated my first foster mum. She was so old and so grumpy! And I kept telling my social worker but she just said it was OK, the foster carer had no problems with me – as if she was the only one who mattered, not me. Then the foster carer didn't want me any more so that's when my social worker started to look around for someone else. I was introduced to a new family where there were other children in the house. We met a couple of times. Then I was placed with them. I'm still there but it's not working out. Although we have the same background I don't really know anything about it, you know, the food, the religion and stuff because I'd never been included in any of that in my dad's house. And I don't get on with my new foster carer's children. They pick on me all the time and accuse me of everything, like using their shampoo and stuff. And again, I've been telling my social worker but she's still not saying we'll look for another placement. They always say they listen to you but they don't. I mean there are some good social workers and they do their job properly but I think, because I'm one of the good kids, I don't run away or cause so many problems, so they just put me to one side. They don't listen to what I have to say. But then other times they do, like when I said I didn't want to take my dad to court. It was too soon for me then and I think maybe if they'd put it a bit differently, I might have been able to do it; because they told me then that they couldn't really do anything because my dad and step mum had denied everything so, obviously, I thought well that's that. So now my social worker is telling me that my carer thinks everything is ok with the placement, so there's no need to move me again. But it's not ok for me. I mean I've been with them for nearly two years now and I don't even have a key to the house! But they just write their reports and they all twist my words.

"Talking about race makes me uncomfortable but I don't tell my social worker"

Sherina's story

I came into long term foster care when I was three years old. I think I'd been in and out of care before that but I don't really remember much; and I don't really remember much of the first few years I was with the foster family. I'm still with them now. At first I got quite a lot of extra help at school, like extra maths and English tuition. I did that for about a year but then I stopped it because I didn't really need it. And I also stopped going to the regular meetings they used to have at the school to review my progress. My social worker still went and she would pass on anything I had to say and tell me about what went on in the meetings. But now I don't have a social worker any more. I have a personal advisor because I'm in transition. That means I'll be leaving care soon but I don't really know my personal advisor yet. I've only just met her.

With my last social worker, I had a bit more contact. I used to email her if I needed to discuss something and that was quite helpful. My social worker before that was quite good too because I felt comfortable talking to her but because their time is so short, I didn't really feel like I needed to talk to them. My foster mum is ok too although I think she's a bit strict but I still have contact with my mum, I think I see her maybe four times a year. And my foster mum is quite sensitive about racial stuff. She's always asking me, so do you think you're black or white. And I always tell her I don't care about that but she's always going on about race and stuff. It makes me uncomfortable but I don't tell my social worker as that would just make more problems for me at home. If my foster mum thought I would rather talk to my social worker it wouldn't be good because she doesn't like to think of the social worker having more power than her, because it's her house sort of thing. And I think it's hard for social workers to find these things out, especially when they rarely visit.

I know too that my foster mum has had her ups and downs and at some point social services were thinking of moving me to another placement. They explained everything although they didn't really consult with me and give me a choice. In the end I stayed where I was and I was happy with that.

So now I've been learning about budgeting and accommodation because if I get good enough grades I will be going to university and I'll be living semi-independently. It's a bit scary because I've never lived on my own but if I get to university I'll feel a bit better. I'll be with other people. And I've applied to a university close to where I live now so there could be an option to stay with my foster carer but I think I might quite like to try and live semi-independently. I can always go back and stay with her in the holidays. And I might be able to go and stay with my mum more.

Child physical abuse & neglect

Stories and experiences of young people with intervention

Germany

Ich bin in einer großen süddeutschen Stadt geboren worden, mein Vater kommt aus dem Irak und meine Mutter ist Deutsche. Als ich klein war, hat meine Mutter mich und meinen Bruder oft irgendwo vergessen, in Kneipen und so, und wir wurden dann immer ins Kinderheim gebracht und da später von meiner Mutter wieder abgeholt. Irgendwann, ich war damals fast drei Jahre alt, hat das Jugendamt dann aber zu meiner Mutter gesagt, dass es jetzt reicht und dann haben sie uns nicht wieder zurückgegeben. Wir sind dann stattdessen erst in ein Kinderheim und dann in diese Pflegefamilie gekommen. Wir waren erst zur Probe mal übers Wochenende hier und sind dann ganz hierher gezogen. Ich bin froh, dass ich in dieser Familie lebe, weil sie für mich eher wie meine richtigen Eltern sind und wenn ich bei meiner Mutter geblieben wäre, wüsste ich nicht, was dann mit mir passiert wäre und wie es mir heute gehen würde.

Ich habe eine Vormundin, die mich regelmäßig hier in der Pflegefamilie besucht. Ich kann ihr alles erzählen. Wenn ich irgendwas über meine Eltern erfahre, kann ich ihr das sagen oder sie fragen, ohne dass sie es irgendwem weitererzählt. Und sie hört mir zu und hilft mir auch, wenn irgendwas ist. Manchmal finde ich es aber auch ein bisschen nervig, dass ich mich immer mit ihr treffen muss. Sie fragt mich aber auch, zu was für Sachen ich Lust habe, und dann unternehmen wir manchmal was zusammen, fahren in einen Freizeitpark oder backen Kuchen oder so. Sie versucht auch nie mir etwas auszureden, wenn ich was will. Sie sagt dann zwar, ob sie das gut oder schlecht findet und dass ich mir etwas zum Beispiel noch mal gut überlegen soll. Aber wenn ich was wirklich will, unterstützt sie mich auch dabei.

Mein allergrößter Wunsch ist, dass ich meine Mutter wiedersehen kann, die habe ich seit sieben Jahren nicht gesehen und sie ist ja meine leibliche Mama. Erst hatten wir regelmäßig Kontakt, aber dann hat sie sich nicht mehr gemeldet und jetzt ist meine Mutter auch im Gefängnis. Da wäre zwar möglich, dass ich sie sehe, aber dazu müsste sie mir halt erst mal Briefe schreiben und wir müssten mal telefonieren und das klappt halt nicht. Meine Vormundin unterstützt mich auch bei diesem Wunsch, sie sagt aber, wir müssen jetzt halt hoffen, dass meine Mutter das wirklich will und sich darum auch bemüht.

I grew up in a big town in South Germany, my dad is from the Irak and my mother is German. When I was little, my mother often forgot me and my little brother somewhere, in bars and stuff. We were usually brought to a children's home, then my mother picked us up there later.

One day, when I was three years old, the people from the Youth Welfare Office said to my mother that it was enough and then they didn't give us back to her. First they took us to a children's home and then we came to this foster family. First we came here for a weekend test only but then we moved here completely. I am glad to live in this family because they are more like real family and if I had stayed with my mother I wouldn't know what would have happened to me then and how I would be today.

I have a guardian and she visits me here in my foster home regularly. I can tell her everything. When I get to know anything about my family, I can tell her or ask her about it, without her telling anybody else. And she listens to me and helps me if I need anything. Sometimes I think it's a little bit annoying that I have to meet her so often. But she does ask me what I would like to do and then we do something together sometimes, go to a leisure park or bake a cake together. And she never tries to talk me out of something, when I want something. She says what she thinks, if it's good or bad, or if I should think it over again. But when I really want something she supports me.

My greatest wish is to see my mother again. I haven't seen her since I was seven, and, I mean, she is my biological mother. First, we were regularly in contact but then she didn't get in touch with me any more and now my mother is in prison. There it would be possible that I see her but then she would have to write me letters first and we would have to talk on the telephone and that's just not working. My guardian supports me with this wish as well. But she says we need to hope that my mother really wants it, too, and that she really makes efforts to realize it.

Jans Geschichte

Ich bin jetzt 17 und bin mit meiner Mutter und meinen Geschwistern aus Ungarn nach Deutschland gekommen, als ich zwei Jahre alt war. Mein Vater ist in Ungarn geblieben und ich habe zu ihm keinen Kontakt. Hier in Deutschland haben meine Mutter und mein Stiefvater mich oft geschlagen, einmal hatte ich ein geschwollenes Auge, weil mein Stiefvater mir einen Kochlöffel ins Gesicht gehauen hat. Ich musste dann in der Schule sagen, dass ich wogegen gelaufen bin. Meine Lehrerin hat schon gemerkt, dass ich Probleme hatte, öfter blaue Flecken, vor allem aber aggressiv war. Ich selber wollte mit niemandem reden, weil ich Angst hatte, dass es dann zuhause noch mehr Ärger gibt. Meine Lehrerin hat dann meine Mutter angesprochen. Um gut dazustehen, hat meine Mutter mich dann zum Psychologen geschickt, aber weil sie gleichzeitig Angst hatte, dass ich da was verrate, war es in dieser Zeit zu Hause noch schlimmer als vorher. Nur vorm Psychologen hat sie mich in den Arm genommen und einen auf Supermutter gemacht. Bei dem Psychologen fand ich es ganz gut, mit ihm konnte ich einfach reden und er hat mir auch versprochen, niemand etwas weiterzusagen. Nach 12 Sitzungen hatte ich dann keine Lust mehr und dachte, ich schaff das auch alleine.

Mein Stiefvater war zu dieser Zeit schon im Gefängnis, wegen dieser Gewalt und Misshandlungen und auch Missbrauch an meinen Geschwistern. Ich musste in dem Verfahren nicht gegen ihn aussagen, ich glaube, die wollten mir das ersparen. Aber sie hätten mich ruhig fragen können, ich hätte ihn noch länger in den Knast gebracht.

Später hatten wir dann für ein Jahr lang einen Familienhelfer, den hatte uns das Jugendamt geschickt, ich glaube, weil ich oder meine Schwester öfter nachts von zuhause abgehauen sind und dann von der Polizei aufgegriffen wurden. Ich selbst habe nie mit jemandem vom Jugendamt gesprochen, aber die haben uns eben diesen Familienhelfer geschickt. Mit dem Familienhelfer konnte ich auch gut reden und er ist mit mir auch mal was essen gegangen oder er hat mir was beim Bäcker gekauft, weil es bei uns zuhause eigentlich nie was Richtiges gab. Ich mochte den echt gerne, konnte ihm alles erzählen, er war ein bisschen wie ein Vater für mich.

I am 17 now, and I came with my mother and brothers and sisters from Hungary to Germany when I was two years old. My father stayed in Hungary and I'm not in contact with him. Here in Germany my mother and my stepfather were hitting me a lot, one time I had a swollen eye because my stepfather had hit me in the face with a big spoon. I had to tell everybody in school that I had bumped into something. My teacher did notice that I had problems because I often had bruises but especially because I was aggressive in school. But I didn't want to talk to someone because I was afraid that I would be in even more trouble at home. My teacher talked to my mother then and, to look good, my mother sent me to a psychologist. But because she was at the same time afraid I might tell something it was even worse at home during that time. Only when the psychologist was watching she took me into her arms and faked the super-mom. I pretty much liked going to the psychologist, I could just talk to him and he promised to keep everything secret. But when I had been there 12 times I had enough and I thought I could manage it alone from then on.

At that time my stepfather was already in prison because of that violence and maltreatment and also abuse of my sisters and brothers. In the court proceedings I didn't have to give testimony, I believe they wanted to spare me that. But they could have asked my opinion, I would have sent him to prison even longer.

Later we had a family helper for a year who was sent by the Youth Welfare Office, I believe because my sister and I had often run away from home at night and had to be brought back by the police. I myself have never talked to someone at the Youth Welfare Office, but they just sent us this family helper. With him I could talk well and sometimes he even went out to eat somewhere with me or bought me something at the bakery because we never had proper food at home. I really liked him, I could tell him everything and he was a bit like a father to me. My mother was strictly opposed to the support right from the start and afterwards she said they had destroyed her family. But in reality it was my mother herself who destroyed it. The family helper also helped me to get away from my mother and come to live in this institution. He told me again and again that I should rather go to a children's home, but at first I didn't want to, mostly because of my little sister whom I didn't want to leave with my mother.

Meine Mutter war von Anfang an strikt gegen die Familienhilfe und nachher hat sie gesagt, die hätten unsere Familie kaputt gemacht. Aber tatsächlich hat meine Mutter sie kaputt gemacht. Der Familienhelfer hat mir dann auch geholfen, von zuhause weg- und hier in die Einrichtung zu kommen. Er hat immer wieder gesagt, ich soll doch lieber ins Heim gehen, aber ich wollte erst nicht, vor allem wegen meiner kleinen Schwester, die ich nicht bei meiner Mutter lassen wollte. Aber irgendwann, als ich 14 Jahre alt war, hab ich gedacht, es hat ja keinen Zweck mehr und bin dann halt hierher in die Einrichtung gezogen, die der Familienhelfer mir vermittelt hat.

Und seit ich im Heim bin, hat sich vieles für mich verändert. Die haben mich hier ganz herzlich empfangen und sind jetzt quasi meine neue Familie. Ich kann mit jedem reden und hier wird jeder respektiert, egal wie der aussieht. Natürlich gibt es manchmal Streit wegen unnötigem Scheiß. Aber sonst eigentlich ganz friedlich. Und vor allem stehen die wirklich zu mir.

Ich hatte dann eine Freundin, die war der erste Mensch in meinem Leben, den ich geliebt habe. Als mit der Schluss war, war es zu viel für mich, da wollte ich dann gar nicht mehr leben und hatte suizidale Gedanken und habe mich geritzt und viel geweint. Da war ich auch ein paar Tage in der Psychiatrie. Da hat mich mein Erzieher hin geschleift, ich wollte gar nicht, aber er hat gesagt, wenn ich da jetzt nicht hingehe, dann kann ich meine Sachen packen und mir ein anderes Heim suchen und da bin ich dann halt gegangen. Und da habe ich wieder gemerkt, dass die aus der Einrichtung wirklich zu mir stehen, denn sie haben mich jeden Tag besucht, weil sie nicht wollten, dass ich mehrere Tage alleine bleibe. Aber nach ein paar Tagen habe ich gemerkt, dass ich was anderes brauche, als die Medikamente, die man da bekommt. Man hatte da auch niemand zum Sprechen die haben einfach aufgepasst, dass man sich nichts antut. Und da habe ich einen Erzieher aus meiner Einrichtung gefragt, was ich machen muss um da wieder rauszukommen und er hat gesagt, wenn ich zu einem Psychologen gehe, dann holt er mich da raus. Und seither mache ich eine Therapie und das hilft auch wirklich, denn der Psychologe hat mir gezeigt, dass es auch was anderes gibt und dass man das Leben ernst nehmen muss. Seitdem mache ich ganz viel Sport und ich versuche auch den anderen zu zeigen, dass Sport gut tut. Zum Beispiel ist hier so ein anderer Jugendlicher der ganz viel kifft und ich habe ihn jetzt dazu gebracht, dass er mit mir laufen geht und er seit zwei Wochen schon nicht gekifft hat.

Nachdem ich hierher gezogen war, gab es dann ein Verfahren vor dem Gericht, da ging es um die Vormundschaft, weil meine Mutter nichts unterschreiben wollte, als ich ins Krankenhaus musste mit einem gebrochenen Daumen. Meine Mutter hat mich auch früher nie zum Arzt geschickt, wenn ich was hatte. Sie hat immer nur gesagt, och, das ist nichts Schlimmes, deshalb muss man nicht zum Arzt. Das ist hier ganz anders. Ich muss mich hier nicht schämen, wenn ich ein Problem habe, zum Beispiel zum Arzt muss, weil mir etwas weh tut. Dann fahren die mich sofort dahin.

But at some point I thought, well, there's no point in all this any more and then I just moved to this home which the family helper had found for me.

And since I am in this home a lot has changed for me. They welcomed me warmly and are like my new family now. I can talk with everyone and everyone is respected here no matter how he looks. Of course there are sometimes arguments because of unimportant stuff but apart from that it's actually quite peaceful. And what's most important, they really stand behind me.

I had a girlfriend then and she was the first person I really loved in my life. And when she broke up with me it was all too much for me, I didn't want to live anymore and had suicidal thoughts and cut myself and cried a lot. I came to a psychiatric clinic for a few days then. My carer had dragged me there, first I really didn't want to but he said if I wouldn't go there I could pack my stuff and look for another home and so I rather went to the clinic. And there I realised once again that everybody from the children's home really stood behind me because they visited me every day and didn't want me to be alone even for a few days. But after a few days I realised that I needed something different from the medicine you get there. There was no one to talk to, they only took care that nobody harmed themselves. And so I asked one carer from the children's home what I had to do to get out of there again. And he said if was willing to go a psychologist he would get me out of there. And since then I am in therapy and it really helps me because the psychologist showed me that there is something else and that you have to take your life seriously. I have now been doing a lot of sports and I also try to show others that sport is a good thing. For example there is another boy here who smokes dope a lot and now I have brought him to go jogging with me and now he hasn't smoked weed for two weeks.

After I had moved here there was a court proceeding to establish the guardianship because my mother didn't want to sign the papers when I had to be treated in the hospital with a broken finger. And when I was younger my mother also never sent me to a doctor when I was ill. She always used to say, oh well, that's not so bad, you don't need a doctor for that. And that's really different here. I don't have to be ashamed of any problem I have, like when something hurts and I have to go to the doctor. They drive me there right away.

"Najprej nisem hotel. A na neki točki sem pomislil, da vse to nima več nobenega smisla"

Janova zgodba

Zdaj sem sedemnajst. V Nemčijo sem prišel z Madžarske, in sicer z mamo, brati in sestrami, ko sem imel dve leti. Oče je ostal na Madžarskem in nisva v stikih. Tu v Nemčiji sta me mama in očim veliko pretepala; enkrat sem imel otečeno oko, ker me je očim udaril po obrazu z veliko žlico. Vsem v šoli sem moral reči, da sem se v nekaj zaletel. Učiteljica je opazila, da imam težave, ker sem pogosto imel modrice, a še posebej zato, ker sem bil v šoli agresiven. Nisem pa hotel z nikomer govoriti, ker sem se bal, da bom zato imel doma še več težav. Potem je moja učiteljica govorila z mojo mamo in, da bi dobro izgledalo, me je mama poslala k psihologu. Ker pa se je hkrati bala, da bi lahko kaj povedal, je takrat bilo doma še hujše. Le ko je psiholog gledal, me je objela in se pretvarjala, da je supermama. Rad sem hodil k psihologu, ker sem se lahko pogovarjal z njim, on pa je obljubil, da bo vse ostalo med nama. Po dvanajstem obisku sem imel dovolj, verjel sem, da bom naprej zmogel sam.

Takrat je bil očim že v zaporu zaradi tistega nasilja in trpinčenja in zlorabe sester in bratov. Na sojenju mi ni bilo treba pričati; mislim, da so mi to hoteli prihraniti. A lahko bi me prosili za mnenje, še za dlje bi ga poslal v zapor.

Kasneje smo imeli družinskega pomočnika, ki ga je poslal urad za mladino. Mislim, da zato, ker sva s sestro ponoči pogosto zbežala od doma in naju je morala policija pripeljati nazaj. Sam nisem nikoli govoril z nikomer na uradu za mladino, a so nam enostavno poslali tega družinskega pomočnika. Z njim sem se lahko lepo pogovoril in včasih je celo šel z mano ven kaj pojest ali mi je kupil kaj v pekarni, ker doma nismo nikoli imeli prave hrane. Res mi je bil všeč, vse sem mu lahko povedal, bil mi je malo kot oče. Mama je bila od samega začetka odločno proti podpori in potem je rekla, da so ji uničili družino. A v bistvu jo je uničila mama sama. Družinski pomočnik mi je tudi pomagal, da sem odšel od mame in da sem prišel živet v to ustanovo. Kar naprej je ponavljal, naj grem raje v otroško zavetišče, a najprej nisem hotel iti, predvsem zaradi svoje mlajše sestre, ki je nisem hotel pustiti pri mami. A na neki točki sem pomislil, da vse to nima več nobenega smisla, potem pa sem se enostavno preselil v to zavetišče, ki mi ga je našel družinski pomočnik.

Odkar sem v tem zavetišču, se je zame veliko spremenilo. Toplo so me sprejeli in so zdaj kot moja nova družina. Z vsemi se lahko pogovarjam in vsi tu so spoštovani, ne glede na to, kako izgledajo. Seveda včasih pride do prepirov o nepomembnih stvareh, a razen tega je dejansko precej mirno. In kar je najpomembnejše, zares me podpirajo.

Takrat sem imel punco, ki je bila prva oseba, ki sem jo kdaj ljubil. Ko me je pustila, je bilo to zame preveč, nisem želel več živeti, imel sem samomorilske misli, rezal sem se in veliko jokal. Takrat sem za nekaj dni šel na psihiatrično kliniko. Tja me je zvlekla moja skrbnica; sprva res nisem hotel iti, a je rekla, da če ne grem, lahko spakiram in poiščem drugo zavetišče, tako da sem raje šel na kliniko. In tam sem spet spoznal, da so me vsi iz zavetišča res podpirali, ker so me vsak dan obiskali in niso hoteli, da bi bil sam, četudi le nekaj dni. Po nekaj dneh sem ugotovil, da potrebujem nekaj drugačnega od zdravil, ki jih dobiš tam. Nisem se imel s kom pogovoriti, skrbeli so le za to, da se nihče ni poškodoval. Zato sem enega od skrbnikov iz zavetišča vprašal, kaj moram narediti, da pridem spet ven. Rekel je, da če sem pripravljen hoditi k psihologu, me bo spravil ven. In od takrat hodim na terapijo, ki mi res pomaga, ker mi je psiholog pokazal, da obstaja nekaj drugega in da moraš svoje življenje vzeti resno. Zdaj se veliko ukvarjam s športom in tudi drugim skušam pokazati, da je šport dobra stvar. Na primer, tu je še en fant, ki se veliko zakaja s travo; pripravil sem ga do tega, da hodi z mano džogat, in zdaj že dva tedna ni kadil trave.

Potem ko sem se preselil sem, so sprožili sodni postopek za ugotovitev skrbništva, ker mama ni hotela podpisati papirjev, ko so me v bolnici obravnavali zaradi zlomljenega prsta. Ko sem bil mlajši, me mama nikoli ni poslala k zdravniku, ko sem bil bolan. Vedno je govorila: »Oh, ja, to ni tako hudo, za to ne potrebuješ zdravnika.« In to je tukaj res drugače. Ni se mi treba sramovati kateregakoli problema, ki ga imam, če me, recimo, kaj boli in moram k zdravniku. Takoj me peljejo tja.

"Das beste war, dass ich das erste Mal im Leben wirklich jemanden zum Reden hatte"

Jasmins Geschichte

Ich komme aus Lybien und bin mit meiner Familie nach Norddeutschland geflohen, als ich vier Jahre alt war. Vor drei Jahren, als ich 13 war, begann ich Probleme zu haben, Stress mit meinen Eltern, falsche Freunde und so. Als ich beim Klauen erwischt wurde, sind meine Eltern durchgedreht und haben mich schlimm geschlagen. Ich hatte das Gefühl, meine Eltern würden für mich nicht mehr existieren und lief am nächsten Morgen weg. Ich bat meine Lehrerin, zu der ich ein gutes Verhältnis habe, mir mit meiner Verletzung von den Schlägen zu helfen. Sie fragte mich, wie das passiert sei und ich erzählte es ihr. Sie war sehr schockiert und fragte mich, ob ich Angst hätte, wieder nach Hause zu gehen und ob ich mit ihr zusammen zum Jugendamt gehen wollte. Ich wusste zwar nicht genau, was das Jugendamt ist, aber ich wollte wirklich Hilfe und deshalb war ich einverstanden. Die Frau im Jugendamt war sehr hilfsbereit und besorgte mir einen Platz in einer Einrichtung, aber sie war auch sehr streng und erklärte mir viele Regeln und Verbote. Zum Beispiel durfte ich das Haus nicht ohne Erlaubnis verlassen außer um zur Schule zu gehen. Aber trotzdem hat sie mir sehr geholfen und ich bin sehr froh darüber, weil ich keine Ahnung habe, wo ich sonst heute sein würde. Ich habe dann gehört, dass meine Eltern sehr aggressiv geworden sind, als ihnen gesagt wurde, dass ich für eine Weile nicht nach Hause kommen würde. In unserer Kultur ist das ein No-Go, dass ein Mädchen sein Zuhause verlässt, bevor sie 18 oder verheiratet ist.

Im Louise-Hase-Haus kam ich mit den Betreuern gut zurecht. Das Beste war, dass ich das erste Mal wirklich jemanden zum Reden hatte, das gab es bei mir zuhause damals nicht. Sie haben mir wirklich zugehört und ich habe mich wirklich angenommen gefühlt. Nach einer Weile durften meine Eltern mich besuchen kommen und es gab auch Gespräche mit meinen Eltern und dem Jugendamt, in denen meine Eltern auch versprachen, dass so etwas nie wieder passieren würde. Deshalb beschloss ich nach Hause zurückzuziehen. Eine Weile lang ging das gut und wir hatten auch Kontakt zum Jugendamt aber dann bekam ich wieder Probleme mit Drogen und meine Eltern drehten wieder durch und schlugen mich auch wieder. Ich ging dann wieder zu der Frau vom Jugendamt, die mir beim ersten Mal geholfen hatte. Sie war froh, dass ich kam um Hilfe zu suchen, aber sie traf auch wieder alle Entscheidungen für mich,

I come from Libya and my family fled to North-Germany when I was four years old. Three years ago, when I was 13, I started having problems, stress with my parents, wrong friends and so on. When I was caught shoplifting my parents freaked out and punished me by beating me badly. I felt like my parents might as well no longer exist for me and left the next morning though they had forbidden me to leave the house. I went to school and asked my teacher, with whom I had a good relationship, for help with the injuries from being beaten. When she asked me how that had happened I told her and she was shocked and then she asked me if I was afraid of going back home and if I wanted to go to the Youth Welfare Office with her to seek help. I didn't know exactly what the Youth Welfare Office was, or I didn't know they would help young people like me but I really wanted help and so I agreed. And then my teacher went there with me directly and I told everything again. The woman in the Youth Welfare Office offered me a place in a youth institution. At first I was shocked but I didn't know what else to do and so I accepted. The woman in the Youth Welfare Office was very helpful but also very strict and told me that there were many rules and prohibitions, like I was not allowed to leave the house without permission except for going to school. But still she did help me and I am very happy that they helped me because I have no idea where I would be now if they had not. I heard that my parents got very aggressive when they told them that I would not come home for a while because it's a no-go in our culture, a girl leaving her home before she's 18 or married.

In the Louise-Rabbit-Home I got along very well with the carers, we played together and talked together. The best was that I had someone to talk to for the first time in my life and they were really listening to me and I felt really appreciated. After a while my parents were allowed to visit and there were conversations with my parents and the Youth Welfare Office and my parents promised that nothing like before would happen again. So I decided that I wanted to go back to them. For a while that went well and there were also contacts with the Youth Welfare office but then I got problems again with drugs and my parents freaked out and hurt me again. I went to the woman from the Youth Welfare Office again who was happy that I came to seek help but she also made all the decisions for me again, like she was the boss, and sent me back to the Louise-Rabbit-Home.

als wäre sie der Chef, und schickte mich zurück ins Louise-Hase-Haus.

Es gefiel mir wieder dort zu sein, obwohl ich in der ersten Woche das Haus nicht verlassen durfte. Aber sie kümmerten sich wirklich um mich und beschützten mich, wenn ich Angst vor meinen Eltern hatte. Bei einem Treffen mit meinen Eltern fragte mich die Frau vom Jugendamt, ob ich wieder zu meinen Eltern zurückgehen wollte. Ich war total überrascht, dass sie mir so eine Frage in Anwesenheit meiner Eltern stellten, aber ich antwortete dann trotzdem "Nein", obwohl meine Eltern mich deshalb die ganze Zeit beschimpften. Es wurde dann entschieden, dass ich in einer anderen Einrichtung wohnen sollte, weil das Louise-Hase-Haus nur für vorübergehende Aufenthalte ist. Am Anfang war ich unzufrieden, weil ich nicht woanders hingegeben werden wollte sondern da bleiben wollte, wo ich mich sicher und wohl fühlte. Aber es gab ein paar wirklich coole Betreuer, die jugendlicher und nicht so moralisch waren und dann begann ich, ihnen wieder zu vertrauen.

Eines Tages bekam ich einen Anruf von einem Familienrichter. Ich war total erschrocken und er erzählte mir am Telefon, dass er meinen Eltern das Sorgerecht entzogen hatte. Ich hatte dann totale Angst wegen meiner Brüder und Schwestern, weil ich nicht wollte, dass ihnen etwas Ähnliches passiert. Und ich war auch etwas traurig, weil er mir erzählte, dass meine Eltern voll locker damit umgegangen sind. Als Kind wünscht man sich eigentlich, dass die Eltern um einen kämpfen und sagen: „Nein, das ist unser Kind, das wird unser Kind bleiben und wir wollen nicht, dass es von irgendjemand weggenommen wird." Später erfuhr ich dann auch, dass ich einen Vormund hatte. Ich finde, jemand hätte mich vorher darauf und auf den Anruf vom Richter vorbereiten können, weil die Betreuer das ja schon wussten. Das hätte mir sehr geholfen, aber sie haben das nicht gemacht.

Es ging dann wieder los, dass ich Probleme hatte und ich begann wieder Drogen zu nehmen. Manchmal bin ich auch für eine Nacht oder ein paar Tage abgehauen. Eines Tages kamen mein Vormund und die Frau vom Jugendamt und brachten mich in so eine Art Krankenhaus ohne mir das vorher zu sagen. Ich musste da dann ein paar Wochen bleiben. Zuerst wollte ich gar nicht und hasste es da und war sauer. Aber im Nachhinein finde ich es super, weil ich weiß, dass sie nur um mich besorgt waren und mich beschützen wollten. Und wenn sie mich nicht dahin geschickt hätten, dann wäre ich jetzt wahrscheinlich auf der Straße, mit falschen Freunden oder so.

Aber was für mich wirklich negativ war, war, dass ich da in der Klinik so einen Test machen musste und sie mir nachher sagten, ich sei nicht intelligent genug. Die haben mich da voll doof dargestellt, quasi als wäre ich behindert. Und mein Vormund sagte dann, ich werde keine Ausbildungsstelle finden, und es wäre doch besser, ich ginge in eine andere Einrichtung, in der ich etwas lernen könnte wie in der Küche zu arbeiten. Und im Jobcenter sagten sie mir dann das Gleiche und mein Vormund, der mit dabei war, unterstützte mich überhaupt nicht. Ich habe mich dann alleine auf die Suche nach einem Ausbildungsplatz gemacht und habe auch ganz allein einen gefunden. Ich bin darüber sehr froh und stolz, denn ich kann jetzt das lernen, was ich immer wollte.

I liked being there again even though they didn't let me go out for the first week, not even together with one of the carers. But they were really caring for me and protecting me when I was afraid of my parents. Then there was a meeting with my parents and the Youth Welfare Office and the woman from the Youth Welfare office asked me if I wanted to go back to my parents. And I was surprised that they would be asking such a question when my parents were there, but I still said no even though my parents scolded me the whole time because I said that. Then it was decided that I should go to another, permanent home for a longer time, because the Louise-Rabbit-Home wasn't meant for a longer stay. At first, I didn't like that decision, I didn't want to be put somewhere else again but wanted to stay in the Louise Rabbit-Home where I felt safe and comfortable and I didn't want to get to know all the new people in the new home. And I wasn't allowed to go out during the first time again. But there were some carers who were really cool, talking like us young people and not being so moral and then I started trusting them again.

Then one day a family judge called me and I was shocked and he said he had withdrawn custody from my parents. Then I was very afraid for my sisters and brothers because I didn't want something similar to happen to them. And I also was a little sad, because they told me my parents had taken the decision easily. I mean, as a child you wish that your parents do not agree with such a decision but fight for their child and say: "That is our child and will stay our child and we don't want someone to take it away from us". Later I was informed that I had a guardian now. I think the carers from the home should have prepared me for that call, because they already knew about it. They could have said: "Hey someone might be calling you because of parental custody". That would have been helpful for me. But they didn't tell me.

I then started having problems again, my parents made trouble and I started taking drugs again and sometimes I ran away for a night or for a few days. And one day my guardian and the woman from the Youth Welfare Office came and told me to pack my stuff and then they brought me to a kind of hospital without telling me before. There I had to stay for a few weeks. At first, I didn't want that and hated it and was angry that they didn't ask me about it but just brought me there. But when I thought about it afterwards and think about it now I find it was great because I know they were just caring about me and wanted to protect me and if they had not sent me there I'd probably live on the streets with the wrong friends now.

But what was really negative was that they gave me some kind of test and told me I was not intelligent enough, as if I was really stupid or somehow retarded. Then my guardian said it wouldn't work for me to find a training position in the job I hoped for, but I should go to another institution where I could learn something like working in a kitchen. And in the Job Centre they were saying the same and my guardian wasn't supporting me and my wishes in any way. But then I searched for a training position on my own and found one all by myself without any help of the carers or my guardian. I'm really glad, because now I can do what I always wanted to do.

Meine Mutter, eine Sinti, musste mich und meine Schwester weggeben, als wir neun Monate alt waren, weil es ihr nicht gut ging. Wir kamen dann in eine Pflegefamilie in Berlin, in der es uns aber gar nicht gut ging. Es war ein totaler Messy-Haushalt und es gab auch häufig Übergriffe, vor allem durch unsere älteren Pflegebrüder. Einmal im Jahr kam zwar jemand vom Jugendamt zur Kontrolle, aber vorher wurde immer aufgeräumt und wir saßen dann immer nur alle zusammen, mit der ganzen Familie am Tisch in der Küche und es wurde ein bisschen geredet.

Erst viel später hatten wir auch wieder Kontakt zu unserer richtigen Mutter und als wir 13 Jahre alt waren, sind wir zu ihr abgehauen. Sie hatte wegen ihrer anderen Kinder so einen Familienhelfer aus einer Beratungsstelle für Sinti und Roma, Herrn K. und der hat uns dann geholfen und beim Jugendamt bewirkt, dass wir nicht zurück zur Pflegefamilie mussten und denen auch die Pflegeerlaubnis, glaube ich, entzogen wurde. Mit meiner richtigen Mutter und unseren Brüdern gab es aber schnell Streitereien, weil wir plötzlich deren Kultur leben sollten und ich nicht so über mich bestimmen lassen wollte. Ich bin dann manchmal in eine Jugendschutzstelle abgehauen, nach einer Weile aber immer zurück zu meiner Mutter gegangen.

Einmal war ich auch drei Wochen lang in einer psychiatrischen Klinik, weil ich mich immer geritzt habe. Da war es ganz furchtbar für mich, so eingesperrt. Herr K. hat mir dann wieder geholfen, dass ich raus und zurück zu meiner Mutter durfte. Da habe ich dann einen Jungen kennengelernt, mit dem ich dann zusammen war. Weil er ein Freund meines Bruders war, war diese Beziehung in unserer Familie tabu, und es gab dann wieder häufig schlimme Streitereien, bei denen meine Mutter und meine Brüder mich auch geschlagen haben. Ich bin dann wieder in die Schutzstelle gegangen, von da aber oft zu meinem Freund abgehauen, weil ich mich sowieso schon so alleine gefühlt habe. In der Schutzstelle waren die zwar nett, aber ich hatte niemanden, dem ich vertraut hab und mit dem ich richtig reden konnte. Wenn ich abgehauen bin, hat mich immer die Polizei gesucht und wieder aufgegriffen und zurück in die Schutzstelle gebracht. Als ich 16 war, haben sie mich wegen meiner Ausrisse in so ein geschlossenes Kinderheim gesteckt, wo es für mich ganz furchtbar war. Einmal war ich sogar ein paar Tage in einen kleinen Raum eingesperrt, wo ich nur einen Eimer zum Reinmachen hatte.

*My mother, a Sinti, had to give me and my sister away when we were nine months old
because she wasn't feeling well. We came to a foster family in Berlin then but we were
doing badly there. It was totally messy and there was often violence, especially from
our older foster brothers. Once a year someone from the youth welfare office did come
visit our foster family, but then they tidied up everything beforehand and then we just
all sat together around the table and talked a bit.*

*It was only much later that my sister and I got in contact with our real mother again,
and when we were 13 years old, we ran away from our foster family to our mother.
Because of her other children she had a family helper from an advice centre for Sinti
and Roma, Mr. K. He helped us and talked to the Youth Welfare Office so we didn't
have to go back to our foster parents and, I believe, their care-permission was also
withdrawn then. But after living together with our mother and our brothers for a while
we started having fights because I was supposed to live in their culture from one day
to another and I didn't want to let them tell me what to do. Sometimes I ran away to a
Youth Protection Centre but after a while I always went back to my mother.*

*One time I had to stay in a psychiatric clinic for three weeks because I had been cutting
myself. It was terrible for me in there, being so locked up. Mr. K. helped me again then
to get out and back to my mother. Then I got to know a boy and we became a couple.
But our relationship was a taboo in our family because he was a friend of my brother.
We started fighting badly again and my mother and brothers were also beating me. I
went to the protection centre again then but ran away to my boyfriend often because
I was feeling so alone anyway. The people in the protection centre were nice but there
was nobody I could trust or really talk to. When I ran away the police used to look
for me and then they picked me up and brought me back to the protection centre.
Because of me running away they put me in a closed children's home when I was 16
years old. It was terrible there. Once they even locked me up in a little room and I only
had a bucket to pee into. I really cannot cope with being locked up. I always need to be
outdoors a lot. Finally I managed to run away and then I hid at my boyfriend's place in
the cellar.*

*I got pregnant then from my boyfriend and when I was 18 I gave birth to my little son.
During that time a man from the Youth Welfare Office supported me, for example
when I had to apply for clothing allowance for my son or something.*

Ich kann das gar nicht ertragen, wenn ich eingesperrt bin, ich muss immer viel raus in die Natur. Endlich ist es mir gelungen von da abzuhauen und ich habe mich dann bei meinem Freund im Keller versteckt.

Von meinem Freund bin ich dann schwanger geworden und als ich 18 war, habe ich meinen kleinen Sohn bekommen. In dieser Zeit hat mich ein Herr vom Jugendamt unterstützt, z.B. wenn ich Anträge stellen musste für Kleidung für den Kleinen oder so. Ein paar Monate nach der Geburt habe ich mich aber von meinem Freund getrennt, weil es da auch viele Probleme mit Alkohol und so gab, und bin erst mal wieder zu meiner Mutter. Aber weil es da bald wieder viel Streit mit ihr und meinen Brüdern und Aggressionen und Gewalt gab, habe ich wieder Hilfe gesucht. Herr K. hat mir dann wieder geholfen und ich habe dann bei der Bahnhofsmission gebeten, dass sie mir ein Frauenhaus sagen, in das ich gehen kann. Sie waren auch hilfsbereit und haben rumtelefoniert, aber es war nirgends ein Platz frei. Deshalb musste ich erst mal wieder nach Hause, habe dann aber noch bei der Frauennothilfe angerufen und die haben dann auch noch mal rumtelefoniert und dann für mich diesen Platz hier in L. gefunden. Hier geht's uns ganz gut, ich kann eigentlich machen, was ich will, und ich bin unglaublich froh, endlich meine Ruhe zu haben. Ich kann hier halt nur begrenzt bleiben und muss meine eigene Wohnung finden. Ich habe immer noch Kontakt zu Herrn K., der mich die ganze Zeit über bei allem unterstützt hat. Ich möchte jetzt auch gerne eine Therapie machen um das alles zu verarbeiten. So was kann ich mit Herrn K. auch alles planen und wie es sonst so weitergeht, mit vielleicht einer Ausbildung und so.

A few months after the birth I broke up with my boyfriend because there were a lot of problems with alcohol and so on, and I moved back to my mother then. But soon the fighting started again and there was aggression and violence as well, so I looked for help again. Mr. K. was the one who helped me again and I asked the drop-in centre at the train station if they could find me a woman's shelter where I could go. They were very helpful, ringing around a lot but there were no vacancies. So I had to go home again but I called the women's help line then and they rang around again and then they found this place for me here in L. Here we are doing quite well, actually I can do what I want and I am unbelievably glad to be left alone at last. I mean I can't stay for an unlimited time and have to find my own apartment. I am still in contact with Mr. K. who has supported me all the time. I want to start therapy now to cope with everything that has happened. Things like that I can plan with Mr. K. and how everything is going to move on, perhaps with a traineeship or something.

"Tam mi je bilo grozno, ker sem bila tako zaprta"

Jelenina zgodba

Moja mama, ki je pripadnica skupnosti Sintov, naju je s sestro pri devetih mesecih morala dati v rejo, ker se ni počutila dobro. Prišli sva k rejniški družini v Berlin, a sva se tam počutili slabo. Bilo je svinjsko in pogosto sva bili podvrženi nasilju, še posebej nasilju najinih starejših rejniških bratov. Enkrat na leto je nekdo z urada za mladino obiskal najino rejniško družino, a so takrat vse vnaprej pospravili, potem pa smo vsi skupaj samo sedeli pri mizi in se malo pogovarjali.

Šele veliko kasneje sva s sestro spet vzpostavili stik z najino pravo mamo in pri trinajstih letih sva zbežali od najine rejniške družine k mami. Zaradi njenih ostalih otrok je imela družinskega pomočnika s svetovalnega centra za Sinte in Rome, gospoda K. Pomagal nam je in se pogovoril z uradom za mladino, tako da se nama ni bilo treba vrniti k najinim rejniškim staršem in mislim, da so jima tudi odvzeli rejniško dovoljenje. A ko sva nekaj časa živeli z mamo in brati, smo se začeli prepirati, ker naj bi kar naenkrat živela v njihovi kulturi in nisem hotela, da mi ukazujejo, kaj moram. Včasih sem pobegnila v center za zaščito mladine, a sem se po določenem času vedno vrnila k mami.

Enkrat sem morala iti v psihiatrično kliniko za tri tedne, ker sem se rezala. Grozno mi je bilo tam notri, ker sem bila tako zaprta. Gospod K. mi je spet pomagal, da sem prišla ven in se vrnila k mami. Potem sem spoznala fanta in postala sva par. Toda najino razmerje je bilo tabu v naši družini, ker je bil bratov prijatelj. Spet smo se začeli hudo prepirati, mama in bratje pa so me tudi pretepali. Spet sem šla v center za zaščito, a sem pogosto zbežala k fantu, ker sem se itak počutila tako samo. Ljudje v centru za zaščito so bili prijazni, a ni bilo nikogar, ki bi mu lahko zaupala ali zares govorila z njim. Ko sem pobegnila, me je policija iskala, potem so me prijeli in pripeljali nazaj v center za zaščito. Ker sem bežala, so me pri šestnajstih letih dali v zaprto otroško zavetišče. Grozno je bilo. Enkrat so me celo zaklenili v majhno sobico in sem lahko lulala le v vedro. Ne prenesem tega, da sem zaprta. Moram biti zunaj na deželi. Na koncu mi je uspelo pobegniti in sem se skrila v fantovi kleti.

Zanosila sem s svojim fantom in pri osemnajstih rodila sinčka. V tistem času mi je podporo nudil nek moški z urada za mladino; ko sem se morala prijaviti za dodatek za obleke za sina, na primer, ali kaj podobnega. Nekaj mesecev po porodu sem se razšla s fantom, ker so bile težave z alkoholom in sem se preselila nazaj k mami.

A so se prepiri kmalu spet začeli, pa tudi agresivnost in nasilje, zato sem spet poiskala pomoč. Spet je bil gospod K. tisti, ki mi je pomagal, svetovalni center pa sem prosila, da mi pove za žensko zavetišče, kamor bi lahko šla. Bili so zelo uslužni, veliko so klicali naokoli, a ni bilo prostih mest. Zato sem se morala vrniti domov, a sem takrat poklicala linijo za pomoč ženskam, tako da so oni potem spet klicali naokoli in so mi našli tole mesto tu v L. Tukaj nama gre kar dobro, dejansko lahko počnem, kar hočem in sem neverjetno zadovoljna, da imam končno mir. Mislim, ne morem ostati neomejeno časa, moram si poiskati lastno stanovanje. Še vedno sem v stiku z gospodom K., ki me je ves čas podpiral. Zdaj bi rada začela s terapijo, da se spopadem z vsem, kar se je zgodilo. Take stvari lahko načrtujem z gospodom K. in kako se bo vse premaknilo naprej, mogoče z vajeništvom ali kaj takega.

Marcos Geschichte

Als ich zwei Jahre alt war, haben meine Eltern sich getrennt und ich habe meine Mutter seitdem nicht mehr gesehen. Mein Vater verließ Kenia und ließ mich zunächst bei meiner Großmutter. Aber als ich acht Jahre alt war, holte er mich und meinen Bruder zu sich nach Deutschland. Hier lebten wir in einer kleinen Stadt in Norddeutschland, wo ich erst Klassen besuchen musste zum Deutsch lernen und dann in die richtige Schule kam. In der Schule wurde ich oft wegen meiner Hautfarbe geärgert. Ich wusste nicht, was ich tun sollte und manchmal weinte ich sogar, aber auch die Lehrer merkten das nicht oder unternahmen zumindest nichts dagegen. Ich wurde dann aggressiv und prügelte mich oft mit Kindern, die mich angriffen. Die Schule schickte mich deshalb zu einem Anti-Aggressions-Training. Für mich war das ok, dass ich da mitmachen musste, vor allem weil ich da mit jemandem reden und auch Sport machen konnte. Aber dann bekam mein Vater einen Job in einer anderen Stadt und wir zogen um.

Als ich 14 war, bekam ich auch Probleme mit meiner Familie, weil ich meine Stiefmutter nicht mochte, und es gab dann oft Streit mit ihnen. Ich half auch nicht mehr im Haushalt, blieb nur in meinem Zimmer, war meist allein. Eines Tages nahm mein Vater mir mein Bett weg, weil ich nicht aufgeräumt hatte, und von da an musste ich auf dem Fußboden schlafen. Sie schlossen auch die Küche ab und ließen mich nicht mehr mitessen, und dann ließen sie mich auch nicht mehr in die Wohnung, wenn ich nachhause kam (ich hatte ja keinen eigenen Schlüssel). Manchmal bin ich deshalb sogar zur Polizei gegangen aber die haben mich gar nicht ernst genommen und mir überhaupt nicht geholfen. Eines Tages bin ich dann zum Jugendamt gegangen, weil mir ein paar Freunde erzählt hatten, dass man da Hilfe bekäme. Aber das Büro war über die Ferien geschlossen und ich sollte ein paar Wochen später noch mal wieder kommen. Als ich das tat, sagten sie mir, sie würden meinem Vater einen Brief schreiben und ihn zu einem Gespräch einladen. Sie fragten, ob ich bei dem Gespräch dabei sein wollte, was ich ablehnte. Sie hatten nicht viel Zeit und ich hatte nicht das Gefühl, dass sie mir wirklich zuhörten oder mich verstanden. Ich glaube, dass mein Vater dann wirklich zu diesem Treffen ging, aber es passierte jedenfalls nichts weiter.

When I was two years old, my parents broke up and I haven't seen my mother since. My father left Kenya and went to Germany. I stayed behind with my grandmother for a few years but when I was 8, he came for me and my brother to live in Germany with him. Here we lived in a small town in North Germany, where I first had to go to classes to learn German and then came to the regular school. There I was often bullied because of my skin colour. I didn't know what to do about it and sometimes even cried but the teachers didn't realize this or didn't do anything about it. I started being aggressive, sometimes fighting with children who were offending me. So they sent me to an Anti-Aggression-Training. It was ok for me to take part, especially because I was able to talk to someone there and do sports. But then we moved to another town because of my father's job.

When I was 14 I started having problems with my family, because I didn't like my stepmother, I started arguing with them often, stopped helping in the household, started staying in my room by myself. One day, when I didn't tidy up my room my father took my bed away, so I had to sleep on the floor afterwards. They also locked the kitchen and didn't let me eat with them and then started not even opening the door of the flat when I came home (I didn't have my own key). Because of that I sometimes even went to the police but they didn't take me seriously and didn't help me in any way. Then I went to the Youth Welfare Office to seek help, because some friends had told me they might help me there. But the office was closed for the holidays and I had to come back a few weeks later. When I went there again, they told me they would write a letter to my father and invite him to a meeting and asked me if I wanted to be part of that meeting, which I refused. They didn't have much time for me and I didn't feel like they were really listening to me or understanding me. I think my father went to the meeting but nothing really happened afterwards.

But then, I think because often I was late in school, a school social worker came to me one day and talked to me and asked if I was feeling alright at home and if I wanted to tell her anything. So I told her of my missing bed and not getting any food and stuff, and that I had already been to the Youth Welfare Office but they had not really helped me.

Aber in der Schule kam dann eines Tages so eine Sozialarbeiterin auf mich zu - ich glaube, weil ich oft zu spät kam - und redete mit mir und fragte, ob ich mich zuhause wohl fühle und ob ich ihr irgendetwas erzählen wolle. Also erzählte ich ihr von meinem nicht vorhandenen Bett und dass ich nichts zu essen bekäme und so und auch, dass ich schon beim Jugendamt gewesen war, die mir aber nicht geholfen hätten. Sie fragte mich dann, ob sie einmal gemeinsam mit mir zum Jugendamt gehen sollte und brachte mich dann auch mit dem Auto dahin. Ich sagte dann aber, dass ich alleine reingehen wolle und deshalb wartete sie draußen auf mich. Und ich sprach dann noch mal mit denen, aber es passierte wieder nichts. Aber dann erzählte mir mein Vater, dass er mit der ganzen Familie nach Leipzig ziehen aber mich nicht mitnehmen wollte. Und er sagte, er hätte die Wohnung schon gekündigt und ich müsse nun selber sehen wo ich bleibe. Ich ging dann zu dieser Schulsozialarbeiterin, die dann mit mir gemeinsam zum Jugendamt ging und mit mir zusammen mit denen sprach. Und das war das erste Mal, dass sie mir wirklich zugehört haben und mich ernst nahmen, als ein Erwachsener mich begleitet hat. Deshalb denke ich, es ist gut, dass es dieses Angebot der Schulsozialarbeit gibt. Denn wenn Du als Kind alleine zum Jugendamt gehst, nehmen sie Dich nicht ernst. Sie nehmen sich nicht genügend Zeit und bieten Dir auch nicht an, wirklich zu helfen. Sie hören Dir nur zu, wenn ein Erwachsener Dich begleitet.

Aber an dem Tag, an dem ich mit der Schulsozialarbeiterin da war, gaben sie mir sofort einen Platz in der Einrichtung, in der ich jetzt lebe. Hier fühle ich mich wohl, und die Betreuer sind in Ordnung. Ich lebe hier jetzt seit einem halben Jahr, aber ich kann nicht viel länger bleiben, weil es nur für vorübergehende Aufenthalte von Jugendlichen gedacht ist. Deshalb ist es auch schwer Freunde zu finden, weil alle nur kurz da sind. Ich glaube, dass sie mir bald meine eigene Wohnung geben werden.

Was meine ausländische Herkunft angeht, so habe ich oft das Gefühl, dass die generelle Einstellung in Behörden und so ist: „Die können ja nix". Aber ich habe kein konkretes Beispiel für dieses Gefühl.

She asked me if she should go with me to the Youth Welfare Office again and she drove me there but I said I wanted to go in alone and she should wait outside for me. So I talked to the Youth Welfare Office again but nothing happened again. But then my father told me they (my whole family) were going to move to Leipzig and he didn't want me to come with them. And he said he had already cancelled the apartment and I would have to look out for myself and see where I could live. So I went to the school social worker again who went to the Youth Welfare Office with me and talked to them with me. And that was the first time they really listened to me and took me seriously, when an adult was with me. So I think it's good when schools provide a school social worker, because when you come alone to the Youth Welfare Office as a kid they don't take you seriously. They don't really offer you enough time to talk or offer you real help, I think. They only really listen to you if an adult is accompanying you.

But that day, when I went there with the school social worker they gave me a place in the home which I'm living in now. Here I feel alright and the care workers are ok. I've been living here for half a year now but I can't stay much longer because it's not a permanent home for young people but only temporary. That's why it's difficult to find friends here because everybody is leaving again. I think they are going to give me my own flat soon.

Regarding my foreign origin I often have the feeling, the general attitude in institutions and the like is: „They are good for nothing". But I have no concrete example for this feeling.

"Fremd mochte ich einfach nicht"
Nediz' Geschichte

Ich bin hier in M. geboren worden, meine Eltern kommen beide aus der Türkei, meinen Vater habe ich aber nie gesehen, weil er vor meiner Geburt zurück in die Türkei gegangen ist. Meine Mutter hatte immer Probleme damit, sich richtig um meine ältere Schwester und mich zu kümmern, sie war auch psychisch krank und deshalb hat sie uns in ein Kinderschutzhaus gegeben, als ich zweieinhalb Jahre alt war. An diese Zeit habe ich wenige Erinnerungen, da war aber eine Erzieherin, die sich auch viel gekümmert hat, mich gefüttert und mit uns Kindern gespielt hat. Aber ich weiß, dass ich niemanden irgendwie näher rangelassen, nicht geredet, nie offen eigene Gefühle gezeigt habe und deshalb auch erst ein Verdacht auf Autismus bei mir bestand.

Nach einer Weile sind uns dann unsere späteren Pflegeltern in dem Schutzhaus besuchen gekommen, wir haben auch mal einen Ausflug mit ihnen gemacht und später sind meine Schwester und ich dann zu ihnen gezogen. Ich erinnere das als fließenden Übergang. Meine Mutter war an dem Prozess auch beteiligt und hat das mit entschieden, dass wir in die Pflegefamilie kommen sollten. Aber gesehen habe ich sie dann erst mal nur sehr selten.

Als wir dann bei den Pflegeeltern wohnten, sind wir auch in den Kindergarten gekommen, aber da wollte ich am Anfang gar nicht hin und habe da viel Randale gemacht, auch meine Kindergärtnerinnen geschlagen und gekratzt und die Kindergärtnerinnen waren dann böse und haben mich aus der Gruppe gesetzt, wo ich mich beruhigen sollte. Und wenn das nicht ging, musste ich abgeholt werden. Ich glaube ich hatte damals halt auch Angst, dass wir wieder woanders hin müssen und unsere Pflegeeltern uns da nicht wieder abholen kommen. Fremd mochte ich einfach nicht. Da war nur eine Erzieherin, die anders war und auch immer gucken wollte, warum ich so bin und die wurde dann meine Lieblingskindergärtnerin und später bin ich richtig gerne dahin gegangen. Sie hat dann später auch meinen ersten Liebesbrief bekommen. Und meine Pflegeltern haben auch einen Freund, der Psychologe ist und öfter zu Besuch kommt und viel mit uns Kindern redet und der hat mir auch verklickert, dass Kindergärtnerinnen nichts Schlechtes sind.

Meine Pflegemutter hat dann vor allem in den ersten Jahren eine Mutterrolle für mich übernommen, ich war ein richtiges Muttersöhnchen, wollte mich nur von ihr ins Bett bringen lassen. Erst später habe ich dann selbst gemerkt, dass sie nicht meine richtige Mutter ist, sondern eben meine Pflegemutter und dann habe ich sie auch nicht mehr Mama genannt.

"I just didn't like strange"

Nediz' Story

I was born here in M. My parents are both from Turkey and I have never seen my father because he went back to Turkey before I was born. My mother always had problems caring for me and my older sister. She also was mentally ill and therefore gave us away to a children's home when I was two and a half years old. I don't remember much of that time but there was one caregiver who cared for the children a lot feeding me and playing with the children. But I also know that I didn't let anyone get close to me, I didn't speak and never showed feelings openly so at first they thought I might suffer from autism.

After a while our future foster parents came to visit us in the children's home or we went on a trip together and later we moved in with them. I remember this as a gradual change. And my mother also participated in this process and also in the decision that we should live with our foster parents. But I saw her very rarely during the time right afterwards.

When we lived with our foster parents we also went to the kindergarten. But at the beginning I didn't want to go there and acted up, also hitting and scratching my kindergarten teachers. They used to get angry and separated me from the group to calm down. And when that wasn't enough my foster parents had to come and pick me up. I believe at that time I was afraid that we would have to live somewhere else again and that our foster parents would leave us there and not come to get us home again. I just didn't like strange. And there was only one kindergarten teacher who was different and who also wanted to find out why I behaved like that and she became my favorite kindergarten teacher and later I liked going to the kindergarten very much. She was the one who got my first love letter later. And also, my foster parents have a friend who is a psychologist and visits quite often and talks to us children. And he also made clear to me that kindergarten teachers aren't bad.

During the first years my foster mother took over the role as my mother. I was a real Mama's boy, only she was allowed to put me to bed. Only later I realized that she wasn't my real mother but just my foster mother and then I stopped calling her Mum. My foster dad gets along especially well with teenagers, he's doings sports and stuff together with them and for me he's somewhat like a father. I mean it's kind of like in a real family, where the parents ask if everybody has done his homework or his housekeeping duties or why someone comes home late.

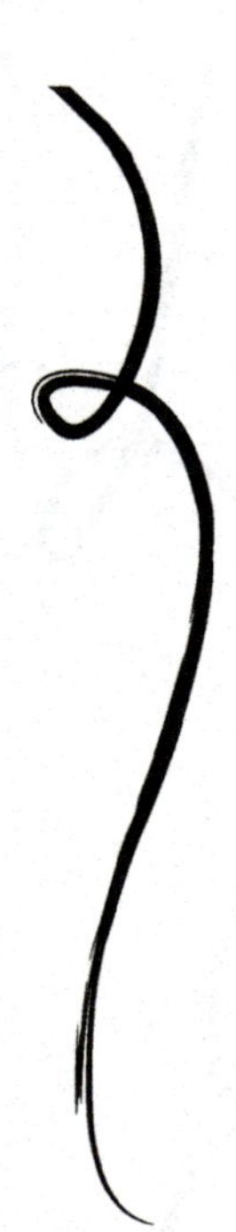

Mein Pflegevater kommt vor allem gut mit Jugendlichen klar, mit ihm mach ich auch Sport und so, und hat für mich auch sozusagen die Vaterrolle inne. Es ist halt bei uns so ziemlich wie in einer richtigen Familie, wo die Eltern fragen, ob man schon seine Hausaufgaben oder seine Aufgaben im Haushalt gemacht hat oder warum man so spät nach Hause gekommen ist oder so. Man versteht sich gut und man streitet halt auch, das ist eben ganz anders als im Heim, wo man nicht so Familie miteinander ist und kein Erzieher wirklich Zeit für die einzelnen Kinder hat. Ich finde, das ist hier auch so wie auch in anderen Familien, dass, wenn man älter wird, einem nicht mehr Verantwortung gegeben wird sondern Eltern erst recht klammern. Aber mir geht es so, dass ich immer unterwegs sein muss, ich mag nicht so viel zu Hause sein, eigentlich lieber nur zum Schlafen und Frühstücken. Und je älter man wird, desto wichtiger werden eben Freunde, und Erwachsene werden eher unwichtiger.

Insgesamt finde ich aber schon, dass wir eigentlich mehr Freiheiten haben als Kinder in den meisten normalen Familien. Da gibt es immer gleich richtig Ärger, wenn man zu spät nach Hause kommt mit Hausarrest oder Computerverbot oder so. Meine Pflegeeltern sind dann eher nur sauer und sagen, man kann auch anrufen, aber bestrafen das nicht mit was, das damit gar nichts zu tun hat. Und ich meine, sie wollen eben, dass wir unser Leben auf die Reihe kriegen. Das ist ja auch noch wichtiger als bei Kindern mit einer eigenen Familie, denn bei uns ist mit 18 Schluss, dann müssen wir unser Leben selbst hinkriegen.

Ich habe auch auf jeden Fall vor, Abi zu machen. In der Schule komme ich auch gut klar. Einmal hatte ich eine richtig schlechte Phase und da hat mir meine Lehrerin sehr geholfen. Die hat das halt so gemerkt und dann gesagt: Junge, was ist da los? Du kannst dich nicht so gehen lassen. Und dann habe ich auch zwei Mal die Unterschrift gefälscht, weil ich eine schlechte Arbeit hatte und das nicht zeigen wollte und dann hat sie das gemerkt und dann hat sie gesagt: „So, Unterschriftfälschung, jetzt fliegst du eigentlich von der Schule. Aber sie hat dann gesagt: Wir vergessen das, das bleibt ein Geheimnis. Aber krieg dein Leben in den Griff!" Und dann sollte ich ihr versprechen, in Zukunft besser zu werden und dann ging das auch. Sie hat mich so ein bisschen hochgepusht, dass ich wieder besser werde. Sonst, ohne sie wäre ich schon längst von der Schule geflogen.

Meine Mutter besuche ich manchmal, wenn ich Lust habe. Sie hat auch immer noch das volle Sorgerecht für uns und bestimmt auch mit, z.B. wann wir hier ausziehen dürfen und dass wir vorher die Schule zu Ende machen müssen.

Like in other families people get along well with each other, of course also argue with each other, and that's totally different than in a children's home where people are not family with each other and no caregiver really has time for the individual children. But it's also the same here as in other families that you are not given more responsibility when you get older but instead your parents are getting even clingier. But with me it's like I always like to be on the move, I don't like to hang around at home so much, actually I prefer to be home just for sleeping and having breakfast. And the older you get the more important friends and the less important grownups become.

But actually all in all I think that we have more freedom than children in most normal families. In some of them children really get into trouble when they are coming home late, like they are grounded or get a computer ban or stuff like that. My foster parents just get angry in cases like that and tell you that you could have called. But they don't punish you with something that hasn't got anything to do with what you've done wrong. And I mean, they just want us to get our lives under control. And that's even more important for us foster children than for a child from another family because when you turn 18, it's the end, then we have to get our lives under control just by ourselves.

And I am really planning to accomplish my Abitur and I get along well in school. One time I was having a really bad time and then my teacher helped me. She just realized it and said: "Boy, what's going on? You can't get let yourself go like that". And then I faked two signatures because I had gotten bad grades and I didn't want to show them. But she realized it and then she said: „So forging signatures, that usually means you flunk out of school!" But then she said: "We'll forget about this, that's our secret. But get a grip on your life!" And then she wanted me to promise her to do better and that worked. She did push me a bit just to get better. And otherwise, without her I would long since have been expelled from school.

Sometimes, when I want to, I visit my mother. She still has parental custody and for example can decide when we are allowed to move out of this home or that we have to finish school first.

"Ich wusste ja gar nicht, wer das war und habe geweint"

Ninas Geschichte

Ich bin mit meinen Eltern aus den Niederlanden nach München gekommen, als ich ganz klein war, weil mein Vater da immer Ärger mit den Behörden hatte. Meine Eltern haben immer Drogen genommen und hatten auch oft Streit, bei dem sie sich geschlagen haben und manchmal mussten wir dann deshalb ins Krankenhaus. Einmal ist meine Mutter aber extra nicht ins Krankenhaus gegangen, weil sie Angst hatte, dass unsere Familie dann zu auffällig wird und die vom Jugendamt mich dann holen kommen. Leute vom Jugendamt waren auch öfter bei uns zuhause. Einmal hat jemand mit meinen Eltern gesprochen und mir dann auch viele Fragen gestellt, wie es mir geht und so. Der war zwar nett aber hat sich gar nicht vorgestellt. Und es war schon komisch, dass so ein Mann zu mir kam und mich irgendwelche Sachen fragte. Die vom Jugendamt haben dann öfter geklingelt aber meine Mutter hat die Tür nicht aufgemacht und wir mussten dann ganz leise sein, damit sie denken, wir wären nicht zuhause. Einmal haben sie gerufen: Wir wissen, dass Sie da sind. Wir kommen wieder!". Meine Mutter hat dann gesagt, das seien böse Menschen und ich fand das sehr gruselig. Wir sollten auch immer die Gardinen zumachen, damit uns keiner sehen kann.

Als ich vier Jahre alt war, war einmal das Küchenfenster auf und ich saß auf dem Tisch, wo die mich von draußen sehen konnten. Ich glaube, die haben dann die Tür aufgetreten oder so. Und dann wollten die mich mitnehmen und haben mich gepackt und meine Mutter hat an mir gezogen und geschrien: „Lasst sie los, lasst sie frei." Und ich habe auch geschrien: „Lasst mich los". Ich wusste ja gar nicht, wer das war und habe geweint. Der eine hat dann nur so gesagt: „Wir sind gut für dich, wir wollen nichts Böses." Und dann haben die mich mit in ihr Auto genommen und gesagt, sie sind vom Jugendamt und holen mich da raus." Ich durfte noch nicht mal irgendwelche von meinen Sachen mitnehmen. Dann haben sie mich ins Jugendamt gebracht, da sollte ich mir ein Buch aussuchen und angucken, aber ich wollte gar nichts und habe da nur so gesessen und auch geweint. Dann kam ein Jugendamtsmitarbeiter und wollte mit mir reden, aber ich fand den voll gruselig, weil er ganz fremd war und ich ganz klein und ich hatte auch immer so Filme gesehen, wo jemand geraubt wurde und daran musste ich denken.

Später kam dann eine Frau vom Heim, die hat gesagt: „Du bleibst jetzt erst mal bei mir!"

"I didn't know who they were and I was crying"

Nina's Story

When I was little, I came from the Netherlands to Munich with my parents because my father had trouble with the authorities. My parents were always taking drugs and were often arguing and then sometimes hitting each other and because of that we sometimes had to go to the hospital. One time, my mother decided not to go to the hospital because she was afraid that our family would raise suspicion and then someone from the Youth Welfare Office would come and get me. And sometimes people from the Youth Welfare Office came to our apartment. One day, one of them talked to my parents and then asked me a lot of questions, how I felt and stuff like that. He was kind of nice but didn't even introduce himself. And I thought it was kind of strange that some man just came to me and asked me questions like that. Later, the people from the Youth Welfare Office rang at our door quite often. But my mother never answered the door and we had to be very silent to let them think we weren't home. One day, they were calling: „We know you're there. We are coming back!" My mother told me then they were bad people and it was very scary for me. She used to tell us as well to close the curtains so nobody could see us.

One day, when I was four years old, the kitchen window was open and I was sitting on the table so that they could see me from outside. I believe they kicked the door in or something. And then they wanted to take me with them and they grabbed me and my mother pulled me and screamed: "Let her go, let her free!" And I was screaming as well: "Let me go!" I mean I didn't know who they were and I was crying. One of them just said then: „We are good for you. We don't want anything bad". And then they took me to their car and told me they were from the Youth Welfare Office and were there to get me out of my family. I wasn't even allowed to take any personal stuff with me. Then they brought me to the Youth Welfare Office and there they told me to choose a book and look at it. But I didn't want anything and was just sitting there, crying. Then a man came to talk to me but I found him too scary because he was strange and I was so small and sometimes I had also watched such movies in which someone got robbed and that's what I had to think about.

Later, a woman from a children's home came to me and told me that I was going to stay with her. That was scary as well and in the children's home I didn't eat for three days and just stayed in my room.

Die fand ich auch fremd und gruselig und im Heim hab ich dann erst mal drei Tage lang nichts gegessen und bin nur in meinem Zimmer geblieben. Das Heim war eigentlich für Jugendliche und nicht so kleine Kinder wie mich, aber es gab wohl keinen anderen Platz. Deshalb war auch in meinem Zimmer noch eine Jugendliche, die immer Ärger gemacht hat und auch so mit Drogen zu tun hatte, glaub ich. Außerdem hatten die Erzieher so viel mit den Jugendlichen zu tun, dass die für mich nicht so viel Zeit hatten. Als ich dann in den Kindergarten kam, war es nicht mehr ganz so schlimm, weil ich dann nur noch den halben Tag im Heim sein musste. Dann endlich, im nächsten Sommer, durfte meine Mutter zu Besuch kommen und ich habe mich wahnsinnig gefreut. Aber irgendwie durfte ich nie zu ihr hinrennen, wenn ich sie gesehen habe, sondern musste immer in der Tür stehen und warten, bis sie ganz da war. Ich hatte keine Ahnung warum, und sie durfte auch immer nur ganz kurz bei mir bleiben, eine Stunde oder so.

Später kam dann manchmal eine Frau vom Jugendamt, die meine Vormundin ist. Als die Erzieherin mir erzählte, dass sie kommen würde, hatte ich zuerst Angst und sagte „nein, ich will nicht, dass die kommt", weil ich immer an die Leute vom Jugendamt denken musste, die mich einfach von zuhause weggenommen hatten. Aber die war dann sehr nett und hat sich auch gut vorgestellt und mit mir geredet und mir auch das erste Mal ein bisschen erzählt, warum ich im Heim sein musste. Und sie hat dann auch gesagt, dass es vielleicht besser wäre, wenn ich nicht mehr im Heim lebe sondern woanders und dass vielleicht bald jemand kommen würde. Dann kamen mich meine jetzigen Pflegeeltern im Heim besuchen und haben mich manchmal auch zu Ausflügen abgeholt. Und dann, mit sechs Jahren, bin ich zu ihnen gezogen. Von meinen Pflegeeltern wurde mir dann auch zum ersten Mal richtig erklärt, warum ich von meinen Eltern weg musste, dass die nämlich drogenabhängig waren und was das bedeutet. Überhaupt kann ich mit meinen Pflegeeltern gut reden und auch Freizeit miteinander verbringen und das ist ganz anders als im Heim. Ich habe auch Freunde, die im Heim leben, und denen geht es echt nicht sehr gut, also, die sind echt anders. Zum Beispiel müssen die immer, auch am Wochenende, schon um neun Uhr ins Bett und dürfen nicht fernsehen. In einer Pflegefamilie gibt es mehr Vertrauen und man muss sich gleichzeitig nicht so eingeengt fühlen.

Meine Vormundin treffe ich regelmäßig, meistens kommt sie zu uns und meistens finde ich das gut, weil ich ihr auch Fragen stellen und mich anvertrauen kann, wenn was ist. Die kenne ich ja schon, seit ich klein bin. Manchmal finde ich es auch ein bisschen viel, dass die jetzt schon wieder kommt, weil ich gar keine Fragen gerade habe. Aber eigentlich ist das schon ok. Und ich kann sie auch jederzeit anrufen, wenn was ist und dann würde sie sich sofort mit mir treffen und ich habe auch Vertrauen zu ihr. Gut finde ich, dass sie alles bei sich behält, was ich ihr erzähle. Das ist bei meinen Pflegeeltern halt anders, die tauschen halt immer alles untereinander aus, was ich einem von ihnen erzähle. Außerdem hat sie halt, wenn wir uns treffen, nur für mich und meine Probleme Zeit.

Meine Eltern kommen mich gar nicht mehr besuchen, meine Mutter will das irgendwie nicht, aber ich habe noch Kontakt zu meiner Schwester und meinen Großeltern und Onkeln und Tanten in den Niederlanden.

The children's home was actually for teenagers and not for small children like me but there was probably no other place for me. So I had to share my room with a teenage girl who caused a lot of trouble and, I believe, also did something with drugs. And besides, the caretakers had to deal with the teenagers a lot and didn't have much time for me. When I started going to kindergarten it wasn't as bad any more because then I only had to be in the children's home half the day. And then, finally, in the next summer, my mother was allowed to visit and I was so, so glad. But somehow I was never allowed to run to her but had to keep standing in the door and wait for her until she was really there. I had no idea why and she was also only allowed to stay for a short time, one hour or so.

Later, a woman from the Youth Welfare Office sometimes came to visit me and she was my guardian. When the caretaker told me she would be coming, I was scared at first and said: "No, I don't want her to come." Because I always had to think of the people from the Youth Welfare Office who just took me away from my home. But then she was very nice and really introduced herself and talked to me and for the first time told me a little about the reasons why I had to stay in the children's home. And then she also said that it might be better for me not to live in the home any more but somewhere else and that soon someone might be coming for me. Then my foster parents came to visit me in the children's home and sometimes they also picked me up for trips. And then, I was six years old by then, I moved to them. My foster parents then were the ones who explained to me properly for the first time why I could not live with my mom and dad, that they were drug addicts and what that means. And generally, I can talk well with my foster parents and also spend time with them and it's really different than in the children's home. I have some friends, now, who live in a children's home and they are not doing so well, I mean they are really different. For example, they always have to go to bed at nine, even at the weekend and are not allowed to watch TV. In a foster family there's more trust and at the same time you don't have to feel so hemmed in.

I'm regularly meeting my guardian, usually she comes to my foster family and usually I think it's good because I can ask her questions and confide something to her if there is anything. I mean I know her since I was really small. Sometimes I think it's a little too much that she's coming again because I don't really have any questions. But actually that's ok. And I can always give her a call when something's the matter and then she would immediately meet me. And I also trust her. What I think is good is that she keeps everything I tell her to herself. That's different than with my foster parents because they tell each other everything whenever I tell something to one of them. And besides, she has time just for me and my problems when we meet.

My parents do not visit me anymore; my mother doesn't want that somehow. But I still have contact with my sister and with my uncles and aunts in the Netherlands.

Pierres Geschichte

Meine Mutter ist Indianerin und mein Vater Italiener, er ist aber früh von der Familie
weg und wieder nach Italien zurückgegangen. Er wollte mich und meinen ältesten
Bruder zwar gerne mitnehmen, das hat meine Mutter aber nicht erlaubt. Sie ist
aber alleine mit uns fünf Kindern nicht zurechtgekommen, war total überfordert
und oft aggressiv und gewalttätig. Sie hat uns erst nicht mehr geschlagen als wir
selber zu groß und stark waren und sie Angst hatte, wir würden sie zurück schlagen.
Außerdem musste ich ganz viel vom Haushalt machen, auch mitten in der Nacht
noch den Boden wischen oder so. Und ich hab mich halt auch nicht anerkannt,
richtig gemocht gefühlt von ihr. Als ich 11 war, ist meine ältere Schwester von
zuhause abgehauen und in ein Heim gekommen und dann ist mein anderer Bruder
mit 14 auch abgehauen, weil meine Mutter ihm mit dem Besen das Ohr ganz blutig
geschlagen hat. Er ist dann in eine Pflegefamilie gekommen. Wir hatten zwar mal
ein Jahr lang eine Familienhilfe, die zweimal wöchentlich kam, aber der haben
wir von den Schlägen nicht erzählt, weil es ja schließlich doch um meine Mutter
ging und wir dann Mitleid mit ihr hatten. Während dieser Zeit war es zuhause
ein bisschen besser, zumindest ist meine Mutter nicht mehr auf so viele Partys
gegangen, aber aggressiv war sie immer noch zu uns und hat uns geschlagen. Den
Familienhelfer mochte ich auch ganz gerne, der war immer nett zu mir und hat
auch viel mit mir geredet. Aber die Familienhilfe war halt befristet und dann ist der
halt nach einem Jahr nicht mehr gekommen. Die Lehrer in der Schule sind zwar mal
aufmerksam geworden und wollten mit mir reden, weil ich immer so müde war und
meine Leistungen so nachgelassen haben. Aber ich wollte nicht mit denen reden
und hatte auch Angst.

Als ich 13 war, hat meine Mutter mich mal wieder zuhause eingesperrt, weil
ich immer gegen ihre Ausgangszeiten verstoßen hab. Und da bin ich dann aus
dem Fenster gesprungen und von zuhause abgehauen. Ich bin dann zur Polizei
gegangen und die haben zu mir gesagt: „Ach, das kann doch gar nicht so schlimm
sein. Rede doch nicht so viel. Niemals ist deine Mutter so."

My mother is American Indian and my father comes from Italy. He left our family early and went back to Italy. He wanted to take me and my oldest brother with him but my mother didn't allow it. But she didn't get along well being alone with us, the five children, she was totally stressed and often aggressive and violent. She only stopped hitting us when we were big and strong ourselves and she was afraid we might hit her back. I also had to do a lot of household chores, even wiping the floor in the middle of the night or stuff like that. And I never felt she really appreciated, really liked me. When I was eleven years old my older sister ran away from home and came into a children's home. And some time later my brother left as well when he was 14 years old, because my mother had beaten him with a broom until his ear was bloody. He came into a foster family then. I mean, we did have a family helper who came twice a week but we didn't tell him about the beating, because after all she was my mother and we pitied her. During that time things were getting a little better at home, at least my mother wasn't going to parties so often but she was still aggressive and beat us. And I liked the family helper, he was always nice to me and talked to me a lot. But the family support was only limited in time and after a year he stopped coming. The teachers in school started paying attention though and tried to talk to me because I was always so tired and my school performance had gotten worse. But I didn't want to talk to them and was afraid, too.

When I was 13 my mother had once again locked me in at home because I had broken her curfew. And then I jumped out of the window and ran away. I went to the police but they said to me: "Oh, it can't be that bad. Don't talk so much. Your mother is never like that." They didn't take me seriously. But I stayed tough and said I would never go back to her and at last they brought me to the Baker-Home. There my brother already lived who had run away earlier. I was acting up a lot there because of my grief and anger, until I got thrown out. I came to another children's home then, the Rousseau-home.

Die haben das nicht ernst genommen. Aber ich bin zäh geblieben und hab gesagt, ich geh auf keinen Fall dahin zurück, und dann haben sie mich doch ins Gläser-Heim gebracht. Da wohnte schon mein Bruder, der vor mir abgehauen war. Ich hab da aber extrem viel Ärger gemacht, wegen meinem Zorn und meiner Trauer, solange, bis ich rausgeflogen und in ein anderes Heim, ins Rousseau-Kinderheim gekommen bin. Da hatte ich mehr Freiheiten, hab aber dann auch noch mehr Mist gebaut, die Fenster eingeschlagen und solche Sachen, oder ich bin abgehauen und von der Polizei aufgegriffen worden. In dem Heim hatte ich zwar Betreuer, die haben sich aber nicht so richtig um einen gekümmert, mehr so bloß um die körperlichen Grundbedürfnisse, sonst sollte ich gucken, was ich mache. Einmal die Woche hatte ich zwar ein psychologisches Gespräch, aber das hat nicht so richtig was gebracht. Es gab einfach nicht so richtig Regeln und vor allem Sanktionen und deshalb konnte ich da auch nicht lernen, was es heißt, Verantwortung zu übernehmen für sich selbst. Nur mit einem Gitarrenlehrer, bei dem ich Unterricht bekommen habe und der auch Pädagoge war, hab ich mich gut verstanden und auch viel geredet. Auch darüber, dass ich meine Ausraster immer hatte, weil ich aus meiner Kindheit traumatisiert war und nur, wenn man mich auf eine bestimmte Art angesprochen oder angefasst hat, die das dann bei mir ausgelöst hat. Aber ich hatte da einfach keine richtige Vertrauensperson und war dann auch kaum noch da, sondern immer nur bei meiner Freundin und hab eben auch viel Scheiße gebaut und deshalb haben die mich da auch wieder rausgeschmissen.

Ich bin dann erst mal wieder zu meiner Mutter gezogen, aber nach einem Monat bin ich wieder abgehauen. Ich bin dann wieder zur Polizei gegangen und die haben dann wieder im Gläser-Kinderheim angerufen. Erst wollten die mich gar nicht, aber dann haben sie gesagt, sie nehmen mich in die Notaufnahme und versuchen es nochmal mit mir. Da war ich erst wieder ziemlich aggressiv und dann hab ich so Angststörungen, so Panikattacken bekommen, dass sie mich in eine Klinik geschickt haben. Da war ich drei Wochen und der Psychologe da hat mir wirklich weitergeholfen, erklärt, woher so Panikattacken kommen und was man dagegen tun kann. Aber da waren auch echt Verrückte in der Klinik, mit denen ich da zusammen war. Dann bin ich zurück ins Heim. Ich habe dann auch eine richtige Therapie gemacht. Die wurde abgeschlossen mit dem Bericht, dass ich ein kerngesunder junger Mann bin und mich gut verhalten kann. Mache jetzt bald mein Abitur. Und auf meinem Weg, auf meinem langen Weg, bis ich einen Platz gefunden habe, an dem ich bleiben kann, an dem ich mich entwickeln konnte, in eine positive Richtung, mich um 180 Grad drehen konnte, habe ich ein paar Personen kennengelernt, mit denen habe ich natürlich jetzt noch Kontakt, die dazu beigetragen haben, dass ich mich halt ins Positive entwickle. Die wichtigste Bezugsperson in meinem Leben ist mein Bezugsbetreuer, den ich dann im Heim bekommen habe. Mit dem bin ich gleich super klar gekommen und mit dem konnte ich immer gut reden und so. Und man braucht halt eine echte Vertrauensperson, damit man sich entwickeln kann, wenn man die nicht hat, geht alles nicht.

There I had more freedom but I was also acting up even more, punching in the windows and stuff like that. Or I ran away and got picked up by the police. There were carers in the home but they weren't really caring for us children, only for our physical needs, aside from that I had to look out for myself. Once a week I talked to a psychologist, but there was no point in that either. The thing was that there just were no real rules and especially no sanctions and so I couldn't learn what it means to take responsibility for yourself. My guitar teacher who was also a pedagogue was the only one I got along with well, and I talked to him a lot, also about how my outbreaks of anger came from the traumas in my childhood, and that I only freaked out if someone talked to me or touched me in a certain way that set this off. But aside from that I had no real relationship of trust there. I was usually not there but with my girlfriend. And, well, like I said, I acted up a lot and so I was thrown out again.

After that I moved back to my mother for a while but after a month I ran away again. I went to the police again and they called the Baker-Home once more. First they didn't want me but then they said they would take me in Emergency Care and try it one more time. In the beginning I was acting aggressive again and then I got such panic attacks so that they sent me to a psychological clinic. I stayed there for three weeks and the psychologist really helped me, explained where panic attacks come from and what you could do against them. But there were real maniacs in there, too, who were staying there together with me. Then I got back to the Baker-Home. Then I started a real therapy which has now finished with the report that I am in good health and can behave well. I am going to take my Abitur soon. And on my way, on my long way, until I had found a place where I can stay, where I can develop positively, make a 180-degree turn, I have met a few people who really helped me to be able to develop positively. The most important person in my life is my carer whom I got when I came back to the Baker-Home. I got along with him from the beginning on and could always talk to him. And you just need a real person of trust to be able to develop positively. If you don't have someone like that nothing can work.

Child physical abuse & neglect

Stories and experiences of young people with intervention

Portugal

"Na instituição fiquei mais responsável"

História de Afonso

Eu nasci em Cabo Verde e vivi lá até aos 8 anos. Em Cabo Verde, tive a melhor a infância que podia ter tido. Aquilo foi espetacular! Nós não tínhamos nada destas tecnologias todas mas divertia-me. Até com uma roda dum carro conseguia divertir-me. E aqui, a única coisa que fazemos é jogar playstation, o que eu não gosto muito.

Nunca entendi porque é que eu vim para Portugal. Em Cabo Verde, sinceramente, tínhamos uma vida boa. Tínhamos uma loja, tínhamos um carro, tínhamos tudo. Só que depois tive de vir para aqui, porque a minha mãe estava cá. Aconteceu de um dia para o outro. A minha mãe ligou e disse: "Já tenho as vossas passagens, venham para aqui". Viemos todos, eu e os 3 meus irmãos. E dei por mim, estava em Portugal. E eu fiquei assim: "O que é que se passou aqui?" Foi muito estranho. Eu pensava que ia ser melhor aqui, mas, como a minha mãe não tinha assim muitas condições, eu e os meus irmãos tivemos que ir para uma instituição.

Quando entrei na instituição, fiquei mais responsável porque eu antes, em Cabo Verde, nem conseguia ir à escola. O meu pai dizia-me sempre: "Vai para a escola", e eu, em vez de ir para a escola, ia para o monte brincar. Esquece, odiava a escola! Eu acho que não ia para a escola porque tinha liberdade a mais. As escolas não tinham grades, só ficava lá se quisesse. Eu aos 8 anos já tinha feito coisas que acho que nenhum rapaz de 8 anos daqui fazia. Eu acho que aquilo me atrasou bué.

Não fui vítima de violência. Fui para a instituição mais para ganhar responsabilidade porque ninguém me punha a mão. Quando fui para a instituição a minha mãe disse-me: "Vais para um colégio porque isto não está assim tão bem". E eu chorei, chorei, mas também era pequenino. As pessoas falavam comigo e diziam: "Olha, é melhor ires para lá, porque isso vai-te fazer bem no futuro" e essas coisas todas. No início o tempo nunca mais passava, um dia pareciam três. Quando cheguei à instituição, comecei a ter uma rotina. Tive um horário pela primeira vez na vida mas aquela rotina, escola, instituição, instituição, escola... Ei! Aquilo desfazia-me a cabeça toda. Eu dizia assim: "Eu não sou assim, por amor de Deus, o que é que eu estou aqui a fazer?" Mas depois falavam comigo e eu comecei a atinar. Só que eu ficava bué revoltado mas não dizia a ninguém. Mas, um dia, todos temos que nos abrir com alguém e na instituição ajudaram-me com isso.

"At the institution I became more responsible"

Afonso's Story

I was born in Cape Verde and lived there until I was 8 years old. In Cape Verde I had the best childhood. It was amazing! We didn't have all this technology but we had so much fun. Even with a tire of a car we had fun. Here, the only thing we do is play videogames, which I don't like very much.

I never understood why I had to come to Portugal. In Cape Verde, honestly, we had a good life. We had a store, a car, we had everything. But then I had to come to Portugal because my mother was here. It happened from one day to the other. My mother called and said: "I already have the tickets for you to come over". We all came, my three older brothers and I. Suddenly I found myself in Portugal. I was like: "What is happening here?" It was very strange. I thought things would be better here but my mother didn't have resources to have us with her so we had to go to the institution.

At the institution I became more responsible because before, in Cape Verde, I didn't want to go to school. My father always told me to go to school but instead I usually went to play outdoors. I hated school! I think the reason for me to not go to school was because I had too much freedom. The school didn't have fences and we only stayed there if we wanted. At 8 years of age I already did things that were not appropriate for a boy of that age. I think this delayed my development.

I wasn't a victim of violence. I went to the institution to become more responsible because no one could handle me. When I went to the institution my mother told me: "you have to go to an institution because things are not going well here". I cried and cried because I was little. Other people also told me: "Look, it's better for you to go to the institution because it will be good for your future." In the beginning time hardly passed, one day felt like three days. When I arrived in the institution I started to have a routine. I had a schedule for the first time in my life but the routine school-institution-school... It messed me up. I used to say: "I'm not like this! For God's sake, what am I doing here?" But then, in the institution, they talked with me and I started to gain more sense. Sometimes I felt very angry but wouldn't let anybody know. But sooner or later we all have to open up with somebody and they helped me to do that. At the institution I saw psychologists and social workers. The director of the institution was always talking with us too and he used to say to everybody:

Na instituição, fui acompanhado por psicólogas e assistentes sociais. O Diretor também estava sempre a falar connosco e dizia a toda a gente: "Não sejas cão de trela de ninguém". Hoje, eu percebo, porque às vezes juntam-se muitos e sai porcaria. E essa frase nunca mais me saiu da cabeça.

As coisas ficaram mais fáceis quando fiz 15 anos. Agradeço quase todos os dias o que eles fizeram por mim. Espetacular! Eu não queria estar lá no início mas depois comecei a gostar daquilo. E agora vejo que me fez bem. Eu gosto daquilo e ajudou-me a crescer bué! Comecei a fazer o meu caminho sozinho, fiz alguns amigos, e acho que me dei bem. Sempre mantive contacto com a minha família. No fim de semana vou ver a minha família. Gosto de ir a Cabo Verde passar férias, mas não quero ficar lá porque a minha vida agora é aqui.

Acho que a instituição piorou muito. Antes, era rigoroso mas funcionava com as pessoas. Mas agora, eu acho que as pessoas entram lá e fazem o que querem. Não passaram o que eu passei no início. Também acho que é por causa de as pessoas entrarem lá cada vez mais velhas. Algumas com 17, 18 anos. E assim já não dá para os mudar, eles já vão ser sempre aquilo, na minha opinião. Acho que aquilo está a cair. É o que todos os que estiveram comigo desde o início também dizem.

Eu agora estou na casa de autonomia porque eles selecionaram os 6 melhores e eu fui um deles. A transição correu bem. Sempre quis ir para a casa de autonomia porque, apesar de não fazermos tudo o que queremos, temos muito mais liberdade. Somos nós que cozinhamos e fazemos tudo. Foi bom ir para lá, já estou lá há 2 anos.

Estou a tentar ficar com cidadania portuguesa mas é mesmo complicado porque tenho de esperar 6 meses. Estou mesmo cansado daquilo. Acho que já devia ter feito o pedido antes porque, depois de estar aqui 4 anos, já podia fazê-lo, mas estive sempre a adiar. Muitas vezes, as pessoas tratavam-me de forma diferente por ser cabo-verdiano, especialmente quando era mais novo. Eu ficava agressivo mas agora não ligo. Os monitores não me tratavam de forma diferente, eles são mesmo espetaculares. Mas os colegas, quando eu era pequenino, chamavam-me "preto", essas coisas todas, "vai para a tua terra". Mas eu acho que era por brincadeira. Depois passou, as pessoas vão mudando, com o tempo! E depois, já nos dávamos todos bem. Na escola, ninguém me tratava de forma diferente porque eu não queria ser o mais fraco e juntava-me aos grupos. Há portugueses e portugueses, uma parte é racista, mas em geral eu acho que não.

Agora estou a acabar o 12º ano e pretendo ir para a universidade. Mas, para isso, tenho que fazer os exames nacionais, e vai ser muito complicado. O que eu gostava mesmo de fazer era ser professor de educação física ou treinador num ginásio.

"Don't be somebody else's leash dog!" Today I understand this, because sometimes boys get together and bad stuff happens. That saying is always in my head.

Things got easier after I turned 15. Everyday I'm grateful for what they have done for me. It has been great! In the beginning I didn't want to be there but then I started to like it. Now I recognize that it was really good for me. I like to live there; it helped me a lot to grow up. I have started to forge my own path, making a few friends and I am doing well now. I always maintained contact with my family. On the weekends we go visit the family. I enjoy going to Cape Verde for vacation but I don't want to live there because my life is here now.

I think the functioning of the institution worsened a lot. Before it was more rigorous but it helped people. Now I think kids enter in the institution and do whatever they want. They don't go through what I went through in the beginning. I think this is also because the boys who enter there are gradually older. Some are 17, 18 years old. In my opinion, it's too late to change them. I think the institution is failing. This is what the people who have been there from the beginning think too.

I now live in the autonomy house because they selected the 6 best kids and I was one of them. The transition was good. I always wanted to be in the autonomy house because, even though we can't do everything that we want, we have much more freedom there. We cook and do everything. It is good to live there. I have been there for two years.

I'm applying for Portuguese citizenship but it's very difficult because I have to wait for six months. I'm really tired of that. I think I should have applied sooner because after living 4 years in Portugal I could have applied but I was always postponing it. Oftentimes people treat me differently because I'm from Cape Verde, especially when I was young. I used to get very angry but now I ignore it. The monitors didn't treat me differently; they are really amazing. However, the kids at the institution used to call me "nigger" and tell me things like: "go to your country". I think they were just kidding. Then they stopped. People change with time and we started to have good relationships. At school no one treated me differently because I joined groups so I wouldn't be the weakest kid. There are different types of Portuguese people, some are racist but in general people are not racist.

Now I'm finishing high school and I want to go to college. In order to do that I have to pass the national exams and it will be very difficult for me. I really want to go to college and be a physical education teacher or a trainer at a gym.

"Ninguém me explicou nada, aconteceu de um dia para o outro"

História de Alberto

Tenho 20 anos. Vivo em instituições para jovens desde os 12 anos. Antes disso vivia com a minha mãe, padrasto e avós. Fui para a primeira instituição porque a minha mãe não me dava um bom viver. O meu avô morreu quando eu tinha 12 anos e eu sofri muito. Depois disso eu ficava com a minha avó sozinho em casa. A minha avó tinha Alzheimer. Eu fugia e ia muitas vezes para o hospital, porque, quando era mais novo, adorava brincar lá com as outras crianças. A assistente social do hospital é que me mandou para a primeira instituição. Ninguém me explicou nada. Foi de um dia para o outro.

Eu era vítima de bullying na primeira instituição. Os outros eram maus comigo. Chamavam-me nomes e batiam-me. Contei à subdiretora e ela disse: "Tens que ser forte, ignora." Mas eu tinha muito medo deles. Isso não me ajudou. Depois foi lá a minha técnica, e então falei com ela: "Bem, o que é que tu queres?" E eu: "Eu queria ir para outra instituição, porque eu aqui não estou bem." Ela disse que estava bem e fui para a instituição onde vivo hoje. Eu gosto de estar nesta instituição. É fixe. As pessoas são o que eu mais gosto aqui. Quer dizer, só me chamam uns nomes, mas faço queixa aos monitores e eles castigam. Isso ajuda. A coisa pior que aconteceu aqui foi o que me fizeram, outros daqui da casa. Mas já foi há muitos anos. Um há 2 anos e outro há 5 anos. Levaram-me ao Instituto de Medicina Legal. Trataram-me bem lá.

Um dos dias mais felizes foi quando fiz 18 anos. Bebi o meu primeiro copo de vinho do Porto. Foi tão bom! Adorei! A coisa que mais me marcou foi quando a diretora se que foi embora. Ela disse: "Eu vou-me despedir mas vocês estão no meu coração".

Uma coisa que me ajudou foi poder ir para os meus tios todos os fins de semana. Eu não posso estar com a minha mãe. Falei com a minha assistente social e ela disse: "escreve a carta para a Dr.ª Juíza, a ver se ela te autoriza". Foi quando eu disse: "e como é que se escreve uma carta?" Ela ensinou-me e passou ao computador. A carta dizia: "Meritíssima Juíza, venho por este meio pedir-lhe se me autoriza ir passar os fins de semana a casa dos meus tios." E ela aceitou: "Sr. Alberto, autorizamos a passar os fins de semana em casa dos seus tios. Serão os responsáveis por si até sair daqui."

"Nobody explained anything to me, it happened from one day to the other"

Alberto's Story

I am 20 years old. I have been living in institutions for young people since I was 12 years old. Before that I lived with my mother, stepfather and grandparents. I went to the first institution because my mother did not give me a good life. When I was 12 years old my grandfather died and I suffered a lot. After that I spent a lot of time with my grandmother and she had Alzheimer's disease. I ran away many times and went to the hospital, because I loved playing there with the other kids. A social worker at the hospital sent me to the first institution. Nobody explained anything to me. It happened from one day to the other.

I was a victim of bullying in this first institution. The other kids were mean to me. They called me names and beat me. I told one of the administrators and she said: "you have to be strong, ignore it." But I was very afraid of them. This did not help me. Then, my social worker went there and I talked with her: "What do you want?" she asked. I said: "I want to go to another institution because I'm not well here." She said: "OK" and I went to the institution where I live today. I like being in this institution. It's cool. What I like the most are the people here. Sometimes, the other kids call me names but I complain to the monitors and they punish them. That helps. The worst thing here was what other kids did to me but it was 5 and 2 years ago. They took me to the forensic medicine. They treated me well there.

One of the happiest days was when I turned 18 years old. I drank my first glass of Port wine. It was so good! I loved it! The thing that someone said that struck me the most was when the director left to go to another job. She said: "I will say goodbye but you are in my heart".

One thing that also helped me was the possibility to go visit my aunt and uncle every weekend. I can't be with my mother. I asked for help to one of the social workers here and she said: "write a letter to the judge to see if she authorizes." I said: "and what should I say?" She taught me and wrote the letter on the computer. The letter said: "Honourable Judge, I would like to request to spend the weekends with my aunt and uncle". The judge accepted: "Mr Alberto, we grant your request to spend the weekends with your aunt and uncle. They will be responsible for your until you leave the institution."

"Nihče mi ni nič razložil. Zgodilo se je i danes na jutri"

Albertova zgodba

Star sem dvajset let. V ustanovah za mladostnike živim že od dvanajstega leta. Pred tem sem živel z mamo, očimom in starimi starši. V prvo ustanovo sem šel, ker mi mama ni nudila dobrega življenja.

Ko sem imel dvanajst let, mi je umrl dedek in sem zelo trpel. Potem sem veliko časa preživel z babico, ki je imela Alzheimerjevo bolezen. Velikokrat sem zbežal in šel v bolnico. Rad sem hodil tja, ker sem se lahko igral z drugimi otroki tam. Socialna delavka v bolnici me je poslala v prvo ustanovo. Nihče mi ni nič razložil. Zgodilo se je iz danes na jutri.

V tej prvi ustanovi sem bil žrtev nasilništva. Ostali otroci so bili hudobni do mene. Zmerjali so me in tepli. Povedal sem eni od upravnic, ki mi je rekla: »Moraš biti močen … Ne meni se za to.« A sem se jih zelo bal. To mi ni pomagalo. Potem pa je prišla moja socialna delavka in se pogovorila z njo. »Kaj hočeš?« je vprašala. Rekel sem: »Rad bi šel v drugo ustanovo, ker mi tu ni v redu.« Rekla je: »V redu.« In poiskala ustanovo, kjer živim danes.

V tej ustanovi mi je všeč. Kul je. Tu so mi najbolj všeč ljudje. Včasih me ostali otroci zmerjajo, a so potem kaznovani. Pritožim se rediteljem in ti kaznujejo otroke, ki me trpinčijo. To pomaga.

Najhujša stvar, ki se je zgodila tu, je bilo to, kar so mi naredili drugi otroci, a to je bilo pred petimi in dvema letoma. Peljali so me na oddelek za forenzično medicino. Tam so lepo ravnali z mano.

Eden najsrečnejših dni je bil, ko sem dopolnil osemnajst let. Spil sem prvi kozarec portovca. Tako dober je bil! Zelo mi je bil všeč.

Besede, ki so se me najbolj dotaknile, so bile, ko je direktorica, ki nas je zapustila zaradi druge službe, rekla: »Poslovila se bom, a si v mojem srcu.«

Kar mi je še pomagalo, je bila možnost, da vsak vikend obiščem teto in strica. Z mamo ne morem biti. Neko socialno delavko tu sem prosil za pomoč in mi je rekla, naj napišem pismo sodnici in jo prosim za dovoljenje.

Rekel sem: »Kaj pa naj rečem?« Naučila me je in napisala pismo na računalniku. V pismu je pisalo: »Spoštovana sodnica, prosim vas, da mi odobrite preživljanje vikendov pri teti in stricu.« Sodnica je ugodila prošnji: »Gospod Alberto, sodišče je ugodilo vaši prošnji, da vikende preživite s teto in stricem. Odgovorna bosta za mladostnika, dokler ne zapusti ustanovo.«

"Nunca acreditaram que ia sequer fazer o 9º ano"

História de Emanuel

Entrei na instituição há 15 anos, quando tinha 7 anos. A minha mãe teve-me muito nova, quando ainda era adolescente e nunca conheci o meu pai. Vivíamos com os meus avós, bisavós e o meu tio mais velho. Havia sempre conflitos e violência entre eles, principalmente quando entrei para a escola. Andavam sempre à porrada! Estava sempre a ver a minha mãe a chorar e isso. Muitas das vezes esses conflitos eram por minha causa. Pelo menos, era o que eles estavam sempre a dizer. Agora, os verdadeiros motivos não sei porque ainda era muito pequeno.

Sei que um dos motivos pelos quais fui para a instituição foi porque eu ia para a escola e estava sempre a dormir nas aulas. Uma vez, a stôra viu-me uma marca nas costas. A professora deixou a aula a meio e levou-me para o hospital sem o conhecimento dos meus pais e eu nem sabia para onde é que ia. Ela depois também fez queixa que a minha mãe andava a bater-me em casa. No entanto, eu tinha uma marca nas costas porque me tinha aleijado, não era de me chicotearem. Ninguém sabia de mim e estavam todos em casa à minha espera e eu sem aparecer. Não sei quanto tempo é que estive no hospital. Acho que estive lá pelo menos um mês. Não me lembro da minha família me ter ido lá visitar. Depois, quando fui para casa, a minha mãe contou-me que a stôra não tinha avisado para onde é que me tinha levado e que houve stresses na escola quando a minha mãe foi lá saber de mim. Foram momentos difíceis! Do hospital fui para casa e depois a minha mãe e o meu padrasto levaram-me para a instituição. Quando fui para lá, lembro-me da minha mãe ter dito que tinha de ir por causa do meu sistema nervoso e por me portar mal. Mas o motivo mesmo não sei. Nunca falaram muito sobre isso. À parte de ir para o hospital e não terem dito nada à minha família, porque acho mal isso, o melhor para mim foi ter ido para a instituição.

Os primeiros 2 anos na instituição foram muito complicados porque eu estava sempre a fazer asneiras e a fugir, não queria estar lá. Não queria ir às aulas, não queria nada, era um rebelde por causa dos problemas em casa e por ter ido para a instituição. Preocupava-me muito com o que acontecia em casa. Depois de algum tempo, a minha atitude e o meu comportamento melhoraram muito. Se tivesse ficado em casa... pff! Se calhar, hoje, não era assim tão calmo e ainda estava pior do que era antes. No início diziam que se quiséssemos ligar para casa era só pedir aos assistentes sociais. Durante a semana não falava com ninguém da minha família.

"They never believed that I would even pass 9th grade"

Emanuel's Story

I went to the institution 15 years ago, when I was 7 years old. My mother was a teenager when she had me and I never met my biological father. We used to live with my grandparents, great-grandparents and my older uncle. There were a lot of conflicts and violence in my family especially when I first went to school. They were always beating each other! I was always seeing my mother crying and all that. Many times these conflicts happened because of me. At least that was what they said. I don't know the real reasons because I was very young.

I know that one of the reasons why I went to the institution was because I was always sleeping in school. One time my teacher saw bruises in my back. She stopped the class and took me to the hospital without my parents knowing and I also had no idea where I was going. She made a complaint against my mother accusing her of beating me at home. However, I had bruises in my back because I had hurt myself and not because I was whipped. My family didn't know anything and were all expecting me at the end of the day. I don't know how long I was at the hospital. I think it was at least one month and I don't remember my family going there to visit me. Then, when I came back home, my mother told me that she was not informed about what had happened to me and that there were conflicts in school when she went there to know where I was. Those were hard times! From the hospital I went back home and after some time my mother and my stepfather took me to the institution. When I went to the institution I remember that my mother said it was because I was very nervous and behaved badly. But I don't know the real reason. They never talked about it. Although I don't agree with my family not being informed when I went to the hospital, going to the institution was the best thing for me.

The first two years at the institution were very difficult. I didn't want to stay there and was always messing up and running away. I didn't want to go to school and was a rebel due to the family problems and having to be at the institution. I worried a lot about the problems at home. After some time my attitude and behaviour improved a lot. If I had stayed at home maybe today I wouldn't be so calm and would be worse off. In the beginning they said that if we wanted to call our families we just needed to ask the social workers. During the week I didn't talk with anyone of my family just on the weekends when I went home. This way I was distant from the problems at home, which helped me.

Só ao fim de semana, quando ia a casa. Por isso, também estava, de certa forma, longe dos problemas de casa, o que me ajudava.

Nos primeiros tempos, não tinha à vontade para falar sobre o que se estava a passar mas depois consegui e tenho evoluído bastante. Na instituição, tinha uma psicóloga que me ajudou a evoluir, a deixar os problemas de lado e seguir a minha vida. Quando tinha 15 anos deixei de ir porque deixou de haver problemas, achei que já não era preciso ir. Tinha 15 anos. Este processo nem foi rápido, nem foi muito lento. Também tive dois monitores que me ajudaram bastante. Conheço-os desde o início e quando preciso de apoio eles estão sempre lá e ainda hoje me ajudam.

Nunca tive contacto com a polícia, nem o tribunal. Só tive que ir à Comissão de Proteção de Crianças e Jovens (CPCJ) duas ou três vezes. A última vez que fui lá, tinha 17 ou 19 anos e era para saber se queria continuar na instituição ou não. Quando ia à CPCJ, só eu podia entrar e ficava sempre tudo entre nós. Das vezes que fui era sempre uma senhora a perguntar se estava tudo bem e se estava a correr tudo bem no lar. Uma das vezes que fui foi para decidir as visitas do fim de semana.

Os meus pais emigraram há 13 anos. Eles ligam sempre ao domingo, a uma certa hora que nós combinamos. Nas férias ou eles vêm cá ou eu vou lá. Os meus pais queriam que eu fosse viver com eles mas eu queria acabar os estudos, sempre quis fazer o 12º e prefiro estar aqui.

Foi bom ter vindo para a instituição. Já estou bastante ligado e agora vai-me custar sair. O objetivo que eles queriam de mim ao menos consegui. Nunca acreditaram que eu ia fazer sequer o 9º ano, quanto mais o 12º. Mas eu fiz o 12º. Eles não acreditavam que eu conseguisse por causa da minha maneira de ser e dos conflitos que eu arranjava no início. Todos os dias havia sempre queixas de mim, que eu faltava às aulas ou estava a fazer asneiras e desconcentrava a turma. Agora estou a trabalhar. Assinei contrato a semana passada. O emprego não é mau; não é bem a minha área mas arranjei emprego. Eu queria continuar para a universidade mas via as outras pessoas com licenciaturas que não arranjavam emprego e por isso desisti da ideia. Ter feito o 12º ano foi o que mais me marcou porque toda a gente que me acompanhou desde o início dizia que eu não ia chegar nem ao 9º ano.

A instituição mudou muito nos últimos anos. A identidade da instituição não é aquilo que era antigamente. Antes, era mais restritivo, não se podia usar telemóveis. Agora já deixam usar tudo e deixam sair. Agora é mais livre e as pessoas que vão para a instituição vão por outro tipo de problemas e são mais velhas. Se eu entrasse com essa idade, se calhar não melhorava. Por isso, foi bom ter entrado naquela altura, com aquelas regras.

Early on, I didn't feel comfortable to speak about what was going on but then I started to open up and have grown greatly. In the institution I had a psychologist who helped me grow, leave the problems behind and keep going with my life. When I was 15 I decided to stop the psychological support because I no longer had problems and didn't need this anymore. I also had two workers of the institution who helped me a lot. I have known them from the beginning and when I need support they are always there for me, even to this day.

I never had contact with the police or the court. I just had to go to the child protection commission two or three times. The last time I was there I was 17 or 19 years old and it was for me to say if I wanted to stay at the institution. The times I went to the child protection commission I had to go alone; everything we said was kept between us. It was always a lady that used to ask me if everything was all right with me at the institution. One of the times I had to go there was to determine the weekend visits.

My parents emigrated 13 years ago. They always call me on Sundays. During the holidays I go visit them or they come to Portugal. Some time ago, my parents wanted me to go live with them but I wanted to finish high school and I preferred to stay here.

It was good that I came to the institution. I am very attached to it and now it will be hard to leave. The main goal they had for me, I got it. They never believed that I would even pass 9th grade, much less high school. But I did finish high school. They didn't believe I would get this far because of my attitude and the conflicts I had in the beginning. Every day there were complaints that I skipped classes or was disruptive. Now I am working. I signed a contract last week. The job isn't bad; it's not really my area but I have a job. To finish high school was my biggest accomplishment because everyone used to tell me that I would not pass 9th grade.

The institution changed a lot in recent years. The identity of the institution is not the same. Before it was more restrictive and we couldn't use cell phones. Now they let us use everything and let us go out. Now it's more liberal and people who are going to the institution have other kinds of problems and are older. Maybe I wouldn't have gotten better if I went to the institution older. So it was good to come to the institution in those old times, with those rules.

"Quero sair em breve para poder encontrar a minha irmã"

História de Filipa

Antes de ir para uma instituição vivia com a minha mãe, com o meu pai e com os meus irmãos. Nós morávamos num bairro difícil e eu tinha medo de lá estar. Numa noite em que a minha mãe teve que ir trabalhar, eu fiquei em casa com o meu irmão mais velho, tive muito medo e fugi com os meus irmãos para casa da madrinha da minha irmã. Ela escondeu-nos e chamou a polícia. Foi assim que aconteceu.

Primeiro, a polícia levou-nos para um colégio temporário onde estivemos 3 meses. Depois levaram-nos para outra cidade muito longe. Naquela altura só me disseram que eu tinha sido retirada à minha mãe. Eu tinha 6 anos. Nunca pensei que me levassem para tão longe. Nem sequer sabia o que era um colégio.

Quando tinha 9 anos, disseram-me que tinha de mudar-me para outro colégio, mas não me disseram onde é que era, nem como era, não me disseram nada. Só me disseram que eu ia mudar de colégio. Nessa altura só estava com a minha irmã porque o meu irmão já tinha saído do colégio. A única coisa que eu perguntei foi o que é que ia acontecer com a minha irmã, e eles disseram-me que ela ia ser adotada. A partir desse momento, eu já não quis saber de mais nada. Comece a chorar e saí do escritório. Depois disso também não quis falar mais. Eu sabia que ia sofrer assim que saísse de lá e, por isso, não queria estar sempre a tocar no mesmo assunto. A minha irmã tinha 5 anos na altura e eu ainda penso nela todos os dias. Nunca mais a vi depois de sair de lá. Desde que nos separamos, tenho andado a perguntar por ela e a tentar descobrir onde ela está mas eles dizem-me sempre que não me podem dar nenhuma informação. Quero sair em breve para poder encontrar a minha irmã. Ainda tenho contacto com a minha mãe mas com o meu pai nem tanto. Normalmente vou passar os fins de semana com a minha mãe.

Na instituição tentam juntar as meninas que têm mais ou menos a mesma idade. Depois estamos divididas por quartos e há uma educadora em cada unidade. Eu estava num quarto mas depois houve mudanças e eu disse que queria mudar para a unidade com as meninas mais novas mas eles não deixaram. Quando abriu uma vaga, tornei a insistir e eles deixaram-me ir para lá. Eu adoro a minha educadora.

"I want to leave soon so I can find my sister"

Filipa's Story

Before I went to an institution I used to live with my mother, father and two brothers. We lived in a tough neighbourhood and I was afraid of being there. One night my mother had to go to work and I stayed home with my older brother. I felt so afraid I ran to my sister's godmother's place with my siblings. She hid us and called the police. That's how it happened.

First, the police took us to a temporary institution where we stayed for 3 months. After that, they moved us to a city far away. At that time, I was only told that I had been taken away from my mother. I was 6 years old. I never thought they would take me so far away. I did not even know what an institution was.

When I was 9 years old they told me I had to move to another institution. They did not say where it was, how it was, they did not say a thing. They only said that I was going to move to a new place. My little sister was the only one still with me because my brother had already left the institution. The only thing I asked was what was going to happen to my sister and they said she was going to be adopted. From that moment on I did not want to know about anything else. I started crying and then left the office. Then I did not want to talk anymore. I knew I would suffer as soon as I got out of there so I did not want to talk about that all the time. My sister was 5 years old and I still think about her every day. I never saw her again after I left. Ever since we separated I have asked about her and I have tried to find out where she is but they always say they cannot give me that information. I want to leave soon so I can find my sister. I still stay in touch with my mother but not that much with my father. I usually spend the weekends with my mother.

At the institution they try to group girls according to their age. Then they split us in rooms and we have a monitor for each unit. I was in one room but there were some changes and I said I wanted to move to the unit with the younger girls but I wasn't allowed to. Then, when there was room available, I insisted again and they allowed me to move there. I love my monitor.

A pessoa responsável por mim é a assistente social da Comissão de Proteção de Crianças e Jovens (CPCJ). Quando estava longe, não sei quem era responsável por mim mas também devia ser alguém da CPCJ. Quando preciso de alguma coisa, falo com a minha assistente social e ela depois fala com a minha educadora.

Agora tenho de decidir se saio já da instituição, ou se saio só quando acabar o curso. Durante alguns meses, pensei em ficar até acabar o curso. Mas depois mudei de ideias e queria sair logo depois ao fazer 18 anos mas agora já mudei outra vez de ideias. É difícil decidir sozinha depois de ter estado numa instituição tanto tempo e tendo sempre alguém a tomar as decisões por mim. Quando queria fazer uma coisa vinha alguém e dizia: "Ah, não, não fazes isto, fazes aquilo". Arrependo-me de ter saído do colégio anterior, mas na realidade a escolha não foi minha.

Neste momento, estou no 11º ano e ainda me falta um ano para acabar o curso de cozinha. Quero acabar o 12º ano com uma boa média para depois tirar pastelaria ou, quem sabe, outro curso melhor. Na instituição aprendemos a ser mulheres, a tornar-nos mais autónomas e mais responsáveis. Eles preparam-nos para o futuro. Por outro lado, não temos tanta liberdade. Por exemplo, quando não tenho aulas, eles podiam deixar-me sair com os meus colegas, ou com o meu namorado para não estar sempre na instituição. Estar na instituição, ir para a escola, estar na instituição, ir para a escola, sempre assim todos os dias a mesma rotina, também me custa. Com esta idade, já percebemos mais as coisas e queremos um bocado o nosso espaço e não o temos. Foi importante ouvir as monitoras dizerem que não queriam que eu me fosse embora. Eu sabia que gostavam de mim mas não até chegar ao ponto de dizerem para eu não me ir embora.

Hoje faço 18 anos e sinto-me contente, mas ao mesmo tempo triste. Porque, como diz a maior parte das pessoas, 18 anos só se fazem uma vez. E nessa data era para estar tudo reunido, amigos, família; as pessoas mais importantes. E não é isso que vai acontecer. Só vou estar com a minha mãe, mas a minha irmã não vai estar lá.

The person responsible for me is a social worker from the child protection commission (CPCJ). When I was sent to a distant city I do not know who was responsible for me but I assume it was someone from CPCJ as well. When I need anything I talk to my social worker first and then she talks to my monitor.

Right now I have to decide if I leave the institution right away or only when I finish school. For many months I thought I would stay until I finish my course. Then I changed my mind and decided I would leave right after my 18th birthday but now I changed back again. It is difficult to decide for yourself after being in an institution for so long and having someone else doing it for me. I would say I want to do this and then someone would come and say: "no, you don't do this, you'll do that". I regret leaving the first institution but in the end that was not my decision.

I am in 11th grade now; I still have one more year to finish my course to become a cook. I want to finish 12th grade with a good overall mark so that I can enrol in the pastry course, or even a better course. At the institution we learn how to become women, how to become more independent and more responsible. They prepare us for the future. On the other hand we do not have that much freedom. For example, when I do not have school in the afternoon they could let me go out with my friends or boyfriend so that I am not at the institution all the time. I am at the institution, then I go to school, then I go back, then school again, every day the same routine and it gets hard to deal with it. At our age we already understand a few things and we feel the need to have our own space but we do not have it. It was important to hear the monitors say that they did not want me to go away. I knew they liked me but not to the point of telling me not to leave.

Today is my birthday, I am 18 years old now and I feel happy and sad at the same time. It is, as they say, you are only 18 once. Today I should be surrounded by family and friends; the most important people. But that is not going to happen. I will be with my mother but my sister will not be there.

"É muito difícil ser estrangeiro em Portugal"

História de Henrique

Nasci na Guiné Bissau. Lá passávamos por muitas dificuldades. Os meus pais não tinham possibilidade de nos criar. Muitas vezes, os pais preferem não comer para poderem dar aos filhos. Foi a minha avó que me criou. Ela é a melhor pessoa que tenho na vida porque foi a pessoa que me criou apesar de todas as dificuldades que tinha. A minha avó é uma mãe e um pai para mim. Ela é tudo para mim. A primeira coisa que vou fazer quando estiver por minha conta é ajudar a minha avó e enviar dinheiro todos os meses, se conseguir.

Vim para Portugal com 11 anos e vim fazer o 7º ano aqui. Nesse ano não passei porque não falava português muito bem. Eu estava a viver com o meu pai e com uma madrasta com quem não me dava muito bem. O meu pai decidiu levar-me para casa da minha tia e eu fiquei lá um ano. Eu dormia no sofá porque não havia outro sítio onde dormir. A minha tia começou a pensar que seria melhor que eu fosse para um colégio por causa das despesas e também porque na instituição eu teria um sítio para dormir. Ela depois falou com o meu pai, o meu pai concordou e depois falaram comigo. Eu aceitei essa ideia e depois eles levaram-me para lá. Eu aceitei porque vi que estava a precisar de ajuda e nem a minha tia, nem o meu pai, me iam conseguir ajudar. Então achei que o colégio me podia ajudar. Entrei lá quando tinha 13 anos.

Os primeiros tempos no colégio foram muito difíceis. Não estava habituado àquilo. O ambiente e as pessoas eram muito diferentes. Havia lá muitas pessoas malucas, por assim dizer. Muitas pessoas tomavam comprimidos para dormir; alguns eram mal educados e não tinham respeito pelos monitores. Eu sentia saudades de casa e, muitas vezes, no quarto, à noite, levantava-me da cama, punha-me à beira da janela a olhar para fora, a pensar. Depois, ao longo do tempo, fui conhecendo as pessoas e criei algumas amizades. Um dos monitores aqui é, para mim, das melhores pessoas que podem existir numa instituição. É uma pessoa com princípios. Quando uma pessoa está errada, ele fala, como dois amigos, não berra. Ele ajuda as pessoas, em tudo o que a gente precisa. Nunca diz não. A mim nunca me recusou a nada.

No princípio, os outros rapazes chamavam-me "preto" e coisas assim. Isto no princípio deitava-me abaixo, mas agora já não ligo a isso. Dou valor àquilo que sou.

"It's very difficult to be a foreigner in Portugal"

Henrique's Story

I was born in Guinea-Bissau. We had many difficulties there. My parents did not have resources to raise us. Oftentimes, parents there prefer not to eat so they can give food to their children. My grandmother raised me. She is the best person I have in my life because she raised me in spite of all the difficulties she had. My grandmother is a mother and a father to me. She is everything to me. The first thing I will do when I am on my own is to help my grandmother and send her money every month, if I can.

I came to Portugal when I was 11 years old and went to 7th grade here. I didn't pass that year because I didn't speak Portuguese very well. I was living with my father and a stepmother with whom I didn't really get along. My father decided to send me to my aunt's house and I lived there one year. I would sleep on the couch because I didn't have any other place to sleep. She thought it might be best for me to go to an institution because of the expenses and because at the institution I would have a place to sleep. She then talked with my father about it, my father agreed and then they talked with me. I accepted their idea and they took me there. I agreed because I thought that I needed help, because I saw that my aunt would not be able to help me, nor would my father. So, I thought that the institution could help me. I entered the institution when I was 13 years old.

The first times at the institution were very difficult. I was not used to it. The environment and the people were very different. A lot of people there were crazy, so to speak. A lot of people took pills to sleep; some of them were rude and disrespectful even with the staff. I missed home, and sometimes, in the room, at night, I got out of bed and sat by the window looking outside and thinking. Over time, I got to know people and was able to make friends. One of the monitors here is one of the best people that can work at an institution. He is a person with values. When people are wrong he talks with them, like two friends, he doesn't scream. He helps us in anything we need. He never says no. He never refused anything to me.

In the beginning, the other kids called me "nigger" and things like that. This used to put me down but now I don't care about it. I value myself. A few years ago there were many Portuguese people who were racist and called out those kinds of names. Nowadays, I see many black and white people interacting together.

Há alguns anos atrás havia muitos portugueses que eram racistas e chamavam esses tipos de nomes. Mas hoje vejo pretos e brancos a conviverem.

É muito difícil ser estrangeiro em Portugal. Nós não temos os mesmos direitos. Temos que estar sempre a renovar a autorização de residência e, se fica fora da validade, não podemos fazer nada. A autorização de residência às vezes dura um ano, às vezes dura dois anos. Depende. Por exemplo, é fácil para quem trabalha. Se uma pessoa tiver 18, 19 anos e não tiver um trabalho, vai ser mais complicado porque tem de se pagar impostos, essas coisas todas, para poder renovar a residência. Eles pedem o passaporte, cartão das vacinas, e uma data de informação. No colégio eles também ajudam a obter e organizar esses documentos. Já tive de abdicar de atividades que eram muito importantes para mim por causa de ser estrangeiro.

Estou contente por poder ficar no colégio até aos 21 anos porque isso vai-me dar tempo para organizar a minha vida. Há alguns meses mandaram-me para a casa de pré autonomia. Tem sido uma experiência muito boa. Esta casa serve para nos preparar para o futuro: levantar a horas, lavar a roupa, limpar, cozinhar, fazer tudo por nossa conta. Acho que tem ajudado imenso. Antes não sabia cozinhar e agora já sei, mais ou menos. Tem sido um grande apoio viver nesta casa.

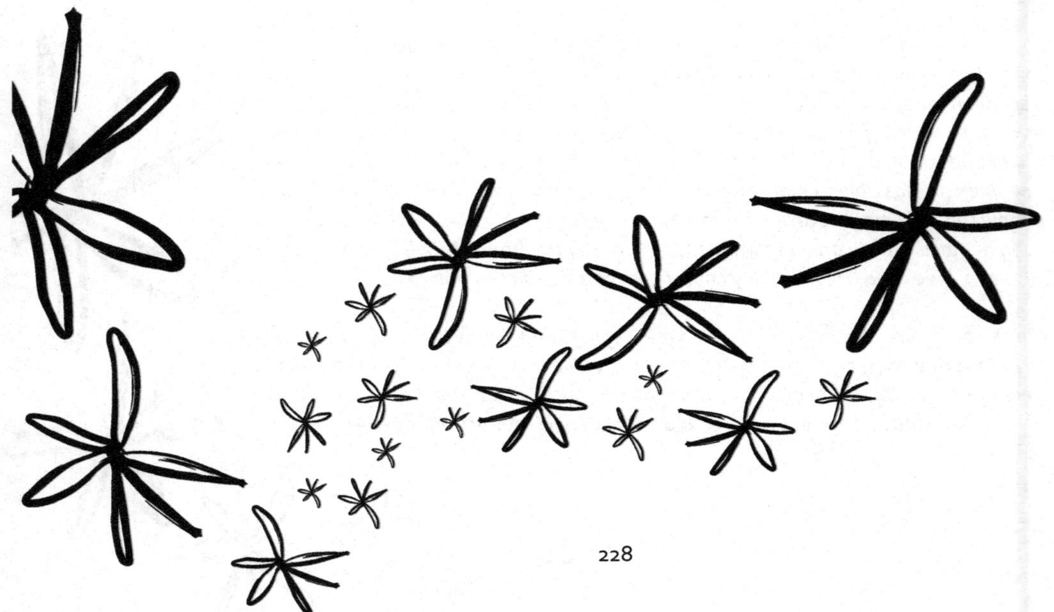

It's very difficult to be a foreigner in Portugal. We don't have the same rights. We have to renew the residence permit all the time and if it is expired we can't do anything. Sometimes the permit is good for one year, other times it lasts two years. It depends. For instance, it is easier if you have a job. If you are 18, 19 years old and you don't have a job, it will be more difficult because you have to pay taxes, all that stuff, to be able to renew the residence permit. They ask for passport, vaccination card, and a lot of other papers and information. The institution also helps with gathering all the documents. I have been unable to participate in activities that were very important to me because I am a foreigner.

I am glad I can stay in the institution up until I am 21 years old because this should give me enough time to get my life on track. Some months ago, they sent me to the pre-autonomy home. It has been a very good experience to stay at this home. This home is meant to prepare us for the future: wake up every day on time, do our laundry, clean up, cook, do everything on our own. I think this will help me a lot. Before I didn't know how to cook and now I can cook a bit. It has been a great support to live in this home.

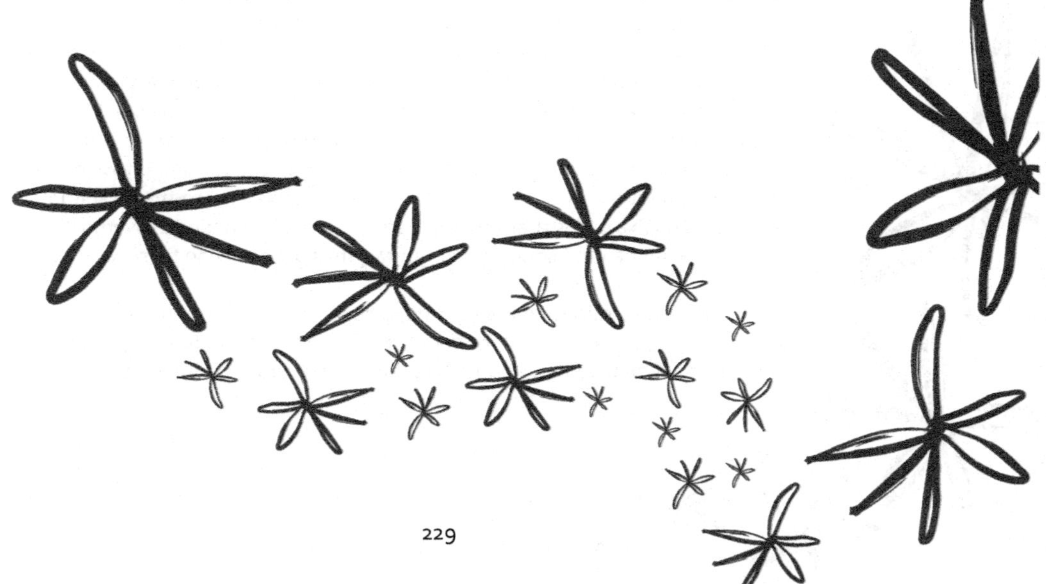

"Muitas vezes disseram-me que não ia conseguir certas coisas na vida"

História de Liliana

O meu pai e a minha mãe não tinham um casamento feliz. Infelizmente a minha mãe tinha autismo e não cuidava de nós em condições, era eu que tomava conta dos meus irmãos. Sou a mais velha dos meus irmãos todos. Mudava-lhes a fralda e dava-lhes de comer. A minha mãe não cuidava de nós e o meu pai, quando chegava a casa, batia na minha mãe. Ninguém merece mas, neste caso, a minha mãe metia a vida dos filhos em risco. Não era a melhor maneira do meu pai responder, que isso não se faz. Mas apesar de tudo sempre amei muito o meu pai. A minha vida na escola foi boa. Aos 6 anos perdi os meus pais. Eles não morreram, mas fomos abandonados. Os meus padrinhos já tinham feito queixa várias vezes e eu já estava à espera que isto acontecesse. O meu irmão tinha 5 anos e a minha irmã tinha 12 meses. Na altura, nós tivemos que ser adotadas. O meu pai sempre nos seguiu, sempre nos foi visitar. A minha mãe só nos foi visitar uma vez, mas tratou-me mal e a nova família disse que não queria que isso voltasse a acontecer.

A assistente social que seguia o meu caso falava comigo porque eu era a mais velha. Na altura, eu e o meu irmão fomos para uma família de acolhimento mas a senhora teve um acidente e faleceu. Então, passámos para outra família, onde estivemos 5 anos, os dois. Entretanto a minha mãe também foi entregar a minha irmã. A meio da estadia nessa família, fomos para outra família e estivemos lá 17 dias. Essa família tinha adoptado uma criança negra, e tratavam-na mal. Não queriam que eu estudasse nem nada. Só os meus irmãos. Eu tinha que ir trabalhar para a empresa deles. Eram pessoas com dinheiro. Fiz queixa na altura, sem saberem, telefonei para a minha assistente social. Isto já foi há muitos anos, não me recordo muito bem como é que foi a conversa, mas lembro-me perfeitamente de ter feito queixa e eles tiraram-nos. Depois da família em que estivemos 17 dias, eu e a minha irmã continuámos juntas, mas o meu irmão foi separado.

A minha irmã andou sempre comigo, e depois encontrámos uma família de acolhimento, que na altura queria ter filhos mas já era tarde. Tentaram adotar-me, a mim e à minha irmã, só que as coisas não correram muito bem comigo.

"Many times I was told that I
would not achieve certain things
in life"

Liliana' Story

My mum and dad did not have a happy marriage. Unfortunately my mother had autism and did not take care of us, I was the one who looked after my younger siblings. I am the oldest of my siblings. I would change their diapers and feed them. My mother did not take care of us and my father would hit her when he got home. No one deserves that but in this case she was putting our lives at risk. My father's response wasn't the best. However, I have always loved him. My life at school was good. When I was 6 I lost my parents. They did not die, we were abandoned. My godparents had reported the situation several times so I was already expecting this to happen. My brother was 5 and my younger sister was 12 months old. At that time, we had to be adopted. My father always visited us. My mother only visited us once but she treated me badly so the new family said they did not want this to happen again.

The social worker who followed my case talked to me because I was the oldest. At that time, my brother and I went to a foster family but the lady had an accident and passed away. We had to move to another family where my brother and I stayed for 5 years. Meanwhile, my mum also handed in my younger sister. Halfway through this stay we went to another family for 17 days. This new family had already adopted a black kid and treated him badly. They did not want me to go to school, only my younger siblings. I had to work at their company. They were people with money. I was the one who reported the situation and called my social worker. This was many years ago, I cannot remember the words exactly but I do remember reporting it and that was why we left their house. After this, my sister and I stayed together but my brother was separated from us.

My sister was with me until we found a new foster family who wanted to have children but it was too late for them. They tried to adopt us both but things did not go that well with me. At that time I really wanted to be adopted, but then I saw that things were not ok and I was fed up with going back to the institution, then back to being adopted, over and over again. One day I said: "I will stay at the institution for good!" and so I've been there since I was 9 years old and I am ok. Meanwhile, my sister was adopted and I still get to see her now and then, but it is not as it used to be.

Eu na altura queria muito ser adotada, mas vi que as coisas não estavam bem, e estava farta de tentar ser adotada, voltar para o colégio, tentar ser adotada, voltar para o colégio. Até que disse: "eu fico no colégio definitivamente", e estou aqui desde os 9 anos e estou bem. A minha irmã entretanto foi adotada e ainda a vou vendo, de vez em quando, mas não é como era dantes.

Quando vim para o colégio, fiquei com uma tutora. A pessoa que eu tive como tutora foi uma pessoa incrível. Foi a diretora da instituição e para mim ela é uma mãe. Além de ser muito profissional, dentro da instituição, ela trata-me igual a toda a gente, lá fora é uma mãe e trata-me como uma filha. Muitas vezes fui a casa dela passar o Natal, quando era mais nova. Vou muitas vezes a casa dela passar os fins-de-semana, porque lá fora, somos amigas. Ela foi minha tutora até aos 18 anos. Qualquer tipo de autorização era tratado com ela mas sempre tive muita liberdade. Desde os 16 anos já podia ir sair com os meus amigos. Também eu nunca dei problemas com namorados.

Tudo o que eu passei até agora de mau foi positivo porque fez-me crescer. E fez-me ver as coisas de outra forma. Muitas vezes disseram-me que não ia conseguir certas coisas na vida. E muitas pessoas insistiam em tocar sempre na ferida, em atirar-me certas coisas à cara, mas perderam o seu tempo, porque eu sou muito forte, sei aquilo que valho e não me deixo calcar por qualquer pessoa.

Se calhar se as coisas tivessem corrido melhor, eu não me tinha separado do meu irmão. O meu irmão, para mim, era como se fosse meu gémeo. Se calhar se eu tivesse reagido de outra forma, também estava ao pé da minha irmã. Mas, por outro lado, não me arrependo de ter ido para a instituição. Foi o melhor para mim.

Temos que dar ouvidos às pessoas que estão ao nosso lado, porque às vezes aquelas que nós ignoramos são as que mais depressa nos apoiam quando nos vamos abaixo. Cresçam como pessoas, porque tudo é possível. Como comigo, tive a possibilidade de ter um final feliz na minha vida: sempre tive o sonho de encontrar um irmão que há mais de 15 anos não sabia nada dele. Neste momento, estou radiante porque no Natal vou poder reviver a minha infância com a família com quem estivemos 5 anos e com os meus irmãos. Desistir nunca, lutar sempre pelos nossos sonhos.

When I went to the institution I was assigned a tutor. My tutor is an incredible person. She is the Director of this institution and to me she is like a mother. In addition to being very professional, inside the institution she treats me like anyone else, outside the institution she is like a mother and treats me as if I was her own daughter. A lot of times I went to spend Christmas at her place, when I was younger. I often spend the weekends with her because outside the institution we are good friends. She was my tutor until I was 18. Any authorization was treated with her but I always had a lot of freedom. I could go out with my friends since I was 16 and I never got myself into trouble when it comes to boyfriends.

Every bad thing I have been through has been positive because it made me grow up. It changed the way I see things. Many times I was told that I would not achieve certain things in life. Many people insisted on hurting me and saying bad things to my face but they have wasted their time because I am very strong, I know what I am worth and I do not let people hurt me.

Maybe things could have been better and I would not be separated from my brother. He was like my twin. Maybe if I reacted differently I would still be with my sister. But on the other hand I do not regret going to the institution. It was the best for me.

We should listen to people who are by our side because sometimes the ones we ignore are those who are willing to help us get back on our feet when we fall. We should grow as human beings because everything is possible. Like for example with me, I had the chance to have a happy ending in my life: I always had a dream that I would find my brother who had been separated from me for over 15 years and right now I am so happy because we will spend Christmas together and I will be able to relive my childhood with my siblings and the family we lived with for 5 years. Never give up, always fight for your dreams.

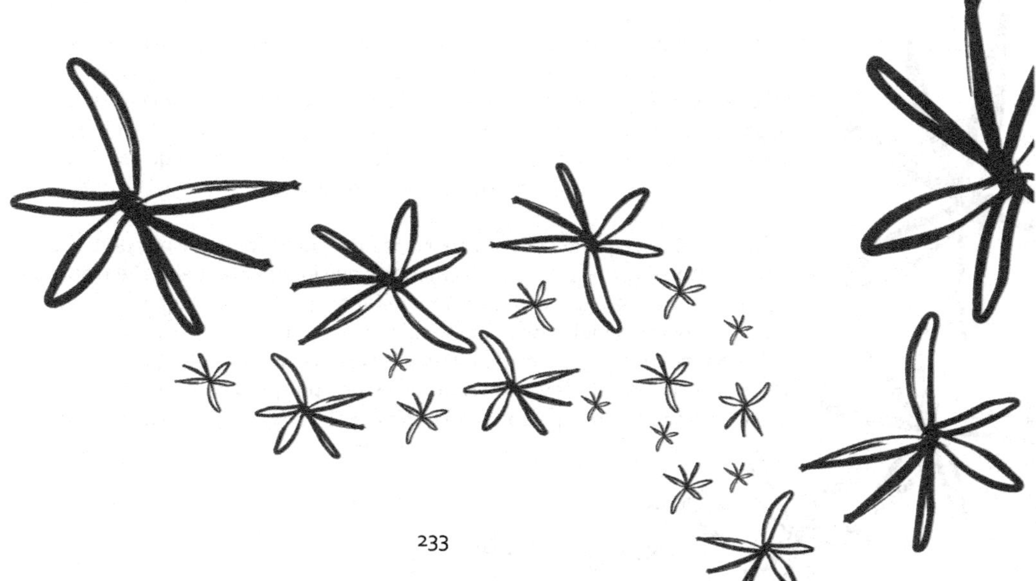

"Ia para casa e voltava, era sempre aquele receio"

História de Mónica

A primeira vez que vim para a instituição foi a pé, porque moro mesmo aqui ao lado. A minha irmã e eu viemos para a instituição há uns 10 anos. A minha irmã só veio porque quis e foi por causa de mim. Os meus dois irmãos mais velhos ficaram em casa porque eram melhores alunos. Quando vim para a instituição, achei estranho mas lembro-me que a minha mãe disse: "Vais para o colégio para ver se sobes essas notas". Não me habituava à ideia, ia para casa e voltava, era sempre aquele receio e era muito chato. Tanto sente-se tristeza como felicidade. A primeira semana é sempre complicado, estar afastada dos pais mas a minha irmã sentiu mais tristeza ao separar-se do pai do que da mãe. Nós estávamos mais ligadas ao meu pai do que à minha mãe. A assistente social disse que, mal entrasse aqui, era óbvio que ia sentir aquela tristeza por não estar com os meus pais, mas depois que eu me ia habituar à ideia de estar aqui. Os meus pais perguntaram se eu gostava de estar na instituição. A primeira semana disse que não, porque me estava a habituar à ideia. Mas habituei-me à ideia de gostar de sopa e tudo. Sinto-me bem aqui. Percebi logo que, se viesse para aqui, era para aprender. Foi bom. Comecei a subir as notas. Aqui, o mais positivo é sabermos que temos aquele apoio, que nos arranjam tudo o que precisamos, e em casa já nem temos tanto esse apoio como temos aqui. Todos os fins de semana vou a casa dos meus pais. Os meus pais estão desempregados há bastante tempo.

Antes de vir para esta instituição, estive noutra. Não gostei nada desta instituição. A Diretora até era simpática, mas com aquelas horas para dormir, horas para não sei quê. Quando éramos muito desarrumadas, a subdiretora punha todas as nossas coisas num saco e só nos entregava no final do semestre. Nem sequer ia aos fins de semana a casa. Custou-me muito a adaptação e tive que sair porque as empregadas não gostavam nada de mim.

Gosto muito de praticar desporto. Na instituição gostam que nós pratiquemos desporto escolar e somos várias meninas que jogamos andebol. Tem aqui um professor que dá explicações e também faz desporto. Foi ele que nos meteu no andebol e no futebol e assim. Eu sempre gostei muito da escola, especialmente do segundo ciclo. Agora, estou no secundário e também gosto. Estou a gostar da minha turma e fazemos várias visitas de estudo porque a minha diretora de turma dizia, e com razão, que passar quatro anos inteiros dentro da escola é muito mau e cansativo.

"I went home and came back, I always had that fear"

Mónica's Story

The first time I went walking to the institution because we lived nearby. My younger sister and I both went to live at the institution some 10 years ago. My younger sister went there because she wanted to stay with me. I have two older brothers but they stayed at home because they had better grades at school. When I came to the institution, I thought it was weird but I remember that my mother told me: "You will go to the institution to raise your grades." I couldn't get used to the idea, I went home and came back, I always had that fear and it was very difficult. One feels sadness and happiness. The first week was very difficult because we were away from our parents. My sister was especially sad to be separated from our father. We were more connected to our father than our mother. The social worker told us that, in the beginning, it's natural to feel sad from being separated from our parents but after a while we would get used to the idea of living in the institution. My parents asked me if I liked the institution. In the first week my answer was "no" but then I got used to the idea and eventually even got used to the soup and everything. Now I feel good there. I understood that the purpose to go to the institution was to learn more and that was good. My grades started to increase. The most positive thing in the institution is to know that we have support. They give us everything we need and at home we don't have this type of support. I go to my parents' home every weekend. My parents have been unemployed for a long time.

Before I went to this institution I spent some time at another one. I didn't like this institution at all. The director was friendly, but all those rules, hours to sleep, hours to everything. And when we were untidy the subdirector would put all our stuff in a bag and would only give it back at the end of the semester. I also didn't go home on the weekends. The adaptation was very hard and I had to leave because the staff didn't like me.

I love practicing sports. In the institution they like that we play school sports and there are a lot of girls who are playing handball. We have a teacher who tutors us and also practices sports. He was the one who introduced us to handball and football. I have always loved school, especially middle school. Now I am in high school and I also love it I like my class and we make lots of field trips because our class director says, and rightfully so, that spending four years in school is very tiring. Now in high school, I'm taking a culinary and pastry course and I'm almost finishing it. I have never considered going to college.

Estou a fazer um curso de cozinha e pastelaria que gosto e já estou quase a acabar.
Nunca considerei seguir para a universidade.

Aos 18 anos, fui à assistente social, para saber se queria ou não ficar na instituição,
mas eu disse que queria ficar até acabar este curso e arranjar um emprego. E quando
tiver um emprego garantido penso sair logo daqui. Foi bom ter vindo para a instituição
porque estou a evoluir. Aqui, ensinam-nos a crescer mais, a ter autoestima e a ser mais
autónomas. No futuro, gostava de ser jogadora de andebol e trabalhar numa confeitaria.

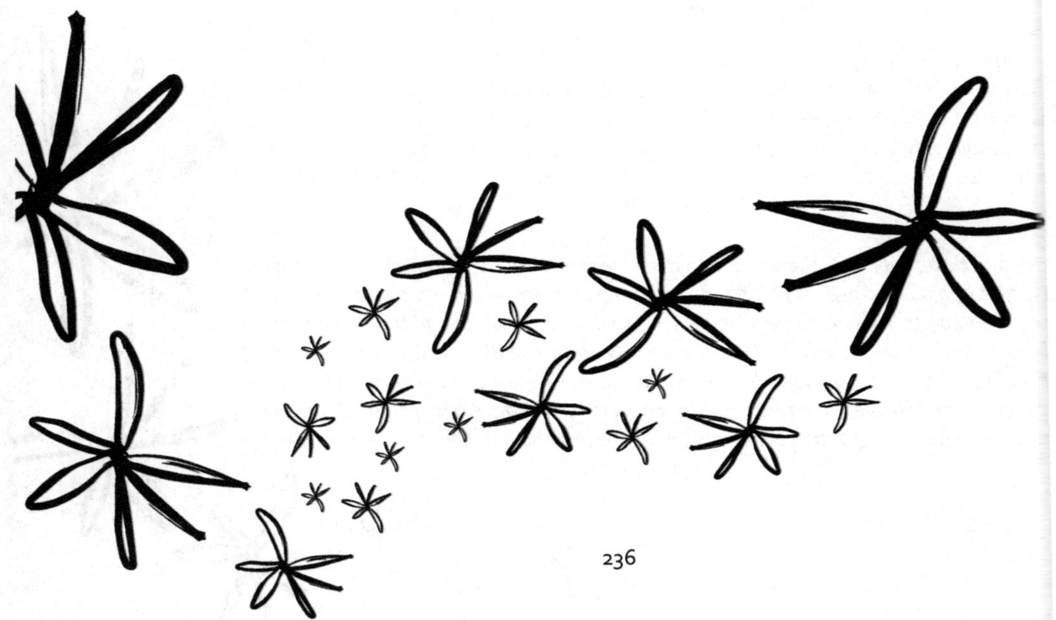

When I turned 18, I went to the social worker to decide if I wanted to stay at the institution and I decided I wanted to stay until I finish my course and find a job. Once I find a stable job I will leave the institution. I am glad I am at the institution because I feel that I am evolving. Here they teach us to grow, to have self-esteem and to be more autonomous. In the future I would like to be a handball player and work in a bakery.

"Tu nas učijo odraščanja, samospoštovanja in večje avtonomije"

Mónicina zgodba

V ustanovo sem prvič šla peš, ker smo živeli blizu. Z mlajšo sestro sva obe šli živet v ustanovo pred približno desetimi leti. Moja mlajša sestra je šla tja, ker je hotela biti z mano. Imam dva starejša brata, a sta ostala doma, ker sta imela boljše ocene v šoli. Ko sem prišla v ustanovo, se mi je zdelo čudno, a se spomnim, da mi je mama rekla »V ustanovo boš šla, da izboljšaš ocene.« Prve dni se nisem mogla privaditi na idejo. Težko je bilo hoditi sem in tja med domom in ustanovo. Imela sem veliko mešanih občutkov strahu, žalosti in sreče.

Prvi teden je bil zelo težek, ker sva bili daleč od staršev. Moja sestra je bila še posebej žalostna, da je bila ločena od očeta. Bolj sva bili povezani z očetom kot z mamo. Socialna delavka nama je povedala, da se je na začetku naravno počutiti žalostno zaradi ločitve od staršev, a se bova čez čas navadili na idejo življenja v ustanovi. Starša sta me vprašala, če mi je ustanova všeč. Prvi teden je bil moj odgovor 'ne', a sem se potem navadila na idejo in na koncu celo na juho in vse ... Zdaj se tam dobro počutim. Razumela sem, da je namen obiskovanja ustanove učenje in to je bilo dobro. Ocene so se začele višati. Najbolj pozitivna stvar v ustanovi je, da vemo, da imamo podporo. Dajo nam vse, kar potrebujemo, doma pa nimamo take podpore.

K staršem domov grem vsak vikend. Starša sta že dolgo brezposelna.

Preden sem šla v to ustanovo, sem kratek čas preživela v drugi. Tista mi sploh ni bila všeč. Direktor je bil prijazen, a vsa tista pravila, čas za spanje, čas za vse ... in če smo imeli razmetano, je pomočnik direktorja vse naše stvari dal v vrečo in nam jih vrnil le na koncu semestra. Pa tudi čez vikend nisem hodila domov. Prilagajanje je bilo zelo težko in sem morala oditi, ker osebju nisem bila všeč.

Rada se športno udejstvujem. V ustanovi jim je všeč, da se ukvarjamo s šolskim športi, in veliko deklet igra rokomet. Imamo učitelja, ki nas inštruira in se tudi športno udejstvuje. On je bil tisti, ki nas je seznanil z rokometom in nogometom. Šola mi je bila vedno všeč, posebej višji razredi osnovne šole.

Zdaj sem v srednji šoli, ki mi je tudi všeč. Moj razred mi je všeč, hodimo na veliko izletov, ker razrednica upravičeno pravi, da so štiri leta, preživeta v šoli, zelo utrujajoča. Zdaj v srednji šoli hodim na kuharski in slaščičarski tečaj, ki ga bom kmalu končala. Nikoli nisem razmišljala, da bi šla na fakulteto.

Ko sem dopolnila osemnajst let, sem šla k socialni delavki, ki me je vprašala, če sem se odločila ostati v ustanovi. Odločila sem se, da ostanem, dokler ne končam tečaja in ne najdem službe. Ko si najdem redno službo, bom zapustila ustanovo. Zadovoljna sem, da sem v ustanovi, ker se mi zdi, da se razvijam. Tu nas učijo odraščanja, samospoštovanja in večje avtonomije. V prihodnosti bi rada igrala rokomet in delala v pekarni.

"Deviam alertar as pessoas de que há instituições como esta"

História de Ricardo

Tenho 19 anos. Quando nasci a minha mãe vivia com os pais dela, os meus avós. Ela teve muitos problemas durante a gravidez porque ainda era adolescente. Os meus avós não aceitaram muito bem a gravidez e houve muitos conflitos graves entre eles. A minha mãe acabou por me abandonar quando eu ainda era muito pequeno. Quando eu tinha 10 anos voltei a ver a minha mãe e soube que ela tinha casado e tinha outro filho. Fiquei feliz por saber que estava tudo bem com ela, mas, ao mesmo tempo, fiquei um bocado revoltado porque vi que o meu irmão tinha tudo. Eu nunca conheci o meu pai, nunca soube quem ele é. Vivi com os meus avós todo esse tempo e essa foi, provavelmente, a pior fase da minha vida. Eles fizeram-me tudo e mais alguma coisa que há de mal: desde agressões, humilharam-me, tudo o que possa ser imaginado. Vivia mesmo num clima de terror. Cheguei a ficar cheio de negras mas nunca me levaram ao hospital, se calhar com medo. Eles tratavam-me como se eu fosse um animal. Os meus tios também não me levavam ao hospital porque iam chegar lá e iam-lhes perguntar: "quem é que fez isto?" Os meus avós diziam muitas vezes que me iam entregar a uma instituição porque não queriam saber de mim.

Quando tinha 15 anos, alguém fez uma queixa anónima à polícia e tive de ir à Comissão de Proteção de Crianças e Jovens (CPCJ). No entanto, nessa altura, menti e disse que os meus avós me tratavam bem. Apesar de todo o mal que os meus avós me fizeram, eles eram a minha família e eu não queria ficar longe deles. Olhando para trás, quando fui dessa vez à CPCJ, eles deveriam ter investigado mais. O meu avô estava na consulta comigo e eu não me senti à vontade para dizer a verdade. Além disso, não tinha marcas nenhumas no corpo para provar que estava a falar a verdade.

Quando tinha 17 anos, fizeram de novo uma queixa anónima. A polícia contactou a CPCJ que foi a casa do meu avô. Eles disseram que o meu avô e eu tínhamos de ir à CPCJ no dia seguinte. Na CPCJ, fui o primeiro a ser ouvido. Eles disseram que alguém tinha feito queixa e perguntaram-me se tinha algumas negras ou arranhões. Como eu tinha uma prova física do que tinha acontecido, senti-me mais confiante. Foi por isso que confirmei imediatamente o que tinha acontecido sem pensar duas vezes. Depois, saí do gabinete e senti-me muito nervoso. Mal o meu avô saiu do gabinete eles disseram-me: "tu já não voltas para casa do teu avô."

I am 19 years old. When I was born my mother lived with her parents, my grandparents. She was in a lot of trouble during her pregnancy because she was a teenager. My grandparents did not accept that very well and there were serious conflicts between them. Eventually, my mother abandoned me when I was a toddler. At the age of 10 I met my mother again. I learned that she was married and had another child. I was happy that she had a good life but at the same time, I was a bit angry because I could see that my brother had everything. I never met my father, never knew who he is. I lived with my grandparents all that time and that was probably the worst phase of my life. They did terrible things to me; from aggressions to humiliation. I lived in a horror environment. I would get bruises all over my body but they never took me to the hospital, probably out of fear. They treated me like an animal. My aunt and uncle could not take me to the hospital either because they would get asked: "who did this?" My grandparents often said that they would send me to an institution because they did not care about me.

When I was about 15 years old someone made a report to the police and I had to go to the child protection commission (CPCJ). However, at that time I lied and told them that my grandparents treated me well. Despite all the bad things they did to me, they were still my family and I did not want to stay away from them. Looking back, I think that when I went to CPCJ, they should have investigated further. My grandfather was there with me and I didn't feel that I could tell the truth. I also did not have any marks on my body to back me up.

When I was 17 someone made an anonymous complaint. The police went to my grandfather's place. They said that my grandfather and I had to go to CPCJ in the next day. At the CPCJ, I was the first to be heard. They told me about the report and asked if I had any bruises and scratches. I had physical proof of what had happened so I felt more confident. This was why I confirmed immediately what had happened without thinking twice. Then I left the office feeling very nervous. As soon as my grandfather left they told me "You are not going back to your grandfather's house". I knew this would happen sooner or later. Later on that same day we had to go to the police because of the complaint. They asked me if I wanted to give up the complaint and I said: "no, I want to proceed with the complaint". After that we went to the court, I went to many places that day.

Eu já sabia que, mais cedo ou mais tarde, isso iria acontecer. Depois ainda tivemos que ir
à polícia, por causa da queixa. Perguntaram-me na altura se eu queria desistir e eu disse:
"não, quero avançar com a queixa". Depois disso fomos ao tribunal, andei por muitos
sítios nesse dia. À noite, os meus tios foram-me buscar e eu estive em casa deles durante
3 ou 4 meses. Nesse período em que estive em casa deles, a minha família quase toda foi
chamada a tribunal. Foi um tempo difícil. Até os meus tios estavam com medo do que
pudesse acontecer. Eles estavam a tentar fazer-me desistir da queixa mas eu disse-lhes:
"Eu é que vou decidir!"

Quando fui a tribunal, eles disseram-me "se quiseres desistir tens agora esta
oportunidade. Se não quiseres, as coisas depois podem-se complicar para os teus avós."
Eu não queria que eles sofressem como eu sofri; não os queria ver na prisão. Optei por
desistir da queixa e não estou arrependido. Depois, vivi com os meus tios mais uns 2
meses e, durante esse tempo, a CPCJ foi lá visitar-me duas vezes para ver se eu estava
bem. Eu estava muito melhor do que antes. No entanto, a casa era pequena e eu não
me estava a sentir muito confortável. Foi difícil mas decidi que era melhor ir para uma
instituição. Depois de estar na instituição também tive que ir a tribunal. A minha mãe
também teve que ir lá assinar uns papéis mas já não me lembro o que eram.

Quando fui para a instituição, vi que era uma coisa completamente diferente do que eu
imaginava. Se quisesse sair a algum lado podia ir, se quisesse falar com alguém podia
falar. Até achei um bocado estranho porque não estava habituado. Já concretizei alguns
dos meus sonhos que, se calhar em casa dos meus tios, ou dos meus avós, nunca se
teriam concretizado. Fiquei contente por poder ficar na instituição até aos 21 anos.
Assim, tenho mais tempo para organizar a minha vida. Acho que é uma oportunidade
única poder chegar a uma instituição e ouvir "se quiseres podes estudar, se quiseres
podes ir para a faculdade, garantimos-te tudo, ninguém te vai proibir de fazeres o
que queres, desde que te portes bem e cumpras as normas"; e estas regras não são
nada do outro mundo. Deviam alertar as pessoas, por exemplo na televisão, de que há
instituições como esta. O que aconteceu comigo, infelizmente, acontece a muita gente
aqui em Portugal e em todo o mundo.

At night my aunt and uncle picked me up and I stayed at their place for 3 or 4 months. During that time almost all my family was called to court. It was a difficult time. Even my aunt and uncle were afraid for what could happen. They were trying to make me give up the charge but I told them "I will decide on my own!"

When I went to court they told me: "if you want to give up you have this opportunity. If you don't, then things might get complicated for you grandparents". I did not want them to suffer like I did; I didn't want to see them in prison. I decided to give up the complaint and I do not regret it. After that I lived with my aunt and uncle for about 2 months and during that time people from CPCJ came to visit me twice, to check if I was doing OK. I was much better than before. However, the house was small and I did not feel very comfortable. It was hard but I eventually decided to go to the institution. I also had to go to court. My mother had to go there too to sign some papers but I do not remember what it was.

When I went to the institution I noticed it was completely different from what I thought. If I wanted to go out I could, if I wanted to talk to someone I could. I even thought it was a bit weird because I was not used to it. Some of my dreams already came true and maybe this would not have been possible if I stayed with my family. I am glad I can stay in the institution up until I am 21 years old. This will give me enough time to get my life on track. I think it is a unique opportunity to get to an institution and being told: "If you want you can study, you can go to university, we'll provide everything, no one will forbid you doing what you want as long as you comply with the rules" and these are nothing out of this world. They should let people know, for example on the TV, about institutions like this. Unfortunately, what happened with me happens to a lot of people in Portugal and all over the world.

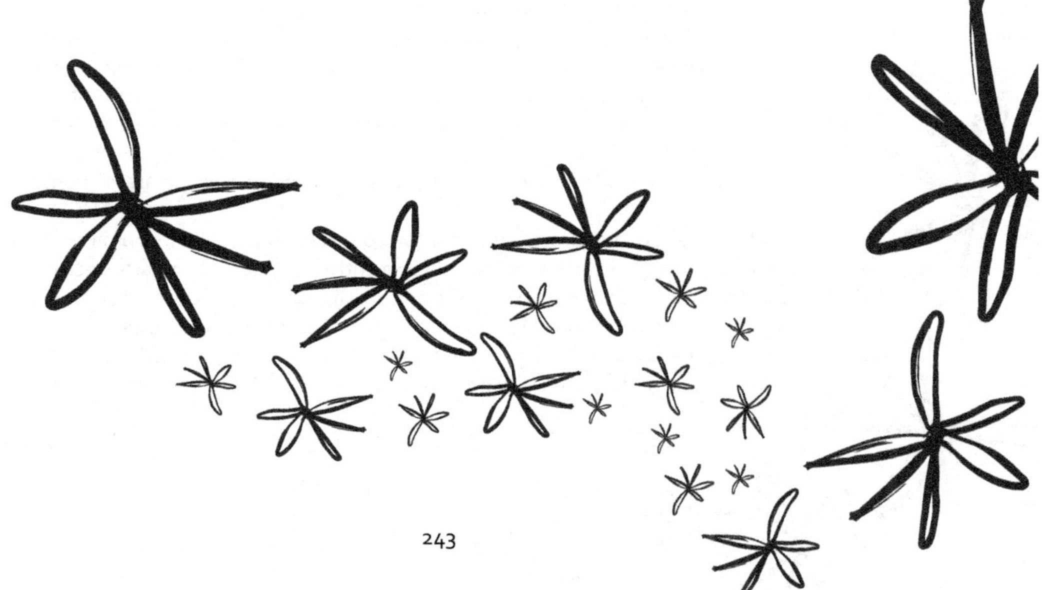

"Fiquei confuso com a ideia de mudar para outra instituição"

História de Rui

Tenho 18 anos. Andei em dois colégios antes deste onde estou agora. Antes de ir para o primeiro colégio morava com a minha família mas não quero falar sobre isso. Entrei na primeira instituição quando era bebé. A minha adaptação foi fácil. Habituei-me à professora e eles lá conheciam-me desde bebé. Foi lá que conheci um monitor que estava a começar a trabalhar. Voltei a encontrá-lo há 5 anos nesta instituição onde estou agora. O mundo é tão pequeno! Foi uma grande coincidência!

Não me lembro com que idade fui para a segunda instituição. As coisas foram muito difíceis lá. Eu portava-me mal e fugia. E lá uns miúdos batiam-me. Contei aos monitores e eles ouviram-me. Acho que foram corretos comigo. Mudei para a terceira instituição por causa disto e também porque não podia ficar lá mais, por causa da idade. Entrei nesta instituição aos 13 anos. Entrei e habituei-me. Custou um bocadinho quando a diretora foi trabalhar para outro sítio. Tinha-me habituado a tê-la aqui. Agora, dou-me bem com os monitores e os outros jovens. Sinto-me bem aqui. Eu, antigamente, portava-me mal e fugia às vezes, de manhã. Era pancada. Fugia para a praia. Uma vez, pedi comida e conheci uma amiga. Fugia muitas vezes, e depois telefonava para o 112 a pedir ajuda. Inventava muitas desculpas. Outras vezes chamei a polícia. Uma vez um senhor ajudou-me a voltar para a instituição. Agora arrependo-me, já não fujo. Nesta casa têm tudo. Pronto, têm cama, têm comida, têm tudo. Pessoas que me ajudam e apoiam quando eu preciso. Tenho momentos bons, momentos maus, como toda a gente tem. O meu monitor também me ajudou muito e os meus amigos também me ajudaram imenso.

Vou ter de ir para outra instituição porque vou fazer 19 anos. Eu tive uma entrevista no outro dia. O meu monitor foi comigo à entrevista. Ainda não há certeza mas é melhor contar que vou para esta instituição. Um dia vou sair desta casa, porque é só miudagem. Não vou estar aqui toda a vida. Estou nesta instituição há muitos anos. Esta casa vai ser sempre a minha família. No início, fiquei confuso com a ideia de mudar para outra instituição. Agora já sei que é bué da fixe.

"I was confused with the idea of having to move to another institution"

Rui's Story

I am 18 years old. I lived in two other institutions before the one I live in today. Before I went to the first institution I lived with my family but I don't want to talk about that. I was still a baby when I went to the first institution. My adaptation there was easy. I got used to the teacher and they also got to know me since I was a baby. I also met a teacher who was starting out at the time. I encountered him again at my current institution when I moved there five years ago. It's a small world! It was such a nice coincidence.

I don't remember at what age I moved to the second institution. Things were very difficult there. I used to misbehave and run away. Also, some kids beat me and I told the people in charge. They listened to me. I think they did the right thing. I moved to the third institution because of this and also because I could not stay there anymore due to my age. I moved to the current house when I was 13 years old. I got in, I got used to it. It was very difficult for me when the director moved to another job. I had gotten used to having her. Now I get along with all the staff and the other young people. I feel good here. Before, sometimes, I used to misbehave, run away in the morning. It was a bit of an obsession. I ran away to the beach. I asked for some food and made a friend there. I ran away many times. Then I called the 112 and asked for help. I made up so many excuses. Other times, I called the police. Another time, a man helped me get back to the house. I regret it now. I don't run away anymore. They have everything here. There is a bed; there is food; there is everything. There are people who help me, who support me in what I need, in the good and bad moments like everybody has. My teacher has also helped me a lot and so have my friends.

I will have to leave to another institution soon because I am turning 19 years old. I had an interview the other day. My teacher went to the interview with me. I don't know for sure if I am going there or not but it is better to think that it will happen. One day I will have to leave this house anyway. The kids here are too young. I can't stay here my entire life. I have been here for many years and this house will always be my family. In the beginning I was confused with the idea of having to move to another institution. Now I know it is cool.

Child physical abuse & neglect

Stories and experiences of young people with intervention

Slovenia

"Krizni center je bil najboljša rešitev"

Andrejeva zgodba

To je bilo pred štirimi ali petimi leti, bil sem v zadnjem razredu osnovne šole, brat pa je bil v dveh razredih nižje. Najmlajši je bil star deset let. Socialna delavka me je poklicala k sebi, ker je izvedela za nasilje v naši družini, to, da nas očim pretepa. Povedala mi je, da to ni prvi tak primer, da jih je imela že nekaj. Predlagala je, da bi nasilje prijavili policiji. Jaz pa sem rekel, da to še ni nujno, da še ni tako hudo. Poklicala je tudi mojo mamo in se pogovorila z njo. Vendar se ni končalo, imel sem dovolj in moral sem nekaj storiti, konec koncev sem najstarejši brat. Zato sem šel do socialne delavke in na mojo pobudo je poklicala policijo. Prišli so na šolo, kjer smo se pogovorili. Tudi moja brata sta morala podati izjavo. Ne vem, kako naj se izrazim … to je bilo precej kruto. Potem so nas vse tri odpeljali v mladinski krizni center nekam na sever. Mama je povsem podpirala to odločitev za zaščito njenih otrok. Očim ni nič vedel, dokler ga niso poklicali s policije, da bi podal izjavo. Nekaj dni je bil pridržan, a so ga morali izpustiti. Vse je zanikal.

V krizni center so nas peljali en dan po tem, ko smo govorili s policijo. Bilo je konec šolskega leta in smo na srečo že imeli zaključene ocene. Zdelo se mi je, da se je to zgodilo prehitro, bil sem nekoliko presenečen, da so se tako hitro odzvali. Tega nisem pričakoval. Nobenih svojih stvari nisem imel s sabo, nisem mogel domov, v center so nas peljali naravnost iz šole. Po eni strani sem bil vesel, da so nas odpeljali, ker sem upal, da se bo očim odselil. Po drugi strani pa je bilo neprijetno, da so me odpeljali iz šole, saj sošolci niso vedeli, kaj se dogaja. Ko sem jih kasneje srečal, sem jim povedal, da je bil očim do nas nasilen in da sem imel vsega dovolj in da zdaj več ne živi z nami in je bolje.

Naslednji dan je socialna delavka naše stvari prinesla v krizni center, saj niti mama niti očim nista smela vedeti, kje smo. Kasneje nas je mama obiskovala, enkrat na dva tedna recimo, kolikor ji je socialna delavka dovolila. Vsakič je ostala eno ali dve uri. V bistvu sta to bili edini dve uri, ko nismo bili v stiku z nobenim socialnim delavcem v kriznem centru.

V kriznem centru smo ostali en ali dva meseca ali nekaj takega – dokler se stvari niso umirile in dokler mama ni vložila zahtevka za ločitev.

"The crisis centre was the best solution"

Andrej's Story

It was four or five years ago, I was in the last year of primary school and my younger brother was two years after me. There was also the youngest, he was ten. The social worker at the primary school called me in, because she learned that there is family violence going on, that our stepfather was beating us. They informed the social worker at my school. She told me that this was not the first time that something like this was happening and that she has had several such cases. She suggested reporting the violence to the police. But I said that wasn't necessary, that it is not that bad yet. She also called my mother and talked to her. But it didn't stop, I had enough and I had to do something, after all I was the eldest brother. So I went to the social worker and on my initiative she called the police. They came to the school and we talked. My siblings also had to give a statement. I don't know how to say... that was quite cruel. Then they took all three of us to the youth crisis centre, somewhere in the north. My mother was all for it, that her kids are protected. Our stepfather didn't know about this until the police called him for a statement. They even detained him for a couple of days but then they had to let him go. He denied everything.

They took us to the crisis centre the day after we talked to the police. It was the end of the school year, luckily we already had our grades. I thought this happened too quickly, I was a bit surprised that they reacted so quickly. I didn't expect that. I didn't have my things with me, I couldn't go home, they took us to the centre straight from the school. On the one hand I was happy that they took us because I hoped our stepfather would move away. On the other hand it was unpleasant that they took me from school as my school mates didn't know what was going on. When I met my school mates later, I told them that our stepfather was violent towards us and that I was fed up with everything and that he is no longer living with us, that now things are better.

The next day the social worker brought our stuff to the crisis centre, as neither our mother nor stepfather could know where we were. Later my mother came to visit, let's say once every two weeks, as much as the social workers allowed her. She stayed one or two hours at a time. Basically these were the only two hours when we weren't in contact with any of the social workers at the crisis centre.

V centru so bili nekako štirje socialni delavci, ki so se menjavali. Imeli smo delavnice, hodili smo na izlete in tako. Zelo so nam pomagali in veliko smo se pogovarjali. Tam so bili tudi drugi otroci s podobnimi izkušnjami in tudi z njimi smo se pogovarjali. V bistvu so zelo upoštevali naše želje. Vprašali so nas, ali mislimo, da se bo očim spremenil. Hotel sem, da se vse čim prej konča, a se nisem hotel vrniti k njemu. Brata sta se strinjala, da se vrneta domov, tudi če bi on še vedno živel tam. Jaz sem bil proti, nobenemu od nas očim ni bil všeč. Na koncu so prepričali mlajša brata in počakali smo, da se je izselil.

Ni se mi zdelo, da me obravnavajo kot otroka brez svojega mnenja. Če so hoteli kaj izvedeti, so večinoma poklicali mene. Z bratoma so govorili le zato, da so dobili izjave vseh treh. Policiji sem moral večkrat podati izjavo. Tudi socialna delavka je večkrat prišla v krizni center in sem ji dal svoje izjave. Jaz sem jih zapisal, ona jih je vzela, jih prebrala in odnesla na sodišče. Kot najstarejši sem moral na sodišče kot priča. Počutil sem se, kot da moram narediti nekaj, česar nisem hotel narediti. Ni imelo smisla, da sem moral kot petnajstletnik na sodišče pričat. Mami in socialni delavki sem rekel, da se tam nisem hotel srečati z očimom, a sta mi rekli, da moram podati izjavo, da bo sodnik lahko videl, kaj se dogaja. Tisti dan, ko sem moral na sodišče, sem bil zelo živčen. Vendar je zaslišanje potekalo dan kasneje in mi ni bilo treba v sodno dvorano. Svojo izjavo sem dal gospe v pisarni, jaz sem govoril, ona je zapisovala. Potem so mojo izjavo uporabili na sodišču.

Prišlo je do sodbe, a nisem prepričan, kakšna točno je bila. Vem, da je mama zahtevala prepoved približevanja. Dobil je nekaj dni družbenokoristnega dela, ne spomnim se natančno. Mislim, da ni dobil toliko, kot bi lahko. Glede na to, da nas je pretepal, to ni kaj prida kazen.

Kasneje sem upal, da ne bom naletel nanj, a sem, saj še vedno živi tam blizu, kjer treniram nogomet. Ker sem šel tja peš ali s kolesom, sem ga srečeval vsak dan. Sprva sem se mu izogibal, a enkrat me je poklical po nadimku in sem se obrnil. Pozdravil me je in spregovorila sva nekaj besed. A nisem hotel govoriti z njim o tem, kar se je zgodilo. Če je otrok starejši, recimo 17 ali 18, se že lahko zaščiti, a če je mlajši, bi ga morali karseda zaščititi. Otrok ne bi smeli pustiti samih, še posebej če oseba, ki jih ogroža ali s katero so bili v konfliktu, živi blizu njih.

V celotni situaciji je meni najbolj pomagal krizni center. Nismo imeli stika z očimom in krizni center je bil najboljša rešitev. Prej bi ga morali izseliti in mu ne dovoliti, da je med sojenjem živel pri nas doma. To pravim predvsem zaradi mame, saj smo mi takrat tako ali tako bili v kriznem centru. Potem ko smo se vrnili domov k mami, smo imeli nekaj srečanj na centru za socialno delo, da so lahko spremljali stvari. Potem nisem imel več nobenega stika z nikomer.

We stayed at the crisis centre for one or two months or so – until things calmed down and my mother filed for divorce. At the centre there were about four social workers who took turns. We had some workshops and went on trips and such. They helped us a lot and we talked a lot. Other kids with similar experience were also there and we talked with them, too. Basically they took into account what we wanted a lot. They asked us if we thought our stepfather would change. I wanted everything to be over as soon as possible but I didn't want to go back to him. My siblings agreed to go home even if he was still living at our place. I was against it, none of us liked our stepfather. At the end they convinced my younger brothers and we waited for him to move out.

I didn't feel that they were treating me as a child without his own opinion. If they wanted to know something, they mostly called me. They talked to my brothers just to have statements from all three of us. I had to give my statement to the police several times. The social worker came to the crisis centre many times and I gave statements to her. I wrote them down, she took them, read them and took them to the court. As the eldest, I had to go to the court as a witness. It felt like I had to do something I didn't want to do. It didn't make sense that I as a fifteen-year-old had to go to the court and testify. I told my mother and the social worker that I didn't want to meet my stepfather there, but they told me I had to give the statement so that the judge can see what was going on. On the day I had to go to court I was very nervous. But the hearing took place the day after and I didn't have to go to the courtroom. I just gave a statement to a lady in an office, I was talking and she was writing. They then used my statement in court.

There was a judgement but I am not sure what it was exactly. I know my mother asked for a restraining order. He got a few days of community service, I can't remember exactly. I think he didn't get as much as he could. Considering that he was beating us, that is not that much of a punishment.

Afterwards I hoped I wouldn't run into him but I did, as he still lives near the place where I have my football training. Since I walked or went by bike I ran into him every day. At first I avoided him but one time he called me by my nickname and I turned around. He said hello and we spoke a few words. But I didn't want to talk to him about what had happened. If a child is older, let's say 17 or 18, he can already protect himself. But if the child is younger, he should be protected as much as possible. Children shouldn't be left alone, even more so if the person who is threatening them, or they had a conflict with, is living near them.

In this whole situation, the crisis centre was most helpful for me. We didn't have contact with our stepfather and the crisis centre was the best solution. They should have evicted him sooner and not let him stay at our place during the trial. Mostly I say that because of my mother, we were at the crisis centre at the time anyway. After we returned home to our mother, we had a couple of meetings at the social work centre so they could monitor things. After that I didn't have any contact with anyone else.

Intervention against sexual exploitation

Stories and experiences of trafficked women

Intervention against sexual exploitation

Stories and experiences of trafficked women

England & Wales

"You couldn't do anything, we had to stay shut in"

Anna's story

I ran away. I can't talk about anything that happened before then but I ran away and I went to find some police. I told the police and they helped me. They arrested the man and so I received help from the police. The first night, they organised accommodation at the hotel. For three nights, they were paying for my room in the hotel and then I was moved to a hostel. A woman was taking care of me. She came and gave the money for survival for a few days. Then the police officer came and told me I was to leave this city and that I would be going to another city with the Salvation Army. They did not talk to me about this or tell me why, only that I was to be ready the next day so I was very confused because I did not know what was going to be happening.

The next day the car came with the Salvation Army people. There was no interpreter and no-one talked to me. They put my belongings in the car and they took away my mobile telephone. And three times we changed cars in this city. I was driven to one part, then put in another car, then the same again, twice more. I was scared because I didn't know what was happening and I thought these Salvation Army people are usually connected with moving people from country to country. So without my consent I thought I was being taken to my country, the country I come from. But instead they brought me to this different city. And I was given a room in a house and I had a key worker who made a plan. Basically they were trying to do their best to work out a plan. The only bad thing being over there in that city was that I hadn't got any contact with any other people. Because it was a safe house. Only with other people in the house, or with the police and that was it. You couldn't do anything. Then we had to stay shut in. Then they took me to see a solicitor. That was about this case but I can't talk about that and I don't know what is happening about this case.

Then they brought me back here to this city and to this organisation. I think this was part of the plan because my key worker said I would come back here when something was available. So that it how I came to this organisation. First I stayed in their house with other women. That was alright. They took me to a GP to register. That was very important because of my medical condition.

And they helped me with the money, the benefits and I went to college, I am still going to college to learn to speak English because I want to be a resident here and I want to stay in the UK and get a job here. So all this they helped me with and I got the support. They took me to a solicitor and we went for an appointment with the Home Office. They filled in the forms for the visa so that I could be a resident and now I have this card which says I can be here for a year and that I can work. And I have a little flat – a studio and I am learning how to manage. When my English is better I will get a job.

The only thing is with the Salvation Army, I would say it wasn't very good – and it should be done in a different way. It should be planned earlier, not just from one day to the next. And the police, I don't know what is happening with the case but when they arrested… they took all my belongings and I don't know where they are. All my clothes and my documents, all the medical records. I have lost everything and these are important to me. I had my medical records right back to when I was a little child and this is important because of my condition. But now everything is gone and no-one can tell me where they are. So this has been very difficult for me.

"If I could go to school, then I wouldn't be so upset and lonely"

Ardita's story

I am from an Eastern European country but I came to the UK from Italy. I was brought in a lorry. I was on the street and I heard a woman talking on a mobile phone. She was speaking my language and I went to her and I asked her to help me. She took me to an organisation, I think it was for refugees but I don't remember much. There was a man in this organisation and the woman spoke to him for about ten minutes, then she left. The man made a telephone call. He asked me to wait. Some time later another woman came in a car and she picked me up and brought me to this organisation. That was about six months ago.

First, they took me to a doctor because I was very bad. I was depressed and I couldn't sleep at night. There was a translator and the doctor spoke to me and gave me a paper to get some medicine. Then I spoke to my support worker. Again, I had a translator. She told me I could stay in a room in a house they had until the Home Office made a decision. She said she had to send information on a form to the Home Office because they had to decide whether I was a victim. Then I would also need to see a solicitor to apply for asylum. So she took me to see this solicitor and I had to tell her my story again. She said to me what I could I do and I said to apply for the asylum so that is what she did.

I don't know if anyone understood my situation but I felt saved. I felt safe. And they helped me with my English but the classes were not long enough, only two months and I wanted to have counselling but the counsellor was too busy. In the house sometimes it is nice. The support workers prepare snacks and bring them to the house and that's nice because we stay inside and we have got problems and we can talk to each. That's nice, but in the house three women have children and three do not. It's noisy because they cry, they sleep, and they cry and this is not good for me. Also, there is not enough to do. This organisation, they have events but it would be better if there were more events. It's better because we forget about things and if I could go to school, spend at least half the day at school and then I wouldn't be so upset and lonely.

Now I have had a refusal from the Home Office. They don't believe I have been trafficked and I have to move to another house to wait for a decision about the asylum. My solicitor has said to wait but I don't know what will happen.

ism *"The government needs to learn more about our culture, how much we are in danger"*

Ciwana's story

Before I came to this country I had a big family but, apart from my mum, I had a horrible life. Then my dad forced me to come to the UK to marry. I was locked in a room in my husband's home and I was tortured by his family. Another relative here called the police. I was scared when the police arrived. Because I didn't know much English back then I was only able to tell them that I needed help and I was in danger. The police talked to me, told me you will be safe, we will help you and I felt so happy. They found me a hotel room overnight and then the next day a man and a woman came from the Salvation Army. The woman was really nice and caring and made me feel better. She told me about the NGO for women from minority backgrounds and they sorted out my hostel place for me. If it were not for this NGO or Salvation Army maybe I would die or I would be in street.

My caseworker at the NGO helps me and I am becoming independent. The Job Centre provides me with money. They provide English classes too and counselling. I am sad though, because my counsellor left after only a few weeks and I have not talked about what happened to anyone else. I don't like being asked all the time about what happened to me. I remember that at the beginning all the time they say, tell me what happened to you, what happened, and all the time I cry, it's like you have a cut on your hand and it is making all the time again new cut. I would prefer that they only ask once and then send information to each other, not ask all the time. But I get support here and I have friends. Friends are very important and stop me feeling very lonely. I have friends here from everywhere, many cultures, so I am learning more. They share with me same situation I learn more about culture, their culture and everywhere. And every day you learn a new thing and your thinking will be bigger and seeing, having picture about this world.

It is very different in the UK from my country. I am safe. And I have my choice. I can choose everything in my life – no-one can force me to do that. If you have freedom it means you have everything – you can be everything in this life. There is no difference between woman and man here. Everyone is equal here.

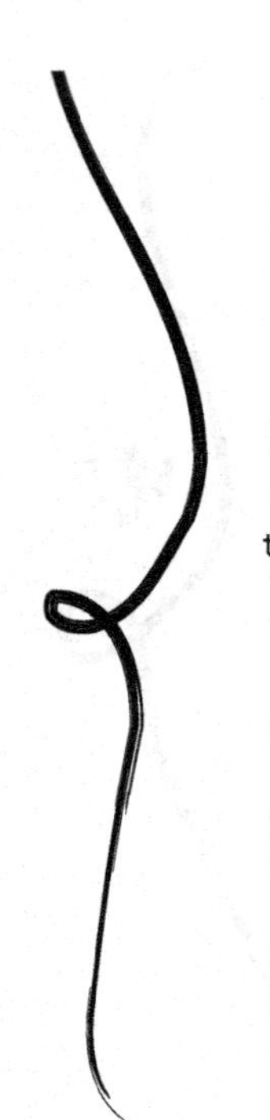

The police did not make me feel like I am not from here or I am different, and they treat me nicely and they show how much they care about me and for my life be safe. I don't feel I am stranger or I am different from this country, or I am not British – they help me – there is no difference with government or police; but I feel angry that my husband and his family still have their freedom. No action was taken against them. The police could not do anything because I don't have any proof or evidence to show them because they are so clever, they don't do anything to show anything to my body. It is not fair. The lack of evidence is also making me very scared. My immigration solicitor is a very clever woman but I am worried that without it she can't help me stay in the UK. The Home Office cancelled my marriage visa and then gave me a temporary visa which was extended. But I have not been granted indefinite leave to remain in the UK and I don't understand why. I can't imagine going back to my country. I know what's waiting for me there. My family wants killing me for honour and here the family of my husband wants killing me too. The Home Office people know I can be killed, and I am in danger so why is the decision taking so long?

Other women I know get their indefinite leave very quickly but they are not like me, they are not in danger really. But I am in danger. In this country too I am in danger. I think the government need to learn more about our culture because they have a little bit imagined, but not all of it. They don't have imagined what's happening in real terms – how much we are in danger. If the Home Office said yes, then I can stay, then I can make a new start. A new beginning I can start thinking about my future. Having indefinite leave would feel good.

"Vlada se mora naučiti več o naši kulturi, o tem, kako ogrožene smo"

Ciwanina zgodba

Preden sem prišla v to državo, sem imela veliko družino, imela sem mamo, toda grozno življenje. Potem me je oče prisilil, da sem prišla v VB, da bi se poročila. Zaklenili so me v sobo na moževem domu, njegova družina pa me je mučila. Nek drug sorodnik tu je poklical policijo. Ko je policija prišla, me je bilo strah. Ker takrat nisem govorila veliko angleško, sem jim lahko povedala le, da potrebujem pomoč in da sem v nevarnosti. Policija se je pogovorila z mano, rekli so mi, da bom varna, da mi bodo pomagali, in bila sem zelo vesela. Za tisto noč so mi našli hotelsko sobo, potem pa sta naslednji dan prišla moški in ženska iz Salvation Army. Ženska je bila zelo prijazna in skrbna, po pogovoru z njo sem se počutila bolje. Povedala mi je za nevladno organizacijo za ženske, pripadnice manjšin, in ta mi je uredila hostel. Če ne bi bilo te nevladne organizacije ali Salvation Army, bi mogoče umrla ali pa bi bila na cesti.

Moja socialna delavka pri nevladni organizaciji mi pomaga in postajam neodvisna. Zavod za zaposlovanje mi nudi denar. Prav tako nudijo tečaje angleščine in svetovanje. A sem žalostna, ker je moja svetovalka odšla po le nekaj tednih in z nikomer drugim nisem govorila o tem, kar se je zgodilo. Ne maram, da me vedno sprašujejo, kaj se mi je zgodilo. Spomnim se, da so na začetku ves čas govorili, naj jim povem, kaj se je zgodilo, kaj se je zgodilo, jaz pa sem ves čas jokala; tako je, kot bi imel ureznino na roki in to povzroča vedno nove ureznine. Raje bi, da bi samo enkrat vprašali in potem poslali informacije drug drugemu, ne pa da ves čas sprašujejo. A tu dobim podporo in imam prijatelje. Prijatelji so zelo pomembni in se zaradi njih ne počutim tako zelo osamljeno. Tu imam prijatelje od vsepovsod, veliko kultur, zato se več naučim. So v isti situaciji kot jaz, naučim se več o kulturi, njihovi kulturi in drugih. In vsak dan se naučiš nečesa novega in tvoje mišljenje bo širše in boš dobil sliko tega sveta.

V VB je zelo drugače kot v moji domovini. Varna sem. In imam svojo izbiro. Vse v svojem življenju si lahko izberem – nihče me ne more prisiliti, da to naredim. Če imaš svobodo, pomeni, da imaš vse – lahko si vse v tem življenju. Tu ni razlike med žensko in moškim.

Tu so vsi enakopravni. Policija mi ni vzbujala občutka, da nisem od tu ali da sem drugačna, lepo ravnajo z mano in pokažejo, da jim je mar zame in za mojo varnost. Ne počutim se kot tujka ali da sem drugačna od te države ali da nisem Britanka – pomagajo mi – ni razlike pri vladi ali policiji; a sem jezna, da so moj mož in njegova družina še vedno na prostosti. Proti njim niso ukrepali. Policija ni mogla narediti ničesar, ker jim ne morem pokazati nobenega dokaza, ker so tako pametni, da niso naredili nič, kar bi se videlo na mojem telesu. To ni pravično. Pomanjkanje dokazov me tudi plaši. Moja odvetnica za imigracijo je zelo pametna, a me skrbi, da mi brez tega ne more pomagati ostati v VB. Ministrstvo za notranje zadeve je preklicalo mojo poročno vizo in mi izdalo začasno vizo, ki je bila podaljšana. A mi niso odobrili vize za prebivanje v VB za nedoločen čas in ne razumem, zakaj. Ne predstavljam si, da bi se vrnila v domovino. Vem, kaj me tam čaka. Družina me hoče ubiti zaradi časti in tu me želi ubiti družina mojega moža. Ljudje na Ministrstvu za notranje zadeve vedo, da me lahko ubijejo in da sem v nevarnosti. Zakaj potem traja tako dolgo, da se odločijo?

Vem, da druge ženske dobijo prebivanje za nedoločen čas zelo hitro, a niso kot jaz, niso zares v nevarnosti. Jaz pa sem v nevarnosti. Tudi v tej državi sem v nevarnosti. Mislim, da bi se vlada morala naučiti več o naši kulturi, ker si nekaj malega predstavljajo, a ne vsega. Ne predstavljajo si, kaj se realno dogaja – kako ogrožene smo. Če bi Ministrstvo za notranje zadeve reklo 'ja', potem lahko ostanem, potem lahko začnem znova. Z novim začetkom lahko začnem razmišljati o svoji prihodnosti. Če bi dobila bivanje za nedoločen čas, bi se počutila dobro.

Lisa's story

I was brought to the UK several years ago from my home country. I thought it was to work, to find a proper job but I was taken to a house where there were lots of other women. We were all there, we had no choices, day or night, we couldn't go out. It was very stressful and often I felt ill. I said to them, I am ill and I need to see a doctor but they didn't believe me and no doctor came. I felt hopeless. All I was allowed to do was phone my mother, maybe once a month or once every couple of months, from a phone they had there. I did not have my own phone. But I could not tell my mother what was happening, she would have been too upset.

Then one day I saw that I could get out of that house and I ran away and I kept running. I didn't know where to go but I decided I would find some police and I would tell them about what was done to me. I didn't know if they could or would help, I thought maybe they would put me in jail because what I was doing was wrong and because I didn't have any papers. But I didn't know what else to do. So I asked people in street, where are the police? Then someone told me and I went into the building. I was very scared. But the police were very nice to me. I sat and I told them what had happened to me and they listened even though my English was very poor. I said I have no phone and no family, no-one to call and no-one to call me. Then the police said they were my family and I was so happy. I cried. So, first the police took me to see a doctor and this was good because I had so much pain and the doctor helped me. Then they took me to stay somewhere. They said this is only for a short while until they find somebody who can help me more. So that is when they brought me here to this organisation, that was six years ago.

When I first came here, they brought me in the office, there was an interpreter, and they talked to me for a long time. They asked me many questions and I cried a lot because it was the first time I could tell anybody what had happened to me and how much I needed help. And so they helped me. I stayed in a room in a house with other women and we were together. My support worker was an English woman but she was very, very nice. She took me to register with a doctor so that I could see the doctor when I needed to, and she took me to see a solicitor.

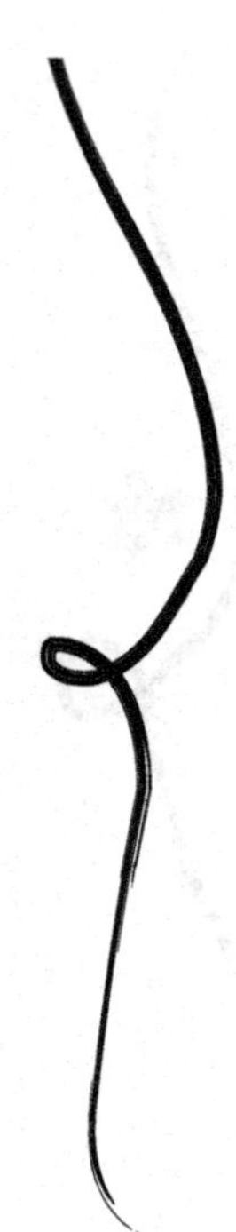

This was because I didn't have any papers to be in the country so the solicitor sorted out my immigration. They sorted out my benefits and I attended English classes at a college and this was very good and quickly my English improved. And I had the counselling, this helped me so much and slowly I could go out, I could be on my own a little, I could stay on a bus. Then after about one year, I couldn't stay in this house anymore and I had to move to a hostel. This was not good for me. I was there for two years and I should have had a key worker there too but I did not get anyone and no-one listened to me. And because this organisation thought I had the key worker, they didn't know that I had no support at all. I was very upset and when I was ill they accused me of acting, it was just like before....I was too upset. I felt treated differently to the other girls there. Sometimes they were drunk but still they listened to them but they didn't listen to me or believe me. If I said there was something I was not happy with, they told me to go back to my own country. Then they told me I had to leave this hostel and they found me new accommodation but it was not safe. I said to them I am not safe here so they took me to another place, maybe two or three more but these places were no good to me. Then they asked me to leave the hostel.

I was homeless for about a month. Sometimes I had to stay out, sometimes I stayed with other people I knew. I slept on the floor or on the sofa. Then I went myself to the Council and they gave me temporary accommodation. This is where I am now and it is very hard because I still need help. So this year I came back to this organisation and they are helping me again. They have contacted the Council and now the Council has said they will find me permanent accommodation. This is what I am now waiting for.

I was in a very bad condition. The last four days that I was in the house I was very, very, very sick: either I was going to die there, or I was going to escape. And so I escaped. I had no money, only the clothes I was wearing. I took the small roads because I knew if walked straight ahead, he would take the car and find me. And I managed to find a tiny train station and I got the first train and stayed on until the last stop. That was London. If the train had stopped somewhere else then I would have gone there. I found a park and saw a lady so I went and sat beside her and I said, excuse me I need help. And she asked me where I was from. I told her. She took me to her house. She said I have a friend. I will call her and then the friend said I should go to the Home Office.

So the next day she took me to the Home Office and then she went away. As soon as I got inside I spoke to someone. I had like a small interview, then I had to wait for the afternoon to have another interview. In the second interview there was an interpreter. I tried to show the woman all my scars but she told me, don't do that in here, like it's not proper. She said they would send me somewhere safe when I would be taken care of by a nurse and doctors and everything. I didn't feel safe. I had lots of feelings, because I was really in pain, I was feeling like I had needles all over my body. They took me and some others to a place that used to be a church.
The thing I remember is that I was starving! So I was grateful when they gave me something to eat. Then they sent me and another girl somewhere else. And they left us there for one week. I had to go out and ask people for food. No nurse came, there were no towels or soap and no sanitary towels. Then they brought us back to the church place and I was there for two months. At least there was food and shower facilities but no-one came to help me see a nurse or tell me what was happening.

After that they took me to a hostel in another city. I had a single room. There was a main office where we went every week to collect some money. So at least I could buy some food, I could choose something of my desire. And the girl I had shared with at the church, she gave me a top and a pair of trousers so I could change my clothes. And there they did take me to a hospital but I no longer needed to see a nurse. But I was happy in the house. The only thing I wasn't comfortable with is that I had felt secure in the first place because I didn't know where I came from.

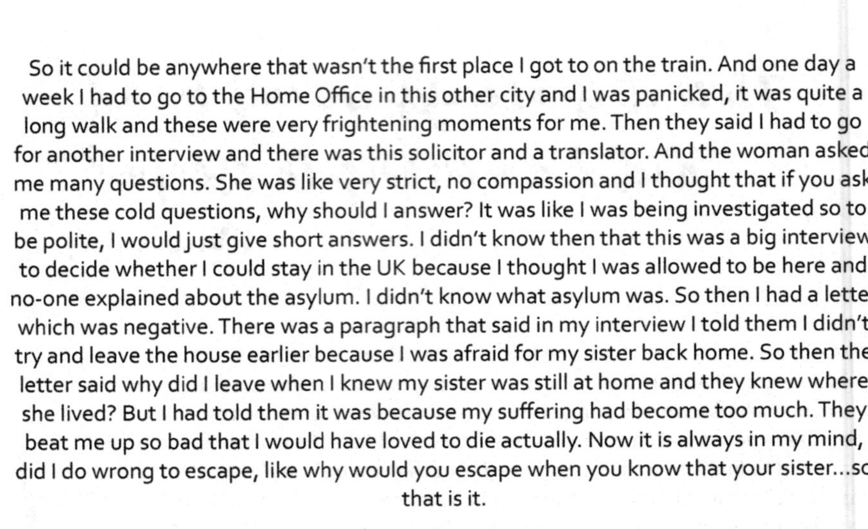

So it could be anywhere that wasn't the first place I got to on the train. And one day a week I had to go to the Home Office in this other city and I was panicked, it was quite a long walk and these were very frightening moments for me. Then they said I had to go for another interview and there was this solicitor and a translator. And the woman asked me many questions. She was like very strict, no compassion and I thought that if you ask me these cold questions, why should I answer? It was like I was being investigated so to be polite, I would just give short answers. I didn't know then that this was a big interview to decide whether I could stay in the UK because I thought I was allowed to be here and no-one explained about the asylum. I didn't know what asylum was. So then I had a letter which was negative. There was a paragraph that said in my interview I told them I didn't try and leave the house earlier because I was afraid for my sister back home. So then the letter said why did I leave when I knew my sister was still at home and they knew where she lived? But I had told them it was because my suffering had become too much. They beat me up so bad that I would have loved to die actually. Now it is always in my mind, did I do wrong to escape, like why would you escape when you know that your sister…so that is it.

So I left that city. I found an internet cafe and I googled 'Help for trafficked women' and so many organisations came up, I sent them all messages. I thought the biggest one was the Salvation Army. I called and called them. Several times they said they would come but they never did and then one organisation said the best place would be this one and so I came here. This was when my life began to change. They said they would talk to me and ask me very deep questions but it was OK. I was OK talking to them. It didn't feel like I was being investigated. They found me a room in a safe house and they got me another solicitor to make a fresh claim to the Home Office. So now I have a visa for one year and at the end of the year the solicitor will apply for me again. Now my child is born too. So I have help with finding a flat, with the benefits and the child benefit and I have learned English. And now I understand that I can do as I wish. I only knew that after I came here, a long time after because we come from a very difficult situation. We are pushed down so we don't have our own mind, and we don't talk our own mind. But now I can say, like I can say I hate the Salvation Army people as much as I love this organisation but I don't know what will happen, what to expect from the Home Office. My solicitor here is better, but it is not her decision. It is the Home Office and I don't know what will happen.

"Zdaj vedno razmišljam, ali sem naredila napako, da sem pobegnila"

Mirelina zgodba

Bila sem v zelo slabem stanju. Zadnje štiri dni, ko sem bila v hiši, sem bila zelo zelo bolna: ali bi tam umrla ali pa pobegnila. In tako sem pobegnila. Nisem imela denarja, le obleke, ki sem jih nosila. Šla sem po majhnih ulicah, ker sem vedela, da če bi hodila naravnost, bi sedel v avto in me našel. Uspelo mi je najti majhno železniško postajo, sedla sem na prvi vlak in ostala na njem do zadnje postaje. To je bil London. Če bi se vlak ustavil kje drugje, bi šla tja. Našla sem park in zagledala neko gospo, zato sem se šla usest poleg nje in sem ji rekla: »Oprostite, potrebujem pomoč.« Vprašala me je, od kod sem. Povedala sem ji. Peljala me je k sebi domov. Rekla je, da ima prijateljico in jo bo poklicala. Potem pa je prijateljica rekla, da bi morala iti na Ministrstvo za notranje zadeve.

Tako me je naslednji dan peljala na Ministrstvo za notranje zadeve, potem pa je odšla. Takoj ko sem prišla noter, sem z nekom govorila. Imela sem nekakšen mali razgovor, potem sem morala počakati do popoldneva na še en razgovor. Pri drugem razgovoru je bil tolmač. Ženski sem skušala pokazati vse svoje brazgotine, a mi je rekla, naj tega ne počnem tam, češ da ni primerno. Rekla je, da me bodo peljali nekam na varno, kjer bodo sestre in zdravniki poskrbeli zame in vse to. Nisem se počutila varno. Imela sem veliko občutkov, ker me je res bolelo, počutila sem se, kot da imam igle po celem telesu. Mene in še nekaj drugih so peljali nekam, kjer je včasih bila cerkev. Spomnim se tega, da sem bila sestradana! Zato sem bila hvaležna, ko so mi dali hrano. Potem so mene in še eno punco poslali nekam drugam. Tam so naju pustili en teden. Morala sem hoditi ven in prositi ljudi za hrano. Nobena sestra ni prišla, ni bilo brisač ali mila in nobenih higienskih vložkov. Potem so nas pripeljali nazaj v nekdanjo cerkev, kjer sem bila dva meseca. Tam smo imeli vsaj hrano in tuše, a nihče mi ni prišel pomagat, da bi me peljal k sestri ali da bi mi povedal, kaj se dogaja.

Potem so me peljali v hostel v drugo mesto. Imela sem svojo sobo. Tam je bila glavna pisarna, kamor smo vsak teden šli dvignit nekaj denarja. Tako da sem si lahko kupila vsaj nekaj hrane, lahko sem si izbrala nekaj po svoji želji. In punca, s katero sem bila v cerkvi, mi je dala majico in hlače, da sem se lahko preoblekla.

Tam so me peljali v bolnico, a sestre nisem več potrebovala. Vseeno pa sem bila v hiši zadovoljna. Edina stvar, ki mi je vzbujala nelagodje, je bila, da sem se počutila varno v prvem kraju, ker nisem vedela, od kod sem prišla. Tako da bi lahko bilo kjerkoli, samo da ni bil prvi kraj, kjer sem sedla na vlak. Enkrat na teden sem morala na Ministrstvo za notranje zadeve v tem drugem mestu in me je grabila panika; moral si dolgo hoditi in to so bili zame zelo strašljivi trenutki. Potem so rekli, da moram še na en razgovor, kjer sta bila odvetnik in prevajalec. Ženska mi je postavila mnogo vprašanj. Bila je zelo stroga, nobenega sočutja in mislila sem si, da če mi postavlja ta hladna vprašanja, zakaj bi morala odgovarjati. Bilo je, kot bi me preiskovali, zato sem iz vljudnosti dajala samo kratke odgovore. Takrat nisem vedela, da je bil to veliki razgovor, ki je odločal o tem, ali lahko ostanem v VB, ker sem mislila, da mi je dovoljeno biti tu, nihče pa mi ni razložil glede azila. Nisem vedela, kaj je azil. Potem sem dobila pismo, ki je bilo negativno. V enem odstavku je pisalo, da sem jim v razgovoru rekla, da hiše nisem skušala zapustiti prej, ker me je bilo strah za sestro doma. Potem so v pismu vprašali, zakaj sem šla, če sem vedela, da je sestra še vedno doma in vejo, kje živi. A sem jim povedala, da zato, ker je moje trpljenje postalo preveliko. Tako hudo so me pretepli, da bi dejansko z veseljem umrla. Zdaj vedno razmišljam, ali sem naredila napako, da sem pobegnila; zakaj bi pobegnila, če veš, da je sestra ... Tako da je to to.

Zato sem zapustila tisto mesto. Našla sem internetno kavarno in pogooglala 'pomoč za žrtve trgovine z ljudmi' in med zadetki dobila veliko organizacij, ki sem jim vsem poslala sporočila. Zdelo se mi je, da je največja Salvation Army. Klicala sem in klicala. Nekajkrat so rekli, da bodo prišli, a nikoli niso, potem pa je neka organizacija rekla, da bi to bilo najboljše mesto, zato sem prišla sem. Takrat se mi je življenje začelo spreminjati. Rekli so, da se bodo pogovorili z mano in mi postavili zelo globoka vprašanja, a je bilo v redu. Pogovor z njimi je bil v redu. Nisem se počutila, kot da me preiskujejo. Našli so mi sobo v varni hiši in mi priskrbeli drugega odvetnika, da je vložil novo zahtevo na Ministrstvo za notranje zadeve. Tako imam zdaj vizo za eno leto in ob koncu leta bo odvetnik spet prosil zame. Zdaj se je rodil tudi moj otrok. Tako da imam pomoč pri iskanju stanovanja, pri finančni podpori in otroških dodatkih, pa še angleško sem se naučila. In zdaj razumem, da lahko delam, kar hočem. To sem spoznala šele, ko sem prišla sem, dolgo zatem, ker prihajamo iz zelo težke situacije. Tlačijo nas, tako da nimamo lastnih misli in ne povemo lastnega mnenja. A zdaj lahko rečem, lahko rečem, da sovražim ljudi iz Salvation Army toliko, kolikor imam rada to drugo organizacijo, a ne vem, kaj se bo zgodilo, kaj naj pričakujem od Ministrstva za notranje zadeve. Moja odvetnica tu je boljša, a to ni njena odločitev, pač pa Ministrstva za notranje zadeve in ne vem, kaj se bo zgodilo.

At the beginning I didn't look to anyone for help except in the church. Sometimes people let me stay in their houses, maybe sleeping on sofas and the like and in return I would clean or look after their children. Then I met my child's father and he said he would take care of me. We moved to another area and he rented some place. He took me to see a solicitor because I didn't have a passport or any papers but I couldn't understand what was going on as the solicitor just spoke to my boyfriend and then told him he had to come back with money. But I didn't have any money so I never went back.

Later I had to go to the hospital to have my baby and when I came out and got back home, my boyfriend had left. I had to leave then too as I had no money for the rent but now I had my baby and I was very scared. That was when I decided I had to go to the police. I had never thought of going to the police before because I had always been told they will arrest me and put me in jail. So, in my head I am thinking they will put me in jail but I have to go because of my baby and so I went to the police station. Then I was surprised. They put me in room and someone came to speak to me and I told them my story and they said I will need a lawyer because I've come to this country illegally and I will need help with this. So they called a lawyer for me and he told me all my options. Then we went to the Home Office for an interview and they said I was a trafficking case and they would need to make a decision. But I needed somewhere to live while they were making the decision so the police asked me would it be ok for them to refer me to a Migrant Helpline and something called the Salvation Army and I said, yes, it would be ok. So I spoke to Migrant Helpline and to the Salvation Army people but only the Salvation Army people could help me. The Migrant Helpline wanted so many things from me, like letters and things, and I could not do this. But the Salvation Army people said they would just help me and they would take me somewhere else where I could stay. So they came in a car and they brought me to this NGO. That was when I first came here and then things began to change for me.

When I first got here I didn't know where I was or anything that I had to do. But they talked to me and said this person would be my support worker. She took me to a house with other women and said I could have my own room, just for myself and my baby.

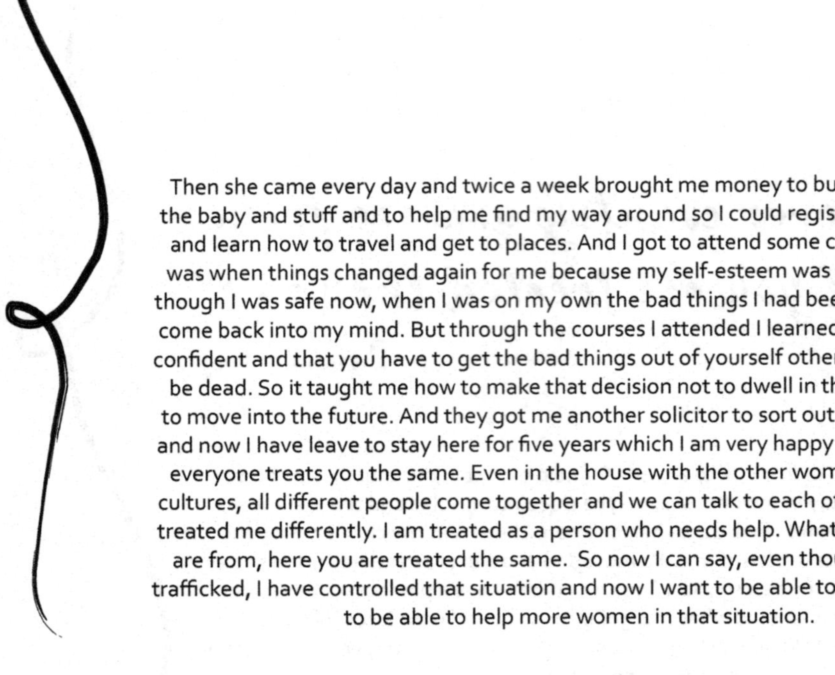

Then she came every day and twice a week brought me money to buy stuff, food for the baby and stuff and to help me find my way around so I could register with a doctor and learn how to travel and get to places. And I got to attend some courses and that was when things changed again for me because my self-esteem was so low and even though I was safe now, when I was on my own the bad things I had been through would come back into my mind. But through the courses I attended I learned how to be more confident and that you have to get the bad things out of yourself otherwise you will just be dead. So it taught me how to make that decision not to dwell in the past and how to move into the future. And they got me another solicitor to sort out my immigration and now I have leave to stay here for five years which I am very happy about. And here, everyone treats you the same. Even in the house with the other women, all different cultures, all different people come together and we can talk to each other. Nobody has treated me differently. I am treated as a person who needs help. Whatever country you are from, here you are treated the same. So now I can say, even though I have been trafficked, I have controlled that situation and now I want to be able to speak out, I want to be able to help more women in that situation.

"They gave me the chance to listen to my story"

Victoria's story

I did not know who to ask for help. I was told never to contact the police as they would arrest me. Then I became sick and had to go to the hospital. They told me I was pregnant and so I had to keep appointments with a midwife.

One time, late in my pregnancy, I had been badly beaten and locked in a room. I rang the midwife to tell her I could not make the appointment because I was bleeding and feeling dizzy. Then I fell unconscious. When I came to, the police were there. They said the midwife had called them and asked them to check up on me. They took me to hospital.

I was in the hospital for five days and during this time I told the midwife I did not want to go back to the house again but that I had nowhere else to go. She asked me why this was and so I told her what had happened to me. After that a police officer came and I was afraid. I said I had not committed any offence and I begged her to let me go home to the house. The police officer told me that was not how things were done in this country, that if they let me go home, there was no knowing what would happen to me or the baby so they said no, and the midwife said no and said they have to call the social service people. So I was scared but they told me they wanted to make me safe because of the baby and they would give me a place to stay until the baby was born. And so I said ok.

Later the social worker called and said she had found a place that was in another area. I said, yes, I wanted that. She told me the Salvation Army would help to move me and the baby. Then the Salvation Army people came and talked to me. They asked me about my passport and how I had come to this country. They said they would bring me to a safe place and see what help there was about my status in this country. They told me about this place and I agreed to come here so they brought me and I thanked them and I waited in the reception.

Then a lady came and I was scared because I didn't know where I was. I was holding my child and she said she was not going to hurt us and so I should calm down. I said OK then. We talked and then I came to this house and I am in one room with my child. They gave me help. They gave me counselling first and they gave me recovery. I did recovery. And we went to a lawyer.

And I said, if there is any help, please help me out to get my future, my daughter's future life. So she read me all the options and I said, ok then, I want the asylum.

Then we went to the Home Office. I went to an interview and I told them all that had happened to me. And they said, OK then, you will hear from us. So I got a letter that said I should come and sign. So that is what I am doing now. I said I cannot go back to my country because I have no money to pay the man my relative sold me to and because that relative can give me to anyone he wants again, and because I have not had the circumcision. My mother did not do this to me. She told me she had been circumcised and so had her sister but her sister died so she will not do this to me, and I will not do this to my child. I would go back if my mother was alive because she would support me; but she is dead. So if I went back they would have to do this to me and to my child because where you don't do it, it shows you are a prostitute. It is the process of womanhood; to show you are a woman that can be successful in life and that is what you face in society. So if you don't so that, they don't count you.

The positive thing is, I would say the Home Office they have given me the chance, they could have sent me back home but they gave me the chance to listen to my story, which I was very grateful for, and they asked me to come in and sign every month which I do. And the thing I like about this NGO, it gives me hope in this life, to have some who will listen to you or have time for you and this is helping me to come out from my fear.

And looking back the midwife saved my life and my baby's life; and the police and the social services who sent me out of that house, because if I went back there I don't know what might have happened to me and my baby. And the police officer said they arrested the man and he is on bail. I don't know what they are going to do with that man. I would say they should let him be because I don't want another trouble but I sense what he has done he has not regretted. So the police said they now have to decide what to do.

In my home country, the men, they treat us very bad. Why? Because that is our culture. You have no authority to doubt that, whatever you are facing in relationship, you have to submit to that because you are a woman. To me in other aspects it's wrong, it's rather killing with the women always to humiliate in our life.

Being here, it has changed my life, building up the confidence; and they give me money for food every week, and the counselling they do for us and they are training us to use our hands and to do some creative things. It's good, they've really done a lot for me. I thank all the NGO people who are now taking the fear from me because you can ask them. When I came here I was afraid to talk to anybody, won't go near people. But now it's going out of me. But I don't know what will happen. I hope they will consider me, that they will help me and my daughter for a better life. I have hope that the Home Office and the British Government will help us, so that my little girl will not go through what I have been through, the slavery.

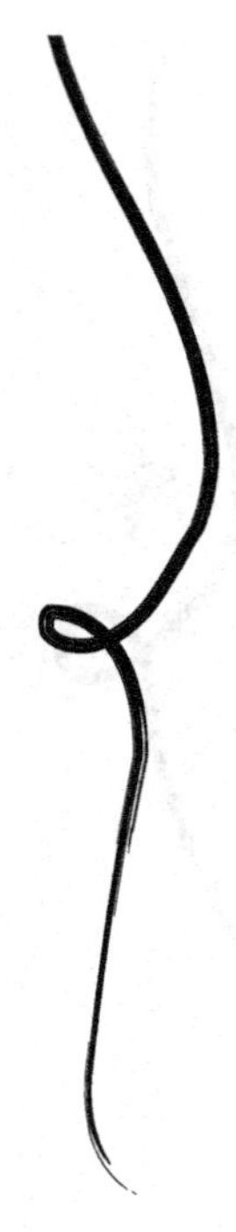

Intervention against sexual exploitation

Stories and experiences of trafficked women

Germany

"Ich habe immer noch Angst, weil ich nicht weiß, wo er ist"

Anitas Geschichte

Ich bin mit meinem ex-Freund mit einem Visum für drei Monate nach Deutschland gekommen, weil sein Onkel, der hier war, uns Geld und Arbeit versprochen hat. Wir konnten erst in einem Haus von Bekannten wohnen, aber nach drei Wochen hatten wir keine Arbeit und kein Geld, der Onkel hat nichts mehr für uns getan, und mein Freund sagte dann, ich müsste im Puff arbeiten gehen, das sei nicht schwierig, ich muss nur 10 Minuten mit einem Klienten bleiben, der mir dann 50 Euro gibt. Ich wollte das nicht, aber er drohte damit, meinen Eltern zu sagen dass ich Prostituierte bin. Meine Mutter hat ein schwaches Herz, ich weiß, dass sie stirbt wenn sie das hört. Er hat mir immer gesagt: „Du musst ein bisschen arbeiten und dann haben wir ein gutes Leben zusammen."

In dem Puff war es sehr schwer, 20 Minuten für jeden Mann und dann nur 20 Euro, ich wollte gehen. Mein Ex-Freund hat dann eine falsche ID-Karte aus einem EU-Land machen lassen, damit ich in einem Puff arbeiten kann, wo ich 50 Euro oder mehr verdienen würde. Aber er hat mich auch geschlagen, viel geschlagen, und er wollte meinen kleinen Hund totschlagen. Er hatte mich in dem Land, wo wir herkommen, auch schon geschlagen, aber nicht so Druck gemacht.

Ich wollte immer gehen und diese Arbeit nicht mehr machen. Einmal habe ich mich im Zimmer im Puff eingeschlossen, und als er an der Tür schlug, rief ich der Frau im Büro zu, dass sie die Polizei rufen soll, das hat sie aber nicht getan. Als er für einen Monat wegfuhr wusste ich nicht, wohin ich gehen und was ich machen könnte. Er kam zurück und hat direkt angefangen, mich zu schlagen. Ich hatte aber mein Handy unterm Bett versteckt und habe vom anderen Zimmer aus die Polizei gerufen. Ich musste leise reden und wusste die Straße nicht richtig, aber die Polizei hat das Haus gefunden. Ich hörte wie er sagte, er ist allein, aber ich rief „bitte helfen!" und in diesem Moment war ich frei. Die Polizei hat ihn in ein anderes Zimmer gebracht und ich konnte meine Kleidung packen, und sie haben mich mitgenommen. Nachher brachte die Polizei mich direkt in diese Beratungsstelle.

Der Polizist, der mich dann befragt hat, ist die beste Person, die ich kenne. Er kommt, wenn ich die Polizei rufe und kontrolliert alles, und geht erst dann. Ich hatte viele Termine gemacht, um alles zu erklären, und er ist immer da, und spricht immer gut mit mir, und fragt auch nach mir, z.B. wie es mit der Schule geht.

"I still live in fear, because I don't know where he is"

Anita's Story

I came to Germany with my former boyfriend and a three months' visa, because his uncle who was living here promised us that we could find work and earn money. First we were allowed to live in the house of acquaintances, but after three weeks we had no work and no money, the uncle didn't do anything more for us, and my boyfriend then said that I would have to go and work in the brothel, that wouldn't be difficult, I would just have to stay with a client for 10 minutes who would then give me 50 Euro. I didn't want that, but he threatened to tell my parents that I was a prostitute. My mother has got a weak heart; I know it would kill her if she heard that. He kept telling me: "You just have to work a little bit and then we will have a good life together."

In that brothel, it was very difficult, 20 minutes for every man and then I only got 20 Euros, I wanted to leave. Then my boyfriend somehow had a false ID card from an EU country made, so that I could work in a brothel where I would earn 50 Euro or even more. But he also beat me, a lot in fact; I love dogs and he tried to club my little dog to death. He had already beaten me before in the country we come from, but he didn't put that kind of pressure on me there.

I always wanted to go away from there and stop doing this kind of work. Once, I locked myself in my room in the brothel, and when he banged on the door, I shouted out to the woman in the office that she should call the police, but she didn't do that. When he went away for a month or so, I didn't know where I should go to and what I could do. He came back and started beating me immediately. But I had hidden my mobile phone under the bed and I called the police from the other room. I had to speak quietly and I didn't really know the name of the street, but the police finally found the house. I heard him saying that he was alone, but I shouted: "Please help! "And at that very moment I was free. The police took him into another room so I could pack my clothes, and then they took me along with them. Then the police drove me to this advisory centre without any further delay.

The policeman who then interviewed me is the best person I have ever known. He always comes when I call the police and he checks everything and he does not leave until he has made sure. I had a lot of appointments to explain everything and he's always there, and he always speaks to me nicely, and he also enquires about me, how things are going at school, for instance.

Die Beratungstelle hat mir viel, viel geholfen, mit meinen Dokumenten und allem; sie hat mir Geld für ein Taxi gegeben, und so kam ich ins Frauenhaus. Ich blieb da ca. 2 Monate, aber das Frauenhaus ist nicht gut. Ich durfte meinen kleinen Hund nicht mitbringen – mein Hund ist alles für mich, da musste ich immer weinen. Dort haben sie um 7 h morgens geklopft „Du musst aufstehen". Wenn du viele Probleme hast, viel Stress, willst du nicht mit anderen Leuten sprechen, aber die haben immer gesagt: „Du musst dies putzen, du musst jenes putzen". Ich habe keine Kinder, ich bin frei, ich muss alles putzen, aber die anderen Frauen haben Kinder, nein, sie haben keine Zeit zu putzen.

Es hat einen Prozess gegen ihn gegeben, aber ich verstehe nicht, was passiert ist. Er hat alles zugegeben, was ich gesagt habe, und am Ende hat er erklärt, dass er freiwillig in unser Herkunftsland zurückgeht. Aber ich sehe im Facebook, dass er wieder in Deutschland ist. Er ist frei und ich verstehe nichts. Im Gericht wurde ein Dolmetscher für mich bestellt, der aus einem anderen Balkanland kam; das war eine Katastrophe. Ich verstand nichts was er sagte, er konnte mich nicht verstehen, die Anwältin sagte immer „Übersetze Anita". Ich sage alles das, eins, zwei, drei, vier, er übersetzt nur eins, zwei. Und war nicht gut. Jetzt habe ich immer noch Angst, weil ich nicht weiß, wo er ist. Die Anwältin hat gesagt, dass er mir Geld geben will, aber ich will nichts, ich will nur meine Ruhe haben.

Jetzt habe ich meine Wohnung und habe eine Arbeit gefunden, zur Probe. Denn wenn ich jeden Monat Geld vom Staat nehme, sagt eines Tages der Staat „Was willst du? Wir bezahlen dich immer." Aber wenn ich arbeite, lerne ich neue Leute kennen, ich finde eine Freundin oder habe Kontakt mit Leuten, spreche mehr, Deutsch kommt schnell mehr. Aber ich kann lernen, Universität machen und dann bessere Arbeit, besser leben.

The advisory centre helped me really a lot, a lot, with my documents and everything; they gave me money for a taxi and that´s how I came to the women´s refuge. I stayed there for about two months, but the women´s refuge is not a good place. I was not allowed to take my dog with me – my little dog means everything to me, and I had to cry then. They would knock on the door there at 7 o´clock in the morning and say "You have to get up." When you have a lot of problems, a lot of stress, then you don´t want to speak with other people, but they always said to me: „You have to clean and wipe here and clean and wipe there …". I don´t have children, so I am free, I always have to do the cleaning of everything, but those other women have children; no, they don´t have the time to do the cleaning.

He was taken to court, but I don´t understand what has happened. He confessed to everything I had said, and in the end he declared that he would return to our home country voluntarily. But on Facebook, I see that he has returned to Germany. He is free and I don´t understand anything about this. At court an interpreter was appointed for me, who came from another Balkan country; that was a disaster. I didn´t understand anything he said, he couldn´t understand me, and the lawyer repeated again and again: "Translate, Anita." I said so much, like points one, two, three and four, and he just translated points one and two. He was not a good translator. Now I still live in fear, because I don´t know where he is. The lawyer told me that he would give me money, but I don´t want it, I just want to be left in peace.

Now I have my apartment and I have found a job, for a trial period. Because if I take money from the state every month, then the state will say one day: „What do you want? We always pay for you." But when I work, I meet new people, I will find a friend or be in contact with people, I have more opportunities to speak and my German improves quickly. So I can study, go to university and then find better work and have a better life.

"Ainda vivo com medo, porque não sei onde ele está"

História de Anita

Vim para a Alemanha com o meu antigo namorado e um visto de três meses, porque o tio dele que estava a viver cá prometeu-nos que poderíamos encontrar trabalho e ganhar dinheiro. Primeiro deixaram-nos viver em casa de uns conhecidos mas, depois de três semanas, não tínhamos trabalho nem dinheiro. O tio não fez mais nada por nós e o meu namorado disse que iria ter de ir trabalhar no bordel, que não seria difícil, só teria de ficar com um cliente por 10 minutos e depois me daria 50€. Eu não queria, mas ele ameaçou dizer aos meus pais que eu era uma prostituta. A minha mãe tem problemas de coração e sei que ela morreria se ouvisse isso. Ele estava sempre a dizer-me: "Só tens de trabalhar um bocadinho e depois vamos ter uma boa vida juntos."

Naquele bordel, era muito difícil, 20 minutos com cada homem e só recebia 20€, queria sair. Depois o meu namorado de alguma forma arranjou um Bilhete de Identidade falso de um país da Europa para que eu pudesse trabalhar num bordel onde iria ganhar 50€ ou até mais. Mas ele também me batia muito, na verdade. Adoro cães e ele tentou matar o meu cãozinho à porrada. Ele já me tinha batido antes no país de onde viemos, mas não me pressionava desta forma.

Sempre quis sair de lá e parar de fazer este tipo de trabalho. Uma vez, tranquei-me no meu quarto no bordel e, quando ele bateu à porta, gritei para a mulher no escritório para ela chamar a polícia, mas ela não o fez. Quando ele esteve fora durante um mês ou assim, eu não sabia onde deveria ir e o que poderia fazer. Ele voltou e começou a bater-me imediatamente. Mas tinha escondido o meu telemóvel debaixo da cama e chamei a polícia no outro quarto. Tive de falar baixinho e não sabia o nome da rua, mas a polícia encontrou finalmente a casa. Ouvi-o a dizer que ele estava sozinho, mas eu gritei: "Ajudem por favor!" E nesse preciso momento fiquei livre. A polícia levou-o para outro quarto para que eu pudesse fazer as malas, e levaram-me com eles. Depois a polícia levou-me para o centro de atendimento sem qualquer demora.

O agente da polícia que me entrevistou, na altura, é a melhor pessoa que já conheci. Ele vem sempre quando eu chamo a polícia e verifica tudo e não se vai embora sem ter a certeza. Tive muitos atendimentos para me explicarem tudo e ele está sempre lá e é sempre simpático para mim. Faz-me perguntas, por exemplo, como vão as coisas na escola.

O centro de atendimento realmente ajudou-me muito, muito, com os meus documentos e tudo; deram-me dinheiro para um táxi e foi assim que eu vim para a casa de abrigo. Fiquei lá durante cerca de dois meses, mas a casa de abrigo não é um bom sítio. Não me permitiram levar o meu cão comigo – o meu cãozinho é tudo para mim e eu tive de chorar. Eles batiam à porta do quarto às 7 da manhã e diziam: "tens de te levantar." Quando tens muitos problemas, muito stress, então não queres falar com outras pessoas, mas eles diziam-me sempre: "Tu tens de limpar e varrer aqui e limpar e varrer ali…". Eu não tenho filhos, por isso estou livre, mas tenho sempre de limpar tudo e as outras mulheres que têm filhos, não, elas não têm tempo para fazer as limpezas.

Ele foi levado a tribunal, mas eu não percebo o que aconteceu. Confessou tudo o que eu disse, e no fim declarou que iria voltar para o nosso país de origem voluntariamente. Mas no Facebook vi que ele voltou para a Alemanha. Ele está livre e eu não percebo nada disto. No tribunal, foi-me apontado um intérprete, que veio de outro país balcânico e foi um desastre. Eu não percebia nada do que ele dizia, ele não me entendia e o advogado repetia sempre: "Traduza, Anita." Eu dizia uma série de coisas, tipo: ponto um, dois, três e quatro; e ele só traduzia os pontos um e dois. Não era um bom tradutor. Agora, ainda vivo com medo, porque não sei onde ele está. O advogado disse que ele me ia dar dinheiro, mas eu não quero, só quero que ele me deixe em paz.

Agora tenho o meu apartamento e encontrei um trabalho por um período à experiência. Porque se eu receber dinheiro do estado todos os meses, então o estado dirá um dia: "O que é que tu queres? Estamos sempre a subsidiar-te." A trabalhar, posso conhecer novas pessoas, fazer amigos ou ficar em contacto com pessoas. Tenho mais oportunidades de falar e o meu alemão melhora rapidamente. E isto é bom para poder estudar, ir para a universidade e depois encontrar um emprego melhor e ter uma vida melhor.

Antonias Geschichte

Ich wurde im Auto mit mehreren anderen Frauen aus unserem Land, das jetzt zur EU gehört, nach Deutschland gebracht. Zu Hause hörte sich der Mann seriös und zuverlässig an; mir hat er Arbeit in einem Lokal versprochen, wo ich meine Fremdsprachenkenntnisse einsetzen kann. Meine drei Kinder blieben zu Hause; ich wollte ihretwegen besser verdienen. Zunächst wohnten wir eine Woche bei einer Bekannten von ihm, die aber dann sagte, wir müssten uns selber helfen. Er bot an, uns in ein „Hotel" zu bringen, aber es war tatsächlich ein Bordell. Für mich war das ein ganz großer Schock. Es ist furchtbar, in so ein Lokal reinzugehen und dass man angefasst wird, und überhaupt sich zu prostituieren.

Er hat mich dazu gezwungen, mit zwei Männern mitzugehen, um das Geld für die Fahrt zu bezahlen, danach habe ich mich mit ihm gestritten und ihm gesagt, dass ich da nicht arbeiten werde. Der Chef des Lokals hatte damit keine Probleme, und eine Frau aus meinem Heimatland, die freiwillig dort arbeitet, hat mich verteidigt und gesagt, sie kennt die Gesetze, und wenn er weiter droht, ruft sie die Polizei; er ging dann weg. Später brachte mich diese Frau zu einem Freund, der zwei Zimmer für Wohnungslose bereitstellt, dass sie ein paar Tage nicht auf der Straße sein müssen. Ich habe am nächsten Tag nach Arbeit gefragt, auch in einem Supermarkt, und der Chef dort hat mich arbeiten lassen und mir auch eine Matratze gegeben, dass ich dort schlafen kann. Nachher hat ein deutscher Mann mir ein Zimmer untervermietet, wo ich dann auch ein Bett hatte und mich im Bad waschen konnte. Mit Hilfe meiner Freundin, die Kontakte hatte, suchte ich nach Arbeit in einem Café, und hatte Erfolg.

Nach einigen Monaten hat mich der Täter zufällig gesehen; er wollte nun 500 Euro, und drohte, meine Kinder im Heimatland entführen zu lassen. Da habe ich ganz große Angst bekommen. Meine Freunde, die dabei waren, haben mir gesagt, dass ich sofort die Polizei rufen muss, und weil ich nicht wusste, wie ich das erklären soll, haben sie für mich angerufen, und bezeugt, dass ich ernsthaft bedroht werde. So hat die Polizei angefangen, nach ihm zu suchen.

I was taken to Germany by car with several other women from our country, which is now in the EU. The man who talked to me at home sounded serious and reliable. He promised me a job in a restaurant where I could use my foreign language skills. My three children were left at home; I wanted to earn more money for their sake. At first we lived for a week with an acquaintance of his, but then she said that we would have to help ourselves. He proposed to take us to a „hotel", but in fact it was a brothel. That was great shock to me. It is terrible to go into such a location, to be touched there, and to work as a prostitute at all.

He forced me to go with two men to be able to pay the money for the journey, and then I quarrelled with him and told him that I would not work there. The boss of the establishment didn´t have any problems with this, and a woman from my country, who was working there voluntarily, defended me and said that she knew the laws, and if he continued to threaten me, she would call the police; and then he left. Later, that woman took me to a friend of hers, who offered two rooms to homeless people, so that they wouldn't have to live on the street for a few days. The next day, I asked around for a job, in a supermarket among other places, and the manager of the supermarket let me work there and also gave me a mattress where I could sleep in the back room. Later, a German man offered to sublet a room to me, where I also had a bed and where I could wash myself in the bathroom. With the help of my female friend, who also had contacts, I looked for work in a café and I was successful.

A few months later, the perpetrator caught sight of me accidentally; then he wanted me to give him 500 € and he threatened to have my children abducted in my home country. I was so terrified by that. My friends who were with me there said I should call the police immediately, and as I didn´t know how to explain things, they called the police on my behalf and testified that I was seriously threatened. And so the police began searching for him. I was so scared, and I even called the police in my home country and asked them to protect my children.

Ich hatte solche Angst und habe sogar bei der Polizei in meinem Heimatland angerufen und sie gebeten, meine Kinder zu beschützen.

Dann habe ich ausgesagt, und der Polizist hat sich sehr für mich eingesetzt, er hat mir erklärt was ich zum Selbstschutz mittragen darf, er ist jede Woche bei meiner Arbeitsstelle vorbeigekommen und hat sich immer erkundigt, ob mit den Kindern alles in Ordnung ist. So habe ich verstanden, dass sie mich beschützen und dass sie immer noch nicht den Täter gefunden haben. Also für mich war es so, es gab jemanden, der auf mich aufgepasst, der mich beschützt hat. Dann haben sie ihn geschnappt und es gab einen Prozess.

Ich war sehr besorgt und beunruhigt, weil es sehr schwierig ist, nach einem Jahr sich an alles zu erinnern und einzeln zu erklären. Im Gerichtssaal war der Dolmetscher nicht so gut. Aber ich freute mich, dass sich die Rechtsanwältin sehr engagiert hat, weil ich sehr beunruhigt war. Ich hatte den ganzen Tag nichts essen können und dann wurde mir schlecht im Gerichtssaal. Aber alle waren neben mir. Die Rechtsanwältin hat mich sogar bis nach Hause gefahren und das ist für mich sehr wichtig. Das was mir Leid tut ist, dass er so wenig bekommen hat, denn er hat noch zwei, drei Frauen misshandelt, also er sollte Minimum 6 bis 8 Jahre bekommen. Drei Jahre vergehen zu schnell. Er kann danach wieder das Gleiche tun. Wenn ich über die Vergangenheit spreche, dann spüre ich so einen Schmerz. Das, was ich erlebt habe, war sehr furchtbar.

Ich bin froh, dass der Täter verurteilt worden ist; zurzeit bin ich zur Ruhe gekommen und deswegen fühle ich mich sehr gut. Die Kinder sind bei mir, das freut mich vor allem. Die Wohnung hat drei Zimmer, sie geht auf meinen Namen, also es ist nicht zur Untermiete: Das war mein größter Wunsch. Arbeit suche ich noch, 3 oder 4 Stunden, denn ich will mich jetzt um meine Kinder kümmern. Die Wohnung wird vom Jobcenter bezahlt. Und ich bin sehr sehr dankbar, dass der deutsche Staat auch den Ausländern hilft.

Then I made my statement to the police, and the policeman I talked to was very concerned, he explained to me what I was allowed to carry with me for my self-protection, and he came to my work place each week and he always enquired whether everything was o.k. with the children. That's how I understood that they were protecting me and that they had not found the perpetrator yet. Well, to me, this meant there was someone who was taking care of me and protecting me. Then they caught him and he was put on trial.

I was very much concerned and worried, because it was very difficult to remember and to explain everything in detail after one year had passed. At court, the interpreter was not so good. But I was pleased with the lawyer, she was really committed and supportive, because I was so upset and worried. I was unable to eat all day long and then I began feeling sick in the courtroom. But they were all on my side. The lawyer even drove me home and that was very important to me. What I am sorry about is that he got so little punishment, because he abused two or three other women as well; he should have been sentenced to 6 or 8 years at a minimum. Three years pass by too quickly. After that, he can do the same things again. When I talk about the past, then I feel such pain. My experience was really terrible.

I am glad that the perpetrator was condemned; meanwhile I have been able to calm down and that's why I feel very good. The children are with me, that's what I am particularly happy about. It's a three room apartment rented in my name, that is, this is not a sub-tenancy: that was my greatest wish. I'm still looking for work for 3 or 4 hours a day, for I want to take care of my children now. The apartment is paid by the job centre. And I am very grateful to the German state for helping foreigners as well.

"Ich hatte gar keinen Plan davon, dass man so viel Hilfe bekommen kann"

Floricas Geschichte

Ich war noch ein Kind, als mein Mann mich mitgenommen hat von zuhause, bin gar nicht zur Schule gegangen, gar nichts; bei uns Roma war ich damit seine Ehefrau. Ich habe so viel mit ihm mitgemacht. Er hat mich immer wieder geschlagen und mir Angst gemacht. Bei der Polizei dort bin so oft gewesen und so oft habe ich Anzeigen gemacht, ich war im Krankenhaus, fast ins Koma geschlagen. Die Polizei wusste das genau, hatten alle Papiere, aber wie ich vom Krankenhaus rauskomme, zerschneiden die einfach die Papiere und sagen „Das ist dein Ehemann, du muss mit dem klarkommen" und fertig.

Jahrelang brachte er mich immer wieder nach Deutschland, damit ich für ihn anschaffen gehe. Nach einem kostspieligen Familienereignis sagte mein Mann „Wir können diese Schulden jetzt nicht bezahlen", ich muss zu seinem Verwandten nach Deutschland gehen und mich da prostituieren. Da meine Großmutter gestorben ist, hatte ich niemanden mehr in dem Land. Und so habe ich eine Chance gesehen, wegzulaufen. Ich wollte auch nicht, dass meine Kinder mitbekommen, dass ihre Mutter sich prostituiert. Deshalb hatte ich dem Verwandten, bei dem ich eine Nacht mit den Kindern war, gesagt, „ich will gar nicht mich prostituieren, ich will auch nicht für Dich arbeiten, ich haue mit meinen Kindern ab." Zwei, drei Tage habe ich dann im Park mit den Kindern gelebt, dann habe ich einen Mann kennengelernt, er war ein Café-Besitzer und dahinter war so ein kleines Zimmer. Und dann hat er gesagt „Du kannst hier übernachten, du brauchst nicht draußen schlafen".

Nach einem Monat ist mein Mann nach Deutschland gekommen mit meinem Sohn, weil ich kein Geld geschickt habe, und hat mich irgendwie gefunden. Er wollte mich schlagen, dann sind alle Männer aufgesprungen, dann ist es ein Riesentheater geworden. Er hat gesagt, „Du wirst sofort jetzt mit mir kommen nach Land G, da wirst du arbeiten, ich brauche Geld." Wegen dieser Schlägerei ist Polizei gekommen, und ich habe gesagt „Ich möchte gerne meinen Sohn haben" und die haben tatsächlich das Kind von ihm weggenommen und mir gegeben und ihn gewarnt, er soll von mir sich fernhalten. Er hat es ein zweites Mal versucht, als die Kinder draußen gespielt haben.

"I had no idea that it was possible to get so much help"

Florica´s Story

I was still a child when my husband took me away from home, I didn´t go to school, nothing like that; so for us Roma that made me his wife. I had to go through such a lot of suffering with him. He beat me again and again and frightened me. I went to the police there so many times and filed charges against him. I was in the hospital, because the beating almost sent me into a coma. The police knew that very well, they had all the papers, but as soon as I had left hospital, they simply tore up the papers and said: "He is your husband, it´s up to you to deal with him", and that was that.

For many years, he brought me to Germany to earn money for him as a whore. After an expensive family event, my husband said „We can't pay these debts", so I would have to go to his relative in Germany and prostitute myself. After my grandmother died, I had nobody in that country, so I saw this as a chance to run away. I also didn´t want to have my children discover that their mother was a prostitute. So I told the relative where I stayed with the children for one night: „I don´t want to prostitute myself, I don´t want to work for you, I´m bunking off with my children." For two or three days I lived in a park with my children, and then I met a man who owned a café, and there was a little room behind that café. And he told me: "You can stay overnight there; there is no need for you to sleep outside."

One month later, my husband came to Germany with my son, because I hadn´t sent him money, and he found me somehow. He wanted to beat me again, and all these men jumped up, and everything turned into a big scene. He told me: "You are coming back with me to Country H right now, and you´re going to work there, I need money." The police had come because of that brawl and I told them that I wanted my son and they actually took the child away from him and gave him to me, and they warned my husband to stay away from me. He made a second attempt when the children were playing outside; he wanted to take the little one with him and then he hit me and the children again right there on the street. They all saw that and called the police again. That was my opportunity to tell my story to the police. I told them how he punched me, where he punched me; and the advisor D came and took me to the doctor who wrote down all my injuries. Then the police said I should go with D, and she found an accommodation right away for me and my children.

Er wollte das Kleine mitnehmen und hat mich und auch die Kinder geschlagen auf der Straße. Das haben die alle nochmal gesehen und haben nochmal Polizei gerufen. Das war die Gelegenheit, meine Geschichte bei der Polizei zu erzählen. Ich habe erzählt, wie er mich geschlagen hat, wo er mich geschlagen hat und die Beraterin D hat mich abgeholt und mich sofort zum Arzt gebracht, der alle Verletzungen festgehalten hat. Dann hat die Polizei hat gesagt, ich soll mit der Beraterin D gehen, und sie hat sofort eine Unterkunft für mich und die Kinder gesucht.

Ich hatte gar keinen Plan davon, dass man so viel Hilfe bekommen kann, dass jetzt die Polizei hilft, dass es Institutionen wie die Fachberatungsstelle gibt, dass die sofort irgendwie alles regeln, und so was kenne ich nicht. Der Umgang der Polizei mit mir war sehr gut. Sehr sehr gut. Auch wie sie mit mir bei der Aussage umgegangen sind, alles, was ich erzählt habe, worüber ich mich zum großen Teil schäme, über Tage lang, die sind super mit mir umgegangen, ich hatte die Privathandynummer von dem Kriminalpolizist, falls was ist, konnte ich da immer anrufen. Und später, egal, was passiert ist, konnte ich immer weiter da anrufen, bei anderen Gelegenheiten, der hat immer geholfen von der Kriminalpolizei. Die haben auch bei der Gerichtsverhandlung ausgesagt. Darüber möchte ich nicht reden, weil es mich so belastet, überhaupt daran zu denken. Ich musste im Saal gegen ihn aussagen. Drei Jahre und sechs Monate hat er dann gesessen.

Der ist immer noch hier in dieser Stadt, aber er bedroht mich nicht mehr und hat mich in Ruhe gelassen. Er darf auch die Kinder nicht sehen, da gab es eine Familiengerichtsverhandlung. Er hat es lange Zeit versucht. Fast ein Jahr hat er mir immer wieder Stress gemacht, aber jetzt hat er das gelassen. Das Jugendamt hat mir sehr dabei geholfen. Die haben mir drei Jahre lang sozialpädagogische Familienhilfe bewilligt, zum Beispiel wenn ich kein Deutsch verstehe oder wenn Sachen für die Kinder von der Schule kommen, die haben mir immer geholfen, um die Kinder haben sie sich gekümmert. Ich war damit sehr glücklich, und wenn es nach mir ginge, würde ich das gerne wieder haben, aber mehr als drei Jahre geht nicht.

Früher, sobald ich ihn gesehen hat, bin ich in Panik gefallen, aber die Beraterin hat mich überall begleitet und hat mir jeden Tag 20 Mal gesagt „Hier ist Deutschland, hier gibt's Polizei, du bist sicher, du brauchst dir keine Angst haben, das ist nicht Land H, hier wird dir geholfen". So hat sie mich immer motiviert. Heute kann ich darüber lachen. Jetzt bin ich sehr glücklich, ich habe eine Wohnung, ich bekomme Sozialhilfe, das ist nicht viel, aber reicht mir vollkommen und jedes Mal, wenn er mich sieht, läuft er weg vor mir. Früher bin ich immer weggelaufen, weil ich Angst hatte, aber jetzt bin ich so selbstsicher, dass er vor mir wegläuft.

I had no idea that it was possible to get so much help, that the police would help, that such establishments as an expert advisory centre exist, and that everything could be arranged somehow and so rapidly, I didn´t know about all this before. And how the police dealt with me, that was very good, very very good. And how they treated me when I made my statement, and everything I told them, things that I´m mostly ashamed of, that took days, they treated me so nicely. I even had the private mobile phone number of the criminal police officer, and he said I could always call him if something should happen. And also later, whatever happened, I could still always call him, on other occasions; he never stopped helping me, that criminal police officer. They also testified in the court proceedings. I don´t want to talk about that, because it burdens me so much just to think of it. I had to testify against him in the court room. Then he had to stay in prison for three years and six months.

He still lives here in this city, but he has stopped threatening me and leaves me in peace. He is not allowed to see the children either, there was a family court hearing about that. He tried it for a long time. He put me under pressure again and again for almost one year, but finally he stopped. The youth welfare office helped me a lot in this situation. They granted me three years of social pedagogical family assistance, when I did not understand German for instance or when there were things coming from school for the children; they always helped me and they took care of the children. I was very happy about that, and if it were up to me, I would like to have this again for me, but three years is the limit.

Formerly, I panicked as soon as I saw him, but my advisor accompanied me everywhere and she told me 20 times a day: "We´re in Germany here, we´ve got the police here, you are safe, don´t be afraid, this is not Country H, you are helped here." And in this way, she always motivated me. Today I can laugh about this. I´m very happy now, I´ve got an apartment, I get social benefits, it´s not much, but it´s quite enough for me; and every time he sees me today he runs away from me. In the past, it was me who ran away from him, because I was scared, but today, I feel so confident that he runs away from me.

"Nisem imela pojma, da je možno dobiti toliko pomoči"

Floricina zgodba

Bila sem še otrok, ko me je mož odpeljal od doma, nisem hodila v šolo, nič takega; za nas Rome to pomeni, da sem bila njegova žena. Z njim sem veliko pretrpela. Vedno znova me je pretepal in strašil. Tam sem velikokrat šla na policijo in ga ovadila. Bila sem v bolnici, ker me je pretepanje skoraj spravilo v komo. Policija je to zelo dobro vedela, imeli so vse papirje, a kakor hitro sem zapustila bolnico, so te papirje enostavno raztrgali in rekli: »Vaš mož je, na vas je, da opravite z njim.« In to je bilo to.

Mnoga leta me je vozil v Nemčijo, da sem služila zanj kot kurba. Po dragem družinskem dogodku je mož rekel, da teh dolgov ne moreva poplačati in bom morala iti k njegovemu sorodniku v Nemčijo in se prostituirati. Potem ko mi je babica umrla, nisem imela nikogar v državi H., zato sem to videla kot priložnost, da zbežim. Prav tako nisem hotela, da bi otroci odkrili, da je njihova mama prostitutka. Zato sem sorodniku, kjer sem z otroki prenočila, rekla: »Nočem se prostituirati, nočem delati zate, mrknila bom s svojimi otroki.« Dva ali tri dni smo z otroki živeli v parku, potem pa sem spoznala moškega, ki je bil lastnik kavarne, za katero je imel eno sobico. Rekel mi je: »Tam lahko prenočite; ni potrebe, da spite zunaj.«

En mesec kasneje je moj mož prišel v Nemčijo s sinom, ker mu nisem poslala denarja in me je nekako našel. Spet me je hotel pretepsti in potem so vsi ti moški skočili in nastala je velika scena. Rekel mi je: »Takoj zdaj greš z mano nazaj v državo H., kjer boš delala, potrebujem denar.« Zaradi pretepa je prišla policija, rekla sem jim, da hočem svojega sina in so mu ga dejansko vzeli in ga dali meni, moža pa so opozorili, naj se mi ne približuje. Drugič je poskusil, ko so se otroci igrali zunaj; malega je hotel vzeti s sabo, potem pa me je kar tam na cesti spet udaril in otroke tudi. Vsi so to videli in so spet poklicali policijo. To je bila moja priložnost, da svojo zgodbo povem policiji. Povedala sem, kako me je boksnil, kam me je boksnil; potem je prišla svetovalka D. in me peljala k zdravniku, ki je zapisal moje poškodbe. Potem je policija rekla, naj grem z D., ki je takoj našla namestitev zame in moje otroke.

Nisem imela pojma, da je možno dobiti toliko pomoči, da bo policija pomagala, da obstajajo take ustanove, kot so strokovni svetovalni center, in da je možno vse nekako urediti in tako hitro, vsega tega prej nisem vedela.

In to, kako je policija ravnala z mano, je bilo zelo dobro, zelo zelo dobro. In kako so me obravnavali, ko sem podala izjavo in vse, kar sem jim povedala, stvari, ki se jih večinoma sramujem, kar je trajalo dneve, obravnavali so me zelo prijazno. Imela sem celo zasebno mobilno številko kriminalista, ki je rekel, da ga lahko vedno pokličem, če bi se kaj zgodilo. In tudi kasneje, karkoli se je zgodilo, sem ga vedno lahko poklicala, tudi ob drugih priložnostih; nikoli mi ni nehal pomagati, tisti kriminalist. Prav tako so pričali na sojenju. O tem nočem govoriti, ker me zelo teži, če samo pomislim na to. Morala sem pričati proti njemu na sodišču. Potem je moral iti v zapor za tri leta in pol.

Še vedno živi tu v mestu G., a mi je nehal groziti in me pusti pri miru. Ne sme obiskovati otrok, o tem je odločalo družinsko sodišče. Dolgo časa je poskušal. Skoraj eno leto je kar naprej pritiskal name, a je končno nehal. V tej situaciji mi je zelo pomagal urad za mladino. Odobrili so mi tri leta socialne pedagoške družinske pomoči, ko nisem razumela nemško, na primer, ali ko so prišle stvari iz šole za otroke; vedno so mi pomagali in skrbeli za otroke. S tem sem bila zelo zadovoljna in če bi bilo odvisno od mene, bi to še enkrat imela, a je omejeno na tri leta.

Prej me je zagrabila panika takoj, ko sem ga zagledala, a me je svetovalka spremljala povsod in mi dvajsetkrat na dan rekla: »V Nemčiji smo, imamo policijo, varna si, ne boj se, to ni država H., tukaj ti pomagamo.« In na ta način me je vedno motivirala. Danes se temu lahko smejem. Zdaj sem zelo srečna, imam stanovanje, dobivam socialne prejemke, ni veliko, a zame je čisto dovolj; in danes vsakič, ko me vidi, zbeži stran. V preteklosti sem jaz bežala pred njim, ker sem se bala, a danes se počutim tako samozavestno, da on zbeži od mene.

"Behandelt mich wie einen Menschen, nicht wie ein Tier das Ihr haltet"

Graces Geschichte

Ich komme aus Afrika, und ich war sehr jung, 14 oder 15, als ich nach Europa gebracht wurde; es war eine harte Reise mit dem Schiff und dem Auto durch verschiedene Länder. Das ist zehn Jahre her. In Deutschland haben sie mich in ein Haus mit ein paar anderen Mädchen gebracht, und ich war überrascht zu sehen, dass die Mädchen kurze, kurze Kleider gekauft haben um zu laufen. Dann haben sie jemanden gebracht um meine Haare zu machen, und ein Laufkleid, und die Frau sagte: „Du weißt, Du wirst mir 100 000 bezahlen" und ich sagte: „100 000? Woher soll ich das bekommen? Sie sagte ja, ich muss laufen und dieses Geld bezahlen, ich habe keine Wahl. Ich sagte ich kann diese Art von Arbeit nicht machen, aber sie sagte ich soll mich an den Schwur erinnern, denn ich am Schrein in M abgelegt habe, und ich wusste es ist sehr gefährlich: Wenn du das Geld nicht zahlen kannst, bist du nicht frei und alles kann passieren. Also muss ich es einfach machen, also versuche ich und versuche ich und versuche ich und bezahle und bezahle und bezahle und bezahle, ich bezahle fast 50.000, und sage der Frau dann, dass ich nicht mehr bezahlen kann.

Die Polizei hat mich oft gefunden wenn sie Papiere kontrolliert haben, und mich zur Polizeistation gebracht, aber weil ich ein kleines Mädchen war brachten sie mich in ein Kinderheim, und ich habe es immer geschafft wegzurennen. Diese Frau hat mir gesagt ich soll einfach in irgendeinen Zug einsteigen und sie dann anrufen, und sie hat mich dann immer getroffen und mich in eine andere Stadt gebracht. Aber in Stadt Z habe ich gefragt ob wir uns an einer U-Bahn-Station treffen können und ihr gesagt, dass ich kein Geld habe, und wir kämpfen und kämpfen und kämpfen, und die Leute schauen uns an und rufen die Polizei. Die Polizei hat mich zur Station gebracht und meinen Namen gecheckt und gesagt, dass sie schon lange nach mir suchen, und mich dort behalten.

Dann kam die Beraterin, sie ruft die Polizeistation immer einmal in der Woche an. Ich traf sie und sie war wirklich lieb, wundervoll, fürsorglich, und sie hat angefangen mich zu fragen was mich dorthin gebracht hat, aber ich hatte zuviel Angst um ihr zu sagen was mit mir passiert.

I come from Africa, and I was very young, 14 or 15, when I was brought to Europe; it was a tough journey by ship and car through different countries. That was ten years ago. In Germany they took me to a house with some other girls, and I was surprised to see that the girls are buying short, short dresses for walking. Then they brought somebody to fix my hair, and a walking dress, and the woman said 'you know you will pay me 100 000' and then I said: 100 000? Where am I going to get this from? She said yes, I have to walk and pay this money, I have no choice. I said I cannot do this kind of work, but she said to remember the oath I took at the shrine in M, and I knew it is really dangerous: If you cannot pay the money you are not free and anything can happen. So I just have to do it, so I try and try and try and try and pay and pay and pay and pay, I pay almost 50.000, and then I tell the woman that I cannot pay any more.

The police often found me when they were controlling papers, and took me to the police station, but because I was a little girl they took me to a children's home, and I was always able to run away. This woman told me I should just get in any train and then call her, and then they always met me and took me to a different city. But in city Z I asked to meet her at a subway station and told her I don't have money, and we fight, we fight and fight, and people are looking and call the police. The police took me to the station and checked my name and said they had been looking for me a long time, and kept me there.

Then the counsellor came, she always calls the police station once a week. I met her and she was really lovely, wonderful, caring, and she started asking me what brought me here, but I was too scared to let her know what is happening to me. The counsellor kept saying "G., be free and talk with me", and she always brought African food with her. It took me about one week to begin talking about my situation and everything. The counsellor was really sad, and then she explained that she has to tell the police some of this or I will be deported, and that it is not allowed for that woman just to take all that money. Then I said 'OK, you can go ahead and do it.'

Die Beraterin hat immer wieder gesagt: „G., sei frei und sprich mit mir", und sie hat immer afrikanisches Essen mitgebracht. Ich habe ungefähr eine Woche gebraucht bis ich anfing, über meine Situation und alles zu sprechen. Die Beraterin war sehr traurig, und dann hat sie erklärt, dass sie der Polizei etwas davon erzählen muss oder ich werde abgeschoben, und dass es nicht erlaubt ist, dass diese Frau einfach das ganze Geld nimmt. Dann habe ich gesagt „OK, kannst Du machen, dann mach's." Danach dauerte es vielleicht zwei Wochen, dann haben sie mich entlassen und zu einem sicheren Haus gebracht, weil nämlich diese Frau gesagt hat, das sie mich umbringen wird hier in Deutschland wenn ich das Geld nicht bezahle. Dort war es sehr schön, und später hat meine Beraterin für mich eine Schule gefunden, so dass ich einen Sprachkurs anfangen konnte.

Dann hat die Polizei die Beratungsstelle wissen lassen, dass sie mir so gerne ein oder zwei Fragen stellen würden, und dass ich mich darauf vorbereiten muss. Diese Frau in der Polizeistation hat wirklich viele Fragen gestellt, und ich habe ihr alles erzählt. Aber sie wollten mehr Beweise, wie „Habe ich ein Foto davon wie ich der Frau Geld gebe?", aber das ist nicht möglich. Oder habe ich Kontakt zu anderen Mädchen die eine Aussage machen könnten? Aber die Mädchen, die auf den Strich gehen, haben alle eine andere Madam und dürfen untereinander überhaupt keinen Kontakt haben. Ich habe mit einer oder zwei geredet, ob sie eine Aussage für mich machen würden, aber sie haben alle zu viel Angst. Wir sind alle Schwarze, wir sind alle afrikanisch, wir wissen was wir machen können.

Als ich in dem geschützten Haus war, gab es einen Mann bei der Ausländerbehörde, der die Termine gemacht hat, um meine Aufenthaltsgenehmigung für drei oder sechs Monate zu verlängern, und er war sehr gut. Aber ich denke generell sind die Leute, die in der Ausländerbehörde arbeiten, kaltherzig, ohne Mitleid, und rassistisch gegenüber Schwarzen. Sie fragen dich nicht, was sie mit dir machen sollen, weil sie meinen, es ist ihr Land und sie werden entscheiden ob du bleibst oder nicht. Die Beratungsstelle und ihre Anwältin haben mir geholfen der Polizei zu sagen, dass es gefährlich wäre in mein Land zurückzukehren, die Madam weiß woher ich komme und hat gedroht mich zu töten. Nach all dem Geld was ich bezahlt habe, muss ich was lesen, ich muss einen Sprachkurs machen, ich muss Krankenpflege lernen und etwas aus meinem Leben machen.

Das Schlimmste ist, die sagen „Wir geben dir drei Monate, bleib in diesem Gebäude, geh nicht raus, geh nicht nach Stadt N, noch nicht mal Stadt D." Du kannst nicht arbeiten, du kannst nicht zur Schule gehen, du kannst nichts machen. Wir haben nur eine andere Farbe, dieselben Augen, Körper, es ist nicht so anders. Also behandelt mich wie einen Menschen, nicht wie ein Tier das ihr haltet. Nach sechs Jahren haben sie mir 2012 eine Aufenthaltsgenehmigung für drei Jahre gegeben. Für Frauen in meiner Situation sollten sie es nicht so lang machen, bevor ihnen bewilligt wird, was sie wollen.

And it was after maybe two weeks that they released me and brought me to a safe house, because this woman had said she would kill me in this country if I don't pay the money. There it was very nice, and later my counsellor found a school for me so I started doing a language course.

Then the police let the counselling centre know that they'd love to ask me one or two questions and I have to prepare for that. This woman at the police station really asked a lot of questions, and I told her everything. But they wanted more proof, like 'do I have a picture where I give the woman money?' but this is not possible. Or do I have contact with other girls who could testify? But the girls who walk all have different madams and are not allowed to have any contact with each other. I tried to talk with one or two if they would testify for me, but they are all too scared. We are all black, we are all African, we know what we can do.

When I was in the safe house there was one man from the foreigners' office who made the appointments to have my permit renewed for three months or six months, and he was very good. But I think in general, the people who are placed in the foreigners' office are hard-hearted, without pity, and racist towards blacks. They will not ask you what they do with you, because they feel it is their country and they will decide if you stay or not. The counselling centre and their lawyer helped me tell the police that it would be dangerous to return to my country, the madam knows where I come from and has threatened to kill me. After all this money I have paid, I have to read something, I have to do a language course, I have to learn hospital nursing and do something with my life.

The worst part is, they say "We give you three months, stay in this building, don't go out, don't go to City N, not even City D." You cannot work, you cannot go to school, you cannot do anything. We are just a different color, same eye, body, it's not so different. So treat me like a human being, not like an animal you keep. They gave me a three-year residence permit after six years in 2012. For women in my situation they should not make it so long before they are granted what they want.

"Gib nicht auf, es ist nicht vorbei"

Lindas Geschichte

Meine Reise von Afrika nach Europa war kompliziert. Meine Madame hat mich in Länder geschickt, wo ich arbeiten und Geld an sie und ihre Agenten überweisen musste. Teile meiner Familie waren darin involviert und ihnen wurde gedroht oder sie mussten auch Geld bezahlen. Ich wurde auch von ihren Agenten hier in Deutschland bedroht. Ich weiß im Moment nichts über die Situation meiner Geschwister. Irgendwann hatte ich genug und ich habe aufgehört Geld zu zahlen. Ich habe meiner Familie geraten, sie sollen den Agenten sagen, dass ich die Polizei in Deutschland kontaktieren werde, wenn sie nicht aufhören Probleme zu machen. Die Polizei hier in Deutschland hat gesagt ich kann sie anrufen wenn die Agenten auf mich zukommen.

Meine Erfahrungen mit der Polizei sind gemischt. Jetzt helfen sie mir, aber ich war zweimal im Gefängnis als ich nach Deutschland gekommen bin. Beim ersten Mal haben sie mich schlecht behandelt, meine Hand verdreht und mir wehgetan. Ich habe die ganze Situation nicht verstanden und drei Tage lang geweint. Wenn du an einem neuen Ort bist, fühlst du dich schlecht weil du nicht verstehst warum die dich so behandeln. Im zweiten Gefängnis habe ich versucht freundlich zu den Leuten zu sein, damit sie freundlich zu mir sind. Irgendwann haben sie mich gehen lassen und ich war glücklich darüber.

Der Kontakt mit anderen Institutionen war auch schwierig für mich. An einem Tag musste ich sehr lange beim Sozialamt warten, obwohl ich einen Termin hatte. Sie sagten ich bräuchte eine Nummer, und dass sie mich davor nicht beraten würden. Ich sagte, dass ich einen Termin ohne Nummer habe, aber sie glaubten mir nicht und gaben mir eine Nummer, so dass ich noch länger warten musste. Ich wollte nicht streiten, weil das nicht mein Land ist. Ich fing an zu weinen. Endlich hat sich jemand den Zettel mit meinem Termin angeschaut und ich konnte direkt in das Büro gehen. An einem anderen Tag in der Ausländerbehörde haben sie einfach meine Tasche genommen und nach meinem Handy gesucht. Sie wollten meine Telefonnummern sehen um herauszufinden woher ich komme. Ich sagte ihnen, dass ich aus Afrika komme und dass sie meinen Anwalt oder die Beratungsstelle anrufen sollten, und dann würden sie wissen woher ich komme. Sie haben das nicht nochmal gemacht, weil mein Anwalt ihnen geschrieben hat, dass sie das nicht mit mir machen sollen. Die Beratungsstelle war die erste, die mir wirklich geholfen hat. Jedes Mal wenn ich jetzt zur Ausländerbehörde muss, kommt eine Beraterin mit.

"Don't give up, it's not over"

Linda's Story

My journey from Africa to Europe was complicated. My Madame sent me to countries, where I had to work and transfer money to her and the agents. Parts of my family were involved in this and have been threatened or had to pay money as well. I have been threatened by agents here in Germany, too. I don't know about the situation of my other siblings right now. At some point it was enough and I stopped paying money. I also advised my family that they should tell the agents that I will contact the police in Germany if they don't stop making problems. The police here in Germany said that I can call them when the agents approach me.

My experiences with the police are mixed. Now they are helping me, but I have been in jail twice when I came to Germany. The first time they treated me badly, twisted my hand and hurt me. I didn't understand the whole situation and had to weep for three days. When you are in a new place, you feel bad because you don't understand why they are treating you like that. In the second jail I tried to be friendly to people so they will be friendly with me. At some point they released me and I was happy about that.

The contact with other institutions was difficult for me as well. One day I had to wait in the social welfare office for a long time, even though I had an appointment. They told me I need to have a number and before that they wouldn't see me. I told them that I have an appointment without number, but they didn't believe me and gave me a number so I have to wait even longer. I didn't want to fight, because this is not my country. I started crying. Finally somebody looked at my appointment paper and I could go to the office directly. Another day in the foreigners' authority, they just took my bag and looked for my cellphone. They wanted to see my telephone numbers to know where I'm from. I told them that I am from Africa and that they should call my lawyer or the counseling centre and then they would know where I'm from. They didn't do that again, because my lawyer wrote to them that they shouldn't do that to me. The counseling centre was the first to really help me. Any time I go the foreigners' authority now, they come with me.

I think if you want to help someone, you have to understand: The person had stress before, so you don't add stress. Money is not everything. When you are happy, the other person is also happy. I talk to others no matter the situation they are passing through and say „Don't give up, it's not over".

Ich denke wenn man jemandem helfen will, muss man verstehen: Die Person war vorher bereits gestresst, also mach ihr nicht noch mehr Stress. Geld ist nicht alles. Wenn du glücklich bist, ist die andere Person auch glücklich. Ich rede mit anderen, egal was ihre Situation ist, und sage: „Gib nicht auf, es ist nicht vorbei". Ich teile das Wort Gottes mit anderen. Weißt du, wenn es dir schlecht geht, du denkst niemand hilft dir, aber jemand ist da. Gott hilft mir immer und macht mich glücklich. Ich habe keine Madame, Gott ist mein Herr. Und es gibt mir ein großes Selbstbewusstsein um mich gegen die zu wehren, die mich bedrohen.

Wenn ich darüber nachdenke, wie man Frauen in meiner Situation am besten helfen kann, ist die Nummer eins viel Ermutigung. Nummer zwei ist, lasst sie von Gott wissen. So viele Menschen leben in Dunkelheit, ich wünschte sie würden Gott finden. Nummer drei ist Unterstützung wie Verpflegung, Geld, oder alles was einem sonst noch einfällt, was helfen könnte.

Wenn ich etwas an meinem Leben ändern könnte, dann würde ich gerne nicht mehr zum Sozialamt gehen müssen und endlich anfangen zu arbeiten. Ich will Steuern zahlen und nicht vom Staat abhängig sein. Es stresst mich, all diese Menschen arbeiten zu sehen und wie sie mit ihrem Geld für uns sorgen. Oder wenn jemand zu mir kommt und mich um Hilfe bittet, will ich meiner Schwester 10 Euro geben können. Aber ich habe es nicht und es fühlt sich schlecht an in mir.

I share the word of God with others. You know, when you are in a bad place, you think nobody helps you, but somebody is there. God always brings help to me and makes me happy. I don't have a Madame, God is my Master. And it gives me a lot of confidence to stand up against those threatening me.

The observation by the authorities was stressing me out and I felt helpless, because I had to tell them about every aspect of my life and was not allowed to make my own decisions. And they question you, it's like you are a prisoner, a slave. This was slavery. You can't walk, you can't do anything, you have to depend. For bread. It's not good for me, I like to be independent. Free. I want to decide how to use my money, what to buy. Because that is what I needed, what I was really looking for. Praying for. But I had to give them a receipt of what I bought to show them how I used the money.

When I finally got the residence permit, my life improved a lot. The horror vision of being deported vanished, and I finally had the certainty that I could call the police if the traffickers should find me without putting myself into danger. When somebody asks me what kind of support I wish for, I have a clear answer: Advice and new ideas to cope with my situation are very helpful, but most importantly, my environment must stay optimistic. I hate it when people discourage me. Whenever I want to do something and somebody discourages me, I just let it go. Nobody should tell me that my plans are not going to work out. Don't say to me it's not going to be ok. With my history, I need to be positive and look forward.

"Sag mir nicht, dass es nicht gut werden wird"

Roses Geschichte

Ich bin in Westafrika aufgewachsen und wollte weg nach Europa als ich 17 war. Schleuser brachten mich nach Italien und seitdem musste ich auf den Strich gehen. Ich war in vielen Ländern und habe oft versucht der Situation zu entfliehen. In einem Land hat jemand mir gesagt, wie ich Dokumente bekommen kann, und das habe ich dann gemacht. Als ich schwanger wurde, entschied ich mich nach Deutschland zu gehen.

Als ich mein Kind hier in einem Krankenhaus zur Welt brachte, stellten sie mir Fragen über meine Vergangenheit und meine jetzige Situation, aber ich war noch nicht in der Lage darüber zu sprechen. Ich habe außerdem den Mitarbeiterinnen der Beratungsstelle, die versucht haben mir zu helfen, zuerst nicht vertraut, weil ich wirklich Angst hatte, dass sie Polizei sind. Zum Glück hat eine Beraterin mein Vertrauen gewonnen und ich war erleichtert, dass ich endlich meine Geschichte mit jemandem teilen konnte. Sie hilft mir immer noch mit rechtlichen Sachen und mit dem Leben in Deutschland allgemein. Es ist wichtig für mich unterstützt und beraten zu werden von ihr, und gleichzeitig die Freiheit zu haben für mich selber zu entscheiden. Niemand außer mir kann mir sagen was ich zu tun habe. Man muss das Recht haben selber zu entscheiden was man tut. Ich brauche meine Freiheit, ich brauche meine Freiheit wirklich. Ich weiß, dass meine Beraterin alles tut was sie kann und ich glaube ihr, wenn sie manchmal nicht in der Lage ist mir zu helfen. Immerhin war sie es, die mir die notwendige Hilfe gegeben hat, um eine Aufenthaltsgenehmigung zu bekommen.

Ich musste trotzdem insgesamt vier Jahre lang auf die Entscheidung warten und fand diese Zeit schrecklich. Ich litt an Bluthochdruck, Panikattacken, starken Kopfschmerzen und hatte sogar einen Schlaganfall. Meine Begegnungen mit der Polizei in den verschiedenen Ländern waren generell sehr negativ, ich habe sogar fünf Monate im Gefängnis verbracht wegen illegaler Einreise. Du hast kein Recht irgendwas zu sagen. Wenn sie dich in einen Raum einsperren, kannst du nicht mehr raus. Du hast nicht das Recht zu reden. Das ist die Art wie sie dich misshandeln, du hast kein Recht zu irgendwas. Deswegen hatte ich die ersten Jahre in Deutschland wirklich Angst, dass die Polizei mich finden würde wenn ich mit jemandem spreche.

Auch meine Erfahrungen mit der Ausländerbehörde hier in Deutschland und vor allem mit dem Sozialamt waren frustrierend. Wann immer du da bist, musst du warten, manchmal sagen sie du sollst zurückgehen, dass sie dich nicht beraten werden.

"Don't say to me it's not going to be ok"

Rose's Story

I grew up in West Africa and wanted to leave for Europe when I was 17. Traffickers brought me to Italy and from then on, I had to walk the streets. I have been in many countries and tried to escape the situation many times. In one country someone gave me a tip how I could get legal documents, and I did that. When I became pregnant, I decided to move to Germany.

When I gave birth to my child in a hospital there, they asked me questions about my past and my current situation, but I was not able to talk about it yet. I also did not trust the staff of the counselling centre who tried to help me, at first, because I was really afraid that they were police. Luckily, a counsellor earned my trust and I was relieved that I could finally share my story with somebody. She still helps me with legal matters and life in Germany in general. It is important for me to be supported and advised by her, while having the freedom to decide for myself. Nobody besides me has to tell me what I have to do. You have to have the right to decide what you have to do. I have to have my freedom, I really need my freedom. I know that my counsellor does everything she can and I believe her, when she is sometimes not able to help me. After all, it was her who gave me the help I needed in seeking a residence permit.

I still had to wait for the decision four years altogether and I found this time to be terrible. I suffered from hypertension, panic attacks, strong headaches and even had a stroke. My encounters with the police in different countries were in general very negative, I even spent five months in prison for illegal entry. You don't have rights to say anything. When they lock you in a room, you can't come out anymore. You don't have the right to talk. That's the way how they are maltreating, you don't have the rights to do anything. This is why the first years in Germany, I was really afraid that the police might find me if I talk to someone.

Also my experiences with the foreigners' authority here in Germany and especially the social welfare office were frustrating. Whenever you are there you have to wait, sometimes they say you should go back, they won't see you. Sometimes I went there in the early morning and was still there in the evening. One time I went for a health insurance certificate because I was sick, and they told me to come back the next day. They treat people like animals. The last time I was there, I cried and they almost called an ambulance for me.

Manchmal bin ich am frühen Morgen dorthin gegangen und war am Abend immer noch da. Einmal bin ich für einen Krankenschein hingegangen, weil ich krank war, und sie sagten mir ich soll am nächsten Tag wiederkommen. Sie behandeln Menschen wie Tiere. Das letzte Mal als ich da war, habe ich geweint und sie haben mir fast einen Krankenwagen gerufen.

Die Beobachtung durch die Behörden hat mich sehr belastet und ich fühlte mich hilflos, weil ich denen über jeden Aspekt meines Lebens berichten musste und nicht meine eigenen Entscheidungen treffen durfte. Und sie befragen dich, es ist als wärst du eine Gefangene, eine Sklavin. Das war Sklaverei. Du kannst nicht auf die Straße, du kannst nichts machen, du musst abhängig sein. Für Brot. Es ist nicht gut für mich, ich möchte unabhängig sein. Frei. Ich will selber entscheiden wie ich mein Geld verwende, was ich kaufe. Weil das ist was ich brauchte, was ich wirklich gesucht habe. Wofür ich gebetet habe. Aber ich musste ihnen eine Quittung zeigen von dem was ich gekauft habe, um zu zeigen wie ich das Geld benutzt habe.

Als ich endlich die Aufenthaltsgenehmigung hatte, hat sich mein Leben sehr verbessert. Die Horrorvorstellung, abgeschoben zu werden, ist verschwunden, und ich hatte endlich die Sicherheit, dass ich die Polizei anrufen konnte, wenn die Schleuser mich finden, ohne mich selber in Gefahr zu bringen. Wenn mich jemand fragt, welche Art von Unterstützung ich mir wünsche, habe ich eine klare Antwort: Beratung und neue Ideen mit meiner Situation umzugehen sind sehr hilfreich, aber am wichtigsten ist, dass meine Umgebung optimistisch bleibt. Ich hasse es wenn Leute mich entmutigen. Immer wenn ich etwas machen will und mich jemand entmutigt, lass ich es einfach sein. Niemand sollte mir sagen, dass meine Pläne nicht klappen werden. Sag mir nicht, dass es nicht gut werden wird. Mit meiner Geschichte muss ich positiv sein und nach vorne schauen.

The observation by the authorities was stressing me out and I felt helpless, because I had to tell them about every aspect of my life and was not allowed to make my own decisions. And they question you, it's like you are a prisoner, a slave. This was slavery. You can't walk, you can't do anything, you have to depend. For bread. It's not good for me, I like to be independent. Free. I want to decide how to use my money, what to buy. Because that is what I needed, what I was really looking for. Praying for. But I had to give them a receipt of what I bought to show them how I used the money.

When I finally got the residence permit, my life improved a lot. The horror vision of being deported vanished, and I finally had the certainty that I could call the police if the traffickers should find me without putting myself into danger. When somebody asks me what kind of support I wish for, I have a clear answer: Advice and new ideas to cope with my situation are very helpful, but most importantly, my environment must stay optimistic. I hate it when people discourage me. Whenever I want to do something and somebody discourages me, I just let it go. Nobody should tell me, that my plans are not going to work out. Don't say to me it's not going to be ok. With my history, I need to be positive and look forward.

"Für mich als Person hat sich nur die Beratungsstelle interessiert"

Tatjanas Geschichte

Ich kam nach Deutschland durch eine große Organisation, die Au-Pair-Mädchen aus Osteuropa hierher vermittelt, und wurde bei einer Familie mit einem Kind untergebracht. Es war alles supertoll organisiert, mir wurde zweimal die Stadt gezeigt. Aber nach einem Monat war von einem Tag auf den anderen das Kind mit der Oma weg und ich wurde vor die Tatsache gestellt, dass ich hergekommen bin, um anschaffen zu gehen. Das Babysitting, das war so eine Fassade, dass man an meine Papiere kommt und dass man mich so richtig in Sicherheit hat, meine ganze Lebensgeschichte weiß, meine ganzen Daten von meiner Familie, wo die alle wohnen, die Namen, dass man die Frau so komplett in der Hand hat, damit man sie erpressen kann. Es waren über 50 Frauen, die von einer Wohnung zur anderen gebracht wurden, damit kein Kontakt untereinander entstehen konnte. Es war eine Anzeige geschaltet für Haus- und Hotelbesuche. Da wird man mit einem speziellen Taxiunternehmen zur Wohnung gebracht und nach der Zeit, wofür der Kunde gezahlt hat, abgeholt; in dieser Stunde kann man nicht nein sagen. Zwei Jahre habe ich das durchgemacht.

Hilfe zu suchen, das geht nicht so, weil man funktioniert die ganze Zeit, und der einzige Gedanke ist, dass es vorbei geht. Dass man irgendwann nach Hause fährt, aber wenn man wegläuft, die kriegen dich da wieder und von diesen Drohungen da ist man so eingeschüchtert, da hat man überhaupt nicht mal den Gedanken zu fliehen oder irgendwie wegzulaufen. Ich habe aber Glück gehabt, dass ein Stammkunde gemerkt hat, dass etwas nicht stimmte, weil ich mich immer melden musste, und der Taxifahrer mich mal gewalttätig angepackt hat. Die Hausbesuche bei ihm wurden dann komplett abgebrochen, aber er hat mich in ein Hotel bestellt und meine Flucht organisiert. Er hat mich zu sich nach Hause genommen, es kamen aber sofort Drohanrufe, und da war unser erster Gang zur Anwältin. Ich hatte überhaupt keine Papiere, die hatten alles vernichtet, meine Familie hatten sie auch schon mit einer Lügengeschichte angerufen, und ich war illegal hier. Die Anwältin sagte, die einzige Möglichkeit sei, dass ich die Menschen anzeigen sollte, und sie hat mich auch an die Beratungsstelle vermittelt, die am selben Tag einen Termin für mich hatte, und die mir erklärt hat, welche Möglichkeiten ich hatte.

Tatjana's Story

I came to Germany through a big organisation that arranged for au-pair girls from Eastern Europe to come here, and I was placed in a family with one child. Everything was perfectly organised, and I was shown around the city twice. But after one month, the child and the grandmother disappeared from one day to the next, and I was confronted with the fact that I had been brought there to work as a prostitute. The babysitting, that was just a false front to get hold of my papers and to make them definitely sure about me, to get to know all my life story and all the data of my family, the places where they all live, and their names, to have the woman completely in their grip, to be able to blackmail her. There were more than 50 women who were moved from one apartment to another, to prevent them from getting in contact one with another. There was an advertisement placed for home and hotel calls. Then you are taken to an apartment with a special taxicab company and after the time that the client had paid for, you are picked up again; during this hour, you cannot say 'No'. I endured this for two years.

Searching for help, this is not so easy, because you just function all the time and the only thought you have is that it will eventually come to an end; that the time will come that you will go home. But if you run away, they will get you again and you are so much intimidated by those threats that you don't even think of taking flight or somehow running away. But I was lucky that one of the regular customers noticed that there was something wrong, because I always had to report and one time the taxi driver grabbed me violently. The home calls with this client were stopped completely, but he called me to a hotel then and organised my escape. He took me to his home, but then, threatening calls started right away, and so the first thing we did was to go to a lawyer. I didn't have any papers at all, they had destroyed everything, they had also even called my family and told them cock and bull stories, and I was here illegally. The lawyer said that my only chance was to report those people to the police, and she also put me in touch with the advisory centre; they gave me an appointment on that same day and explained the possibilities open to me.

Ich hätte damals in eine geschützte Wohnung außerhalb der Stadt gehen können, aber das wollte ich nicht, denn die Menschen dieser Organisation sind auch immer außerhalb. Ich habe mich zur Anzeige entschlossen. Außerdem hatte ich das Versprechen, ein Mädchen, das mir bei der Flucht geholfen hat, auch herauszuholen. Über Tage, über Stunden ging das ganze Verhör bei der Polizei; diese Menschen waren bekannt, und man hat mir Bilder in einem Ordner gezeigt, damit ich sage, wer dabei war, denn ich kannte sie nur unter einem anderen Namen. Die Polizei war nicht wirklich an mir interessiert sondern daran, dass ich möglichst schnell aussage, mehr Orte und mehr Namen nenne. Ich war sehr traumatisiert und hatte viel Alkohol getrunken, und sie haben mir nicht gesagt, wo ich Hilfe bekommen könnte; für mich als Person hat sich nur die Beratungsstelle interessiert.

Der Prozess dauerte etwa zwei Jahre, und ich hatte in dieser Zeit eine Duldung, so ein halblegaler Status. Das war besser als gar keine Papiere, aber es war so richtig eingeschränkt, du konntest hier nichts machen. Nur innerhalb der Stadt kann man sich aufhalten, ich durfte nicht ans Meer fahren, musste immer die Genehmigung von der Ausländerbehörde holen, um überhaupt ein bisschen rauszukommen. Zum Glück musste ich vor Gericht nicht aussagen, denn die Menschen haben alles gestanden, teilweise haben sie Bewährung bekommen und andere sind in den Knast gegangen. Damit war die Duldung zu Ende und ich musste innerhalb zwei oder vier Wochen ausreisen.

Zum Glück wollte der Mann, der mir zur Flucht verholfen hat, mich heiraten, und ich bin nur für die kurze Zeit ausgereist, um meine Papiere wieder herstellen zu lassen. Ich hatte in der Zeit immer Angst, dass mich jemand erkennt, denn die Organisation war in Deutschland vor Gericht gewesen aber in meinem Heimatland war alles frei. Aber es ist mir gelungen und seitdem lebe ich hier.

Ohne die Betreuung durch die Beratungsstelle hätte ich das damals alles nicht durchgestanden. Aber ich weiß jetzt, dass ich damals viel mehr für meine Gesundheit gebraucht hätte. In dieser Situation, wenn man so komplett psychisch erschlagen ist und froh, dass man von dieser Gewalt weg ist, dann überlegt man nicht, was man so tatsächlich selber als Person für sich braucht. Das ist das, was mir gefehlt hat, dass eine Organisation mehr psychologische Unterstützung gibt. Und jetzt habe ich so jahrelang damit zu kämpfen. Fast jede Frau in so einer Situation ist suchtgefährdet, Frauen würden viel mehr psychologische Beratung und Therapie brauchen, ein Krankenhausaufenthalt mit Traumatherapie wäre hilfreich. Eine Hilfe wäre auch, die Sprache lernen zu können und ein Praktikum oder eine Arbeit zu machen, unter Menschen zu kommen. Es sollte irgendwie die Möglichkeit geben sich hier zu integrieren. Denn Frauen, die nach diesem Ganzen und mit diesen Krankheiten in das Herkunftsland zurückgehen müssen, haben gar keine Chance, wieder auf die Beine zu kommen. Sie rutschen in die gleiche Sache rein oder noch schlimmer.

At that time, I could have been taken to a safehouse outside of town, but I didn't want that, because the people who worked in that organisation, they are always outside the towns as well. So I decided to press charges. Moreover, I had made a promise to a girl who had helped me escape that I would try to get her out as well. The police questioning took hours and days; those people were known there, and they showed me pictures in a file, so that I could identify who they were, for I only knew them under other names. The police were not really interested in me, but in getting me to make a statement as quickly as possible, to mention more places and more names. I was seriously traumatized and I had been drinking alcohol a lot, and they did not tell me where I could find help; it was only the advisory centre that showed genuine interest in me as a person.

The trial took roughly two years, and during that time, I had a toleration, some kind of semi-legal status. That was better than no papers at all, but it was really living in a restricted situation, you couldn't do anything here. You could only stay here in this town, I was not even allowed to go to the beach. I always had to request a permit from the Foreigners' Office to get out of here at least a little bit. I was lucky enough not to have to testify in court, because those people confessed everything; some of them got a suspended sentence, and others went to prison. Thus, my tolerated status came to an end and I had to leave the country within a few weeks.

Fortunately, the man who had helped me to escape wanted to marry me and I left the country just for a short while to get my papers restored. During that time, I lived in constant fear of being detected, because that organisation had been before the court in Germany, but everything of this kind was free and unpunishable in my country. But I succeeded and I have lived here since that time.

I would never have endured all this without the advisory centre's assistance. But now I know that I would have needed a lot more help for my health at that time. In this situation, when you are so down psychologically, and just glad to have escaped from the violence, then you don't give a thought to what you really need for yourself as a person. What I was missing then was an organisation that would provide better psychological support. And now I have had to struggle with this for so many years. Almost any woman in such a situation is at risk of addiction, women would need a lot more psychological counselling and therapy, a stay in hospital including trauma therapy would be helpful. It would also be helpful to get an opportunity to learn the language and to do an internship and to work, to meet people. There should somehow be a possibility to get integrated. Because women who have experienced all this and who have to return to their country of origin with all those health problems, they have no chance to bounce back. They will fall into the same sort of problems or even worse.

"Só o centro de atendimento é que mostrou interesse genuíno em mim como pessoa"

História de Tatjana

Vim para a Alemanha através de uma grande organização que tratava de trazer raparigas au pair (trabalhadoras domésticas) da Europa do Leste para aqui. Fui trabalhar para uma família com uma criança. Foi tudo perfeitamente organizado. Levaram-me a ver a cidade duas vezes. Depois de um mês, de um dia para o outro, a criança e a avó desapareceram e fui confrontada com o facto de que me trouxeram para trabalhar como prostituta. Fazer de babysitter foi só uma fachada para ficarem com os meus documentos e para me conhecerem melhor, para ficarem a saber tudo sobre a minha história de vida e todos os dados sobre a minha família: os sítios onde eles moram, os nomes. Para terem a mulher completamente nas suas garras, para poderem chantageá-la. Havia mais de 50 mulheres que foram movimentadas de um apartamento para outro, para impedir que contactassem umas com as outras. Havia um anúncio para encontros em casa e em hotéis. Depois era levada para um apartamento com uma empresa especial de táxis e, ao acabar o tempo que o cliente tinha pago, iam-te buscar outra vez; durante esta hora, não podias dizer "Não". Eu aguentei isto durante dois anos.

Procurar ajuda não é assim tão fácil, porque estás a funcionar a toda a hora e o único pensamento que tens é que isto vai eventualmente acabar; que vai chegar a hora de ires para casa. Mas se fugires, eles apanham-te outra vez e tens tanto medo das ameaças que nem sequer pensas em tentar escapar ou de alguma forma fugir. Mas eu tive sorte que um dos clientes regulares notou que algo estava errado, porque eu tinha sempre de avisar quando terminasse e, uma das vezes, o motorista agarrou-me violentamente. Os encontros em casa com este cliente acabaram completamente mas ele combinou um encontro num hotel e organizou a minha fuga. Levou-me para casa dele, mas nessa altura começaram logo as chamadas ameaçadoras e então a primeira coisa que fizemos foi ir a uma advogada. Não tinha quaisquer documentos. Eles tinham destruído tudo. Até ligaram à minha família para contar boatos sobre mim. Estava aqui ilegalmente. A advogada disse que a minha única hipótese era denunciar aquelas pessoas à polícia. Também me pôs em contacto com o centro de atendimento e eles deram-me uma consulta no mesmo dia e explicaram-me que possibilidades é que tinha.

Naquela altura, podia ter sido levada para uma casa de abrigo fora da cidade, mas eu não quis ir, porque as pessoas que trabalhavam naquela organização estão também sempre fora das cidades. Então decidi fazer queixa. Mais ainda: tinha prometido a uma rapariga que me tinha ajudado a fugir que ia tentar tirá-la de lá também. O interrogatório da polícia durou horas e dias. Aquelas pessoas eram conhecidas lá, eles mostraram-me fotografias numa pasta, para que pudesse identificar quem eram, porque eu só os conhecia por outros nomes. A polícia não estava interessada em mim, mas no meu depoimento, o mais rápido possível. Estavam interessados em saber mais sítios e mais nomes. Fiquei seriamente traumatizada e andava a beber muito álcool, mas eles não me disseram onde é que podia encontrar ajuda. Só o centro de atendimento é que mostrou interesse genuíno em mim como pessoa.

O julgamento durou cerca de dois anos e, durante esse tempo, tive uma tolerância, uma espécie de estatuto semilegal. Isso era melhor do que não ter documentos, mas era, mesmo assim, viver numa situação restrita, não podia fazer nada. Só podia ficar aqui nesta cidade. Não me deixavam sequer ir à praia. Tinha sempre de pedir permissão ao Serviço de Estrangeiros para sair daqui durante um bocadinho. Pelo menos, tive sorte suficiente para não ter que testemunhar em tribunal porque aquelas pessoas confessaram tudo. Alguns receberam pena suspensa e outros foram para a prisão. Assim, o meu estatuto de tolerância acabou e tive de sair do país passado umas semanas.

Felizmente, o homem que me tinha ajudado a fugir queria casar comigo e eu deixei o país apenas durante pouco tempo para voltar a ter os meus documentos. Durante esse tempo, vivi em constante medo de ser detetada porque aquela organização tinha sido levada a tribunal na Alemanha mas, no meu país, o tráfico é livre e impune. Mas consegui e vivo aqui desde essa altura.

Nunca poderia ter aguentado isto tudo sem o apoio do centro de atendimento. Mas agora sei que, naquela altura, precisava de muito mais ajuda para a minha saúde. Nesta situação, quando estás tão em baixo psicologicamente mas contente por ter escapado à violência, não pensas no que realmente precisas para ti própria. O que me faltava era uma organização que me desse apoio psicológico. E, agora, tenho batalhado com isto durante anos. Quase todas as mulheres, numa situação dessas, estão em risco de dependência, e precisam de muito mais aconselhamento psicológico e terapia. Pode ser útil uma estadia no hospital, incluindo terapia para traumas. Também pode ser importante ter oportunidade para aprender a língua e fazer um estágio e trabalhar, para conhecer pessoas. De alguma forma, devia haver possibilidade de nos integrarmos. Porque as mulheres que experienciam tudo isto e que têm de voltar para o seu país de origem, com todos esses problemas de saúde, não têm hipótese de recuperar. Elas vão cair no mesmo tipo de problemas ou ainda piores.

Intervention against sexual exploitation

Stories and experiences of trafficked women

Portugal

"Os agentes batiam para elas falarem"

História de Alexandra

Estou em Portugal há 12 anos. Quando eu vim do Brasil para cá, vim com o propósito de trabalhar. A pessoa que me ligou arranjou-me trabalho na prostituição, numa casa de alterne. No dia de folga da casa, só podíamos sair depois do meio dia e tínhamos de estar de regresso às 22h, quem não estivesse em casa, dormia na rua. Quando completei 3 meses como turista, ela colocou-me porta fora e eu não conhecia nada nem ninguém. Eu era ilegal, num país estranho sem conhecer ninguém. Fui contactar o dono de outra casa e passei lá um ano a trabalhar, ilegalmente. Fui trabalhar para essa casa e a polícia bateu lá. Não me pegaram porque fugi para o meio do mato, fiquei lá durante 2 horas e consegui pegar um táxi para minha casa. Nessa altura, já tinha arrendado um apartamento.

No prédio, morava uma senhora em cima que fazia tráfico de pessoas. Quando cheguei em casa, passado 30 minutos, a polícia começa a rebentar as portas e me pega em casa. Aí prendeu a mulher, prendeu toda a gente que estava lá na casa dela e do prédio; portuguesas não prenderam, prenderam só eu, brasileira. Fiquei presa sábado e domingo. Foram presas várias colegas minhas, todas brasileiras, que estavam na casa de alterne. Os agentes agrediam, batiam para elas falarem quem traficava. E elas não queriam falar porque também já estavam sendo ameaçadas. Quando eles me puxaram para ir para a sala prestar o depoimento, vi um agente apontando o dedo na cara de uma delas e falando assim: "se você não falar agora, vai ficar com os dentes no chão" e pah na cara dela, eu só fechei os olhos. Nessa época, foi muito triste. Direitos, a gente tinha direitos?! Quer dizer, não sabia que direitos a gente tinha?! Como é que apresenta denúncia?! Se apresentar denúncia, vai embora! Ninguém me disse nada de direitos, só disse que se eu falar estava tudo bem e se eu não quisesse falar estava tudo bem. Depois fui no juiz que me deu um termo de coação para eu me apresentar quinzenalmente. O juiz falou para a gente "olha, traga essas, mais ilegais, mais brasileiras". Mas não é só no tribunal que a gente vê discriminação, no dia a dia, é normal. A família do meu namorado ainda hoje não me aceita.

Depois no serviço de imigração não foi igual: conversaram mais, abriram mais. Falaram: "olha aqui funciona assim, se quiser falar, fala, se não quiser falar, não fala"; aí foi onde eu falei com eles.

"The police beat them in order to make them speak"

Alexandra's Story

I have been in Portugal for 12 years. I came from Brazil with a goal, to work. The person who called me offered me a job in prostitution, in a brothel. On my day off I could only get out of the brothel after midday and had to be back by 10 pm. If I wasn't at the house at that time I had to sleep in the street. When the three months as a tourist ended, she kicked me out. I was illegal, in a strange country, without knowing anyone. I contacted a pimp that used to go to the brothel and went to another brothel where I worked for a year. When I was working in this brothel, the police went there. They didn't catch me because I hid in the bushes and stayed there for 2 hours until they left. I then took a taxi home. At this time I was already renting an apartment.

In the apartment building where I lived there was a lady in the upper floor who trafficked people. When I arrived home, the police knocked and then started to burst the doors open and caught me in my apartment. They arrested the lady and all the people that were in her house. They did not arrest any of the Portuguese women that lived in the building, just me the Brazilian woman. I stayed in prison on Saturday and Sunday. The police officers beat the women caught at the brothel, who were all Brazilians, in order to make them speak. They beat them and demanded that they say who the traffickers were. They did not want to talk because they were, already, being threatened. When they pushed me to the room to testify, there was one woman and I heard the police officer telling her: "If you don't speak now, your teeth will be on the floor!" He then hit her in the face. I just closed my eyes. That episode was very sad. Rights? Did we have rights?! We didn't know our rights. How could we make a complaint? If we made a complaint we would be sent away! Nobody told me anything about my rights, they only told me that everything was all right if I denounced and if I didn't want to talk everything was all right too. Afterwards, I went to the judge and he gave me a coercive term. I had to present myself at the police station every two weeks. The judge was saying: "bring them, more illegals, more Brazilians". But it's not just in the court that we see discrimination, in our day-to-day it is normal. The family of my boyfriend doesn't accept me to this day.

Then I had to go to the immigration services but it was not like at the police station, they talked more and were more open. They said: "look, here is how it works: if you want to speak, you speak, if you don't, you don't". One inspector told me that if I wanted to denounce, I would enter a process and the traffickers would not do anything to harm me.

Entretanto, um inspetor dos serviços de imigração disse se eu quisesse denunciar, que eu entrava no processo e que os traficantes não podiam fazer nada contra mim. O inspetor deu-me o número de telefone dele e falou: "qualquer coisa que quiser, liga que a gente vem cá na hora". Passados 2 dias, o dono da casa saiu da prisão e começou a me ameaçar. A mulher dele era brasileira, sabia tudo e, se eu denunciasse, eles iam-me matar. Nesse dia, peguei coragem e liguei para o inspetor. Contei a história, tudo. Ele veio de outra cidade para me ouvir nesse dia. Ele falou que eu podia ficar tranquila que, enquanto o processo dessa casa estivesse a correr, não ia acontecer nada comigo. O processo correu durante 7 anos. Nesse mesmo tempo eu não fui chamada, passei ilesa, mas não me informaram de nada. Sei que o dono da casa, no final do processo, teve que pagar uma multa e saiu em liberdade.

Consegui primeiro arranjar os papéis, através do meu namorado, que é português, e assinou um termo de responsabilidade por mim. Quando consegui arrumar os documentos me restou procurar trabalho. O meu namorado não aceitava eu trabalhar na prostituição. Entretanto, as coisas ficaram muito apertadas, eu não conseguia arranjar trabalho e comecei a colocar anúncio no jornal, mas escondido. Foi quando me ligaram da instituição e disseram que ajudavam as pessoas. Foi há 5 anos que me começaram a ajudar a procurar trabalho. A partir daqui, a minha vida começou a melhorar. Agora, cada vez que vou renovar os meus documentos, já não preciso mais do meu namorado porque já tenho trabalho. A cidadania portuguesa vou pegar o ano que vem. Já não faço parte da instituição, mas quando eu não acho apoio noutro sítio, o apoio que eu tenho é aqui.

Gostava de dizer às mulheres para terem mais os pés no chão, para não se iludirem com conversas, com o trabalho, com o sair do país para vir para outro país. As pessoas que estão no Brasil pensam que aqui a gente chega na árvore e apanha dinheiro, pensam é Europa, é um país de 1º mundo, mas quando chega, vê a realidade, é complicado. Eu digo para não se iludirem, para saberem mesmo o que querem da vida e terem consciência daquilo que fazem.

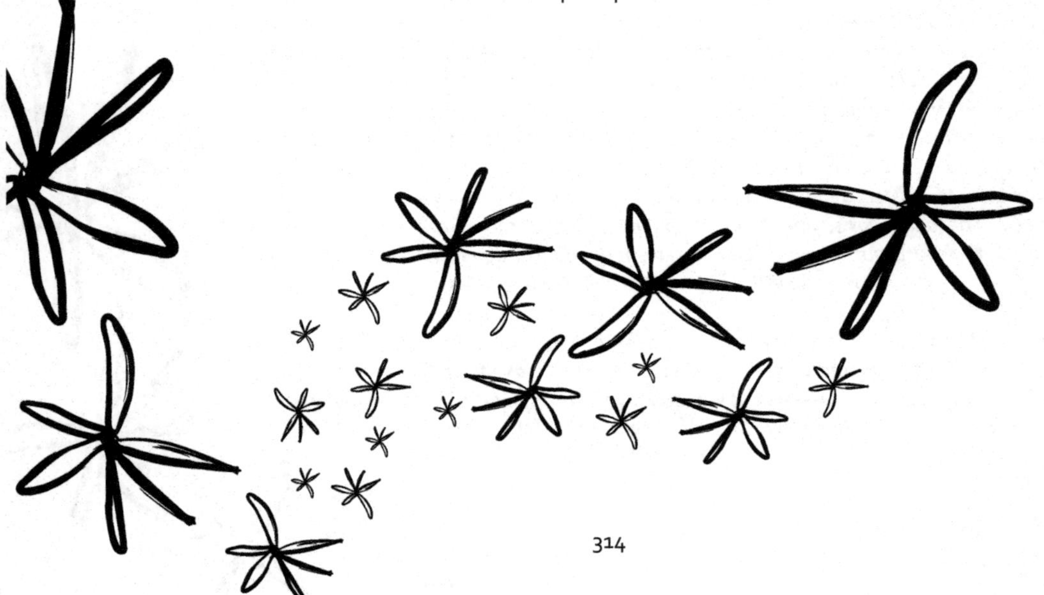

The inspector gave me his phone number and said: "if you need anything call me and we will come immediately". After two days the owner of the brothel was released from prison and started to threaten me. His wife was Brazilian and she knew everything. He said that if I denounced them, they would kill me. That day I got courage and called the inspector. He came from a different city to listen to me that day. He told me to remain calm because while the case was in court nothing would happen to me. The case ran for 7 years. During that time I wasn't called to testify and nothing happened to me but I wasn't informed of anything. I know that at the end of the case the owner of the brothel had to pay a fine and was free.

I first got my immigration papers through my boyfriend. He signed a statement of responsibility for me. When I got the papers I searched for a job. When I met my boyfriend he did not want me to work in prostitution. However our financial situation became very difficult and I couldn't find a job and started to put advertisements in the newspaper and work in prostitution again without my boyfriend knowing. This was when the NGO team saw my advertisement and called me. They told me they were an institution that helped people. This was 5 years ago and since then they helped me find a job. My life started to become better when I went to the NGO. Now, because I have a job, when I want to renew my documents I don't need my boyfriend's signature anymore. I will get Portuguese citizenship next year. I don't belong to the NGO anymore but when I don't find support elsewhere I still go there.

I want to tell other women to get their feet on the ground, to not be naïve when it comes to leaving one's country for work. In Brazil people think that money grows on trees here. They think Portugal is a first world country but when you arrive here you see the reality. It's complicated. I would tell them not to be naïve to find out what they really want in life, and be aware of what they are doing.

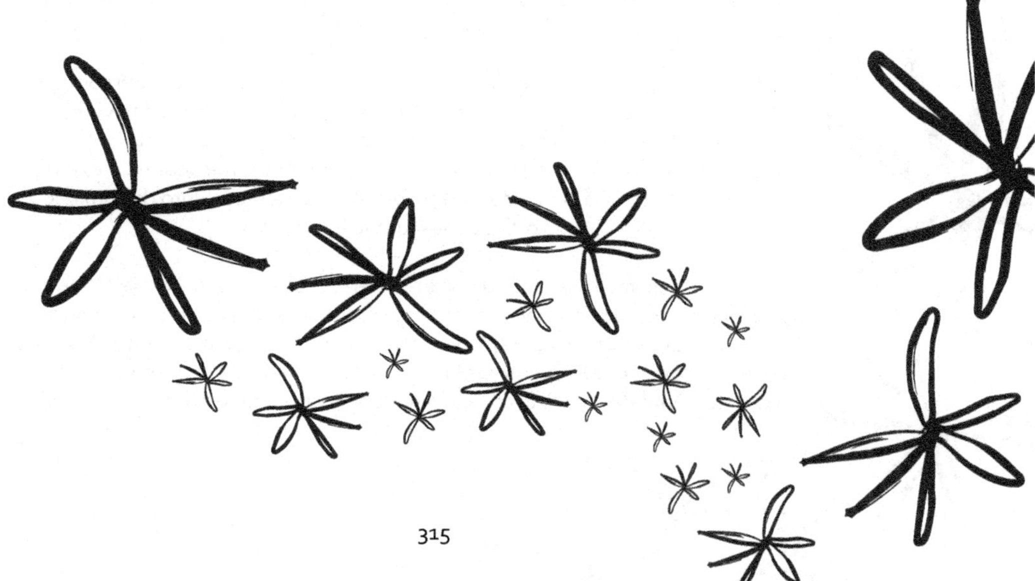

"Tinha muito medo que me mandassem de volta para África"

História de Gina

Nasci em África. Não vim diretamente para Portugal, primeiro fui para Espanha, com 12 anos, e estive lá um ano. Quando cheguei a Portugal, não gostei. Espanha é mais linda. Quando estava a viver com o meu namorado, ele disse-me que não podia sair sem documentos. Uma vez tive de ir ao médico, fui aos serviços de saúde e um enfermeiro disse-me que sem documentos não podia ser atendida. Quando fiz o cartão, já pude ir à médica. Fui bem tratada pela médica que também me informou que podia pedir médico de família. A 1ª médica de família não foi boa, era muito doida, não me ouviu. Voltei a mudar de médica.

Aqui, em Portugal, as forças de segurança não fizeram nada de útil, também não me quero meter com a polícia. Como dizemos na nossa terra, a polícia não é amiga de ninguém. Fui duas vezes presa, por falta de documentos, e fiquei detida na esquadra durante a noite. Estava a trabalhar com outras mulheres na rua e fomos presas. Nas duas vezes que fui presa estava com muito medo que me mandassem de volta para África. Algumas mulheres foram enviadas embora. Não fui informada sobre os meus direitos, mas não me trataram mal e deram comida. Dormi numa cela com as minhas colegas. Tivemos direito a uma advogada oficiosa que não tivemos de pagar e que nos perguntou se queríamos tradução para inglês mas nós não quisemos. A advogada defendeu bem. No tribunal fui bem tratada, e das duas vezes saí em liberdade.

No ano passado, fui à polícia apresentar queixa contra um chulo. Fui com outras mulheres, três eram portuguesas. Até hoje, a gente não sabe nada. A queixa era por agressão contra uma mulher que teve de ser internada vários dias. Ele continua na casa de alterne. A advogada que tenho atualmente já me pediu muito dinheiro, não explica bem as coisas e não me mostra os documentos. Sinto discriminação em Portugal mas fui-me habituando.

O serviço de imigração está a portar-se bem. O que eu faço eles não sabem. A primeira vez, em 2004, quando tentei legalizar-me precisei de um documento, tive de pagar 250€ e estar à espera. No serviço de imigração, fizeram-me ir lá várias vezes para assinar documentos. Mas só em 2006, quando saiu a nova lei, enviaram o documento de autorização de residência. Foi durante estes dois anos que fui presa.

"I was very afraid of being sent away to Africa"

Gina's Story

I was born in Africa. When I left, I was 12 years old, first I went to Spain and was there during one year. When I arrived at Portugal I didn't like the country, Spain is more beautiful. When I was living with my boyfriend he told me that without papers I couldn't get out. Once I had to go to the doctor. I went to the hospital and a nurse told me that without a card I couldn't be seen. When I got the card I could go to the doctor. I had good care from the doctor who saw me and was informed that I had the right to a family doctor. Then I went to search for a family doctor. The first family doctor wasn't good, very crazy, she didn't listen to me. I changed the doctor again.

Since I'm in Portugal, the security forces didn't do anything useful, also I don't want to interact with the police. As we say in my country the police are not friends of anyone. I was arrested two times, due to the absence of documents. I was working with other women in the streets and I was detained during the night. When I was arrested I was very afraid of being sent away back to Africa. Some women were sent away. At the police station they didn't inform me about my rights, although they didn't treat me badly and gave me food. I slept in a cell with my colleagues. We had the right to an officially appointed lawyer which we didn't had to pay for, and she asked if we wanted translation to English but we didn´t want it. The lawyer defended us well. At the court I was well treated and both times I went out free.

Last year I made a complaint to the police against a pimp. I made the complaint with other women, three of them were Portuguese. The complaint was due to an aggression against a woman who was hospitalized for several days. Until today, we don't know anything and the pimp continues to run the brothel. The lawyer I have now already asked for lots of money but doesn't explain things well and doesn't show me the documents of the process. In Portugal I feel discrimination but I'm used to it.

The immigration services are behaving well. What I do in prostitution they don't know about. The first time, in 2004, when I first tried to legalize my situation I needed to get a document and I had to pay 250€ for it and wait. Later, in 2006, there was a new law and they sent me the document. It was during this period without papers that I was detained.

Quando tive documentos já não tive problemas. Mas para ter documentos, precisa trabalhar. Trabalho é difícil sem documentos. Sem trabalho não se desconta para a Segurança Social. Se não descontar para a Segurança Social não tem direito a advogado/a oficioso/a. A Instituição Privada de Solidariedade Social (IPSS) está a ajudar-me com os documentos de legalização. Uma colega minha que foi ao serviço de imigração e não conseguiu os documentos necessários, desistiu porque era muito difícil. Só em Lisboa teve ajuda de uma outra IPSS e conseguiu os documentos de legalização e arranjar um emprego.

Neste momento estão muitas coisas a acontecer e a situação não está fácil, ainda não consegui os documentos de legalização e continuo a trabalhar na prostituição.

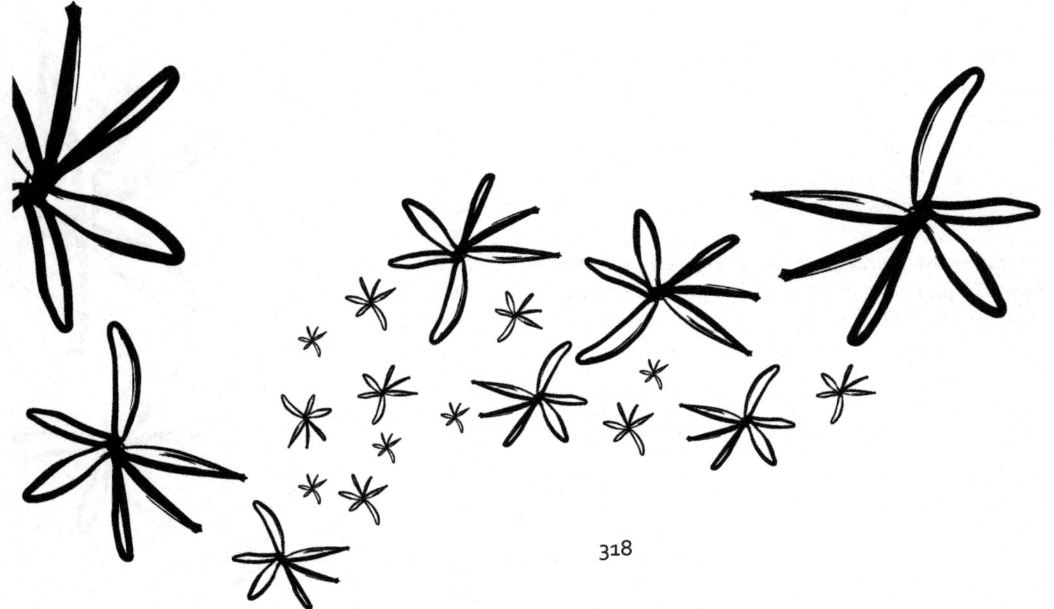

When I had the papers I no longer had problems. It's hard to find a job without documents. To have the documents you need to work. Without work you don't pay for social security. If you don't pay that you don't have the right to an officially appointed lawyer. The Private Solidarity Institution (IPSS) is helping me with legalization. One colleague tried to legalize herself but she gave up because it was very hard. Only in Lisbon with the support of another Private Solidarity Instituion (IPSS) she could get the legalization documents and find a job.

At this moment many things are happening; my situation hasn't been easy because I couldn't get the legalization documents and I'm still working in prostitution.

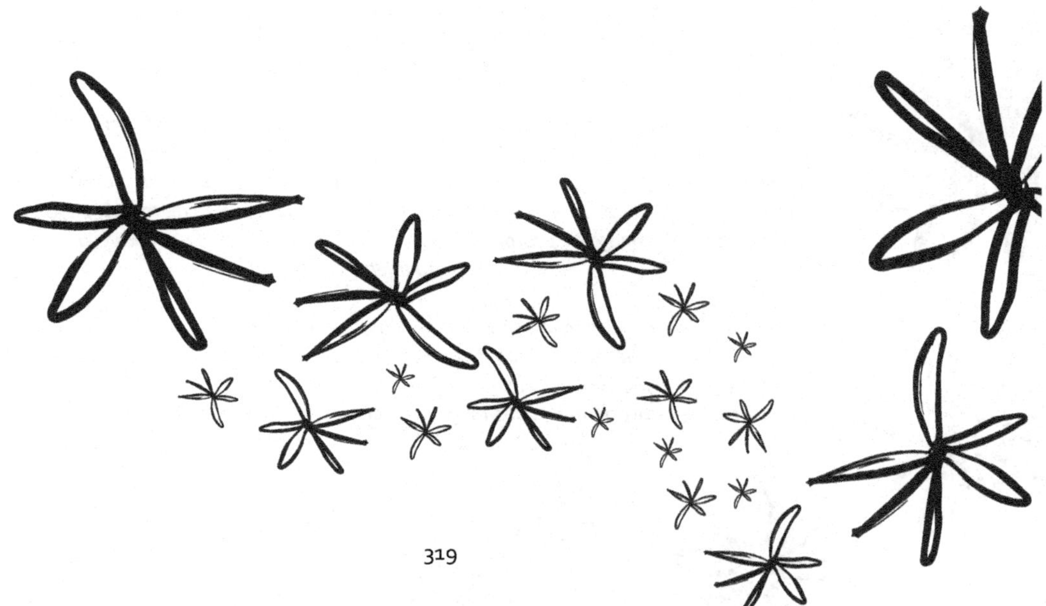

"Bilo me je zelo strah, da me bodo poslali nazaj v Afriko"

Ginina zgodba

Rodila sem se v Afriki. Ko sem odšla, sem imela 12 let. Najprej sem šla v Španijo, kjer sem ostala eno leto. Ko sem prispela na Portugalsko, mi država ni bila všeč, Španija je lepša.

Ko sem živela s fantom, mi je rekel, da brez papirjev ne morem ven. Enkrat sem morala k zdravniku. Šla sem v bolnico, kjer mi je sestra rekla, da me brez kartice ne morejo oskrbeti. Ko sem dobila kartico, sem lahko šla k zdravniku. Zdravnik, ki me je obravnaval, mi je nudil dobro oskrbo in me obvestil, da imam pravico do družinskega zdravnika. Potem sem šla iskat družinskega zdravnika. Prva družinska zdravnica ni bila dobra, čisto nora, ni me poslušala. Spet sem zamenjala zdravnika.

Odkar sem na Portugalskem, varnostne sile niso naredile nič koristnega, pa tudi nočem imeti interakcij s policijo. Kot pravimo v moji domovini, policija ni nikogaršnja prijateljica. Dvakrat so me aretirali, ker nisem imela dokumentov. Z drugimi ženskami sem delala na cesti in so me čez noč pridržali na policijski postaji. Ko so me aretirali, me je bilo zelo strah, da me bodo poslali nazaj v Afriko. Nekatere ženske so poslali nazaj. Na policijski postaji me niso poučili o mojih pravicah, a niso slabo ravnali z mano, dali so mi hrano. S kolegicami sem spala v celici. Imele smo pravico do uradno dodeljene odvetnice, ki je ni bilo treba plačati. Vprašala nas je, če želimo prevod v angleščino, a tega nismo hotele. Odvetnica nas je dobro branila. Na sodišču so lepo ravnali z mano in me obakrat izpustili.

Lani sem nekega zvodnika prijavila policiji. To sem naredila z drugimi ženskami, od katerih so bile tri Portugalke. Prijavile smo ga zaradi nasilja nad žensko, ki je bila za nekaj dni hospitalizirana. Še danes nič ne vemo, zvodnik pa še naprej vodi bordel. Odvetnik, ki ga imam zdaj, je že zahteval veliko denarja, a stvari ne razloži dobro in mi ne pokaže dokumentov v postopku. Na Portugalskem občutim diskriminacijo, a sem je navajena.

Migracijske službe se lepo obnašajo. Ne vlasta, kaj počnem v prostituciji. Prvič, leta 2004, ko sem prvič skušala legalizirati svojo situacijo, sem potrebovala dokument, za katerega sem morala plačati 250 evrov in čakati. Kasneje, leta 2006, so sprejeli nov zakon in mi dokument poslali. V tem obdobju brez papirjev so me pridržali.

Ko sem imela papirje, nisem imela več težav. Brez dokumentov je težko najti službo. Da pa bi imel dokumente, moraš delati. Brez dela ne plačuješ davkov za socialno varnost. Če ne plačuješ davkov, nimaš pravice do uradno dodeljenega odvetnika. Ena kolegica se je skušala legalizirati, a je odnehala, ker je bilo zelo težko. Le v Lizboni s pomočjo IPSS je lahko dobila dokumente za legalizacijo in je našla službo.

V tem trenutku se dogaja veliko stvari, moja situacija ni lahka, ker nisem mogla dobiti dokumentov za legalizacijo in še vedno delam v prostituciji.

"Aqui, arranjar documentos é terrível!"

História de Letícia

Vim do Brasil para Portugal há alguns anos com a promessa de um trabalho, mas quando cheguei aqui, pronto, fui logo para a prostituição. Deixei um filho com um ano e meio e senti-me na obrigação de fazer aquilo. A primeira noite para mim foi horrível, foi o pior dia da minha vida. Na primeira casa de alterne, fiquei uns meses a trabalhar e o dinheiro que sobrava mandava para o meu filho no Brasil. Durante os primeiros anos, foi muito difícil, fui trabalhar em outras casas de alterne e houve situações em que fui parada por agentes de segurança, mas eles não tratavam as portuguesas como tratavam a gente. Quando era uma mulher portuguesa, eles falavam "pode ir embora". Elas estavam lá a fazer a mesma coisa que a gente.

A cidade onde moro agora é maior, tem mais habitantes, mais imigrantes. Há mais abertura; até hoje nunca fui parada pela polícia. Na cidade onde vivia antes, era muitas vezes parada. Uma vez estava com o meu filho que tinha trazido do Brasil, há pouco tempo. Primeiro fizeram a gente ficar dentro do carro da polícia. O meu filho chorava e eles começaram a me interrogar. Eles me levaram para a esquadra com o meu filho e falaram assim para mim: "olha só, não vou mandar você embora agora porque está aqui com o seu filho", e eu falei: "olha, mas o pai dele está cá, eu falei com ele e estou dando entrada no processo de poder paternal. Estou dando também entrada no processo de legalização". E eles me mandaram ir para o serviço de imigração, no outro dia. No serviço de imigração falaram: "minha senhora, é a última oportunidade que a gente dá, se não aparecer aqui com os documentos, vai embora para o Brasil." O serviço de imigração aqui em Portugal é muito complicado. Só fiquei legal depois de três anos de fazer pedido, porque a gente tem que ter três anos aqui, com residência, para ter os mesmos direitos que os portugueses têm: o rendimento mínimo e o abono de família. Para arranjar documentos aqui é terrível! Como se diz, é de sorte. Foi muito difícil, porque, antes, eu ia procurar trabalho e não podia trabalhar porque não tinha documentos.

Durante os primeiros anos que estava ilegal nunca fui no médico, precisei, mas nunca fui. Não era só por medo de ser denunciada, era também porque a taxa é mais cara, como se fosse no hospital particular. E depois para a gente ir no médico tem que ter número de contribuinte. Só fui no médico mesmo quando fiquei legal.

"Here, to get papers is terrible!"

Letícia's Story

I came from Brazil some years ago with the promise of a job but when I arrived I had to work in prostitution. I left my young son, with 1,5 years, in Brazil, and I felt the obligation to do that. The first night was horrible; it was the worst day of my life. At that brothel I stayed a few months working and the money I could save, I sent to my son in Brazil. During the first years it was very hard. I went to work in other brothels and I was stopped by the police. But the police didn't treat the Portuguese women the way they treated us, Brazilian women. When there was a Portuguese woman, they used to let her go. The Portuguese women in the brothel were doing the exact same thing that we were doing there.

The city where I live now is bigger, has more inhabitants, more immigrants. I think here there is more openness. To this day I have never been stopped by the police. There, where I lived before I was stopped many times. One time I was with my son who I had brought from Brazil shortly before. First they made us stay inside the police car. My son was crying and they started to interrogate me. They took me to the police station with my son and they said this to me: "look we are not sending you away to Brazil because you are with your son", and I said: "look but the father is here; I spoke to him and I'm entering in the process for parental rights and I'm also beginning the process of legalization". And they ordered me to go to the immigration services in the next day. In the immigration services they said: "Ms, this is the last opportunity that we give you, if you don't show up here with the documents you go to Brazil." The immigration services in Portugal are very complicated. I became legal after 3 years here with residence permit and to have the same rights that the Portuguese have, like minimum income and child benefits. Here to get the documents is terrible! Like they used to say here: "you need to be lucky!" It was very complicated because before, when I went to find a job I couldn't work because I didn't have the papers.

During the first years when I was illegal I never went to the doctor, I needed it, but never went. It wasn't just because I could be denounced, it was also because the fees are as high as in a private hospital. And then, to go to the doctor you need the VAT number. I just really went to the doctor when I was legal.

O meu filho está na escola e acho que devia haver mais apoio para as crianças porque se ele quer fazer uma viagem de estudo tem que pagar. Se ele quer fazer alguma coisa, eu tenho de pagar. Só recebo 32 euros de abono e o restante tenho que pagar tudo. As polícias deviam ser menos arrogantes e ver também o lado da mulher. Eles só pensam "vão embora para o Brasil, ou falam ou vão embora para a sua terra". Devia haver mais apoios e mais continuados para as pessoas imigrantes.

My son is at school and I think there should be more support for the children because if he wants to go on a fieldtrip I have to pay, if he wants to do something I have to pay. We just get 32 euros of child benefits but the rest I have to pay. Also, the security forces should be less arrogant and see the side of the woman too. They just think: speak or go back to Brazil, go away to your country. They should give more support in a more continuous way to immigrant people.

"Dobiti papirje tukaj je strašno!"

Leticijina zgodba

Pred nekaj leti sem prišla iz Brazilije z obljubo službe, a ko sem prispela, sem morala delati v prostituciji. Ker sem pustila majhnega, leto in pol starega sina v Braziliji, sem se čutila dolžno, da to naredim. Prva noč je bila grozna; to je bil najhujši dan mojega življenja. V tistem bordelu sem ostala tri mesece in sem delala, denar, ki mi je ostal, sem pošiljala sinu v Brazilijo. Tekom prvih let je bilo zelo težko. Delala sem tudi v drugih bordelih in me je zaustavila policija. Vendar policisti ne obravnavajo portugalskih žensk na način kot obravnavajo Brazilke. Ko ustavijo Portugalko jo običajno pustijo. One delajo popolnoma enako stvar kot me v bordelu.

Mesto kjer živim zdaj je večje, ima več prebivalcev, več imigrantov. Mislim, da je tu bolj odprto. Do danes me policija še nikoli ni ustavila. Tam, v mestu kjer sem prej živela, pa me je velikokrat. Enkrat sem bila s sinom, ki sem ga pripeljala iz Brazilije. Najprej sva morala ostati v avtu. Sin je jokal, oni pa so me začeli zasliševati. Odpeljali so naju na policijsko postajo in so mi rekli: »Poglejte, ne bomo vas poslali nazaj v Brazilijo, ker ste s sinom«, jaz sem rekla: »Ampak glejte, oče je tu, sem govorila z njim in vstopam v proces za starševske pravice in proces legalizacije«, oni pa so mi ukazali naj grem v Službo za priseljevanje in meje (SEF) naslednji dan. Tam so mi rekli: »Gospodična, dajemo vam zadnjo možnost; če se ne pojavite tu s papirji, greste v Brazilijo.« Pri SEF-u tu na Portugalskem je zelo zapleteno dobiti en sam dokument. Legalna sem postala šele po treh letih, pomeni da zdaj imam enake pravice kot Portugalci, kot so minimalna plača, otroški dodatki ... Dobiti papirje tukaj je strašno. Kot rečejo tukaj, moraš imeti srečo. Je zelo komplicirano ker nisem mogla niti delati dokler nisem imela urejenih papirjev.

Ko sem bila ilegalka, nikoli nisem šla k zdravniku, potrebovala sem ga, a nikoli nisem šla. Ne le zato, ker bi me lahko ovadili, pač pa tudi zato, ker so tarife tako visoke kot v zasebnih bolnicah. In potem za obisk zdravnika potrebuješ davčno številko. K zdravniku sem šla samo, ko sem bila legalna.

Moj sin hodi v šolo in menim da bi moralo biti več podpore za otroke, ker če on hoče iti na šolski izlet, mora plačati, če hoče kaj početi, mora plačati, plačati mora za vse. Dobimo le 32 evrov otroškega dodatka, ostalo moramo plačati sami. Prav tako organi pregona bi morali biti manj arogantni in razumeti žensko pozicijo. Oni samo mislijo: pričaj ali pojdi nazaj v Brazilijo, vrni se v svojo državo. Morali bi ponuditi več trajnejše podpore migrantom in migrantkam.

Intervention against sexual exploitation

Stories and experiences of trafficked women

Slovenia

"Ni prav, da te prisilijo, da prijaviš lastno družino"

Natašina zgodba

Zbežala sem od očeta. Bila sem noseča, a tega ni vedel in me je prodal. Potem ko sem bila že prodana, sem imela še en teden, preden naj bi prišli pome in bi šla živet v Italijo. Potem pa sem se vrnila v Slovenijo, ker nas je oče prisilil, da smo se vrnili. Bil je nasilen do vseh nas. Kar se tiče intervencij, so na začetku vsi hoteli, da očeta prijavim policiji, da podam izjavo. A jaz tega sploh nisem hotela. Hotela sem le stran od družine. Da ne bi imela več nobenega opravka z njimi, da bi me pustili pri miru, da bi lahko živela normalno življenje. A oni, uradniki ali različni uradi, niso hoteli tega. Rekli so mi, da če ne prijavim, da me je prodal, da je nasilen do nas, nam ne morejo pomagati. A tudi zdaj bi naredila isto in ga ne bi prijavila. Ker vem, da sem s tem zaščitila svojega otroka. Če bi poslušala Društvo Ključ in prijavila očeta, ga niti deset policistov in deset ljudi iz Ključa ne bi moglo ustaviti.

Ni prav, da te silijo, da prijaviš lastno družino. Resnično ne pomaga, ker ne bo prineslo nič dobrega. Tudi če ženska to stori, ji bo potem žal in bo potem težje živela. Vsi, s katerimi sem se pogovarjala, so hoteli, da ga prijavam, a hvala bogu tega nisem storila. To, kar se je meni zgodilo, je bila trgovina z ljudmi. To zdaj lahko rečem. A tega nisem hotela reči policistu, ne takrat ne danes. Ne zaupam jim. To je to. Policisti so zame največji dreki, ker vem, kaj so nam naredili. Oče je skušal ubiti mamo, imela je vse znake, da jo je pretepel, a so ovadili mamo – da je ona udarila njega.

Dekleta in ženske, ki bežijo od svojih družin, se nočejo pogovarjati s tujci. Raje bi se pogovarjala s svojimi ljudmi, ne pa da imam tam prevajalca. Vem, da nočejo tega, ker tudi jaz nisem hotela tega.

Če bi bila tam Rominja namesto tistega tipa, ki je dejansko bil tam v azilnem domu, bi šla. Je povsem drugače, če imaš nekoga svojega, ki ve, kako je, ki razume in ve natančno, kakšno je življenje in kako bo videti potem. Ne pa tiste prazne obljube, da bo bolje, da boš imela varnejše življenje, nihče tega ne verjame. Tudi jaz tega nisem verjela. Prvič: če policist dobi obvestilo, da je prišlo do pretepa v romski družini, mora takoj ukrepati. Takoj, brez zaprtih oči. Prav tako je pomembno: morajo biti pozorni na to, da če dekleta, ki hodi v šolo, nenadoma ni več v šolo, to pomeni, da je že bila prodana. Takoj naj ukrepajo, ne pa da v šolo pošiljajo vabilo na pogovor o tem, zakaj je ne obiskuje.

So I ran away from my father. I was pregnant, but he did not know that and I was sold. After I had already been sold, I had a week before they would come for me and I would be going to Italy to live. And then I came back to Slovenia because my father has forced us to come back. He was violent towards us all. As for interventions, at the beginning they all wanted me to report my father to the police, to give a statement, to report him. But I did not want this at all. I just wanted to go away from my family. So that I would no longer have anything to do with them, for them to leave me alone and that I can live a normal life. But they, the officials or different agencies did not want this. They told me that if I did not report that he sold me, that he was violent towards us, that they cannot help us. But I would do the same even now and would not report him Because I know that with this I have protected my child. If I had listened to Association Ključ and reported my father, not even 10 policemen and 10 people from Ključ could stop him.

It is not right that they force you to report your own family. It really does not help, because it will not do any good. Even if a woman does it, she will feel sorry afterwards and find it harder to live afterwards. Everyone I talked to, they all wanted me to report him, just thank God I did not do this. What happened to me was human trafficking, I can say that now. But I would not say it to a police officer, not then and not today. I do not trust them. That's it. Policemen are for me the biggest piece of shit, because I know what they did to us. My father tried to kill my mother, she had all the signs that he beat her up, but they reported my mother – that she hit him.

Those girls and women who are fleeing from their families, they do not want to talk to strangers. I'd rather talk to my people, not to have an interpreter there. I know that they do not want this, because I also did not want this.

If there was a Roma woman there instead of that guy that actually was there in the Asylum home, I would go. It's completely different if you have one of your own people, who knows what's it like, who understands and knows exactly what life is like, and how it will look afterwards. But not those empty promises that it will be better, that you'll have a safer life, nobody believes that. I also did not believe this. First of all: if a policeman gets notification of the fact that there is a fight in the Roma family, he needs to take immediate action. Immediately, without closed eyes.

Ker če dekleta, starega 14 ali 15 let, nenadoma ni več v šolo, morate vedeti, da je to zato, ker je bila prodana na tuje. Ti dve zadevi sta tu najpomembnejši.

Ko smo se vrnili v Slovenijo, mi je bilo v azilnem domu najhujše, ker je enako kot v zaporu. Po enem tednu je prišel naš odvetnik. Bil je edini, ki nas je razumel in je res hotel pomagati. Tudi moje izkušnje z zdravniškim osebjem so slabe; ko so videli kartico iz azilnega doma. Nihče nam ni pomagal, niti zdravniki niti kdo drug.

Po nekaj mesecih v azilnem domu je prišel nek tip iz Društva Ključ in mene in mojo sestro začel spraševati, kaj se nama je zgodilo, zakaj sva ušli. Razložil nama je, kaj Ključ je, kaj počnejo in kako pomagajo ljudem, a je sestra na začetku takoj rekla, da ne greva. Nisem hotela h Ključu, ker je rekel, da moram prijaviti očeta policiji, razložiti vse, kar se je zgodilo in kako se je zgodilo, česar pa sploh nisem hotela narediti, ker vem, kakšen je moj oče in kakšna je ostala družina. Potem je prišla druga oseba, ki mi je rekla, da svojo izjavo o tem, kaj se je zgodilo, lahko podam le Ključu, ne policiji. To me je prepričalo. V vseh letih me je poslušala le ena ženska pri Ključu. Vedno znova me je spraševala, kaj hočem in kako hočem postopati naprej. Prav tako je vedno znova prihajala kot prijateljica in ne le kot nevladnica. Nekajkrat je prišla le na pogovor, sedeli sva, pili kavo in se pogovarjali.
Ko res nisem imela več moči, mi je rekla: »Pomisli na svojega sina. Potrebuje svojo mamo, potrebuje mamo, ki je dovolj močna, ki se je zmožna prebiti skozi mesec.« S temi besedami mi je dala moč, da sem zdržala.

Kar mi je najmanj pomagalo, je bilo, da me je vsaka oseba, ki sem jo srečala, vprašala, zakaj že prej nisem pobegnila od očeta, zakaj nisem šla prej. Boleča so bila tudi vprašanja o mojih osebnih dokumentih. Hudo mi je bilo, kadarkoli so me to vprašali, ker sem bila izbrisana.[1] Če bi me oče uspel ubiti, sploh nihče ne bi vedel. Ker v Sloveniji, tudi če bi živela tu, nisem obstajala, ker nimam nobenih dokumentov.

---

[1] Slovenija je izbrisala 25.673 oseb, večinoma iz republik nekdanje Jugoslavije, iz registra stalnih prebivalcev. S tem so izgubili pravice, vezane na ta status, nekateri pa so ostali tudi brez državljanstva.

Also important: they need to pay attention if a girl who goes to school is suddenly no longer in school, they need to know immediately what it means – she has already been sold. Take immediate action, rather than sending one invitation to an interview in school, why she's not attending school. Because if a girl who's 14, 15 years old, is suddenly not in school anymore, you should know that it is because she's been sold abroad. These are two things that are most important here.

When we came back to Slovenia, Asylum Centre was the worst time I had, because there it is the same as in prison. A week afterwards, our lawyer came. He was the only person who understood us, and he really wanted to help us. Also my experiences with the medical staff are poor; when they saw that card from the Asylum Centre. We received no help from anyone, not from the doctors, nor from any other.

After a few months in the Asylum Centre, a guy came from the Association Ključ and started asking me and my sister what we have experienced, why we fled. He explained to us what Ključ is, what they do and how they help people, but my sister at the beginning immediately said that we're not going. I did not want to go to Ključ, because he told me that I have to report my father to the police, to explain all what happened and how it happened, but that I did not want to do at all, because I know what my father is like and what the rest of my family is like. Later on someone else came and she told me that I could give my statement only to Ključ about what happened, not to the police. This convinced me. In all these years I was just listened to by one woman from Ključ. She has repeatedly asked me what I want and how I want to go forward. She also repeatedly came as a friend, not only as the NGO person. Several times she only came for a chat, we sat, drank coffee while talking. When I really did not have any more strength, she told me this: "Think of your son. He needs his mother, he needs a mother who is strong enough, who is capable of making ends meet." With these words, she kept me going.

What was the least helpful was that every person I encountered had asked me why I did not escape from my father earlier, why I did not go sooner. Painful were also questions about the personal documents. I felt bad whenever I was asked because I was erased.[1] If my father managed to kill me, no one would even know. Because in Slovenia, even if I lived here, I did not exist, because I do not have any documents.

---

1 Slovenia erased 25.673 persons, mostly from former Yugoslav republics, from the register of permanent residents. With this they lost their residence rights, and some of them remained without citizenship as well.

Afterword

The CEINAV Story
an Afterword to the Anthology

In 2011, five researchers in four countries – Carol, Vlasta, Liz, Maria José and Thomas – who had worked for many years, singly or together, on the challenges of stopping violence, began seeking ways to collaborate more closely. We wanted to explore in depth why intervention approaches differ despite apparent agreement across Europe on what needs to be done, and also why intervention sometimes fails to reach its goals, especially with the women and children who might need support the most. All of us had worked on a European level, building networks and using funding opportunities, and we shared a commitment to research that could contribute to the practical and political work of intervening against the many forms of violence and injustice that play out in everyday life.

But we were not satisfied with what we had been able to do. Too many of our research opportunities were tied to political expectations of a "quick fix". The EU programs that have supported cooperation on issues of gender equality and of violence have enabled professionals to share their experiences and strategies, but rarely made in depth research possible. And due to limited time and resources, there was almost never space to hear the voices of the women and the children who have suffered violence. Surely "good practice" should be accountable to those who are presumed to benefit from it!

The program "Cultural Encounters" promised, firstly, an opportunity to explore how the differences in national history, culture, language and traditions shape the frameworks of intervention and the work of professionals. But importantly, with three years for a project we could focus on how the usual practices of intervention affect women and young people from ethnic or cultural minorities or immigrant communities. Were the standards for "good practice" that were circulating internationally – in recommendations, policy seminars and declarations, with a Council of Europe Convention being prepared and demands for an EU directive being raised – actually able to respond to the needs of the women and of children with ever more diverse backgrounds, but no less burdened by violence in their families, in their close relationships, and in the sex industry?

That the programme did not set any external policy goals, except that of encouraging collaboration in research within the EU, was a further benefit, echoed by the independent reviewers focusing entirely on the quality of the proposals: we even had the opportunity to respond to the questions and concerns expressed by the reviewers – although we had to do this between Christmas and New Year's while the Coordinator was in a town in the US that was struck by a severe ice storm, with the public library as her only access to e-mail! But everyone pitched in, and we were successful.

Our collaboration, both in developing our ideas for the project and in thinking about how to respond to critical questions, gave us a strong sense that we could work together closely. Instead of the partners each delivering their own separate "work packages", we committed ourselves to a unified research process to be done in parallel in the four countries. That meant, as we soon discovered, that we were working through our own cultural differences as we went along.

We were most fortunate in the younger researchers who joined us as the project proceeded; without their engagement and enthusiasm this anthology would not have been possible. As a first step all five teams wrote background papers on the laws, institutions of intervention, migration history and intervention systems in our four countries. This enabled us to understand how intervention is organised across our four countries and for three forms of violence —child physical abuse and neglect, domestic violence and trafficking for sexual exploitation. We had also hoped to agree on which minorities we might look at specifically, but this was simply not possible. The migration and minority histories of our four countries are too different, and not even the concept of a "minority" has the same meaning from one country to the other. The only thing we could do was to leave the choice of what minorities they encounter in practice to the professionals, who put us in touch with survivors of violence who were interested in telling us their stories.

CEINAV began in the field with multi-professional workshops, two for each form of violence in each country (a total of 24). We invited the participants to discuss a fictional case story in three stages, and at each stage to discuss who might notice that violence was present and what the various agencies and professions could, should, or would do if they became aware of the situation. They were particularly asked to reflect on difficult decisions and ethical dilemmas that they might experience. Later, they were asked to think about what might be different if the woman or the child in the story came from an ethnic or cultural minority or a migration background. As we had agreed on a common list of the relevant agencies and professions, and devised a storyline that was realistic for all four countries, being almost entirely identical except for minor adaptions, we saw these discussions as an opportunity to uncover the cultural premises underlying the intervention practices of the countries. Analysing and comparing the discussions in our workshops indeed gave us a good deal of insight into both commonalities and differences in what professionals think about violence in general and about the minority groups they encounter, and how they understand the role of intervention with regard to the various forms of violence. As we discussed this in our meetings, a foundation of our own perspectives took shape.

We did not embark on this research alone; all five of us had cooperated for years with practitioners and organisations whose work involved advocacy and support for women and for children and their families facing different forms of coercion and violence. Networks of practitioners were our associated partners in this project. They helped us devise realistic fictional cases and re-work them until they could make sense in all four countries, and they steered us towards concerned professionals with intervention experience in all the different agencies and positions we sought to include.

Our next step, and the basis for this anthology, was listening to women and young people who had travelled through a history of violence and intervention, and who belonged to a minority. We did not ask them to recount the violence they had endured, but invited them to tell us how they experienced intervention, beginning from when they first thought of seeking help. Acutely aware of the lasting impact of violence and the possibility of further harm, we asked our associate partners and their networks to help us find interviewees who were now in a stable situation but were linked to support. Ideally we would have done seven interviews for each form of violence, 21 in all, in each country, but this was not always possible. Finding women and young people to be interviewed proved challenging, and interviews with trafficked women were almost impossible to arrange in Slovenia and Portugal.

Again, the understanding of "minority" depended on the country, the support services and their practical experience. Many of the interviewees had a migration background, often fairly recent, but some had come to the country quite a long time ago, or one or both parents had. Some saw themselves as belonging to a minority community, others saw this connection primarily in terms of how others reacted to them. Depending on the country, a larger or smaller proportion of the women and young people came from within the EU or from more distant regions of the world. Some had only very recently escaped a violent situation and found their way to an agency that could help them; others had had their first encounters with intervention (police, a school social worker, a specialized counselling center or some statutory agency) many years ago, in a few cases even decades back. The journey towards finding genuinely effective protection and support could be very long and winding, or rather brief.

In taking these two approaches, the workshops and the interviews, we wanted to understand each perspective on intervention in their own terms, not to compare them. The professionals reflected on what they do today and how it could be improved; in the interviews, we heard about what had happened in the past, and what their encounters with intervention professionals and agencies meant to the women and young people. What kinds of responses made them feel stronger and gave them hope, what discouraged them or made them feel more helpless? How did professionals give them the feeling that they were being listened to, or on the contrary, that they were not being heard? Were there moments when they were made to feel less deserving of attention or help, and what was it like to be recognised as a person with rights? How important was it to be helped by third parties such as people they accidentally met? Such experiences can be pivotal in the search for ways to end or to escape violence. Some of the women and young people still felt very strongly about things that happened many years ago, good things or bad things, and these crucial moments are still present for them, carrying them forward or holding them back.

To enable the voices and experiences of women and young people to be more widely heard through storytelling, each country team read and re-read each interview, pulling out the descriptions, sentences and words that seemed most intensely meaningful and expressive of what was important to the woman or young person in their encounters with intervention.

While interviews are long and move back and forth in time as recollections awaken and the interviewee hesitates and tries to find the right words, the researchers used a creative process of narrative to craft a short story for this anthology. We then returned the story to the person concerned to ask if it reflected what she or he would like to say to those responsible for intervention. It was equally important to hear whether they felt that the story, as it is told here, protects the confidentiality and safety promised at each and every interview.

Some of the women and young people thought there would be no more risk for them today even if we used their real names, and a few would have liked the opportunity to make their experiences public. Telling the story with a wider audience can be an important part of moving on, but it needs a context of support that we could not provide: we have thus followed the honored tradition in literature and the arts of giving each storyteller a pseudonym. It would be a challenge for support services, were they well and securely funded and recognised, to find more ways for victims to tell their stories. From her own experience, Susan Brison writes that after trauma "one must (physically, publicly) say or write (or paint or film) the narrative and others must see or hear it in order for one's survival as an autonomous self to be complete" (Aftermath 2002, p. 62). We invited all of the interviewees to participate in art workshops led by an artist-researcher in each country, and those who wished or could manage to come were provided with art materials and encouraged to express their experiences with intervention. In a later dialogue meeting with intervention professionals the interviewee-artists took part and their work was exhibited: Now they were the experts and the professionals the ones seeking enlightenment – an empowering experience, we were told.

If we had had more time and more resources, it would have been wonderful to organise writing workshops as well as art workshops where women and young people could develop their own stories for publication, enabling them to work around the language barriers that many still had, and reflect carefully, as Brison says (p. 97), about "whom, how, when, where, and – we must be especially aware of this – why" each person decides to tell her or his story.

In this anthology, all stories are offered in English translation as well as the original language. In Portugal and Slovenia, the intervention system did not make it possible to do as many interviews as hoped for in some areas, so they translated some stories from the other countries that they believe could "speak" to professionals and other readers in their own country. We learnt a great deal from the stories, and they have helped us work out the "Transnational Foundations for Ethical Intervention" that we are publishing alongside this anthology, and which we hope will spark many reflections and discussions among professionals and those who set the conditions and frameworks for intervention.

Carol Hagemann-White & Bianca Grafe

Die CEINAV-Geschichte

Ein Nachwort zur Geschichtensammlung

2011 begannen fünf ForscherInnen aus vier Ländern – Carol, Vlasta, Liz, Maria José und Thomas – die seit vielen Jahren, einzeln oder zusammen, über Strategien gegen Gewalt forschen, nach Wegen zu suchen, intensiver zusammen zu arbeiten. Wir wollten tiefgründig untersuchen, warum Ansätze der Intervention sich unterscheiden, obwohl doch europaweit scheinbar Einigkeit darüber herrscht, was getan werden muss. Wir wollten auch verstehen, warum Intervention manchmal ihr Ziel nicht erreicht, besonders bei den Frauen und Kindern, die Unterstützung am nötigsten haben. Wir alle hatten auf europäischer Ebene gearbeitet, Netzwerke aufgebaut und verschiedene Förderungsmöglichkeiten genutzt. Gemeinsam war uns ein Engagement für Forschung, die einen Beitrag zu praktischer und politischer Arbeit leisten kann, um die Intervention gegen die vielen Formen von Gewalt und Ungerechtigkeit im Alltag zu unterstützen.

Aber wir waren nicht zufrieden mit dem was wir erreicht hatten. Zu viele Forschungsaufträge waren an die politische Erwartung einer „schnellen Lösung" geknüpft. EU Programme haben zwar Kooperation für Geschlechtergerechtigkeit und gegen Gewalt unterstützt, und Fachkräfte konnten ihre Erfahrungen und Strategien austauschen, aber tiefergehende Forschung war selten möglich. Zeit und Ressourcen reichten fast nie aus, um die Stimmen der Frauen und Kinder zu hören, die Gewalt erlitten hatten. Dabei sollte "gute Praxis" diejenigen einbeziehen, denen sie dienen soll!

Das Programm "Cultural Encounters" bot uns die Chance zu erkunden, wie sich die Unterschiede in der Geschichte der Länder, der Kultur, Sprache und Traditionen auf den Rahmen von Intervention und die Arbeit von Fachkräften auswirken. Wichtiger war noch: Bei einer Laufzeit von drei Jahren konnten wir der Frage nachgehen, wie die Vorgehensweisen der Intervention bei Frauen und Jugendlichen aus ethnischen oder kulturellen Minderheiten oder einem Migrationshintergrund ankommen. International kursieren Standards für "gute Praxis" in Empfehlungen, Tagungen und Beschlüssen, eine Europakonvention wurde erarbeitet und Forderungen nach einer EU-Direktive wurden laut. Aber sind diese tatsächlich in der Lage, auf die Bedürfnisse von Frauen und Kindern einzugehen, deren Hintergründe unterschiedlicher denn je, aber nicht weniger belastet von Gewalt in ihren Familien, in Beziehungen und im Sexgeschäft sind?

Dass das Programm keine externe politische Ziele außer Förderung der Forschungskooperation in der EU setzte, war ein weiterer Vorteil, der sich bei den unabhängigen Gutachtern wiederfand, die ausschließlich auf die Qualität der Anträge achteten:

Wir hatten sogar die Gelegenheit, auf ihre Fragen und Bedenken zu antworten – obwohl wir das zwischen Weihnachten und Neujahr tun mussten, während die Koordinatorin in einer Kleinstadt in den USA weilte, wo ein schwerer Eissturm tobte und der einzige Zugang zu Email die öffentliche Bibliothek war! Aber jeder sprang ein und wir waren erfolgreich. Unsere Zusammenarbeit, sowohl im Entwickeln unserer Ideen für das Projekt als auch bei der Beantwortung kritischer Fragen gab uns das sichere Gefühl, dass wir sehr eng zusammen arbeiten konnten. Anstatt dass jeder Partner sein eigenes "Arbeitspaket" abliefert, nahmen wir uns einen einheitlichen Forschungsprozess parallel in allen vier Ländern vor. Das hieß auch, wie wir bald merkten, dass wir uns im Laufe des Projekts auch durch unsere eigenen kulturellen Unterschiede arbeiteten.

Wir hatten großes Glück mit den jüngeren Forscherinnen, die zu uns stießen, als das Projekt fortschritt; ohne ihren Einsatz und ihren Enthusiasmus wäre diese Sammlung nicht möglich gewesen. In einem ersten Schritt schrieben alle fünf Teams Hintergrundpapiere zu den Gesetzen, Institutionen, Migrationsgeschichte und Interventionssystemen in unseren vier Ländern. Das machte es uns möglich zu verstehen, wie Intervention jeweils für die drei Formen von Gewalt – Körperliche Misshandlung und Vernachlässigung von Kindern, Gewalt in der Paarbeziehung und Menschenhandel zum Zweck der sexuellen Ausbeutung – organisiert ist. Wir hatten auch gehofft, uns auf Minderheiten einigen zu können die wir einbeziehen wollten, aber das war schlichtweg nicht möglich. Die Geschichten von Migration und Minderheiten in unseren vier Ländern sind zu unterschiedlich und nicht mal der Begriff "Minderheit" bedeutet dasselbe. Wir konnten nur den Fachkräften die Entscheidung überlassen, welchen Minderheiten sie in ihrer Arbeit begegnen. Entsprechend vermittelten sie uns Betroffene, die bereit waren uns ihre Geschichten zu erzählen.

Die empirische Arbeit begann mit multiprofessionellen Workshops, zwei pro Gewaltform pro Land (insgesamt also 24). Wir luden Fachkräfte ein, drei Stufen einer Fallgeschichte zu besprechen und jeweils zu überlegen, wer etwas von der Situation mitbekommen könnte, und was die verschiedenen Einrichtungen und Berufe tun könnten, sollten und würden, wenn sie darauf aufmerksam würden. Insbesondere sollten sie über schwierige Entscheidungen und ethische Dilemmata nachdenken, denen sie begegnen könnten. Danach fragten wir sie, was vielleicht anders wäre, wenn die Frau oder das Kind in der Geschichte aus einer ethnischen oder kulturellen Minderheit käme oder einen Migrationshintergrund hätte. Da wir uns länderübergreifend über die wichtigen Institutionen und Berufen einigten und einen Handlungsstrang erfunden hatten, der für alle vier Länder realistisch und außer kleinen Anpassungen beinahe identisch war, sahen wir dies als Möglichkeit, kulturelle Vorannahmen in der Intervention der vier Länder aufzudecken. Die Analyse und der Vergleich unserer Workshops gab uns in der Tat ziemlich viel Einsicht in die Gemeinsamkeiten und die Unterschiede in dem, was Fachkräfte über Gewalt allgemein und über Minderheiten denken und wie sie die Rolle von Intervention bei der jeweiligen Form von Gewalt sehen. Als wir dies im Gesamtteam diskutierten, nahmen Grundzüge unserer eigenen Sicht Gestalt an.

Wir haben uns auf diese Forschung nicht allein eingelassen; wir hatten alle schon seit Jahren mit Fachkräften und Organisationen zusammengearbeitet, die gewaltbetroffene Frauen und Kinder und deren Familien praktisch unterstützen.

Netzwerke von Fachkräften waren unsere assoziierten Partner in diesem Projekt. Sie halfen uns eine realistische Fallgeschichte zu entwickeln und sie so lange zu überarbeiten, bis sie in allen vier Ländern sinnvoll klang. Sie vermittelten uns dann engagierte Fachkräfte mit Erfahrung in Intervention in den verschiedenen Positionen, die wir einbeziehen wollten.

Der nächste Schritt und die Grundlage für diese Geschichtensammlung war, mit Frauen und Jugendlichen zu sprechen, die Gewalt und Intervention erlebt hatten und die einer Minderheit angehörten. Wir fragten nicht so sehr nach der erlittenen Gewalt, sondern luden sie ein, ausgehend von ihrer ersten Hilfesuche zu erzählen, wie sie die Intervention erlebten. Da uns die langfristigen Auswirkungen von Gewalt sowie die Möglichkeit einer erneuten Gefährdung sehr deutlich bewusst waren, baten wir unsere assoziierten Partner und ihre Netzwerke uns zu helfen InterviewpartnerInnen zu finden, die nun stabilisiert waren, aber noch Kontakt zu ihren Beratungsstellen hatten. Idealerweise hätten wir sieben Interviews pro Gewaltform geführt, zusammen 21 in jedem Land, aber das war nicht immer möglich. Frauen und Jugendliche zu finden, die den Suchkriterien entsprachen, war eine Herausforderung und Interviews mit Frauen die zur sexuellen Ausbeutung gehandelt worden waren in Slowenien und Portugal nahezu unmöglich.

Das Verständnis von "Minderheit" hing nicht nur vom Land ab, sondern auch von den Unterstützungseinrichtungen und ihren Praxiserfahrungen. Viele InterviewpartnerInnen hatten einen Migrationshintergrund, oft auch erst kürzlich, aber einige waren vor langer Zeit ins Land gekommen, oder ein Elternteil war das. Manche sahen sich selbst als einer Minderheitengruppe zugehörig, andere sahen diese Verbindung vornehmlich darin, wie andere auf sie reagierten. Je nach Land kam ein kleinerer oder größerer Anteil der Frauen und Jugendlichen von innerhalb der EU oder aus weiter entfernten Regionen der Welt. Manche hatten gerade erst vor kurzem den Weg aus einer Gewaltsituation und zu einer Institution gefunden, die ihnen helfen konnte. Andere hatten ihre erste Begegnung mit Intervention (Polizei, Schulsozialarbeit, Fachberatungsstelle oder staatliche Behörde) schon vor vielen Jahren, in Einzelfällen lag dies sogar Jahrzehnte zurück. Die Suche nach wirklich effektivem Schutz und Unterstützung konnte lang und kurvenreich sein, oder auch recht kurz.

Durch die Kombination der Workshops und der Interviews wollten wir die beiden Perspektiven auf Intervention je für sich verstehen, ohne sie zu vergleichen. Die Fachkräfte reflektierten, was sie heute tun, und was verbessert werden könnte; in den Interviews hörten wir, was in der Vergangenheit passiert war und was die Begegnungen mit Interventionsfachkräften und Behörden für die Frauen und Jugendlichen bedeutete. Welche Reaktionen ließ sie sich stärker fühlen und machte ihnen Mut, was hat sie entmutigt oder das Gefühl von Hilflosigkeit verstärkt? Wie gaben Fachkräfte ihnen das Gefühl, dass Ihnen zugehört und geglaubt wurde, oder im Gegenteil, dass sie nicht gehört wurden? Gab es Momente, in denen Ihnen vermittelt wurde, dass sie weniger Aufmerksamkeit oder Hilfe verdienten als andere? Und wie fühlte es sich wiederum an, als Person mit Rechten wahr- und angenommen zu werden? Welche Rolle spielte Hilfe durch Dritte, wie Menschen, die sie zufällig trafen? Solche Erfahrungen können in der Suche nach Wegen aus der Gewalt von zentraler Bedeutung sein.

Manche der Frauen und Jugendlichen hatten immer noch starke Gefühle und Meinungen zu Dingen, die viele Jahre zuvor passiert waren - gute, oder schlechte – und diese entscheidenden Momente sind ihnen immer noch gegenwärtig, ebnen den weiteren Weg nach vorne, oder halten sie zurück.

Damit die Stimmen und Erfahrungen der Frauen und Jugendlichen durch das Erzählen ihrer Geschichten breiter gehört werden, las jedes Länderteam seine Interviews wieder und wieder und zog die besonders intensiven Beschreibungen, Sätze und Wörter heraus, die am besten zum Ausdruck brachten, was für die Frauen und Jugendlichen in ihrer Begegnung mit Intervention wichtig war. Während Interviews lang sind, und in der Zeit hin und her springen, während Erinnerungen wiederkehren und die erzählende Person nach den richtigen Worten sucht, haben die Forscherinnen in einem kreativen Prozess eine verdichtete Kurzgeschichte erstellt. Diese Geschichte wurde an die betroffene Person zurückgegeben mit der Frage, ob sie passend wiedergab, was sie oder er den Zuständigen für Intervention gern sagen würde. Genauso wichtig war von ihnen zu hören, ob aus ihrer Sicht die Geschichte, so wie sie hier erzählt wird, die Vertraulichkeit und Sicherheit schützt, die bei jedem Interview zugesichert wurde.

Einige Frauen und Jugendlichen sahen heute für sich kein Risiko mehr, selbst wenn wir ihre echten Namen benutzten; und ein paar hätten die Gelegenheit gern ergriffen, ihre Erlebnisse öffentlich zu machen. Die Geschichte einem größeren Publikum zu erzählen kann ein wichtiger Teil für die Verarbeitung sein, aber dies braucht einen Rahmen von Unterstützung, den wir nicht bieten konnten. Wir haben daher, in der bewährten Tradition der Literatur und Kunst, jeder erzählenden Person ein Pseudonym gegeben. Es wäre eine Herausforderung für Unterstützungseinrichtungen, wenn sie gut und sicher finanziert und anerkannt wären, mehr Wege zu finden, wie Betroffene ihre Geschichten erzählen können. Aus eigener Erfahrung schreibt Susan Brison, dass es nach einem Trauma notwendig ist, physisch und öffentlich die Geschichte zu erzählen oder zu schreiben (oder malen oder filmen), und andere müssen sie hören oder sehen, damit das autonome Selbst vollends überleben kann (Aftermath 2002, p. 62, Übers. d.V.). Wir haben alle InterviewpartnerInnen eingeladen an Kunstworkshops teilzunehmen, die in jedem Land von einer forschungserfahrenen Künstlerin geleitet wurde. Diejenigen, die kommen wollten und konnten, wurden mit Material versorgt und ermutigt, ihre Erfahrungen mit Intervention künstlerisch auszudrücken. In einem späteren Dialogtreffen mit Fachkräften nahmen auch die Interview-Künstlerinnen teil und ihre Kunst wurde ausgestellt. Nun waren sie die Expertinnen und die Fachkräfte diejenigen, die nach Aufklärung suchten - eine ermächtigende Erfahrung, wie uns gesagt wurde.

Hätten wir mehr Zeit und Ressourcen gehabt, wäre es wundervoll gewesen, zusätzlich auch Schreibworkshops zu organisieren, wo Frauen und Jugendliche ihre eigenen Geschichten für die Veröffentlichung hätten entwickeln können, ihnen dabei zu helfen die Sprachbarrieren zu überwinden, die viele noch hatten und sorgfältig zu reflektieren, wie Brison sagt (S. 97) „wem, wie, wann, wo und – besonders wichtig – warum" jede Person entscheidet, ihre Geschichte zu erzählen.

In dieser Sammlung bieten wir neben der Originalsprache auch immer die englische Übersetzung an. In Portugal und Slowenien hat das Interventionssystem teilweise nicht so viele Interviews ermöglicht wie erhofft, daher übersetzten die Teams einige Geschichten aus anderen Ländern, von denen sie glauben, dass sie zu Fachkräften und anderen Lesern in ihrem eigenen Land „sprechen". Wir haben von den Geschichten viel gelernt, und sie haben uns geholfen die " Transnationale Grundlagen für eine ethische Praxis" zu erarbeiten, die wir neben dieser Geschichtensammlung veröffentlichen, und wir hoffen, viele Reflektionen und Diskussionen unter Fachkräften und mit denen, die die Bedingungen und Rahmen für Intervention setzen, entfachen zu können.

Carol Hagemann-White & Bianca Grafe

A história do CEINAV

um posfácio à antologia

Em 2011, cinco investigadoras/es em quatro países – Carol, Vlasta, Liz, Maria José e Thomas – que haviam trabalhado durante vários anos, individualmente ou em conjunto, nos desafios de acabar com a violência, iniciaram uma procura de colaboração mais próxima. Queríamos explorar em profundidade o porquê de as abordagens de intervenção diferirem, apesar da aparente concordância na Europa sobre o que precisa ser feito, e também o porquê das intervenções por vezes não atingirem os seus objetivos, especialmente com mulheres e crianças que são quem mais precisa de apoio. Todas/os nós havíamos trabalhado a um nível Europeu, criando redes e usando oportunidades de financiamento, e partilhávamos o compromisso com uma perspetiva de investigação que se constitua como contributo para o trabalho prático e político de intervir contra as várias formas de violência e injustiça que acontecem no dia-a-dia.

No entanto, não estávamos satisfeitos/as com o que tínhamos conseguido fazer até àquele momento. Demasiadas oportunidades de investigação estavam ligadas a expetativas políticas de uma "solução rápida". Os programas da UE que têm apoiado a cooperação em questões de violência e de igualdade de género têm permitido que os/as profissionais partilhem as suas experiências e estratégias, mas raramente têm tornado possível uma investigação em profundidade. E devido a recursos e tempo limitados, quase nunca houve espaço para ouvir as vozes das mulheres e crianças que sofreram violência. Certamente, as instituições devem prestar contas das "boas práticas" a quem deve benefiar com elas!

O programa "Encontros Culturais" prometia, em primeiro lugar, uma oportunidade de explorar como as diferenças na história, cultura, linguagem e tradições nacionais moldam os quadros teóricos da intervenção e o trabalho dos profissionais. Mais ainda, com três anos para um projeto, podíamos focar-nos no modo como as práticas comuns de intervenção afetam mulheres e jovens de minorias étnicas ou culturais ou de comunidades migrantes. Seriam os padrões de "boas práticas" que circulavam internacionalmente – em recomendações, seminários e declarações, como, por exemplo, na Convenção do Conselho da Europa que estava a ser preparada, e na Diretiva da UE que viria a ser aprovada – realmente capazes de responder às necessidades das mulheres e das crianças com backgrounds cada vez mais diversos, mas não menos sobrecarregadas/os de violência nas suas famílias, nas suas relações próximas, e na indústria do sexo?

Um benefício adicional foi o facto de que o programa não definiu objetivos políticos externos, exceto o de encorajar a colaboração na investigação dentro da UE, benefício que as/os revisores/as independentes ecoaram pois focaram-se principalmente na qualidade das propostas: tivemos até a oportunidade de responder a questões e preocupações expressas pelos/as revisores/as – embora tivéssemos de o fazer entre o Natal e o Ano Novo, enquanto a Coordenadora Internacional estava numa cidade nos EUA que foi atingida por uma tempestade grave, com a biblioteca pública como único acesso ao e-mail! Mas todas/os contribuíram, e tivemos sucesso. A nossa colaboração, tanto no desenvolvimento das nossas ideias para o projeto, como em pensar sobre como responder a questões críticas, deu-nos um forte sentimento de que poderíamos trabalhar em maior proximidade. Em vez de cada parceiro entregar o seu "pacote de trabalho" em separado, comprometemo-ros a um coeso processo de investigação a ser concretizado em paralelo. Esta estratégia de organização significou, como depressa descobrimos, que, à medida que avançávamos, estávamos a trabalhar através e no cruzamento das nossas próprias diferenças.

As/os jovens investigadoras/es, que se juntaram a nós, deram um importante contributo, pois sem o seu envolvimento e entusiasmo esta antologia não teria sido possível. Como primeiro passo, as cinco equipas escreveram artigos dos respetivos contextos nacionais sobre o enquadramento legal, as instituições de intervenção, o historial de migração e os sistemas de intervenção nos nossos quatro países. Estes documentos permitiram-nos compreender como é organizada a intervenção para as três formas de violência – abuso físico e negligência contra crianças, violência doméstica contra mulheres e tráfico de seres humanos para exploração sexual. Esperávamos também concordar sobre que minorias iríamos abordar especificamente, mas isto simplesmente não foi possível. Os historiais de migração e minorias dos quatro países são demasiado diferentes, e nem sequer o conceito de "minoria" tem o mesmo significado de um país para outro. A única coisa que podíamos fazer era deixar que fossem as/os profissionais no terreno a escolher que minorias encontram na sua prática, e foram eles e elas que nos colocaram em contacto com sobreviventes de violência que estavam interessados/as em contar-nos as suas histórias.

O trabalho de campo do CEINAV iniciou com workshops multiprofissionais, dois para cada forma de violência em cada país (um total de 24). Convidámos as/os participantes a discutir e refletir sobre uma história ficcional dividida em três fases e, em cada fase, foi proposto discutir quem poderia detetar que a violência estava presente e o que as várias instituições poderiam, deveriam ou iriam fazer se tomassem/ou tivessem conhecimento da situação. Foi solicitado às e aos participantes que refletissem, particularmente, sobre decisões difíceis e dilemas éticos que poderiam experienciar. Mais tarde, foi pedido para ponderarem sobre o que poderia ser diferente na intervenção se a mulher ou a criança na história tivessem um background cultural e/ou migrante. Como tínhamos concordado numa lista comum de instituições e profissões relevantes, e elaborado uma história realista para os quatro países, sendo quase idênticas exceto com algumas adaptações menores, vimos estas discussões como uma oportunidade de descobrir as premissas culturais que estão subjacentes às práticas de intervenção dos quatro países.

Analisar e comparar as discussões nos nossos workshops proporcionou-nos, de facto, uma profunda reflexão quer sobre as semelhanças quer sobre as diferenças acerca do que as e os profissionais pensam sobre a violência em geral e sobre os grupos minoritários que encontram, e como compreendem o papel da intervenção em relação às várias formas de violência. À medida que discutíamos em conjunto, nas nossas reuniões, os fundamentos das nossas próprias perspetivas foram-se explicitando e expandindo.

Não nos aventurámos sozinhas/os nesta investigação; todas/os tínhamos cooperado durante anos com profissionais e organizações cujo trabalho envolve a defesa e o apoio a mulheres e crianças e suas famílias que enfrentam diferentes formas de coerção e violência. Redes de profissionais foram os nossos parceiros associados neste projeto. Ajudaram-nos a elaborar casos ficcionais realistas e a retrabalhá-los até que fizessem sentido nos quatro países, e encaminharam-nos para profissionais preocupados/as, com experiência na intervenção em todas as diferentes áreas e posições que procurámos incluir.
O nosso passo seguinte — a base para esta antologia — foi ouvir mulheres e jovens que tivessem atravessado uma história de violência e de intervenção, e que pertencessem a um grupo social minoritário. Não lhes pedimos que recontassem a violência que tinham sofrido, mas convidámo-las/os a contar-nos como experienciaram a intervenção, começando pelo primeiro momento em que decidiram pedir ajuda. Tendo consciência do impacto a longo prazo da violência e a possibilidade de futuros danos, pedimos às nossas associações parceiras e suas redes para nos ajudarem a encontrar entrevistadas/os que estivessem agora numa situação estável mas ainda ligadas/os às instituições de apoio. Idealmente, teríamos feito sete entrevistas para cada forma de violência, 21 no total, em cada país, mas nem sempre foi possível. Encontrar mulheres e crianças para serem entrevistadas mostrou-se difícil, e entrevistas com mulheres vítimas de tráfico para fins de exploração sexual foi quase impossível de realizar na Eslovénia e em Portugal.

Mais uma vez, a compreensão do que constitui uma "minoria" social dependeu do país, dos serviços de apoio e da sua experiência prática. Muitas/os das/os entrevistadas/os tinham um background de migração recente, mas alguns e algumas tinham chegado ao país há bastante tempo atrás; noutros casos, um ou ambos os progenitores tinham vindo também há bastante tempo. Alguns e algumas dos/as participantes identificavam-se com a comunidade minoritária, e outros/as viam esta ligação primeiramente nos termos em como os outros reagiam a eles/as. Dependendo do país, uma proporção maior ou menor de mulheres e jovens são provenientes da UE ou de regiões do mundo mais distantes. Algumas tinham apenas muito recentemente escapado de uma situação de violência e encontrado o caminho para uma instituição ou organização que as pudesse ajudar; outros/as tiveram os seus primeiros encontros com a intervenção (polícia, um/a assistente social, um centro de aconselhamento especializado, ou alguma instituição) há muitos anos atrás, em alguns casos, até há décadas atrás. O percurso em direção à proteção e apoio genuinamente eficazes pode ter sido muito longo e cansativo, ou bastante breve.

Com estas duas abordagens, os workshops e as entrevistas, queríamos compreender cada perspetiva nos seus próprios termos, não compará-las. Os/as profissionais refletiram sobre o que fariam hoje e como poderia ser uma melhor intervenção.

Os/as sobreviventes contaram-nos o que aconteceu no passado, e o que para eles/elas significaram os encontros com profissionais e instituições de intervenção. Que tipos de resposta os/as fez sentir mais fortes e lhes deu esperança, o que os/as desencorajou ou os/as fez sentirem-se mais impotentes? Como é que os/ profissionais os/as fizeram sentir que estavam a ser ouvidos/as ou, pelo contrário, que não estavam a ser ouvidos/as? Terão existido momentos, no percurso de intervenção, em que a ação de profissionais os fez sentirem-se menos merecedores de atenção ou ajuda, ou como foi ser reconhecido/a como uma pessoa com direitos? Quão importante foi ser ajudado por terceiros, por pessoas que conheceram nestas circunstâncias? Tais experiências podem ser fundamentais na procura de formas de acabar ou escapar à violência. Algumas das mulheres e jovens mantinham fortes sentimentos e emoções sobre situações que viveram muitos anos antes, experiências más e boas, e estes momentos cruciais estão ainda presentes para eles/as, constituindo motivo de ânimo e alento ou de retração e desconforto.

Para possibilitar que as vozes e experiências das mulheres e jovens sejam ouvidas através das suas histórias, a equipa de cada país leu e releu cada entrevista, retirando as descrições, frases e palavras que pareciam mais intensamente significativas e expressivas do que foi mais importante para a mulher ou o/a jovem nos seus encontros com a intervenção. Enquanto as entrevistas são longas e andam para trás e para a frente no tempo à medida que as lembranças vêm à superfície e o/a entrevistado/a hesita e tenta encontrar as palavras certas, os/as investigadores/as usaram um processo criativo de narrativa para criar uma história curta para esta antologia. Devolvemos depois a história à pessoa em questão para perguntar se refletia o que ele ou ela gostaria de dizer aos/às responsáveis pela intervenção. Foi igualmente importante ouvir se pensavam que a história, tal como contada aqui, protege a confidencialidade e segurança prometidas em cada entrevista.

Algumas mulheres e jovens pensaram que não haveria risco para eles/as, hoje em dia, mesmo se usássemos os seus verdadeiros nomes, e alguns e algumas teriam gostado de tornar as suas experiências públicas. Contar a história a uma audiência maior pode ser uma parte importante de avançar, mas precisa de um contexto de apoio que não podíamos acautelar: seguimos então a tradição honrada na literatura e nas artes de dar a cada contador/a de histórias um pseudónimo. Os serviços de apoio, se forem bem financiados e reconhecidos, poderão também encontrar formas de publicar as experiências que as vítimas/sobreviventes desejem contar. A partir das suas experiências, Susan Brison escreve que, depois do trauma, "deve-se (física e publicamente) dizer ou escrever (ou pintar ou filmar) a narrativa e outros devem vê-la ou ouvi-la para que a sobrevivência como um eu autónomo seja completa" (Aftermath 2002, p. 62). Convidámos todos/as os/as entrevistados/as a participar em workshops de arte dirigidos por uma investigadora-artista em cada país, e aqueles/as que desejaram ou puderam vir receberam materiais de arte e foram encorajados/as a expressar as suas experiências com a intervenção. Mais tarde, os/as entrevistados/as-artistas participaram numa reunião de diálogo com profissionais de intervenção em que foram expostos os seus trabalhos que resultaram dos workshops criativos: agora eram eles/as os peritos e eram os/as profissionais quem procurava esclarecimento – uma experiência empoderadora, disseram-nos.

Se tivessemos tido mais tempo e mais recursos, teria sido maravilhoso organizar workshops de escrita para além de workshops de arte, onde as mulheres e os/as jovens pudessem desenvolver as suas próprias histórias para a publicação, permitindo-lhes trabalhar as barreiras linguísticas (ainda presentes em alguns/mas participantes), e refletir cuidadosamente, como diz Brison (p. 97), sobre "quem, como, quando, onde, e – devemos ter especial consciência disto – porque" cada pessoa decide contar a sua história. Nesta antologia, todas as histórias são apresentadas nas suas línguas originais e traduzidas em inglês. Em Portugal e na Eslovénia, o sistema de intervenção não permitiu a realização de tantas entrevistas como o esperado, em algumas áreas, por isso, foram traduzidas algumas histórias de outros países que se acredita possam "falar" aos/às profissionais e outros/as leitores/as no seu próprio país. Aprendemos bastante com as histórias, e elas ajudaram-nos a desenvolver os "Fundamentos Transnacionais para a Intervenção Ética", que estamos a publicar a par desta antologia, e que, esperamos, possam servir de mote a muitas reflexões e discussões entre os/as profissionais e entre quem tem o poder e a obrigação de delinear os quadros teóricos e as políticas legais e sociais para a intervenção.

Carol Hagemann-White & Bianca Grafe

Raziskovalke in raziskovalec iz štirih držav – Carol, Vlasta, Liz, Maria José in Thomas – ki smo se več let sami ali skupaj ukvarjali z izzivi zaustavitve nasilja, smo leta 2011 začeli iskati načine za tesnejše sodelovanje. Hoteli smo poglobljeno preučiti, zakaj se pristopi k interveniranju razlikujejo kljub temu, da se celotna Evropa očitno strinja, kaj je treba storiti, pa tudi, zakaj interveniranje včasih ne doseže svojih ciljev, še posebno pri ženskah in otrocih, ki to podporo morda najbolj potrebujejo. Vsi smo delovali na evropski ravni, gradili mreže in uporabljali možnosti financiranja, prav tako pa nam je bila skupna zaveza raziskovanju, ki bi lahko prispevalo k praktičnemu delu in politikam proti številnim oblikam nasilja in diskriminacije v vsakdanjem življenju.

Vendar nismo bili zadovoljni s tem, kar smo lahko naredili. Preveč naših raziskovalnih priložnosti je bilo zvezanih s političnimi pričakovanji »hitre rešitve«. Programi EU, ki so podpirali sodelovanje pri vprašanjih enakosti spolov in nasilja, so raziskovalkam in raziskovalcem omogočali izmenjavo izkušenj in strategij, le redko pa tudi poglobljeno raziskovanje. In zaradi omejenega časa in virov skoraj nikoli ni bilo prostora, da bi slišali glasove žensk in otrok, ki so nasilje trpeli. »Dobra praksa« pa bi menda morala biti odgovorna tistim, ki naj bi jim koristila!

Program »Kulturna srečevanja« je obetal predvsem možnost raziskati, kako razlike v nacionalni zgodovini, kulturi, jeziku in tradicijah oblikujejo okvire intervencij in delo strok. A še pomembnejše je bilo, da smo imeli za izpeljavo projekta na voljo tri leta in smo se tako lahko osredotočili na to, kako običajne prakse interveniranja vplivajo na ženske in mlade iz etničnih ali kulturnih manjšin oziroma imigrantskih skupnosti. Ali se s standardi »dobre prakse«, ki krožijo v mednarodnem prostoru – v priporočilih, seminarjih o politikah in deklaracijah, pripravah Konvencije Sveta Evrope in zahtevah po direktivi EU – dejansko lahko odzivamo na potrebe žensk in otrok iz vse bolj raznolikih okolij, ki pa niso nič manj obremenjeni z nasiljem v svojih družinah, intimnih odnosih in spolni industriji?

To, da program ni postavil nobenih zunanjih ciljev, povezanih s politikami, razen spodbujanja sodelovanja pri raziskovanju znotraj EU, je bila še ena prednost, kar se je odražalo v tem, da so se neodvisni ocenjevalci in ocenjevalke v celoti osredotočili na kakovost predlogov: imeli smo celo možnost, da odgovorimo na njihova vprašanja in pomisleke – čeprav smo to morali narediti med božičem in novim letom, medtem ko je bila koordinatorka projekta v ZDA v mestu, ki ga je prizadela huda ledena ujma, in je imela dostop do e-pošte le v javni knjižnici! Vendar smo vsi zagrabili za delo in uspelo nam je.

Med našim skupnim delom tako pri razvoju idej za projekt kot pri razmišljanju o odgovorih na kritična vprašanja smo začutili, da bi lahko tesno sodelovali. Namesto da bi partnerji prispevali vsak svoj ločen »delovni sklop«, smo se odločili za poenoten raziskovalni proces, ki bi ga izpeljali vzporedno v štirih državah. To je pomenilo, kakor smo kmalu ugotovili, da smo sproti predelovali tudi lastne kulturne razlike.

Imeli smo veliko sreče z mlajšimi raziskovalkami in raziskovalci, ki so se nam pridružili sredi projekta; brez njihovega angažmaja in entuziazma te publikacije ne bi bilo. V prvem koraku je vseh pet ekip napisalo osnovne dokumente o zakonih, institucijah, odgovornih za interveniranje, zgodovini migracij in sistemih interveniranja v naših štirih državah. To nam je omogočilo, da smo razumeli, kako je interveniranje organizirano v vsaki od štirih držav in za vsako od treh oblik nasilja – telesno zlorabo in zanemarjanje otrok, nasilje v partnerstvu ter trgovino z ljudmi za namene spolnega izkoriščanja. Upali smo, da se bomo lahko dogovorili, katerim manjšinam se bomo posebej posvetili, vendar to preprosto ni bilo mogoče. Zgodovine migracij in manjšin v naših štirih državah so preveč različne in celo koncept »manjšine« nima istega pomena v vseh državah. Tako je bila naša edina možnost, da izbiro tega, s katerimi manjšinami se srečujejo v praksi, prepustimo strokovnjakom in strokovnjakinjam, ti pa so nas povezali s tistimi, ki so doživeli nasilje in interveniranje in so nam bili pripravljeni povedati svoje zgodbe.

Projekt CEINAV se je začel na terenu z delavnicami za različne strokovnjake in strokovnjakinje, po dve delavnici za vsako obliko nasilja v vsaki državi (skupaj 24). Sodelujoče smo povabili, da v treh fazah obravnavajo izmišljeni primer ter v vsaki fazi razpravljajo o tem, kdo bi lahko opazil prisotnost nasilja in kaj bi različne institucije in stroke lahko, morale ali bi dejansko naredile, če bi bile seznanjene s situacijo. Zlasti smo jih prosili, naj razmislijo o težkih odločitvah in etičnih dilemah, ki bi jih lahko doživeli. Nato smo jih prosili, naj razmislijo, kaj bi bilo lahko drugače, če bi ženska ali otrok v zgodbi prihajala iz etnične ali kulturne manjšine oziroma bi bila migrantskega porekla. Ker smo se dogovorili o skupnem seznamu relevantnih institucij in poklicev in si izmislili zgodbo, ki je bila realistična za vse države in razen manjših prilagoditev skoraj povsem identična, smo te razprave videli kot priložnost, da razkrijemo kulturne premise intervencijskih praks v posameznih državah. Analiza in primerjava razprav na naših delavnicah nam je resnično dala precejšen vpogled tako v podobnosti kot v razlike med mnenji strokovnjakov in strokovnjakinj o nasilju na splošno in o manjšinskih skupinah, s katerimi se srečujejo, poleg tega pa tudi v njihovo razumevanje vloge intervencije glede na različne oblike nasilja. Ko smo o tem razpravljali na naših sestankih, se je oblikoval temelj naše perspektive.

Tega raziskovanja se nismo lotili sami; vseh pet nas je leta sodelovalo s strokovnimi delavci in delavkami ter organizacijami, katerih delo je vključevalo zagovorništvo in podporo za ženske in otroke ter njihove družine, ki so se soočale z različnimi oblikami prisile in nasilja. Mreže strokovnih delavk in delavcev so bile v projektu naše pridružene partnerice. Pomagale so nam zasnovati realistične fiktivne primere in jih tako dolgo predelovati, da so bili smiselni za vse štiri države, poleg tega pa so nas usmerile k vpletenim strokovnjakom in strokovnjakinjam z izkušnjami intervencije v vseh različnih institucijah in na različnih pozicijah, ki smo jih želeli vključiti.

Naš naslednji korak in osnova za ta izbor zgodb je bil, da smo poslušali ženske, mladostnike in mladostnice, ki so prestali nasilje in interveniranje ter pripadali manjšinam. Nismo jih prosili, naj nam opišejo nasilje, ki so ga trpeli, pač pa da nam povedo, kako so doživljali interveniranje od trenutka, ko so prvič pomislili, da bi poiskali pomoč. Ker smo se globoko zavedali trajnega vpliva nasilja in možnosti nadaljnje škode, smo pridružene partnerice in njihove mreže prosili, da nam pomagajo najti intervjuvance in intervjuvanke, ki so že v stabilni situaciji, a še povezani s podporo. V idealnem primeru bi opravili sedem intervjujev za vsako obliko nasilja, torej skupno 21 v vsaki državi, a to ni bilo vedno mogoče. Izkazalo se je, da je pravi izziv najti ženske, mladostnice in mladostnike, ki bi jih lahko intervjuvali; v Sloveniji in na Portugalskem pa je bilo skoraj nemogoče organizirati intervjuje z ženskami, ki so bile žrtve trgovine z ljudmi.

Razumevanje »manjšine« je bilo spet odvisno od države, podpornih služb in njihovih praktičnih izkušenj. Veliko intervjuvanih je migrantskega porekla, pogosto so v državo prišli precej nedavno, nekateri pa tudi že dolgo nazaj ali pa sta bila migranta oba starša oziroma eden od njiju. Nekateri so se imeli za pripadnike manjšine, drugi so to povezavo videli predvsem v tem, kako so se drugi odzivali nanje. Večji ali manjši delež žensk, mladostnic in mladostnikov, ki so prihajali iz EU ali iz bolj oddaljenih regij sveta, je bil odvisen od posamezne države. Nekateri so šele pred kratkim ušli iz nasilne situacije in so našli institucijo, ki jim je lahko pomagala; drugi so se z interveniranjem (policije, šolske socialne delavke, specialističnega svetovalnega centra ali kakšne zakonsko določene institucije) prvič srečali pred mnogo leti, v nekaj primerih celo pred desetletji. Pot do resnično učinkovite zaščite in podpore je lahko bila zelo dolga in ovinkasta ali pa precej kratka.

Z obema pristopoma, z delavnicami in intervjuji, smo hoteli razumeti vsak pogled na interveniranje v njunih lastnih okvirih in ju nismo želeli primerjati. Strokovnjakinje in strokovnjaki so razmišljali o tem, kaj počnejo danes in kako bi to lahko izboljšali; v intervjujih smo poslušali, kaj se je zgodilo v preteklosti in kaj so srečanja s pristojnimi za interveniranje, pomenila za ženske in mladostnice. Kakšni odzivi so jim zbujali občutke moči in jim dajali upanje, kaj jim je jemalo pogum in jim zbujalo občutke nemoči? Kako so jim strokovnjaki ai strokovnjakinje dale vedeti, da jih poslušajo, ali nasprotno, zakaj so mislili, da niso slišani? Ali so bili trenutki, ko so se zaradi njih počutili, da so manj upravičeni do pozornosti in pomoči, in kako je bilo, ko so bili prepoznani kot osebe s pravicami? Kako pomembno je bilo, da so jim pomagale tretje osebe, denimo ljudje, ki so jih srečali po naključju? Takšne izkušnje so lahko ključne v iskanju načinov za končanje nasilja ali pobeg pred njim. Nekatere ženske, mladostniki in mladostnice so še vedno doživljali močna čustva v zvezi z dogodki izpred mnogo let, pozitivnimi ali negativnimi, in te ključne trenutke še vedno nosijo v sebi, bodisi kot prepreko ali spodbudo na svoji življenjski poti.

Ker smo hoteli omogočiti, da bi bili glasovi in izkušnje žensk, mladostnikov in mladostnic širše slišani prek pripovedovanja zgodb, je ekipa v vsaki od držav večkrat prebrala vsak intervju in izluščila opise, stavke in besede, o katerih se je zdelo, da imajo najizrazitejši pomen in najmočneje izražajo, kaj je bilo za intervjuvane najpomembnejše v njihovih srečanjih z intervencijo.

Intervjuji so dolgi ter polni časovnih preskokov v obujanju spominov in premorov, ko se intervjuvanka obotavlja in išče prave besede, raziskovalci pa smo uporabili ustvarjalen postopek pripovedovanja, da smo sestavili kratke zgodbe za ta izbor. Nato smo zgodbo vrnili osebi, ki jo je povedala, in jo vprašali, ali izraža tisto, kar bi rada povedala odgovornim za interveniranje. Enako pomembno je bilo izvedeti, ali se jim zdi, da zgodba, kakor je povedana, ščiti njihovo zaupnost in varnost, ki smo ju obljubili pred vsakim intervjujem.

Nekatere sogovornice so menile, da danes tveganje zanje ne bi bilo nič večje, tudi če bi uporabili njihova prava imena, nekaj pa bi jih celo želelo imeti priložnost, da svoje izkušnje razkrijejo javnosti. Povedati zgodbo širšemu občinstvu je lahko pomemben del napredovanja, a je za to potreben kontekst podpore, ki ga nismo mogli nuditi: zato smo sledili spoštovani tradiciji v književnosti in umetnosti in vsaki pripovedovalki dali psevdonim. Za podporne službe, če bi bile dobro in zanesljivo financirane in prepoznane, bi bil izziv, da bi našle več načinov, kako bi žrtve lahko povedale svoje zgodbe. Susan Brison na podlagi lastne izkušnje piše, da moramo po travmi »(telesno, javno) povedati ali napisati (ali naslikati ali posneti) zgodbo in drugi jo morajo videti ali slišati, da bi se naše preživetje v obliki avtonomnega subjekta dovršilo« (Aftermath, 2002, str. 62). Vse intervjuvane smo povabili k sodelovanju na umetniški delavnici, ki so jo vodile umetnice-raziskovalke. Tisti, ki so to hoteli oziroma jim je uspelo priti, so dobili umetniške materiale in spodbudo, naj izrazijo svoje izkušnje z interveniranjem. Pozneje so sodelovali v dialogu na sestanku s strokovnjaki na področju interveniranja, njihova dela pa so bila razstavljena. Zdaj so oni bili izvedenci, strokovne delavke pa tiste, ki so iskale pouk – in povedali so nam, da jih je ta izkušnja opolnomočila.

Ko bi imeli več časa in več sredstev, bi bilo čudovito poleg umetniških delavnic organizirati tudi delavnice pisanja, na katerih bi ženske, mladostnice in mladostniki razvili svoje zgodbe za objavo, s čimer bi jim omogočili, da bi zaobšli jezikovne ovire, ki so bile pri številnih še vedno prisotne, in skrbno razmislili, kot pravi Brison (str. 97), o »kom, kako, kdaj, kje in – tega se moramo še posebno zavedati – zakaj« se vsaka oseba odloči povedati svojo zgodbo.

Portugalskem in v Sloveniji sistem interveniranja na nekaterih področjih ni omogočal, da bi naredili toliko intervjujev, kot smo upali, zato smo prevedli nekatere zgodbe iz drugih držav, o katerih verjamemo, da bi lahko »nagovorile« strokovnjakinje in druge bralce v obeh državah. Iz zgodb smo se veliko naučili, prav tako pa so nam pomagale oblikovati »Transnacionalna izhodišča za etično prakso v interveniranju proti nasilju«, ki jih objavljamo poleg tega izbora. Upamo, da bodo spodbudili mnogo razmislekov in razprav tako med strokovnjaki in strokovnjakinjami kot tistimi, ki postavljajo pogoje in okvire za interveniranje.

Carol Hagemann-White & Bianca Grafe

Credits

This anthology was created by researchers who interviewed women and young people, listened for key experiences and messages, and recast them in the shape of stories that could be published.

Germany:
Carol Hagemann-White
Bianca Grafe
Barbara Kavemann
Leonie Teigler
Thomas Meysen
Janna Beckmann
Andreas Seeligmann

England & Wales:
Liz Kelly
Jackie Turner
Madeleine Coy
Nicola Sharp

Portugal:
Maria José Magalhães
Angélica Lima Cruz
Rita de Oliveira Braga Lopez
Raquel Helena Louro Felgueiras
Vera Inês Costa Silva

Slovenia:
Vlasta Jalušič
Veronika Bajt
Lana Zdravkovic
Katarina Vučko

Design:
Ana Paula Mateus, Coimbra

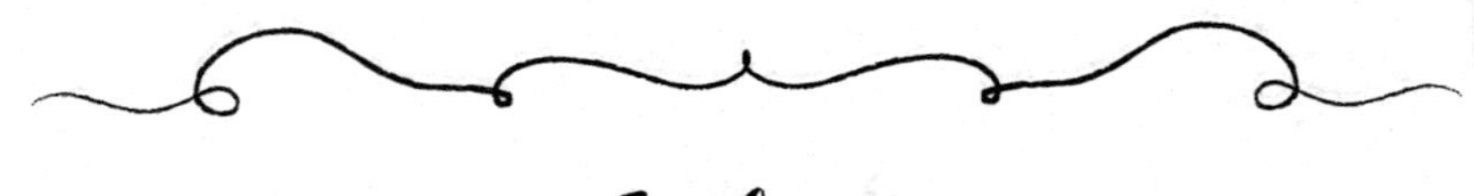

Index

NOTE: throughout the anthology, the original language of the interview is in black and regular font; the translation is in grey and in italics. All translated stories are located next to the original in the section of the country where the story was told.

CPSIA information can be obtained
at www.ICGtesting.com
Printed in the USA
LVOW05s1235060118
562081LV00002B/2/P